The Discipline of

Architecture

Andrzej Piotrowski and Julia Williams Robinson, Editors

The Discipline of

Architecture

University of Minnesota Press   Minneapolis • London

An earlier version of chapter 5 appeared as "Showing What Otherwise Hides Itself," *Harvard Design Magazine* (fall 1998); reprinted with permission from *Harvard Design Magazine*. An earlier version of chapter 11 appeared as "Voices for Architectural Change," *Journal of Architectural Education* (May 1997); reprinted with permission from *Journal of Architectural Education,* published by the Association of Collegiate Schools of Architecture. An earlier version of chapter 12 appeared as "Professional Education and Practice," *Harvard Design Magazine* (winter–spring 1996); reprinted with permission from *Harvard Design Magazine*.

Published by the University of Minnesota Press
111 Third Avenue South, Suite 290
Minneapolis, MN 55401-2520
http://www.upress.umn.edu

Library of Congress Cataloging-in-Publication Data

The discipline of architecture / Andrzej Piotrowski and Julia Williams Robinson, editors.
    p.   cm.
    Includes index.
    ISBN 0-8166-3664-8 (HC) — ISBN 0-8166-3665-6 (PB)
    1. Architectural design—Philosophy.   2. Architecture—Study and teaching.   I. Piotrowski, Andrzej.   II. Robinson, Julia W.
    NA2750.D485 2000
    721'.01 — dc21   00-010663

Printed in the United States of America on acid-free paper

The University of Minnesota is an equal-opportunity educator and employer.

12 11 10 09 08 07 06 05 04 03 02 01   10 9 8 7 6 5 4 3 2 1

Contents

Acknowledgments

The editors express gratitude to Vicky Boddie and Wendy Friedmeyer for their tireless assistance in putting this volume together and Fay Anagnostopoulou for her help during the final phase of preparations. We also thank Professor Ellen Messer-Davidow for her generative role in this project, and the University of Minnesota Press for its realization.

Introduction

Julia Williams Robinson and Andrzej Piotrowski

The disciplinary character of architecture is one of the most important, though underexplored, issues that architects face today. Disciplinarity — the way that architecture defines, creates, disseminates, and applies the knowledge within its domain of influence — is increasingly central to the discussions about the present and future direction of the field. However, we rarely focus on how our seeing, thinking, and understanding of architecture or on how the social construction of our field can obstruct or advance our ability to create a built world viable and valuable for the next century.

Following a line of thought developed by Ellen Messer-Davidow, David Shumway, and David Sylvan (e.g., 1993a, 1993b) and others in which knowledge is seen as "historically and socially contingent," and disciplines as "historically discontinuous" knowledge formations in constant change (Shumway and Messer-Davidow 1991, 218), the essays collected here, many of them presented at the conference "Knowledges: Production, Distribution, Revision,"[1] address this disciplinary question. They suggest that what propels architecture — such as procedures for design, education, research, publication, career advancement — is what has usually been considered to be peripheral to the field. This collection shifts the emphasis to what we believe is the center of the problem — the epistemological and political dimensions of architectural knowledge.

The chapters of this book show that the practices of knowledge[2] production and dissemination do not play a minor supportive role in the discipline. Rather, through application of hidden assumptions in supposedly value-free practices (decisions on such things as what knowledges to pursue, publish, and teach, how to do scholarly research, whether to apply knowledges in design, standards for admitting and advancing students and future practitioners), these practices significantly affect the discipline's direction.

Consequently, the chapters of this book revolve around a set of difficult questions: Is there something uniquely architectural in the way architects know and design buildings? What determines the understanding of value in a building? To what extent is the knowledge of architecture strictly an outcome of particular methods, their epistemological assumptions, and institutional mechanisms that facilitate knowledge production? Are the objectives and methods of knowing architecture similar or different when academia and professional practice are considered? Should they be different or similar? Could these questions even be addressed from perspectives that have dominated architectural knowledge thus far?

As the chapters of the book will elaborate, architectural knowledge is diverse and complex, drawing from a range of fields that influence how a building or environment is imagined, designed, described, constructed, and sold and how it performs, once built. Architectural knowledge is deeply embedded in the network of political relationships. Until quite recently in the United States, with the exception of a small number of institutions, academia primarily disseminated professional knowledge to future practitioners. Professional practice and the building site were the dominant locus of the development of architectural knowledge, the site where architectural knowledge was applied and passed on through apprenticeship. Now the sites of development have expanded to include research centers with well-defined and targeted agendas (located in governmental agencies and business corporations), and many academic institutions, especially those in universities. The discussion of disciplinarity has arisen within academia, perhaps because the presence of other, better-defined fields and the increase of cross-disciplinary work beg the definition of architecture as a discipline. That does not mean that the subject of disciplinarity in architecture is primarily an academic topic, but simply that academia is the place where this discussion has begun.

The discussion of architecture as a discipline is approached through a number of themes. Perhaps most central is the issue of authority. Where does authority lie within the field? Who is given the power of authority, whose interest does it service, and how does the present structure sustain it? Who is denied authority and how? What are the criteria for determining authority, and what are the social structures and mechanisms that maintain it? Arising in many contexts, from the problems of globalism, to the challenges of the increasingly diverse membership of the profession, to the tensions between profession and academia, to how the subfields are arrayed relative to each other, we find a diverse set of responses. The chapters of this book address authority or domination of certain models or attitudes that frame the discipline of architecture. The points they make sometimes reinforce observations in other chapters and occasionally contradict each other.

One of the most important aspects is the existing configuration of the field of architecture and how the knowledge production relates to this configuration—what subjects are central to the field, how it ought to be configured, and how it should be structured. At issue are a variety of structures and practices. One area of discussion is the relation of architecture to other fields. Some argue for maintaining clear and strong distinctions, and others support permeable boundaries, suggesting that increased interdisciplinarity will affect present ways of doing things. Another discussion addresses the relations between the discipline and the subfields. Here again there is no consensus. Authors suggest different subfields and give them different names. In relation to describing the nature of the disciplinary boundaries, authors also propose different definitions of the field. Several authors raise the issue of validating knowledge. Several characterize the present method as based on Western historical precedent and question, variously, whether it can adequately serve non-Western contexts, both genders, all classes, all races and ethnicities, as well as current political realities. All authors address whether the values and ideas that founded the field are still appropriate for today.

The form and content of education is yet another important theme of the discipline of architecture. Because architectural education is unique within the academy, for those who are not familiar with the field, it may be useful to provide information about it. The primary focus of architectural education has been the development of professional competence to construct the buildings that serve society. The architectural curriculum is structured around this content, with architectural design as the core activity. Keith Hoskins (1993) identifies as the locus of higher education the classroom, the seminar, and the laboratory. For the professional education of architects, we must add the design studio, where students are supposed to integrate the divergent knowledges taught in other classes by applying them to particular design projects. The studio resembles the laboratory setting in that students learn by actually doing but differs in that the style of instruction is predominantly criticism. Although the tradition of the studio is felt to be central to professional education and its methods are highly valued for its hands-on, interactive approach to learning, its use of critical pedagogy is currently under severe scrutiny (Anthony 1991). On the other hand, in recent years, the need for specialization and more research has fed nonprofessional advanced education for which the studio may no longer be central, which creates a potentially expanding identity for architectural education beyond the professional orbit.

A third general disciplinary topic related to authority is the legitimacy of different voices within the field in relation to the social responsibility of the architect. Many of the authors see the present social context as challenging existing ideas of authority. The profession of architecture, formerly a bastion of upper-middle-class white males of European descent, has a growing number of people from different classes, genders, nationalities, and ethnic backgrounds. The concepts, methods, and professional practices developed by the original group are often irrelevant and even destructive to the interests and values of the new members.

The fourth area of focus is the relation between academia and the profession. The roles of each can no longer be taken for granted, as academia is increasingly the source of new technology and expertise, and the profession, where ideas are implemented, is not only where the need for new knowledge is identified but also a place where new knowledge is being developed. A new balance of power between the two areas is being negotiated. Following opinions that currently shape this issue, the authors present different perspectives. Some envision academia and the profession as both within the larger discipline; others define academia as the locus of the discipline and argue for its independence from the profession; still others argue that academia and the practicing profession are separate but that each exerts a form of leadership for the other.

Thomas Fisher begins the book with a discussion of the contemporary discipline of architecture as historically growing from two different traditions, scholarly and professional. He says that although in the Western tradition both the academic and architectural professions originated in the Middle Ages, the integrated professional education, as we now think of it, did not exist in most institutions of higher learning until the nineteenth century. Thus the sense of disciplinary authority has been, and still is, a negotiated one. It reflects the uneasy but necessary reconciliation of these two kinds of expertise and modes of operation.

In contrast, Michael Stanton associates the discipline of architecture with the most current cultural phenomenon of commodification of life and, as such, finds it susceptible to intellectual fashions, which legitimize current ways of understanding a building. His concern is that architecture develops a critical apparatus that goes beyond fashion and transcends commercial approaches to architectural knowledge. He argues that the authority of "intuitive creativity" should be replaced with the disciplined, critical, and precise mode of understanding offered by history or theory.

From a similar point of view, Andrzej Piotrowski argues that to understand how the knowledges of buildings are constituted today, one must study the common practices of knowing and representing. Within such a theoretical framework, he studies three particular practices, exploring how each foregrounds certain attributes of a building, defines the relationship between who knows and what is known, and who ensures the truthfulness of such a knowledge.

Julia Williams Robinson contends that fundamental assumptions deriving from earlier conceptions of architecture as a practice need to change to reflect the new knowledges and changing social orientations that now inform design. Seeking to reinforce the synthetic orientation of the field, to link the different subdisciplines, and to strengthen the identity of the field, she proposes a paradigm of architecture as cultural artifact that incorporates and extends beyond the accepted conception of architecture as art.

David Leatherbarrow, on the other hand, argues that the authority and identity of the discipline of architecture reside in subjects and skills that are particular to architecture—representation, architectural reflection, and building technology. He also believes that for professional responsibility and intellectual clarity, it is important to maintain the differences between architecture and related fields such as engineering, painting, and planning.

David J. T. Vanderburgh and W. Russell Ellis critically review the production of architectural knowledge. They address a particular subfield of the discipline that they call "social and cultural factors." They analyze some of the ideas and events that have marked changes in the understanding of social and cultural aspects of architecture over the last three decades, examining particular texts in the context of the changing intellectual environment.

In a study of another subfield, Kay Bea Jones focuses on the practice of traveling to learn about architecture, which, although common among architects and architecture students, seems underexplored as a mode of knowing. Her special concern is with "travel pedagogy," by which she means "experientially centered studies dependent on some cultural, geographic, and paradigmatic shift that radically alters sense perception and challenges visual and spatial cognition" of architecture.

Donald Watson's essay also approaches the knowledge of architecture from a particular subdisciplinary focus. He presents environmental sustainability as one of the most important issues and traces how the function of the knowledge of environment evolved. After examining the structural relation between architecture and the knowledges necessary to create ecological environments, he advocates a number of disciplinary and curricular changes required for environmentally responsible design.

Sharon Egretta Sutton follows Donald Watson's emphasis on environmental issues but reveals a different side of these phenomena. Hers is the first of three chapters that focus on ethical and political aspects of the discipline of architecture. She describes how practices such as professional privilege and land ownership perpetuate existing patterns of domination and not only lead to degradation of biological environments but also create oppressive architectural environments. Sutton argues for radical change in the myth and practice of professional privilege and for a new concept of the architect—a facilitator of social processes.

A. G. Krishna Menon, like Sutton, argues against asymmetries of power behind architectural professional practice and intellectual leadership. Menon's perspective, however, is that of a non-Western architect who practices and thus faces challenges of a global market, and that of an educator who has participated in founding a school in India to develop postcolonial models of architectural education.

The last of the three chapters, the one written by Linda N. Groat and Sherry Ahrentzen, addresses the politics of gender in architectural education. The authors summarize their research on the status of women in architecture, noting that although women are currently marginalized, typically their work is influenced by fields outside architecture. The authors therefore see the present emphasis on interdisciplinarity in academia as presenting leadership opportunities for women in architecture and propose specific ways in which the perspectives of faculty women might transform architecture into a more truly interdisciplinary endeavor.

The next sequence of three interrelated chapters examines the issue of the relationship between academia and the profession. For example, Carol Burns advocates for more connection between academia and practice, proposing a number of possible alignments. Following Burns's argument for the alignment between the two, Garth Rockcastle demonstrates how a similar integration helped his professional practice. Using a case study of a project his company designed in Las Vegas, he discusses how critical insights and reflective modes of thought reveal political and ideological complexities of architectural commissions. In this way, his observations practically substantiate the strategy Carol Burns proposes.

Finally, Stanford Anderson identifies the value in maintaining differences between academia and the profession. He argues for an interdependence of the two areas based on a precise understanding of their complementary functions and perspectives.

In the discussion of disciplinarity that follows, we do not present a definitive text, a cohesive and highly structured framework within which the chapters play clearly defined roles to communicate a singular message. The issue of architectural disciplinarity is too complex and too politically charged to afford a conclusive treatment. Instead, this book presents a multiplicity of critical intersections that demonstrate how knowledges and the systems that produce and reproduce, revise, and disseminate them can no longer be taken for granted. We expect that this book is just the beginning of a timely discussion.

Notes

1. The conference was organized by Ellen Messer-Davidow and David R. Shumway, under the sponsorship of the University of Minnesota and the Group for Research into the Institutionalization and Professionalization of Knowledge-Production (GRIP), and held in April 1994 at the University of Minnesota.

2. The use of "knowledge" in the singular stands for the collectivity of the diverse architectural knowledges and is not intended to suggest the existence of a single integrated "knowledge" in architecture.

1
Revisiting the Discipline of Architecture

Thomas Fisher

The professions in North America are under attack. Surveys reveal widespread public distrust of professions such as law and politics, and the bottom-line management of professions such as medicine and architecture has become equally pervasive, with the rise of entities such as health maintenance organizations and disciplines such as construction management. What has caused this public- and private-sector reaction to professionalism, and how has this affected the disciplines in these fields?

All of the professions have begun to search for answers, and at least in architecture, this has produced a flood of articles, conferences, and books calling for sweeping reform of architectural education and the architectural profession. Some believe that the architectural schools must change to serve the shifting needs of practitioners, others think that the architectural profession has relinquished its educational responsibilities and thus weakened the field, and still others claim that both have become marginalized and need to rethink their mission in order to become more relevant (Crosbie 1995; Kroloff 1996; Fisher 1994, 2000).

In all of this discussion, we need to keep two points in mind. First, the situation we face is not new. The profession of architecture, like the other major professions, has come under attack before, for reasons similar to those generating the current crisis of confidence, and we cannot address the latter without understanding its history. Second, unlike in previous eras, academia has come under as much scrutiny as the

professions in recent decades.[1] This reflects not only the increasing professionalization of higher education but also its inextricable connection
to the professions over the last 150 years. Any reform of the architectural profession must now include reform of higher education, of the
discipline of architecture.

The current critique of the architectural and academic professions
has its origin some eight hundred years ago in the medieval guilds. The
academic profession emerged from the scholars' guild (the *universitas
magistribus et pupillorum,* or guild of master and student) that arose in
Europe in the twelfth century associated with the cathedrals and local
churches. The architectural profession had a similar beginning in the craft
guilds (the masons' and carpenters' guilds) that also arose in part from
service to the church. With the political fragmentation and disorganized
capitalism of medieval Europe, the guilds served as the major way of
organizing work, exerting control over membership, workplace conditions, markets, and relations to the state.[2] The guilds determined who
could join, the length of apprenticeship, the dues and fines members
had to pay, the means of production, the pace and hours of work, and
who could practice in what market. To preserve their monopolies in
particular locations, the guilds also actively lobbied and even occasionally bribed local officials.

The rising power of capitalistic enterprises and the growing influence
of free market thinking in the Renaissance led to a weakening of the
craft guilds, although not the scholars' guilds. Capitalists saw the craft
guilds as a hindrance to free trade, eventually convincing the state that
guild monopolies were more expensive and less efficient than capitalistic
competition. That capitalists also bribed officials, often at higher levels
than the guilds, may have helped this change in perception. As a result, the craft guilds in Europe had largely disappeared by the mid-1500s,
replaced by construction trade groups competing in the marketplace
without a monopoly.

The scholars' guilds generally avoided this fate for several reasons.
Scholars and students were more mobile and would move if governments balked at their guild status, as happened when French scholars
left Paris in 1229 in protest over waning government support and turned
the church schools at Oxford and Cambridge into universities. At the

same time, academics posed less of a threat than the craft guilds to capitalists; education has always been a labor-intensive, low-profit activity. Also, as universities amassed wealth in the form of public sponsorships and private donations, they became less vulnerable to economic pressure. As a result, universities still retain many of the trappings of guild power, such as lifetime membership in the form of tenure, collegial decision making among faculty members, and strict control over contact hours with students.

The architectural and academic professions had relatively little to do with each other as their social and economic positions diverged after the 1500s. Although some specialized architectural schools did emerge, such as the Academy of Architecture in Paris, founded in 1671, professional education as we now think of it did not exist in most institutions of higher learning until the nineteenth century (Draper 1977). The rise of architectural education, at least in the United States, came in the wake of a populist revolt against the idea of professions. From the 1840s through the post–Civil War period, many citizens saw the professions as antidemocratic elites, causing states to repeal certification for professions such as law and medicine. The nascent architectural profession also suffered in this period. Mid-nineteenth-century architects such as Asher Benjamin, A. J. Davis, and Thomas U. Walter bowed to the populist sentiments of their time by producing building guides and plan books for popular consumption. One of the few professions to escape this trend was, again, the academic profession, which retained its guild power largely unscathed.

Their weakened position in that populist, free market era led many professions to form associations (the American Medical Association in 1848, the American Institute of Architects in 1857, the American Bar Association in 1868) in an effort to reestablish some control over their practices. From the 1880s through the 1920s, these associations swung public opinion around, convincing state legislatures to enact licensure laws that became the basis for the professions as we now know them. After decades suffering from quack doctors, crackpot lawyers, and carpenter-architects who built firetraps, the public and politicians needed little convincing; whatever gained in terms of efficiency in a relatively unregulated free market had been lost in terms of public well-being. The professional associations recognized their chance. They emphasized their commitment to the public's health, safety, and welfare and recognized that the monopoly that licensing laws gave them was necessary if they were to advance the state of their knowledge for the greater good.

Key to the latter was a move away from an apprenticeship education toward the establishment of professional schools, often in the newly formed state land grant universities established by the Morrill Act of 1865 and in research-oriented universities such as Johns Hopkins and MIT. In architecture, for example, the first professional program arose at MIT in 1865, followed by programs in land grant schools such as Cornell in 1871 and Illinois in 1873. Here, after centuries of relatively little contact, the academic and architectural communities found themselves interacting once again, but this time, it was the scholars' guild that would undergo the greatest change.

The professional associations had considerable influence over the curricula in these early professional programs, with faculty drawn from either current or former practitioners. This represented a major intrusion into the territory of the academic guild. As a result, the professional schools occupied an uneasy place in universities, tolerated because of the student revenues and outside support that they brought with them, but separated from the traditional academic disciplines. That does not mean that the professional schools offered only a vocational training. In architecture, educators and practitioners worked out a system early on in which the schools would focus on areas such as design, history, and theory, and the profession would educate interns about such matters as running a firm, managing a project, and detailing and constructing a building. But unlike some other professional programs, such as medicine or engineering, architectural schools remained largely teaching oriented, with relatively little funded research or published scholarship (Fisher 1996).

Professional architectural education has remained fairly stable for more than a century. Despite changes in ideology, as a classical education gave way to a modernist and then a postmodernist one, the design-oriented, studio-based pedagogy has remained largely unchanged. But shifts have occurred in the last decade or two that have altered the ground on which both the academic and architectural professions stand and have set in motion the urge for reform in the field.

At one level, these shifts relate to the struggle that goes back to the conflict between guildlike professions and free market capitalism. Guildlike professions thrive when the free market has been either disorganized, as in the Middle Ages, or considered untrustworthy, as happened after the Civil War in the United States. At such times, the state has granted monopoly status to professional groups in exchange for their attending to the needs of the public and their raising the standard of care of their members. But when the ideology of the free market is ascendant, as happened in the eighteenth and early nineteenth centuries or in the last few decades, professional guilds must fend off the criticisms of inefficiency, elitism, and unfair advantage. The rise of fee bidding, the attacks on quality-based selection of professionals, the increasing pace of design and construction — all reflect efforts to measure the architectural profession according to the values of the marketplace.

With the rise of the global economy in the last two decades, the free market critique of the professions has had greater influence and a broader thrust than ever before. In previous eras, the church or the state often served as havens for professional activity, even as capitalists have prevailed in the marketplace. But today, the church has become less of a force, and the government itself has begun to fashion itself in the mold of the private sector, emphasizing its efficient use of taxpayer money and its adoption of business practices. This has resulted in an almost unprecedented alliance between the state and capitalism against professions, evident in the Justice Department's antitrust ruling against the use of fee schedules by architects or in the widespread use in the public sector of design-build as a project delivery method intended to drive down costs and speed up construction.

The free market critique of the professions has also reached into the universities, threatening the guild of scholars as never before. This has taken many forms, from proposals in some schools to eliminate the tenure system, to efforts in others to impose corporate-style management, to attempts in still others to tie budgets to research productivity. Some of this activity has come from outside groups — efficiency-minded state legislatures or free market–oriented university trustees or regents — and some has come from faculty and administrators themselves in an effort to gain flexibility or financial independence in the face of increasingly unstable government support or prescriptive donor requests. Whatever the cause, the result has been an erosion in the power of the scholars' guild akin to what the craft guilds encountered several hundred years ago.

The other allegiance that the professions once could rely on—the public at large—has also withered in recent decades. Public support for the professions exists in proportion to how much the professions devote themselves to the public good and resist taking advantage of their monopoly position in the marketplace for private gain or to unfairly advance the interests of private clients at the public's expense. That often unspoken understanding has existed in periods when the public as well as the public sector have supported the professions. In the late nineteenth and early twentieth centuries, for instance, most architects and educators adhered to this unspoken agreement, advocating public control over the private realm or individual expression, be that in the form of Beaux Arts classicism or modernist urbanism.

Architecture and academia were likewise viewed as a "calling," a devotion to the common good or the truth. But professions now rarely use the word "calling" to describe themselves; instead we see what we do as a career, a way of making a good salary and of finding personal satisfaction while serving the needs of one's paying clients or students. The difference between a calling and a career may be subtle, but it has had a profound effect on the public's support of professionals. As professionals' incomes have risen higher and faster than those of most nonprofessionals, the public has had difficulty believing that the professions still put the common good before private gain. This public disillusionment with the professions has led, in the case of architecture, to proposals in several state legislatures to suspend architectural licensing laws and to eliminate the profession's unfair advantage in the market as we have become too much like just another service business. In the case of the academic profession, public support for such things as tenure or tuition increases has also subsided. Here, too, some faculty have come to seem more interested in their job security than in their devotion to learning, more intent on advancing their careers by hopping from one institution to another than on their service to a particular university in a particular place.

As traditional professions, like architecture or scholarship, face increasing opposition and declining support, many trade groups have achieved professional status, from house inspectors to hairdressers. For trade groups, such status enables them to control their numbers through the process of licensure and to control their markets by demanding that only licensed professionals be able to do certain tasks. Likewise, for a state legislature that licenses such groups, granting them professional status provides a way of protecting the public and ensuring uniformity of service. But this extending of professional status to more people also relates directly to the attacks on the traditional professions. As happened in the early nineteenth century, we have entered a period in which the older professions seem antidemocratic and elitist to many people, which leads not only to reducing the privileges of some but to extending them to others.

Such is the context in which we now struggle to redefine practice and education. The architectural and academic professions face serious challenges in a largely unregulated global economy, with little support from either the public or the private sector. And the situation does not seem likely to change anytime soon. As the sociologist Christine McGuire has argued, "Predictions for the future of individual professions strongly suggest that most, if not all, will continue to be faced by more external regulation, increased competition from outside the field, intrusion of newer occupations, louder public demands for more high-quality service at lower cost, and increasingly rapid and pervasive technological change that drastically alters practice" (McGuire 1993, 15).

Architects and architectural educators have responded to this situation in various ways. Some have argued that the profession must rediscover its calling, its obligation to the public, and attend less to formal concerns of interest largely to architects. That calling can be an explicitly social one, using architecture to support the needs and values of the people who use it, or an ecological one, something that the public may not yet be asking for, but one that it needs and will greatly benefit from.

A related line of thought urges the profession to become more politically savvy, demonstrating its value not only through its buildings but in its ability to navigate public processes. That navigation involves both an empirical understanding of how people use space and a sensitivity to differences of culture, gender, and race, and a pragmatic focus on what we do best, demonstrating our value through our ability to see spatial relationships, to understand form and culture, and to put materials and manufactured assemblies together.

The critique of both the architectural and academic professions has led to a tension between the two unlike that ever experienced before in the field. Some would separate professional practice and education, acknowledging their differences and presumably enhancing the ability of each group to defend itself more effectively against its critics. Others would encourage practitioners and educators to become more aligned, sharing their knowledge and standing together against those who would attack professionalism. A third position emphasizes the discipline of architecture that embraces both practice and education, taking the discussion away from the contested matter of professional privilege and refocusing on the building of knowledge.

A number of other writers have focused on educational reform, although there is a lack of agreement about just what sort of reform is needed. Some see the problem in the subjectivity of design education, wanting us to be more intellectually rigorous, while others see the problem as just the opposite: that architectural education has, for too long, assumed a false objectivity and cut itself off from public narratives and myths. Likewise, some want architectural educators to do more traveling within the academy, connecting to liberal arts disciplines less vulnerable to the critique of professionalism, whereas others want students and educators to do more traveling in the larger world, understanding the various ways in which people of different cultures and genders view architecture. And still others urge us to take a more critical view of how we represent architecture to ourselves as well as to the public, recognizing the multiple ways in which such representations can be interpreted.

How do these views cohere into a workable strategy? One answer is that what worked before can work again. When faced with "market fundamentalism" in the mid–nineteenth century, the professions did several things: they emphasized their public calling as a counter to the private interests of the free market, they left behind hidebound traditions and began to address the problems ordinary people faced in a changing society, they joined practitioners and educators into a common research effort to build their knowledge base, they articulated and demonstrated the value of their core skills, and they opened their membership and extended their expertise to a greater diversity of people. We need to pursue a similar course today if both the architectural and professorial professions are to thrive.

Notes

1. Books such as *Tenured Radicals: How Politics Has Corrupted Our Higher Educations* (Kimball 1998) and *Profscam: Professors and the Demise of Higher Education* (Sykes 1988) typify the critique leveled at the academic profession in recent years.

2. An excellent analysis of the professions vis-à-vis capitalism and the state is in *The Death of Guilds: Professions, States, and the Advance of Capitalism, 1930 to the Present* (Krause 1996).

2
Disciplining Knowledge: Architecture between Cube and Frame

Michael Stanton

This group of elements, formed in a regular manner by a discursive practice, and which are indispensable to the constitution of a science, although they are not necessarily destined to give rise to one, can be called
knowledge.
— **Michel Foucault, *The Archaeology of Knowledge***

Design teaching in architecture school often begins with the cube as its
first topic. The same on all sides, the cube appears neutral, without hierarchies. Its only direction that of gravity, it seems to be free from symbolic content or technical constraints. It is white, pure, available yet
autonomous, waiting to be filled or excavated. Like all designed forms,
this one is a materialization of ideology, for the cube personifies the
subject of teaching, the new student, as much as it is the first object of
architectural work. Its apparently mute regularity points the direction
that architectural knowledge is meant to take and the formats it should
follow.

It may be the distance and simplification of history that allows the
following generalization, but it does seem that the elements of architectural knowledge one hundred years ago were much more identifiable
to those teaching the discipline than they are now. There was then some
agreement that architecture could spring from the classics and other
eclectic formats — Renaissance, Gothic, and so on — that these made a

quantifiable body of rules and precedents to which were added the possibilities of structure and construction, drawing and presentation, all finally augmenting the diagram provided by the past and program. Structural rationalism, art nouveau, and early functionalism provided a fretful counterpoint. If indeed things were more precise then, the surrounding cultural upheaval couldn't much longer support a simple environment for design at the last fin de siècle, and by now the ensuing collapse of master narratives and the proliferation of global media make any relatively terse definition of architectural knowledge quite impossible. Furthermore, its definition will always be a subjective act with political implications. The material we use as architects and pass on to others as teachers is not homogeneous. Although the sources and substance of architectural erudition are essential topics, especially when instruction is discussed, they are rarely candidly presented or critically described. Such a direct approach may seem too pedantic or may threaten doctrines that thrive on unquestioned acceptance, but lack of direction leads directly to the confusion of much contemporary pedagogy.

Not surprisingly, the ideological struggles that accompany teaching often concern knowledge. The principles of a master or theoretical group — New Urbanist, Deleuzean, Beaux Arts, phenomenologist — are passed on to students as formal dogma without the more thorough understanding held by those passing them on. Such agendas, while explicit in attempts to control and reduce, are fortunately nearly impossible to fulfill. Knowledge cannot be so easily managed in a data-saturated environment like the present, for it includes the vast field of information relevant to architecture, including the methods and devices by which these data can be made available in the design process and the criticism that accompanies that process. Only the spin that knowledge is given can be somewhat directed.

> [A]rchitecture problematizes the very differences we depend on for keeping it still and inert: . . . It is the nature of the epistemic to promise presence and deliver absence. (Ingraham 1992, 56)

To be anything other than speculative when deliberating architectural knowledge and its transfer seems just as "historically precluded"[1] as identifying something more precise than its relation to other factors. *Knowledge* itself reverberates with such rhetorical volume as to be almost

Figure 2.1a. From *Encyclopedia*, by Denis Diderot.

indistinguishable from the ideological white noise generated by the charged terms *freedom* or *justice* with which *knowledge* shares a canonical position. Implicitly mercenary and open to self-serving interpretation, these sorts of terms are bound to society and power. It could be said that knowledge is little more than the particular intellectual territory that authority carves out for itself within any particular discipline and thus is of interest only as a foil against which to frame alternatives. To reduce the term in this manner seems to limit its use pointlessly,

Figure 2.1b. From *Encyclopedia*, by Denis Diderot.

or to surrender it to the questionable uses of others,[2] but any discussion must certainly take into account the collusion of knowledge with the status quo, especially when confronting an art as compromised as architecture.

But to defend architectural knowledge is to deconsecrate it at the same time.[3] While buildings are relatively permanent, data pertaining to them are anything but. Knowledge is cheap, pervasive, and indiscriminate. It is everywhere, although we respect little of it, continuing to distinguish "high" knowledge from the rest, with arguments far less sophisticated than those addressing other postmodern phenomena.[4] To avoid evident problems of definition, knowledge will be presented here as material, method, and location, rather than as essence or standard, thus intentionally sidestepping epistemological or hermeneutic structures, both out of respect for their origins and to avoid the delirium of current interpretations. As it did one hundred years ago, *knowledge* still reflects the grandeur of the academy, allowing ideologies both conservative and avant-garde to claim in its name to have tapped into a mother lode of erudition so deep as to be irreducible and incorruptible. While the aura of knowledge is fading in the present climate of co-optation, easy political readings, and soft poststructuralism, it remains essential to continue the process of realignment made possible by the concept's weakness, recognizing the shifting criteria it must confront to regain strength.

In architecture the border between raw information and a conventional notion of refined knowledge is quite fuzzy. The search in this gray zone for a *discursive practice* may help to partially recover these troubled terms — *knowledge, information, practice, discourse.* The juxtaposition of the facts of the practical and the concepts generated by intense discussion could form a rich field in which to both teach and practice. Although the contemporary climate is hostile to them, theory and history should still play an important role in this process. Theory necessarily must determine a knowledge base from which to spring. History both describes and prescribes that base. Theory and history are essential to education, but the former has a bad name, and the latter is considered of little relevance to a culture focused on the future and the market.

Knowledge in the form of an informational commodity indispensable to productive power is already, and will continue to be, a major — perhaps *the* major — stake in the worldwide competition for power. It is conceivable that the nation-states will one day fight for control of information, just as they battled in the past for control over territory, and afterwards for control of access to and exploitation of raw materials and cheap labor. A new field is opened for industrial and commercial strategies on the one hand, and political and military strategies on the other. (Lyotard 1984, 5)

Lyotard and others have emphasized the primary place of knowledge in the late-twentieth-century market. Any attempts to put it elsewhere only seem to ease its merchandising. As with all political phenomena, architectural knowledge is vulnerable to the pressures of a rapidly changing cultural climate and is influenced by a society that not only patronizes production but also is the entity that architecture must depict. This is one of the contradictions that define our practice and muddle our discussions — the dependence on greater culture for sustenance and the simultaneous need to critically engage that culture. Attempts to control knowledge and the architectural forms to which it alludes drive our curricula in school and our goals in practice. The radical epistemological shift that accompanied the rise of the modern movement is an example. Abstraction, new objectivity, the denigration of history, the paradoxically joined accolades to inspiration and the technical, the questionable acceptance of avant-garde postures, the myths of form's purity and of utopia's realization: these modernist criteria still determine the cultural frame in which we find ourselves, a frame in which form, with its ties to power and economics intact, remains the center around which all debate tiptoes.

Like the shapes that pass each other on the runways of architectural enthusiasm, each arguing its immunity from the overheated market it thrives on, the information that accompanies these forms is similarly dependent. As with all commodities, knowledge is susceptible to fashion. The frame changes with the painting. The critical model that had commanded the utmost respect and awe will cause condescension to radiate a few years later in the more refined halls of discourse. Critics continually attempt to absolve themselves of the terms in which they had couched their recent musings. Remember *type, context, autonomy, narrative, semantics, fragmentation, weak form?* Such fashion in thought clearly has problems. It acquiesces to market forces, as was evident during the theoretical *arrière-garde* actions of the 1980s, and it tends to dismiss its predecessors with a scorched-earth vehemence close to critical amnesia.[5] Such fickleness can lead to the worst sort of superficiality, as it discards very important ways of thinking. It encourages posturing and propaganda. But fashion should also be defended, whereas we tend to use the term exclusively to condemn, implying personal distance from a circumstance from which none of us is immune. Fashion purges and rejuvenates. It is inevitable and exhilarating. It polarizes and crystallizes, shining with a flashy brilliance for the short moment that such hot phenomena can survive. It is a necessary and inevitable condition of any aesthetic endeavor and perhaps of any cultural action. To dismiss as "merely fashionable" is to fall under fashion's most potent spell. Hemlines must go up and down, but it is good to remember that they always serve the market.

Current reassessments of knowledge suggest that its potency lies outside the academy, that an epistemological vernacular functions in counterpoint to "high" knowledge, a robust native strain immune from fashion. This subset of the general argument for the "vitality" of indigenous structure over architecture — of rap over poetry, of graffiti over painting — is burdened with the contradictions of the pastoral and with a degree of professional prevarication. It is indeed true that we are swimming in noninstitutional riches. In the United States, specifically, African American and immigrant contributions vitally enrich the necessarily diluted offerings of established cultural bodies. But to assume the value of one over the other is the result of another of the contrived oppositions that confound our existence and hide agendas.[6] It seems wiser to scrutinize our own systems of organized erudition than to presume a savage nobility in those that are more spontaneous or popular. Tangential to the defense of vernacular knowledge, and occasionally co-opting it, are calls for the "real" accompanied by easy interpretations of the architecturally political. Such formulations are indeed current, one might say fashionable. Like all such phenomena, they suffer from a superficiality that allows energy to be directed toward personal goals. This *politics lite* is determining debate in the academies. While taking a stance that could be presumed to be opposed to conservative positions, current political attitudes often thrive on many of the same attitudes.[7] Although it is encouraging to see political criticism become mainstream, at least as long as any popular phenomenon can stay so situated, it is hard to accept the self-righteousness that being mainstream tends to encourage.

Especially in a political economy such as the United States, a focus on knowledge moves immediately to production. Endemic to all American enterprise, the focus on product shapes any discussion of architectural knowledge. It is clear that the making of architectural form depends on diverse sources: history, philosophy, economics, science, political and cultural studies, aesthetics, technology, sociology. It is also clear that form is the bottom line, the end for which these disciplinary borrowings are a means. This is one of the great contradictions of an endeavor that is largely intellectual, verbal, administrative, technical, social, and poetic. Finally, only form is left, built or drawn. Form drives our teaching and the frantic pressure toward realization. Teaching methodologies dissolve into a push for "complete" drawings, for sexy models, for things, proof, culmination.

Given the central role of architecture schools in both defining and producing knowledge, the focus of this chapter will now turn toward teaching procedure. This may indicate a certain critical sleight of hand, since one way to avoid the obvious pitfalls of an atavistic view of knowledge is to move the discussion to the spread of information, here understood as nonantiseptic, contaminated, even promiscuous. The imparting of architectural data and skills will supersede the image of "pure" knowledge as an immaculate ether, an image that, through its reliance on metaphysics, paradoxically advances an intuitive paradigm that is in fact a form of antiknowledge. The shift of emphasis is from a troubled and possibly outmoded concept to didactic procedure, identifying (to turn Jonathan Crary's description of the camera obscura toward teaching) "its multiple identity, its 'mixed' status as an epistemological figure within a discursive order *and* an object within an arrangement of cultural practices" (Crary 1990, 30). The camera obscura is an apt metaphor for the academy—the dark enclosed cube where the fluid image of the world is reversed, solidified, and recorded in another dimension. In that dark space, specific practices and rituals unfold. All are tendentious in their pedagogy. None is without presumption.

If, a few years ago, teachers of architecture urged students not to retreat so readily to the library and the image-mart of the journals and the monographs, now they are asking that same group to gather more material, historical or contemporary, outside their own impulses. Presumably the increasing introversion on the part of students is not due to their faculty's lack of interest or expertise. One can only suppose the opposite, given the continuing migration to faculties of architects trained during a period when analysis and history were considered to be very

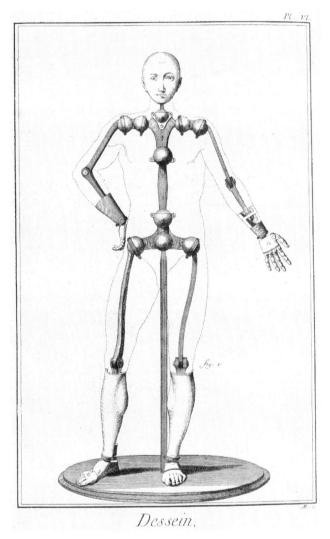

PL. VL.

Dessein,

Figure 2.2a. From *Encyclopedia,* by Denis Diderot.

important. Instead, the lack of inquiry seems related to an expanding belief that such inquiry is more or less irrelevant to the process of designing, that it lies outside pertinent knowledge. With this attitude often comes a general hostility to a priori architectural thinking and to modes of learning that may be analytic or information based in the first place. If we assume that this viewpoint does not come from laziness or a love of ignorance, nevertheless it does eliminate the need for many

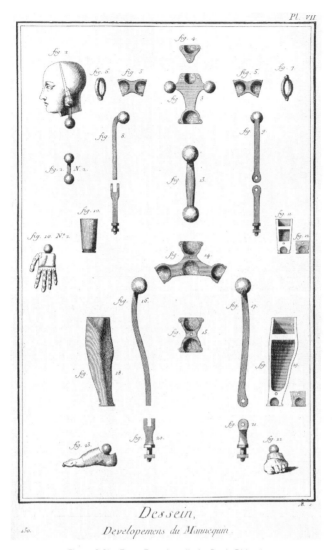

Figure 2.2b. From *Encyclopedia,* by Denis Diderot.

of the more strenuous aspects of learning associated with scholarship, with the study of the past and with logic and the expository, and tends toward an anti-intellectualism that finally argues for an *other* of rigorous thought. Replacing the gathering and analysis of data is a growing faith in intuition and certain historically exhausted notions of creativity that traditionally fueled the modern movement but have been in serious doubt since the first strong critique of that movement more than thirty years ago.[8] It would be repetitious to belabor the obvious problems inherent in easy conflations of "biotechnical determinism and free expression" as outlined as early as 1967 by Alan Colquhoun, but the schools (here I do not include just the students) seem either not to have learned these lessons or to have forgotten them in a reaction against some of their worst dogma. A very precious baby has gone with the tepid bathwater of late modernism, rationalism, and historicist postmodernism.

> The tendency to fetishize the unconscious is inherent in the image of unconsciousness itself. (Lefebvre 1991, 208)

The argument for intuition assumes that this commodity lodges within the individual and is largely independent of, or even compromised by, things external. Design studios become exercises in automatic writing. Professors urge "consciousness lowering," the production of form beneath reason. The focus of these practices, intended to release what Adorno calls the "I of expressionism" (Foster 1985, 63), can also foster self-absorption verging on narcissism. The student is homunculus. In his or her tiny form is the curled creative force, whole and waiting. It would prejudice genius to call students' attention to the given. The goal of pedagogy is then opening, nurturing that which already exists. This takes a lot of responsibility away from the teacher, whose role becomes that of an expediter, excavating the artistic impulse, and perhaps deprogramming information or preconceptions that may block such excavations. This strategy accepts the simple alignment of architecture and the arty, the emotional and the expressive, returning to a theoretically suspect modern pastoral. Although it thoroughly rejected the formats of modernism on one level, architectural teaching returns to them tenaciously on another. What appears to be a rejection of discipline is in fact a particularly rigid historical practice. While Virgilian in origin, this concept gained force during the Enlightenment and the nineteenth century with the canonization of "the innocence of the eye."[9] To propose this paradigm is in fact to revive a troubled and contradictory litany. A historic theme passing from the pastoral, through the romantic, into the modern, finds particularly receptive ears in this millennial New Age, as it did during the late 1960s and early 1970s.

Several factors have led to this revival. In this century, architectural imagery takes its cues from the fine arts, and at least since the mid-seventies, painting has been both figural and decidedly expressionistic in character and doctrine. There were problems with this. Hal Foster writes, "expressionism denies its own status as a language" (Foster 1985, 59–78). By nature, its anarchic charge and solitary persona do not invite the communal impulse that produces discourse. Emotion substitutes rhetorically for a shared communication system. Expressionism markets itself more as an attitude, resisting an easy resurrection of its forms. The contradictions inherent in an academic revival of so impulsive a phenomenon may render the notion of *neoexpressionism* as paradoxical as was *deconstructivism.* Nevertheless, during the seventies and early eighties, the work of Schnabel, Clemente, Chia and Cucchi, Basquiat, Anselm Kiefer, and Elizabeth Murray was readily available in the galleries and, at light speed, in the museums, accessible to architects perpetually hungry for new formal material. Postmodernism, while ineffectual on many levels, returned to a discussion of meaning with such a vehemence that for a long time, it will be difficult to restore the self-proclaimed symbolic silence of the modern movement. Consequently, the alloy of the expressionist and the figural in postmodern painting proposed a new design zeitgeist while avoiding the repetition of prevailing forms.[10] This satisfied an Oedipal need to reject the immediate and suddenly unfashionable predecessor while maintaining its conceptual foundations, and to embrace a formal ancestor safely legitimized and neutered by time and museums. In a discipline in which style still rules, the desire to disengage from that which was popular (and therefore must soon become reciprocally unpopular) is another reason for the rise of a neoexpressionist architecture.[11] On its surface, it seems antithetical to its immediate predecessor, postmodern pastiche. The "anxiety of influence" was diminished. Also, some architects — Gehry, Zenghelis and Koolhaas with Zaha Hadid, Peter Cook, and others at the Architectural Association — had never endorsed the quickly stale excesses associated with the "historicist" phase of architectural postmodernism. Many of po-mo's most zealous practitioners and defenders were also ready to distance themselves from their previous fascinations by the mid 1980s.

At recent international conferences many participants addressing architectural education have made the argument for an early course of study that would "free" the novice designer.[12] Painting, collage, and the sculptural exercises were seen as enabling this "freeing." All derived from the fine arts, which, for architects, still resonate with magical associations to the avant-garde, the aura of creativity, and artistic license. Take, for example, the enormous success of the middling installation artists Diller and Scotidio among architects. That things artistic are automatically freeing was an accepted conclusion, a holdover from early modernism and its beginning design courses, particularly the enormously influential formats of the Bauhaus, that included the arts, architecture, and craft in one regime. This assumption both idealizes and condescends. It is romantic to imagine that the art world is not another relatively calculating professional sphere, bound by its own strictures: entrenched institutions of display and instruction, market pressures, fierce politics, poseurs, trendiness, and snobbism. Furthermore, to assume that art is fundamentally expressive and free is to demean a field that has relied on a complicated synthesis of rationale, history and precedent, skill and technique, theory, mimesis and nonfiguration, as well as economic and curatorial considerations. Great art sometimes produces results that appear expressive. Rarely is it so conceived or made. More rarely is it easy or fun. Titian and DeKooning struggled and ruminated, and worked hard. They gained skill and knowledge in the workshop of Bellini or the academies in Holland. For students to suppose the opposite is understandable. For faculty to promote this supposition is less so.[13]

Most important, the belief in the implicit liberating energy of the arts derives from extremely dubious and antiquated notions that propose "freeing" as the first task of education. It is indeed true that a student is not an aesthetic tabula rasa. He or she brings a lot to school, having been exposed to the media and the rich information stew provided by family, previous instruction, and places lived in and visited. Psychology filters and transforms these data in a period when information has never been more cheap, dense, or hierarchically neutral. The academy's effect is modified by other factors, by the material students bring with them, the vernacular sources previously mentioned, and the inevitable instruction in the practical arenas of the profession provided during and after school. Is this what students need freeing from? Perhaps instead they need to perceive more critically and of course to add the more cosmopolitan data available via the faculty, students, and environment of design school, to develop the material and methods for a "discursive practice" in fact. But then, are art exercises, with their tendency toward more indiscriminate imaging typical of entertainment media, the appropriate mode for this "freeing"? It seems that in an age such as this, one needs to develop the critical ability to gather, filter, order, metabolize, synthesize—those very processes that conventional education has encouraged.

Those who have absorbed the enormously complex data necessary for even rudimentary architectural design work inevitably find ways to "forget," to synthesize subliminally, to not be smothered by information. But to urge, either through curriculum or treatise, those who have not yet assimilated, to resist assimilation a priori seems extremely questionable. Maybe we are again at a moment like that when the modern masters, fully aware of the architectural history that they were consciously overturning, forbade their students from studying that history, arguing its irrelevance and thus producing a generation from whose mediocre work we are still recovering and against which we are still reacting. It seems absurd to assume that because analysis is by nature imprecise, which poststructuralism convincingly illustrates, we should not attempt to use analysis as a temporary framework. To come to this conclusion is as silly as denouncing ideals because life tends to disappoint them. Both ideals and analysis allow us to "throw away the ladder after [w]e ha[ve] climbed up it," as Wittgenstein urges (Wittgenstein 1961, 151).

Here, perhaps, is the root of the problem. The cycles of "freeing," creativity, and so on are accompanied by an innate hostility to the academy and its practices—to ordered thought, disciplined and rigorous assimilation and analysis, study in the most precise sense, and things associated with rationalism, currently the most unsavory of intellectual phenomena. History and urbanism, which has become history's physical manifestation, are considered by many students and faculty to be of no relevance to a culture positioning itself for the twenty-first century. Concern for the urban is reemerging in current political debates about architecture, but the way this concern is manifested seems to avoid engagement, either insisting on an abstraction of the city that appropriates it as more sexy shapes or concentrating on social concerns of such a direct kind that it is difficult to see a place for architecture in their solution given the collapse of utopian teleology. The urban strategy on one hand is to aestheticize to the point of bourgeois acceptability and on the other to materialize to the point of aesthetic impotence.

Owing, in part, to the ideological conflicts that sit at the core of the modern sensibility and that threaten the delicate constructs in which Americans find comfort, we are also experiencing a rejection of the concept of the institution by students and faculty, a rejection that runs parallel to the national aversion to government. That institutions are flawed seems an inevitable result of their existence. On the other hand, an innate hostility to their epistemological apparatus leads to the strange proposition of antigovernment types — that we should try to kick away the chair in which we sit. The hostility to both knowledge and its location is bizarre coming, as it does so often, from within the academies where little else is offered.

Schools themselves are loath to change. Tenure stupefies, mediocrity is self-perpetuating, and entrenched faculties stubbornly defend fiefdoms, along with recycled course syllabi, habit, and tradition — all the innate conservatisms that come with the territory. Meanwhile students and practitioners are alienated from a pedagogy that they feel should support them. Although clearly biased, their attitudes reflect some genuine problems with which schools are struggling.[14] Sometimes in open defiance of teaching institutions, the profession attempts to influence the definition of architectural knowledge through the tendentious content of registration exams, imposing strictures on an academy that intermittently feels it should prepare students for these ordeals. Accrediting boards function similarly, prescribing the values and criteria pertinent to teaching and practice.

In the schools, the actual pressure points remain tightly sealed. Here I refer to change that might unleash curricular innovation without qualification, challenging the Socratic format of the design studio, even its necessity, challenging the obstinate structure of support classes and the intense doctrine embedded in distribution requirements, challenging the integrated curriculum and design as the hub of activity for all students. Such major reassessment is almost always too threatening to established teaching formulas and feudal curricular interests. Consequently a delirious rupture occurs elsewhere, avoiding the tougher issues that a troubled field faces. Sharing imagery with pop music and sartorial fashion, a seventies low-stress pastoral version of "freedom" vies for the hearts and minds of students with more severe "political" postures.[15] A powerful and historically insistent doctrine backs up the former. Rousseau, Nietzsche, Johannes Itten and the early Bauhaus, Marinetti, Kokoschka, Loos and Karl Kraus, Trotsky, Artaud and Mayakovsky, Duchamp, Cage, Bataille, Barthes, Deleuze and Guattari, even Tim Leary have made this a familiar and blindingly exciting call to arms, which should be made with all the opulence and complexity that its turbulent history and recent critiques of the avant-garde have provided. Such an incendiary appeal must also be gauged according to the particular disciplines toward which it is aimed. It can invigorate and debunk and it can, of course, devolve as in the case of Marinetti.[16] Certainly the pitfalls of avant-gardism have been amply marked by writers from Tafuri and Habermas to Foster and Jameson, but nevertheless this remains a primary and unquestioned path for much of architecture's critical and practical elite. Peter Eisenman and Frank Gehry are obvious examples. It is a flawed presumption that meandering into other disciplines or redolent obscurity are *automatically* important or productive (and here I would argue, somewhat polemically, that import and production are desired ends for theory as well as practice). It is a matter of quality and content that distinguishes the fabulous from the fatuous. I question the aura that appears to accompany intrinsically such endeavors, an aura largely evaporated by recent history while furiously invoked by those who believe it still surrounds them.[17]

In the end, the desired "freeing" may be from architecture itself, from its tough facts and tougher paradoxes. And in some cases, this is where both theory and practice have blissfully arrived. Despite the intellectual subtlety demanded by the intricate practice of architecture, our community remains very literal in its hermeneutics. Critical connective tissue is lacking, and theory itself remains largely form driven in its research and conclusions.[18] Theory's flights and its audience's skepticism limit the possibility of an active link between concept and making. This is not particularly surprising, since many contemporary voices have become unhinged from issues or modes of discussion that would continue to interest or inform those outside their immediate penumbra. On the other hand, to assume that architectural thinking is worthless or permanently peripheral must be construed to be an excuse for those unable or unwilling to make the effort to form the vital connections that theory offers, or those made uncomfortable by forming those connections.

> For me it (writing) is very brutal and primitive, because for me architecture is an intellectual discipline and for me writing is the privileged communication of our intellectual disciplines. So writing is absolutely without question necessary. We abuse the alibi of the otherness of our profession. . . . You cannot write if you don't have ideas. I think there is still a very strong section in architecture that somehow hopes that there can be architecture without ideas. (Koolhaas 1993, 43)

The contemporary American climate is hostile to intellectual practices. This is not surprising in the land of action, where the overly contemplative has classically been treated with suspicion in a culture based on certain pastoral and populist exhortations of the nobility of labor, simplicity, and the anti-urbane.[19] It is ironic that a nation with such a strong impulse toward social reconstruction at the same time generates a resistance to the new social entities constructed and to the theories that came into play to construct them. A thick philistine vein runs under our culture and surfaces in the desires expressed in our academies by students and faculty. This vein flows with a media-fed stream of fashion and propaganda. Given that current instructional ideas seem to avoid the most pertinent aspects of culture and are profoundly compromised by the strong discussions of the last thirty years and by the collapse of the doctrines that supported them, must we be tyrannized again by a simplistic notion of artistic liberation and its oafish sidekick, anti-intellectualism?

In the schools, discussion of method, which can be very threatening to entrenched teaching practices and recyclable syllabi, is often replaced by doctrinal bickering over the nature and value of what is taught, culminating in portentous calls for change and quality but little action. I am suggesting that if we are not going to transform our schools radically in response to the pressures of modern culture, if we accept the methodological premises presented by standard curricula and the entrenched mechanisms of the academy, then we should try to use them. These include information gathering and assimilation, analysis and synthesis, the study of the past and of culture, of ideas and aesthetics, the production of ordered thought and presentation of that thought to others. These seem preferable to tacitly agreeing to their irrelevance while maintaining institutions that are primarily equipped to support them. In short, if we cannot or will not do what we should — effect changes in the way we educate architects — then we should use, critique, and transform the instruments we have.

My argument should not be confused with the reactionary call for a restoration of the clarity of the Enlightenment, to a "golden age" before Freud, Marx, Nietzsche, a call that veils a return to a prerevolutionary order few of us want or would be included in.[20] Provisional definitions of "knowledge" and "discipline" can lead to grim conclusions, and therefore a plea for intensity within the many vehicles of knowledge transfer must be continually reformulated. While I have questioned many of the clichés and the presumed progressivism of modernist or avant-garde postures, it was not done to serve convention or reaction. To expose the contradictions and innate conservatism within the glibly progressive should make action possible. It seems necessary to walk a Tafurian line between neoconservative strategies of retrieval on one side and the exhausted paradoxes of the avant-garde and superficially "political" on the other.

Architectural design remains broadly synthetic in its reach from the depths of the artistic impulse to the rarefied heights of capital and the dictates of power. Design seems to be a synthetic process of filtering and interpreting, of metamorphosis in the rich mythmaking sense more than it falls into the exhausted and indefinable, and often unteachable, category of "creativity." It is powerfully cerebral at its roots. In the wide spectrum of possible didactic positions that can be addressed in and out of the academy, schools seem best prepared to aid the synthetic and analytic and to store and provide information. This may seem terribly pedestrian, but design school is a unique opportunity with special attributes, given the lessons provided in other architectural arenas. It is true that most design exercises insist that they do all this, but after closer inspection, they seem to reinforce the dogma of intuition over rigor and of thing over substance. The results of these exercises appear quite uniformly formal, object fixated, and finally consumable, despite accompanying arguments that they are just the opposite.[21]

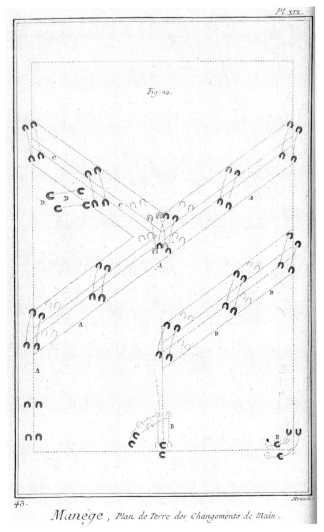

Figure 2.3a. From *Encyclopedia*, by Denis Diderot.

To begin with, there was the scale of the control: it was a question not of treating the body, *en masse*, "wholesale," as if it were a indissociable unity, but of working it "retail," individually; ... In becoming the target for new mechanisms of power, the body is offered up to new forms of knowledge. (Foucault 1979, 155)

A finer focus on the specific example of early design education reveals the criteria that determine the politically charged modes knowl-

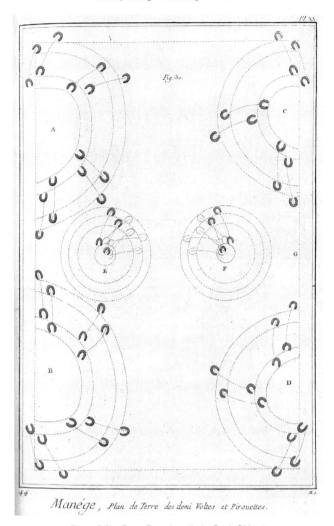

Figure 2.3b. From *Encyclopedia*, by Denis Diderot.

edge will assume. The education of the beginning design student may be seen as an Arcadian time of innocence and sharing, pure and clear. It is all these, but this moment also sits at a cusp where the disordered and intuitive become markedly less so. The crucial first studios instill an ongoing attitude. It is the period of maximum student receptivity generated by novelty and thus the point at which ideology is most readily transferred: the boot camp of architectural education. This fraught period is particularly vulnerable to emphatic doctrine and is complicated by the biases of extremely noninnocent individuals who determine curricula and exercises. The simple promise of beginning becomes immediately compromised by the fact of the academy and the fictions of an information-glutted culture. Struggles rage beneath the standards of "reality," "craft," "new technologies," "diversity," and "sustainability," to name a few of the major protagonists. Beginning design, as practiced in many schools of architecture, is based on debatable definitions of the parameters and issues that the field faces and that school work consequently might address. These issues ought to respond explicitly to the culture architecture serves and to the designer's role in representing that culture. Instead they remain surprisingly hermetic.

A friction exists between *beginning*—smelling of the pastoral, liberty, and spontaneity—and *institution,* redolent as it is of the rational, authority, and order. This, then, is the field in which design teaching starts and the abrasion of discipline and innocence presents enormous problems and great possibilities. The problems have plagued the institution at least since the inception of modernism and its paradoxical design formats. As already stated, the current uneasy truce between romantic notions of the artistic and perfunctory homage to professionalism and technology repeat modernist tensions without the passion that enlivened those tensions.

> When philosophy has finished showing that everything is a social construct,
> it does not help us decide which social constructs to retain and which to
> replace. (Rorty 1994, 227)

In this chapter, architecture is viewed as necessarily compromised by history and by the physical arena in which it expresses itself and of which it becomes part. Consequently, the first teaching of design as a primarily compositional endeavor, with the implied agenda of unleashing innate creative genius in the young designer, is problematic. I refer to the primarily formal exercises—cube transformations, nine-square manipulations, color studies—that shape many elementary design courses. Their roots lie in the interdisciplinary routines of the early modern design education, and they indeed suffer from some questionable presumptions of that era. These exercises are indistinguishable from similar courses taught in art schools, and they display a similar attitude toward education both in the fine arts and in architecture. As an architect, I can only speculate on the function and goals of the fine arts, but a primarily compositional impulse in our particular art seems problematic. Architecture is primarily an aesthetic endeavor, but finally it is a cultural act.

As previously mentioned, the current architectural period is one of partial return to codes of expression, abstraction, and autonomy, though enthusiasm for these attitudes seems to be diminishing.[22] Concurrently there has been a revival of teaching programs with similar objectives. Tough issues — political, economic, disciplinary — are avoided, and beguiling form is achieved. The products look good, and given their universal source and the reductive rules for their alteration and material, they look good together. Students and professors feel good, and a sense of accomplishment leads to the notion that successful design and, by extension, learning have been attained. Given the complex criteria that come into play in design and the discouragement or confusion they can engender, it is indeed necessary to provide reassurance. A sense of achievement should accompany early design work, but it must also be recognized that the restrictive criteria for formal production, while generating instant fulfillments, also promote powerful notions of what constitutes a body of architectural knowledge.

Curriculum is presented in abstract problems permitting certain limited "moves," ensuring an attractive product almost guaranteed by the rules, but at the same time implying an ethos of "design as game" that avoids the messy issues that face a troubled discipline. Architectural design is viewed as a contest to be won through the clever manipulation of its rules, a riddle to be decoded. The rhetorical search for a "solution" employs a terminology linked to mysteries and puzzles and implies a definite teleology. This then ratifies the questionable practice of grading design studio, a practice young students, trained in rote learning, used to be weaned from. This bias continues in the intricate vocabulary of "pieces," in the habitual identification of gambits and strategies. Military action, domesticated on the game board, here finds safe expression in the terms of design.[23] The exquisite thing produced, in the completeness and insistence of its object-hood, confirms the closed perfection of the game. The promise of material success in a gaming process seems strange here, for architectural education and practice actually are much more about means than ends. These games do form a definite knowledge system, but I question their use as a foundation during the vulnerable first exercises of a design education. They are compositional, and their inventors actively or passively propose an armature for later architectural pursuits for which the ideology is put in place in the first years of education.

Exercises that profess, through the actual making of furniture or artifacts that are usually more sculptural than utilitarian, to investigate construction or materiality often arrive at the same conclusion as those that are primarily compositional. They substitute an illusion of craft for the sort of discussion that might confront architecture from the position of our trade's dependence on manufacture. I am not, of course, saying that making is bad for students. But the crafting of beguiling forms avoids the sort of experience that might in fact contribute to an understanding of our art. This sort of work is parenthetical to the crucial interaction of both craft and material with our discipline and its production, while indulging in the pleasure of finishes and the satisfying illusion of labor. Also, it is very literal to presume that action at one scale automatically educates about similar procedures in a very different arena.

Likewise, design teaching that stresses a series of formal transformations and has adopted the loose designation of "process" can move toward a rich methodological discussion but tends toward the sublime vacuum of exponential formal possibilities. If the compositional exercises previously discussed are reductive and propose finally a "solution" that is the inevitable result of limiting possibilities, then "process" arrives at similar form by always expanding them. The operations offer formal variables at every design turn that disengage from signification. The resistance to closure is intense, and the desire for lavish form insistent. "Process" finally puts product first.

> If art contributes to, among other things, the way we view the world and shape social relations, then it does matter whose image of the world it promotes and whose interest it serves. (Haacke 1995)

Whether instructional technique pushes compositional skill through formal exercises, fosters a romantic notion of construction through primarily sculptural production, or arrives at formal entropy through the "exquisite corpse" of "process," the inclination for the beginning design student is to maintain the implied procedures in his or her later work. It is questionable that compositional exploration most effectively releases creativity justified by an automatic connection between pure form and the demiurge. To contest the intrinsic primacy of the latter as the main focus of an architectural education is necessary. It is indeed true that we make a lot of exciting shapes this way. If shape making were the goal of architectural investigation, then the logic of this approach would be irrefutable, and perhaps appropriate, to a commodity-based culture hungry for new consumable images.

Architectural action is never disengaged from the practices of power or economy—if there is a difference between the two. Although form is the product of any architectural action, study of the role of building in culture seems to indicate that "pure" form is profoundly compromised—by historical understandings, by the facts of contemporary culture, by nostalgia for the future, by the actual physical conditions of the realm that buildings find themselves part of and contribute to, by the perceptions of the collective, by the prescriptions of the powerful, by aesthetic concerns, theoretical concerns, technical concerns, economic concerns, political concerns, environmental concerns, by matters codified in allusion to the body, sexuality, and the city, by the burden of received meanings and their shadowy and shifting nature, by the possibilities and limits of reference, by the magic and the real, by a spectrum of information and sensibility that implies that form is in fact much more than just form, that it is mediated by arguments outside its pristine envelope.

> This is not to say, of course, that art is just advertising, only that art, outside the institutional vitrine of therapeutic mystery, is never *not* advertising and never apolitical. (Hickey 1993, 57)

How does one go about providing access to these arguments, assuming that it is not a good idea to suppose that they will come later, after the student has become comfortable, assuming that this comfort will persist as design dogma? I argue instead for an ontogenetic, not homuncular, beginning design curriculum. This argument presumes an architectural model that is figural. Architecture is seen an automatically engaged expression of societal value and collective sensibility. I urge the revival of some apparently outmoded terms, starting with Dave

Hickey's resuscitation of the issue of *beauty* and adding *analysis, history,* maybe even *realism,* not the "real" called for in current simplistic academic discourse, a *real* defined largely by what it excludes, but in the inclusive interpretation that aligns *realism* to, *neue sachlichkeit* to neorealism and magic realism. In fact, the extraordinary extension of the quotidian as promised in this sort of realism may guide the metamorphosis of the terms and institutions discussed in this chapter. This is not a polemic against either imagination or inspiration. In fact, it is one for them, but as implicitly informed by observation. One cannot "forget" what one does not know. One cannot reconfigure an alien field. And this may be the point, that the role of school in the preparation of young designers to practice our art pertains as much to reconfiguration as to invention. Not that the latter is of no importance to the process of making buildings. Obviously it is central, but creativity implies a nebulous and synthetic process largely relying on techniques of transformation and cross-reference, and given its visceral properties, it remains largely nonquantifiable in the framework of conventional architectural teaching. On the other hand, information — dare I say knowledge — is quantifiable and essential. The gathering of that material is largely a process of inquiry, of learning in the most ordinary of senses occurring simultaneously with the most extraordinary of critical actions.

It seems essential that analysis be engaged in immediately, with rigor, by the beginning student. He or she should start to gather and filter cultural conditions and transform them in the design process. Through this means, rather than through gaming or formal manipulation, the complexity of the field can become digestible. Critical inquiry is necessary in seamless conjunction with, and informing, composition. The simple description of forms and their interrelation should be accompanied by the assessment of their collective implications.[24] Then, interpretation, metamorphosis, and misreading may span the breach between the existing and the proposed, between the learned and the imagined, between the rejection of history and its uncritical acceptance. That the study of the relation of forms both manifests similarities and reveals differences and that these then represent shifting codes seems elementary. That study should accompany the first tentative attempts at design seems desirable. In fact, desire is nurtured through experience. Therefore, the plea here is for a pedagogy that, while striving to inspire, is thorough in its attempt to inform, its encouragement to observe, and its incitement to critique the complex vectors that frame architecture and the information-rich culture that architecture both shapes and serves.

This volume is called *The Discipline of Architecture*. This title joins the strengths both of a discursive practice of architecture and of architectural knowledge. To chart a precarious course between the various manifestations of control and pleasure that *discipline* promises while acknowledging the strategies of power that accompany them seems to be a challenging objective. While discipline may have now merged with the forms of what Pierre Bourdieu defines as "symbolic power" (1994, 266), making difficult any moves toward resistance without contradiction, for this same reason, it ratifies a flexible format for architectural action. To echo Eva Hesse's call for "total risk, freedom, discipline" (1969) seems an aim of both teaching and practicing the engaged act of design. The recognition of the potential and limits of knowledge and of such overlapping terms as politics, liberation, and creativity makes a frame for both pedagogy and production.

> Knowledge and power are simply two sides of the same question: who decides what knowledge is, and who knows what needs to be decided? In the computer age, the question of knowledge is now more than ever a question of government. (Lyotard 1984, 8–9)

Notes

This chapter reconfigures two essays written in 1993, "Against the Homunculus" and "The Intuitional Fallacy," and "Trouble in Paradise," written in 1996. All were published in various conference proceedings. I wish to thank Jennifer Gabrys and Frederick Ilchman for their comments on this text.

1. Here I sample Aldo Rossi, "To what then, could I have aspired in my craft? Certainly, to small things, having seen that the possibility of great ones was historically precluded" (1981, 23).

2. Actually, architecture seems to be turning over wholesale to subcontractors, attorneys, politicians, cultural critics, interior designers, engineers, and consultants of all sorts, the skills and activities that might stem the marginalization about which the profession complains so bitterly.

3. The work of Manfredo Tafuri is a model here as in other parts of this chapter. I have never shared the general American view of his project as too dark to be productive. In fact, I find its relentless assault on easy presumptions and doctrinal closure to be encouraging and to propose a paradigm for discursive practice as such. It needs to be pointed out that in a profession as intellectually insecure as architecture, the apparently complex rendered in overblown prose often substitutes for the rigorous inquisition of the evident that Tafuri embodied. To be what Alice Jardine calls "an expediter of the obvious" (Foster 1987, 151) seems one of the main points of intellectual work.

4. Like kitsch and fine art, for example. Where are the Clement Greenbergs, Andy Warhols, or Jeff Koons of architectural epistemology?

5. Stanton 1991.

6. These sorts of invented dichotomies, while historically linked to our understanding of ourselves — like man versus nature, or fashion versus profundity, or mind versus body, or rational versus lyrical — tend to serve productively only when they are understood as temporary and flawed, to be discarded when they have served their discursive purpose. It would appear that we are stuck for now with these oppositions, if only as intellectual form-work. They pepper the language of those who reject them, either leaving those critics mute after destroying the formats that allow speech or uttering phrases in the very language that is attacked in those phrases. Rather than dismissing them while having to use them in a discursive system in which they are so entrenched that their complete eradication remains unattainable, perhaps it is better to understand them as tools, rigid means to a flexible end: like ideals in a post-teleological society, like Wittgenstein's ladder (see "Works Cited").

7. The assumption seems to be that a redirection of conventional information formats toward "nonhegemonic" sources is adequate. Much current "political" criticism in the academies thrives on a less involved refocusing of scholarship toward these new sources without evident recognition of the issues that are implied by such action. Indeed, some of the strongest current criticism comes from these sources, recognizing the complicity of discourse with power and therefore attempting to reroute the entire direction of that discourse. As Cornel West writes, "The issue here is not simply some sophomoric, moralistic test that surveys the racial biases of the interlocutors in a debate. Rather the point is to engage in a structural and institutional analysis to see *where* the debate is taking place, *why* at this historical moment, and *how* this debate enables or disenables oppressed peoples to exercise their opposition to the hierarchies of power" (Kruger and Mariani 1989, 91). To use Diane Fuss's phrase, "romancing the margins" can either enrich or just marginalize. In fact, much current writing is scathingly dismissive of the very critical venues that would make it viable, labeling those venues as "overintellectual," "formalist," "irrelevant," "jargon heavy," "fashionable," or simply not "real."

8. See Banham 1960; Colquhoun 1981; Rowe 1976; and Rossi 1982; and especially the unrelenting critical studies of Manfredo Tafuri (1976, 1987, 1980) point-

ing to the contradictions of the conventional avant-garde and toward a less para-doxical, and more effective, successor.

9. "The whole technical power of painting depends on our recovery of what may be called the *innocence of the eye* that is to say, of a sort of childish perception of these flat stains of colour, merely as such, without consciousness of what they signify." From *The Works of John Ruskin* as quoted in Crary 1990, 95.

10. Theory, quite often political in nature, does sometimes accompany de-sign work that is primarily expressionistic, but it usually stays detached, clipped on to form.

11. I use the word *style* in its nineteenth-century sense: referential and mor-phological.

12. I refer in particular to the ACSA International Conferences in Prague '93, Lisbon '95, Copenhagen '96, and Berlin '97. At each was a much broader cross section of academics from Asia, Europe, Oceania, Africa, and the Americas than the still-substantial pool represented at the many ACSA meetings in the United States I have participated in since 1993 and to which the same comments pertain.

13. At a recent design review, a critic enthusiastically noted that the student work was generated from the study of precedents. In his day such precedents had been Palladio or Aalto—architects. Now they were James Turell, Robert Irwin, or Mary Miss—environmental sculptors. This shift in the field of reference and the uncritical acceptance of this shift by the assembled architectural teachers is indicative.

14. Students often feel that their study is inconsequential to their potential as architects, either too technical or too esoteric, and they feel constrained from doing that which they think will enhance that potential. Student opinion is not always the most accurate barometer of didactic quality. Educational value is not instantly evident, especially to those asked to learn and be judged. Opinion based on immediate perceptions and incomplete data, crossed with emotion, is by na-ture flawed. On the other hand, the irrelevancies felt by students must indicate some systemic problems in the institution, though these problems may lie well to the side of their perceived sources. Professional resentment often does not take into account the educational role that architectural internship is supposed to play, nor does it recognize the particular and scholastic strengths of the academy.

15. Both clichés are reminiscent of sixties revolutionary politics, when ecstatic and austere arguments previously competed for student sympathy. The juxtaposition of liberation and puritanism appears to be a perpetual paradox in the United States.

16. The verve of the *Futurist Manifesto,* of 1909, became Italian political doc-trine after 1922, making Fascism one of the only political movements predicated on aesthetic rhetoric.

17. Stanton 1998a and 1998b.

18. Should an interpretation of Deleuze (1988) have legitimized a strategy for making folded buildings? Does cultural chaos call for its double in architectural form? Such exact transpositions are problematic, but they again confirm that the search for novel form remains a first goal of theory.

19. The reception of Jackson Pollack, the *action* painter, typifies the uncritical American belief in the value of expression and pure image. Stripped of its uncomfortable European ideological charge, and ratified by a culture enthusiastic and naive regarding the complications implicit in such representation, the move to abstraction of the New York school was immediately appropriated by prevalent economic forces. See Stanton 1985.

20. See the neoconservative call for a "return" that in the end rejects the accomplishments — political, philosophical, social — of the last two hundred years. These would place us firmly again in the precise hierarchies and comforting (for some) clarity of prebourgeois culture. See Allan Bloom or William Buckley but also a host of others whose lowest common denominator is the Bushes — father and son.

21. Of course, these are largely available through publications or conference presentations and thus were chosen by the teachers and reflect their preferences over the inclinations of their students.

22. The American scene still clings to neoexpressionism. In a recent "Progressive Architecture Awards," published in *Architecture* 87 (April 1998): 61–93, almost all winning projects continued the faceting, contortion, striation, and biomorphism of late neoexpression. The accompanying text oddly concluded that "design moves away from the big gesture," identifying "subtle shifts" and asking if this was "back to basics." Aaron Betsky's commentary that accompanied the awards may be their most interesting aspect. He argued that "we no longer believe we can save cities . . . through new ways of forming space, solving the need for more or better housing . . . we have little faith anymore in the saving graces of styles." Betsky's insertion of the argument for engagement that I earlier attributed to Aldo Rossi (see note 1) and his insightful if rather hopeless description of the modern condition and its formal discontents as represented by the winners make his piece intriguing. In fact, style seems all powerful in this awards issue. Despite the editorial attempt to keep up, the forms chosen by the jury were quite predictable, as were textual associations to Deleuze and the "dangerous, strange and alien." The presence of Zaha Hadid herself on the jury may explain their preferences, but hers were the strongest critiques of the winning projects, and her discussion of program was the least formal of any on the panel. It seems the jury's Americans (North and Central) were more comfortable with the *style* of their collective choices than Ms. Hadid. Juror Sheila Kennedy remarked, "We looked for things that were deep, being careful not to be fooled by simple, quiet presentations." For her, the simple is deceptive. Noise and formal complexity, with novelty still very much of value, remained preferable criteria.

23. The maintenance, in subsequent architectural education, of an ongoing emphasis on design work primarily at the parti stage indicates a specific game plan. Although often complicating the play by presenting a vocabulary of architectural elements — walls, windows, doors, stairs — as players, these elements are simultaneously dematerialized to the point of intangibility.

24. Here the problem of typology, in the European semiotic sense, taints the discussion. For Americans, typology smacks uncomfortably of rationalism, categorization, systems and logic, of antiquated cosmologies, of pitched roofs and certain Italians, of history itself: all suspect commodities in the New World.

3
On the Practices of Representing and Knowing Architecture

Andrzej Piotrowski

Designing Architecture

Designing architecture is a unique epistemological practice, a unique way of knowing resulting from a complex process of conceptual negotiations. Architects not only solve technical problems and create aesthetic objects but facilitate a process in which visions of a building acquire a particular symbolic or cultural sense. While working on a project, a designer must develop multiple architectural proposals, understand the complexity of issues they manifest, and negotiate them with the parties involved in the project — clients, local authorities, planners, consultants, contractors, bankers, and many others. A designer produces these versions in order to understand what kind of a design problem he or she is actually dealing with.[1] Understanding how a building functions as a cultural artifact is esoteric when compared to, say, the scientific understanding of its physical properties. Unlike, for example, the universality of the principles of physics, a building's symbolic performance is inseparable from time and place. In the design process, the symbolic dimension of architecture is envisioned with the help of models of inhabited reality created in one's imagination or of images retrieved from memory. These conceptual negotiations involve the exchange between different modes of thought and points of view — between verbal and visual interpretations, for example, or between universal scientific laws and the kind of understanding that a particular design process reveals. Everything that an architect produces—conceptual sketches, physical models, functional diagrams, technical drawings, cost analysis spreadsheets, and verbal explanations—supports this process of negotiation. In this way, by testing the spatial and material attributes of architecture, an architect explores the complexity of issues and forces that shape a prospective building.[2] Thus the epistemological uniqueness of designing lies in the double character of this process, of simultaneously defining and resolving the design task. Because of its dual nature, this process is clearly different from that of problem solving, which, even at its most inventive, is based on a scientific paradigm—an assumption that a task becomes a problem that can be resolved when its objectives and limitations are well defined. In contrast, it is impossible to unequivocally define symbolic objectives of architecture and ways of evaluating the symbolic correctness of a particular solution. One could also say that the creative process of designing architecture is similar to writing a novel or painting a picture because all involve revising in the refinement of an idea in one's mind. Yet physical buildings and concepts for prospective architecture relate differently to the material world, everyday life, and culture than do the works of literature or studio arts. First, architecture engages all that surrounds us—all those attributes of our material, social, and political environments that frame everyday life. As a result, the best architecture, without focusing attention on a building, reveals complexity of meanings within those contexts. Second, the architectural design process crystallizes the designer's vision and understanding of reality for all the people involved in the project. Consequently, architects give form to multiple and frequently conflicting or unrealized thoughts concerning reality and, in this way, make them conceptually accessible. Later, when the building exists physically, it manifests a symbolic environment distilled from the ideas, visions, and rationales admitted by the design process. A building's form and the way it functions embody these resulting symbolic concepts of reality.

Such a process is essential for the way buildings are designed. However, only the systematic and purely rational part of the design process has been epistemologically codified, as, for example, the technical knowledge of building systems, taxonomy of architectural styles, or functional typology. All that is really specific to architectural design thought—the mode of interacting with architectural visions that crystallizes concepts of reality—falls outside of established disciplinary categories. Any knowledge, including the traditional history of architecture, that views a building as an unavoidable result of physical or social determinants—for example, climate, dominant political or social forces, or the wishes of a particular client—excludes from its field the symbolically dynamic process of conceptual negotiations I have outlined.

I contend that the discipline of architecture should focus on what is specific to architectural thought: those processes through which architecture shapes understanding of reality. The issue of representation is essential for this kind of epistemological focus. The prevalent understanding of representation in architectural education and profession is still grounded in Aristotle's concept of representation as the imitation of nature and Plato's process of doubling (Aristotle 1984, 194a, 199a; Plato 1924, 214–15). Generally speaking, such traditional approaches assume that as objects of knowing, representation and reality stand in opposition. Thus reality is only that which exists objectively, unaffected by the act of knowing it. Representation, on the other hand, includes everything people construct to be known as a visual record or figurative manifestation of that reality. This opposition reflects the desire for a clear and stable distinction between what actually exists and what was made to appear. Within this approach, architects usually reduce the definition of representation to the creation of such visual forms as drawings or models that selectively double or imitate the physical reality of a building.[3] I would like to move beyond this traditional view to define representation as a culture-specific and dynamic process of establishing the relationships between reality and the signs created to symbolize this reality. In this process, reality becomes *thinkable,* and its meanings are symbolically assigned. That is, through representation the symbolic attributes and structures of a particular concept of reality are rendered accessible to human thought. Although my emphasis is on the visual and experiential aspects of these processes as they occur in architecture, it is noteworthy that Kenneth Surin, Raymond Williams, and Edward Said have already discussed the same issues from a literary perspective, demonstrating that the thinkability of concepts and structuring of feelings, attitudes, and references are essential for the cultural and social specificity of thought.[4] Designing a building involves similar processes of establishing sense in a prospective reality of architecture, but these processes rely only in part on verbal negotiations. In general, buildings do not communicate but represent, a distinction essential to the study of architectural specificity of thought.[5] Architecture represents rather than communicates because the symbolic reality that a building manifests becomes perceivable, but its understanding never reaches the stability of an unequivocal interpretation. This representational process is far more complex and dynamic than the process of sending, preserving, retrieving, and decoding well-formed messages. This is also why, although I see significatory practices as central to conceptualizing and knowing architecture, my approach differs from that of architectural structuralists such as Umberto Eco or Juan Pablo Bonta.[6]

The notion that architecture helps crystallize mental concepts of reality may seem esoteric, but the symbolic practices revolving around this phenomenon are omnipresent in our life, as I will discuss in terms of three practices of knowing typical of architecture: first, when a person interacts with an existing building; second, when knowledge of a building is disseminated through pictures and words; and third, when a building's vision is constructed for commercial reasons. The major objective of my strategy is to identify how these practices constitute knowledge of a building as a symbolic site — which attributes of a building are foregrounded, how knowing a building defines the relationship between who knows and what is known, and how the truthfulness of this knowledge is ensured.

Existing Buildings

Similarly to Jean Baudrillard's description of architecture as that "in which the space is the thought itself" (1999, 32), I assert that a piece of architecture is the *space of representation* — a material environment constructed to interact with human thoughts in such a way that the concepts of reality that the building embodies acquire a degree of tactility.[7] Buildings and cities represent when they serve as repositories of materialized concepts that manifest how people have defined themselves in their lived reality. Bricks and stones last longer than human life, and they transmit these concepts of reality across generations. In this way, a building becomes a repository of cultural memory and helps to expand the sense of reality beyond the here and now. Any piece of architecture functions in this manner when its value is found in the interconnections it establishes with other buildings, practices of everyday life, social structures, attributes of the natural environment, or metaphysical concepts, although many aspects of these relationships may be perceivable only to people identifying with the local culture(s). This process of establishing a symbolic network of relationships can be viewed as analogous to what Jean-François Lyotard calls the emergence of representational consciousness. He observes that the viewer's accumulation of experiences and the delay of the immediacy of reaction to what is being perceived at a particular moment show "how perception stops being 'pure', i.e., instantaneous, and how representational consciousness can be born of this reflection (in the optical sense), of this 'echo,' of the influx on the set of other possible — but currently ignored — paths which form memory" (1991, 42). Through this process, according to Lyotard, human thoughts establish networks of relationships within functioning concepts of reality.

The history of architecture and urban design provides many examples of how public buildings and urban places have given form to and transmitted through time concepts of social structures and value systems. Streets or places of everyday habitation and work, although not fitting into the traditional taxonomy of high architectural styles, provide equally rich symbolic environments.[8] To see how architecture operates as the space of representation, one has to examine the relationship between concepts of reality and the material building itself.

Buildings, unlike scholarly treatises or the rules of law, do not make arguments. As the space of representation, a building only foregrounds concepts of reality and implies modes of thought and perception. For example, it invites a tacit dialogue between old and new, or between a culturally shared and a personal sense of reality. Whatever exists or happens in a building, we interact with it symbolically. Any building admits various and even conflicting concepts of reality. Consider, for example, places where different cultures have coexisted for ages, temples that have been absorbed by different religions, or the recent phenomenon of converting old industrial buildings into public spaces. Such hybridity of meanings is possible because concepts of reality and physical forms of buildings, although symbolically related, are never fully codependent; they are differently constructed. Concepts of reality ultimately aim at clarity and consistency, and if they reach this goal, they result in a verbally organized system of thought, such as laws of physics or principles of theology. As such, these systematic models can be used to unequivocally explain reality; physics, for example, can explain the rationale behind organization of structural members of a building, and theology can be used to interpret the meanings of religious artifacts in a temple. A building, on the other hand, though physically fixed and permanent, remains open to interpretation as a symbolic environment. The materiality of architecture, its construction of space and light, how a building's form implies certain interrelationships among people or metaphorically resembles other places — these are attributes that operate on a level where thought is barely initiated. In this way, buildings engage attention rather than shape rational understanding; they prompt an attitude rather than form a correct knowledge or interpretation. Consequently, because buildings do not impose concepts of reality but make them thinkable, many concepts may coexist and be in symbolic dialogue with one another within a physical space.

When people interact with a building, their understanding of it involves another aspect of this process. A knowledge of reality can relate to life in various degrees — for example, phenomena modeled by quantum physics relate to issues of human existence quite differently than does the knowledge of ethics. Similarly, it does matter how a person interacting with a building finds personal relevance in this interaction. To reveal these kinds of meanings, the building must somehow engage, like Lacan's mirror, a personal sense of reality.[9] I will call this kind of interconnection between the person who knows and the building being known the *subject-object relationship*. For example, a house can be seen as the place where a family shapes and reveals its identity in the never-ending construction of its symbolic environment. Institutional buildings have always been used to simultaneously shape concepts of human subjectivity and the understanding of the world at large. The last two centuries, however, have been crucial for the contemporary understanding of Western subjectivity and its relationship to all others. Architecture has played an important role in these processes. Consider, for example, Foucault's discussion of how the transition in the way individuals related to the society and its power structures between the classical era to the modern world was demonstrated by the design for a particular building. Panopticon, Jeremy Bentham's design for a prison, transformed the individual into a visible "object of information" controlled by omnipresent and invisible power (Foucault 1979, 200). It was the symbolic dimension of this project that made it also useful for designing schools, psychiatric hospitals, and workplaces — the sites of disciplining the society. Later, in the second half of the nineteenth century, when institutional structures equated knowledge with power, architectural designers created different kinds of sites. Museums and world expositions, for instance, created physical places signifying centers of this new abstract power but made them accessible to the masses of the working and middle classes. In this way, architecture facilitated the construction of a totalizing view of the whole world and its history and consequently reshaped Western subjectivity. It was, in the words of Tony Bennett, an order of these buildings "which organized the implied public — the white citizenries of the imperialist powers — into a unity, representationally effacing divisions within the body politic in constructing a 'we' conceived as the realization, and therefore just beneficiaries, of the processes of evolution and identified as a unity in opposition to the primitive otherness of conquered peoples" (1988, 92).

Although these examples describe buildings that explicitly signified power, I believe that contemporary buildings engage human subjectivity the most when they become inseparable, in one's mind, from everyday life. When buildings and the spatial practices they structure become so familiar that they disappear from our field of perception, their impact is the deepest. That is why places that people commonly understand as simply convenient, such as shopping malls, or merely efficient, such as highways, profoundly shape our contemporary way of life. They support a tacit alignment between concepts of reality built into everyday architecture and one's sense of the self.

One elemental question remains: if a person interacting with an existing building becomes aware that this building represents a particular concept of reality, how does this person know that his or her understanding of this concept is true? To say this differently, how does one identify the *authority of signification* in an existing building? The answer seems easy if one believes in the transcendental and transcultural qualities architecture possesses.[10] To answer this question, I return to my discussion of architecture as a repository of concepts of reality. It is noteworthy that nowadays the most likely answer would be that the designer has the final authority over a building's meanings. However, the designer, the one who could supposedly explain the meanings of architecture, is not there to do so. On those rare occasions when design intentions are explained by architects, their explanation of symbolic meanings is usually the most trivial part of their reasoning process. This may result from what Suha Özkan observed as architects' endless "tendency... to redefine architecture in order to accommodate one specific aspect of discourse in theory or practice of the profession" (Özkan 1999, 148). Exploring architecture as the representation of concepts of reality starts with a belief that architecture stands for a certain understanding of reality. This belief, however, does not have to be grounded in a transcendental authority of signification that would have guided the thoughts of a designer centuries ago and thus would allow us to decipher unequivocally representational signs now. As discussed, the design process crystallizes multiple thoughts and interests concerning representational intentions. Consequently, it is exactly the absence of a transcendental authority and the need to consider the intentions of many people that disclose the political hermeneutics in architecture and make it possible to trace how and who has shaped representational processes. The dispersion of the authority of signification and the impossibility, even in the most totalitarian society, of naming a singular authority whose principles totally organize the representational aspects of a building, are the sine qua non of the culturally specific symbolic functioning of architecture. This means that the symbolic negotiations I discussed can be studied only within their network of political and ideological dependencies and that the authority of signification is a part of this dynamic process itself.

Consequently, the practice of interacting with a building constitutes a mode of knowing similar to that of designing architecture. Architecture still initiates symbolic thoughts; cultural negotiations around various concepts of reality still occur; and many people can still participate in this process. In this way, a building continues the transformation and crystallization of concepts of lived reality beyond the design phase.

Published Knowledge

It seems only reasonable to question the constitution of the published knowledge of architecture in the same way as the common knowledge of existing buildings. When one compares what a person who interacts with a building knows versus what a person who studies architecture from books and articles knows, the distinction becomes telling.

Because buildings remain fixed to their locations, learning about them requires that their reality be reproduced to make possible the perception and cognition of architecture from a distance. This way of representing architecture differs from the way a building would present itself to our perception. The complex processes I have discussed before must be replaced by a third party's showing relevant architectural attributes and explaining their significance.

When the authority of signification is considered, it should be noted that whoever explains architecture is placed in a privileged position. By the act of explaining, this new authority repossesses symbolic meanings. This appropriation is easiest when the original designer is no longer available to verify critics' speculations or if the design activity arose out of common social practice and as such could be seen as determined by local traditions, social structures, and the physical environment. Seemingly, if writers can fully understand what the creators "really" intended or had to do and how it was realized, they gain authority almost equal to that of those who created the work. Consequently, the process of analyzing and explaining operates best by foregrounding in architecture all that can be traced as explicitly intentional or necessary. Undoubtedly, this process helps to justify the privileged position of the writers. On the other hand, as a model of knowing based on the clarity of will and logic, it excludes the complex processes of crystallizing and negotiating concepts that I outlined before.

Another important aspect of truthfulness in architectural scholarship is the issue of the epistemological assumptions built into scholarly methods, two of which are worthy of outlining here. One assumption that unites, for example, the traditional history of architecture, the modernist paradigm of architectural sociology, and contemporary cultural studies that explore architecture from a literary perspective is that they all take for granted that societies and cultures first form their concepts verbally and then in architecture — that architecture dresses these verbal concepts up in material forms. Such oversimplification of all processes of symbolic negotiations and the emergence of thought I discussed earlier can be identified when a scholarly publication places architectural form in a binary opposition to meaning; when, for example, a building is dismissed as meaningless if its form does not literally fulfill the expectations created by a supposedly correct narrative, or when a critic approaches it with insufficient experience in analyzing the nonliteral or nonfigural attributes of architecture.

The other assumption lies in the overall taxonomy of architectural knowledge. Although architectural knowledge is frequently presented as interdisciplinary or crossdisciplinary, it is explicitly divided into a set of distinctive subfields, which have been constituted after, and rely on, the epistemological authority of their "pure" models, such as physics, history, or sociology. Thus, when explaining a historic building as an important structural accomplishment, for example, the correctness of the researcher's methodology and conclusions is secured by the principles of physics. How this particular structural solution presents an architectural achievement derives from an understanding of this building's physical performance. Such conclusions stand on their own and do not have to relate to other ways of knowing this building's significance. This right to single out aspects of architectural reality stems directly from the authority that traditional epistemological models have over the segmented knowledge of reality. It is noteworthy, however, that this taxonomy of knowledges resulted from the classical *epistēmē*'s elimination of vagueness in analytical thought and from the nineteenth-century structuring of knowledge (Foucault 1970). Both the elimination of vagueness and the institutional ability to exercise knowledge as power are antithetical to what I have identified as uniquely architectural mode of thought. That a building can make fragile symbolic concepts of reality thinkable and that this can happen in a complex interaction between all aspects of architecture and life is too uncontrolled a knowledge to register within these traditional disciplinary concepts.

When a person reads a book about an existing piece of architecture, the subject-object relationship directly depends on the mediating role of the writer who describes, analyzes, and explains. The subject (the person who studies the book) and the object (the building being studied) relate to each other only as far as the writer implies it in the argument. While reading a book and looking at illustrations, the reader agrees to follow the narration. The ability of the symbolically rich and physically passive form of architecture to imply thoughts is replaced by a writer's or photographer's control of connections between the verbal explanation and the depictions of a building. Reading about architecture is a much more structured practice than the symbolic dialogue a person might have had with an existing building. What the reader perceives, the writer has already selected to be seen and understood. The process of reading, in other words, involves the mode of communication rather than that of representation. The reader reads primarily to understand messages formed by the writer. These mediated observations and conclusions come at the expense of what might have happened between the subject and the object in the space of architecture. Instead of architecture that merely initiates thoughts and confronts the subject with symbolically rich but inconclusive observations, a book embodies a rhetorical practice of arguments and conclusions. A writer may still reflect on symbolic issues that redefine the subject's identity, but this reflection will be devoid of the metaphoric richness that architecture offers.

A book or an article thus creates its own space of representation. Text and illustrations, composed to interact with human thought, foreground particular attributes of architecture very differently from the way a building would. Certain architects of the modern movement, Le Corbusier and Giuseppe Terragni, for example, have recognized and used this representational phenomenon when they published their architectural ideas and buildings, designing the space of representation of their publications like that of architecture.[11] Most frequently, however, books and articles about architecture follow general scholarly patterns. They provide so-called factual information in two forms: verbal and numerical (for example, dates, names, and records of events associated with the building's history, measurements of its physical performance, or empirical statistics resulting from the postoccupancy research) or as illustrations. Visual interaction with illustrations seems to resemble the way a person experiences a building more than does learning from verbal and numerical data. However, a building indiscriminately reveals its symbolic attributes, whereas measured drawings or photographs showing the same building are highly exclusive. Measured drawing conventions, such as plans, sections, and other paraline projections, are, first of all, tools of analysis.[12] They record only what can be measured — the physical size, geometric shape, and location of material elements. Whatever is recorded becomes a coded sign — a line or a number. Attributes that "barely initiate thought," such as the visual and experiential phenomena I discussed earlier, do not register within such a system of analytical notation.[13] Photography, on the other hand, filters reality in a different way. A photograph seems to be an "objective" record of the field of vision that, if not tampered with, is trustworthy because the photochemical process provides a reliable method of recording an image that appears in the box of a camera. This belief is grounded in the same epistemological concept that made camera obscura a symbol of truth in viewing during the classical era.[14] All that makes photography appear believable or objective conceals how much a photograph is a constructed representation. Unlike a person's experience in architectural space, a photographer's picture singles out a particular view and freezes it in time. That which the image illustrates is composed to be seen in certain manner, making particular relationships visible and hiding others. Photographers frequently manipulate light, either artificial or natural, to enhance selected attributes of architecture. All traces of human habitation or symbolic characteristics that exist in the space of the architecture but violate the purity of the master argument are frequently excluded from the picture.

Consequently, the act of publishing architectural knowledge produces a fundamental epistemological and representational shift. Traditional practices of architectural research and knowledge dissemination predetermine their results. That way of knowing aims at certainty and stability of interpretations and, in this way, transforms an existing building into a site of affirmation. Thus, in the mind shaped by this kind of knowledge, a building loses its ability to engage all aspects of life and perception and to negotiate the functioning concepts of reality and be-comes, rather, a place where a "legitimate" interpretation, the one autho-rized by the powers that this knowledge represents, can and should be affirmed on site.

Commercial Promotion

Architects' promoting their work to attract potential clients constitutes another practice of knowing and representing architecture. This mar-ket-driven practice revolves around the business of architectural ser-vices. In a market economy, the ability to disseminate information about a new building is essential if an architect is to achieve popularity and financial success. Generally speaking, commercial strategies stem from an understanding of the market and aim at predicting or, even better, creating demand for a particular product. Although profit remains the driving force behind these strategies, technology provides the means. The history of capitalism shows that the relationship between technol-ogy and power has evolved from that which merely acted on the physical reality into that which transforms reality at its cultural level by chang-ing the way we perceive and interpret the world. Although the work of architects transforms the material world, the business of architecture depends on these new kinds of technologies. Whether called cultural technologies (Bennett 1988, 76), technology of contemporary society (Jameson 1991, 37), or mental technologies (Baudrillard 1999, 33), they have been identified as essential for the cultural changes of the last two centuries. The construction of viewing and the ways of reproducing the visible have been at the center of these processes. Consider, for exam-ple, the stereoscope, an optical device of the first half of the nineteenth century that creates an illusion of three-dimensionality in photographic images. It turned the human body, specifically its optical physiology, into a site where visual sensations could be controlled (Crary 1990, 118–36). The buildings of museums and world exhibitions of approximately the same period used spatial arrangements of objects and visitors to view the knowledge of the past as well as the Western and non-Western worlds (Bennett 1988). But it was the mass media, such as printed catalogs of commercial products, postcards, and movies, that, according to Beatriz Colomina (1994), reshaped the modes of perception and representation at the beginning of the twentieth century. The style of modernism emerged when architects designed buildings to function like mass media. What started with nineteenth-century viewing devices continues now in new technology. Virilio sees digital techniques of visual simulation as "duplication of 'stereoscopy of the real'" leading to "industrialization of the sensations" (1993, 126). It seems that the ultimate goal of these new technologies is to control all forms of perception to the point where the simulated and the real cannot be distinguished—the perfect virtual reality. Today this control of perception reaches far beyond optical tricks of the nineteenth century. On a global scale, mass media and information technology shape our understanding of reality by manipulating the perception of facts and their meanings.[15] In this new world, where the perfection of digital simulation and the flow of information are rapidly increasing, skepticism follows. This technologically mediated sense of reality seems to lose its ability to engage people in a meaningful way, its symbolic relevance becoming diffused by what Gianni Vattimo calls the infinite interpretability of reality (1988, xxi).[16] These cultural phenomena indicate the future that architects face. That the commercial promotion of architecture should be seen as a part of these changes suggests that we should examine popular practices of representation in the business of architecture—the symbolic constitution and functioning of commercial magazines and the use of computer graphics.

When the authority of signification and the subject-object relationship are considered, commercial promotion discloses a different set of issues than those I discussed in the previous two practices of interacting with a building and reading a book. Beautiful photographs of newly constructed buildings or digitally simulated images of structures designed but not yet built may look similar to the photographs in scholarly publications, but their symbolic functioning is radically different. I assert that viewing a commercial photograph erases the distinction between the authority of signification and the identity of the subject.

When published in a commercial magazine, simulated images of new designs or photographs of newly constructed buildings are used to promote architectural products. It is noteworthy, however, that commercial promotion is a symbolic practice that primarily identifies and engages potential clients. The most important aspect of this process is that this practice simultaneously aims at attracting attention and places one's ego in the center of symbolic meanings. A potential client must become the measure of the product's value and its symbolic content. Thus a glossy image depicting architecture must show a new version of what a targeted clientele likes to see, convincing them that what they find exciting in the image is all that matters in the depicted piece of architecture. Consequently, the looking subject becomes the authority of signification. This precludes the complexity of the symbolic dialogue with architecture discussed before. What the beholders find in a picture must affirm what they already like. Promotional photographs of architecture do not want to disrupt this affirmation or force the viewer to reflect critically on his or her subjectivity. The image, rather than supporting a symbolic dialogue between the viewer and a depicted building, encourages the viewer's desire to own a similar kind of architectural commodity. This constructed desire for the represented object shapes the commercial subject-object relationship. If such a picture encourages a reflection on the subject's identity, this reflection is framed only in terms of material possession.

The space of representation created when architecture is commercially promoted is also telling. Attributes of architecture are foregrounded in a new way and for different reasons than those in the practices discussed earlier. Commercial magazines are full of "perfect" or "stunning" illustrations of newly constructed buildings. A reader of an architectural glossy magazine may have difficulty distinguishing which images belong to the section advertising the use of new building materials and which describe new significant architecture. What works for an advertisement works for architectural promotion as well. Editorial boards select buildings that guarantee the popularity of the magazine. Photographs show hyper-real colors, dramatic forms, and amazing locations. Digitally enhanced photo-realism makes these pictures believable. At the same time, they attract and focus attention in a particular way. A picture seduces the viewers by showing something that cannot easily be seen in their lived reality: a glimpse into the exclusive world of the rich, visually perfect places of work or social life, or, at least, incredible light effects. Moreover, the latest stylistic trends or the newest "proper attitude" toward material or cultural environment get translated into distinct visual attributes: fashionable shapes, "high-tech" materials and details, or architectural forms that are characteristically understated to imply social or environmental concerns, for example. In this way, the space of representation that commercial promotion constitutes makes it easy for a potential client to identify with attributes of a particular visual fashion or trendy ideology.

Similar practices can be observed in the way computers simulate the perception of architecture. An architect can now present the appearance of a building to a client before it is constructed. The simulated images show precisely the form of the building and its light distribution, including colors, texture, and reflectivity of materials, even the optical properties of the air. All the dramatic effects and stylistic attributes that can be photographed can be simulated on a computer screen as well. Depending on the hardware and the time available, such an illusion can reach photo-realistic accuracy, where everything looks exactly as if built. Moreover, such a photo-realistic image automatically excludes all those uncontrolled traces of life that could contaminate a photograph. In the future, this kind of visual experience will be interactive, and the client will be able to choose in "real time" what to look at or where to move in the simulated space of the building being designed. On the one hand, this experience appeals to the client's desire to expand the personal freedom of choice over an imaginary product. On the other, the commercially rooted belief that "what you see is what you get" is combined here with the total control of visual perception, and together they create an extremely superficial sense of the space of representation. This way of presenting architecture hides the complexity of symbolic issues behind dazzling effects and literal interpretations. Any technology that aims at replacing imagination with fully controlled visual stimulation may work for the entertainment industry, but it trivializes architecture.

Consequently, because commercial promotion makes the subject the sole judge of represented reality, reduces the subject-object relationship to liking or desiring, and constructs symbolic reality out of attributes that connote fashion, the resulting understanding of architecture differs profoundly from that of inhabited buildings. The processes of instant gratification replace Lyotard's processes of shaping representational consciousness (1991). As discussed earlier, representational consciousness deciphers what we perceive as related to all that we remember and can imagine. Shaping this consciousness is a continual and difficult process of rethinking relevant concepts of reality. In the commercially driven modes of representing architecture, perception must be pure and instantaneous; otherwise the pictures could not dazzle or seduce a client. As Baudrillard observed, in such a process, imagined and remembered reality become prey to "the combined effects of impatience and indifference" (Baudrillard, 1988b, 95). Because images produced in this process are not meant to be read within a complex network of references, representational processes are replaced by the mechanisms of simulation of the symbolic — by the production of the most superficial effects of reality.[17] When promoted in this way, not only images but material buildings lose their ability to engage thought. Famous new buildings become tourist attractions. The tourist industry puts them on the list of attractive travel destinations: sites that are meant to dazzle or intrigue a visitor. In one's mind, such a site, whether it is an ancient temple in a distant country or a new building close to home, is reduced to a symbolic environment that functions when it pleases a visitor. By dismissing the difficult symbolic processes discussed earlier and foregrounding one's ego by making liking or disliking the only measure of any value in architecture, a building is truly commodified.

Conclusion

The separate practices I have discussed are actually highly interconnected. New buildings are frequently designed to meet one primary requirement: to be photogenic. In those cases, instead of designing a building for the way people interact with it, an architect designs for, and benefits from, the effect that the building's image produces. It should not be surprising that often the practice of learning and teaching architecture also follows these patterns. Thus an architectural design studio becomes no more than an implementation of a commercial technique when students, as clients of educational services, are encouraged to seek visual pleasure in the digital effects they produce or to treat their intuitive emotional attachment to certain design ideas as the ultimate sense of value in a design project. It is also difficult to distinguish between dissemination of architectural research and commercial promotion when the knowledge of the latest building technique is packaged to signify progress and disseminated across cultural divisions.

The mechanisms of architectural knowledge production that I have outlined in this chapter are similar to, and in fact they have been a part of, processes of colonization. Edward Said's observation that the colonizing powers epistemologically transformed other cultures, "receiving these other cultures not as they are but as, for the benefit of the receiver, they ought to be," can be applied to the contemporary knowledge of the world's architecture (1979, 67). These processes have reached far beyond the structuring and dissemination of information; they have colonized imagination and sensitivity and consequently predetermined the thinkability of symbolic ideas in architecture for people educated within the Western *epistēmē*. I believe that it was exactly the building's ability to keep the symbolic concepts of reality in a state of nascence, its ability to support a never-ending dialogue between these concepts and the changing conditions of life, that the colonizing forces exploited. The culture-specific mode of enunciation that architecture supports proved to be extremely vulnerable when confronted with the precision of the Western mode of thought imposed to "explain" it.[18] The global market continues these processes by turning the symbolism of architecture into a commodity—that is, emptying lived reality of its cultural specificity and filling that void with the commercial notion of universal exchange value. These processes functioned not only for the colonization of the hybrid complexity of the other realities; they eliminated from the taxonomies of architectural knowledge culturally "impure" or "provincial" Western architecture as well. The world is still full of underexplored and lived symbolic environments. The cultural dimensions of even the most popular commercial buildings still seem transparent to traditional methods of architectural research. The difficulty of acknowledging the epistemological processes through which we "know" architecture and how they predetermine the nature of that knowledge results from the convergence of political and commercial forces to tacitly structure the ways we perceive, think, and communicate. Consequently, to expand the understanding of how buildings have contributed to different cultures and how they participate in contemporary cultural phenomena, the discipline of architecture must develop new critical strategies and change its epistemological assumption.

Notes

1. Usually, the architectural program for a new building states only the requirements concerning its physicality (for example, sizes of spaces) and practical aspects of its function (such as efficient adjacencies of activities).

2. This process may be seen as analogous to the emergence of discursive formations. According to Foucault, the ideological and political processes of the formation and dissemination of concepts lead to the emergence of epistemological statements and then knowledge (Foucault 1972, 106–13). The knowledge that emerges from the process of designing a building follows this model, but the architectural process is local and primarily synchronic and differs from other disciplines in the way nonverbal modes of thought are essential for refining its conceptual statements.

3. Frequently, even the understanding of the symbolic functioning of a completed building is constructed in a similar manner. In such approaches, the interpretation of a building's symbolism follows how the building's form can be broken into a collection of its figural components, as if recognizable and namable figures created the only grounds for symbolic representation. For the discussion of a different point of view, the study of nonfigurative representation, see my essay "Architecture and the Iconoclastic Controversy," in *Medieval Practices of Space,* ed. Barbara A. Hanawalt and Michal Kobialka (Minneapolis: University of Minnesota Press, 2000).

4. Kenneth Surin says that "every culture generates for itself its own 'thinkability' (and concomitantly its own 'unthinkability' as the obverse of this very 'thinkability'), and its concepts are constitutive of that 'thinkability'" (1995, 1183). Similarly, Raymond Williams discusses structures of feelings as a set of "affective elements of consciousness" that could either explicitly manifest existing social structures or be a part of "a social experience which is still *in process,* often indeed not yet recognized as social but taken to be private, idiosyncratic, and even isolating" (1977, 132). He also says that "the idea of a structure of feelings can be specifically related to the evidence of forms and conventions—semantic figures—which, in art and literature, are often among the first indications that such a new structure is forming" (1977, 133). "Structures of feelings" led Edward Said to a similar concept of "structures of attitude and reference" (1994, 52).

5. For many, the processes of conceptual negotiations in architecture could easily be explained as a particular mode of communication. When considered vis-à-vis my definition of representation, communication can be seen as a particular and narrow aspect of representation—a structured exchange of thoughts that are already well formed, ideally like information. Consider, for example, Roman Jacobson's discussion of the process of communication. Although Jacobson studies the poetic dimension of verbal communication, he still follows the primary linguistic model, the one in which the process of communicating a message consists of forming a message, then coding it, intentionally transmitting between a sender and a receiver via a channel, and finally decoding it (1960, 353).

6. Eco (1980) focuses on developing a system of codes that supposedly reflect the culture-specific symbolic functioning of architecture. Bonta tries to establish an elaborate and seemingly highly systematic taxonomy of communication, which treats architecture as a cultural phenomenon operating through signs (1979, 26–30). However, I think that Geoffrey Broadbent discloses the false assumption behind these kinds of studies when he asserts that "any attempt to design buildings consciously for the effects they now have on their users [is] a pragmatic affair," and thus he implies that designers must have always obeyed those practical rules that turn visual phenomena into a system of visual communication (1977, 482).

7. Such a concept of the space of representation is closer to Foucault's discursive formation or the specificity of discursive practice, which describes processes that are not predetermined and are negotiated within the political and ideological networks (1972, 38, 55), than the representational space of Henri Lefebvre, which, though seemingly more "architectural" because inhabitable and containing a coherent system of culturally grounded symbols, is presented as a particular outcome of the production of social space determined by class struggle (1991, 33, 39). Denis Hollier also asserts that architecture is the space of representation, but an oppressive one. Although I do not agree with the notion that architecture, as a symbolic environment, is the "archistructure, system of systems" that predetermines or imposes symbolic meanings, I think that by revolving around formation of thought, Hollier's criticism points out the same specificity in the architectural mode of thought I propose (1989, 31–36).

8. See, for example, de Certeau's text "Walking in the City," where he juxtaposes the view when walking with the totalizing view from above, two spatial practices that reveal different ways of reading the symbolic complexity of the city (de Certeau 1984, 91–110).

9. For Lacan, the primary component in the formation of a child's subject identity is the reliance on how the child perceives himself or herself as an object reflected in a mirror or perceived by other people (1980, 1–7). This approach will help me to challenge another traditional set of polar opposites, that of the object and the subject, and to explore their relationships in architecture.

10. Consider, for example, Karsten Harries's discussion of the symbolic function of architecture. In "Representation and Re-presentation" Harries asserts that "if architecture is to help to re-present and interpret the meaning of our daily life, it first has to open itself to these symbols [of the natural language of space]. Needed today is a recovery of the natural in the inherited conventional symbols" (1997, 132). Harries implies that deciphering these natural signs is possible because of the transcendental ontological character of phenomena and transcultural character of symbolic associations they evoke in the human mind; that is, he argues for the existence of an absolute signifier. In contrast, I believe that it is necessary to identify the authority of signification in the processes of signification.

11. Beatriz Colomina reveals how Le Corbusier created a "collision of images and text" (1994, 119) and thus represented (or, as Colomina implies, exploited) po-

etic and commercial functions of architecture in the world of mass media. Kenneth Frampton (1986) discusses how Giuseppe Terragni composed photographs of his buildings to increase those pictures' ability to engage imagination, in the way similar to architecture.

12. It is not a coincidence that the systematic character of many architectural conventions originated in their analytical usage for military purposes (Scolari 1985).

13. This is another example of epistemological legacy of the classical age. As a system of notation, architectural graphic conventions are based on the concepts of what Foucault calls transparent signs (1970, 63–67). These systems of signs and the rules of their construction, for example, the lines or patterns a draftsman uses to draw a section of a building, were intended to leave no doubt about their analytical functioning; and at the same time, this system was meant to eradicate the murmur of other meanings — interpretations created by "the spontaneous movement of the imagination" seeking resemblances (1970, 58).

14. Jonathan Crary shows that the fact that a person located inside the apparatus of camera obscura could only witness how a picture of the world outside appeared in the black box, never being able to see himself or herself in that picture, made this viewing device a physical manifestation of how the mind objectively views images created in a human eye (1990, 41).

15. See, for example, Jean Baudrillard's reflections on how the illusion of the Gulf War was constructed by mass media (1994, 62–65).

16. Although Vattimo's observations that the operation of mass media in the late modern society is responsible for the "weakening of reality" by weakening the sense of a symbolic thought (1988, 27–28) are pertinent for my study, what I have associated with the specificity of the symbolic functioning of architecture is not grounded in the ontological dimension of reality, but in the very nature of cultural practices. It is the need for making symbolic concepts of reality thinkable, in an individual and collective sense, that prompts the symbolic function of architecture. Moreover, I believe that it is not the process of technological mediation of thought but the commercial purpose for which these new technologies of viewing are developed that weakens symbolic notions of reality.

17. See for example, "Simulacra and Simulations" and "Fatal Strategies" (Baudrillard 1988c, 166–206).

18. It seems telling that in current postcolonial discourses, the subject of culture moves from "an epistemological function to an enunciative practice." Homi K. Bhabha argues for a shift from this approach that treats "culture as epistemology [that] focuses on function and intention" to that in which "culture as enunciation focuses on signification and institutionalization" (1992, 443).

4

The Form and Structure of Architectural Knowledge: From Practice to Discipline

Julia Williams Robinson

In the United States, the field of architecture is in the process of evolving from what has been a practice, informed by other disciplines, into a discipline with its own body of knowledge.[1] Since the nineteenth century, its locus of education has changed from the architecture firm to the higher education institution. Its instructional practices have shifted from a predominantly apprenticeship system to a system of classroom-based teaching supplemented by apprenticeship. The role of architectural instructors is changing from master architect, whose knowledge and theory of making buildings is personally held, implicit, practical, and integrated, and who instructs by demonstration, to that of professor who imparts explicit, specialized knowledges, using explanations based in architectural theory and science. The role of the student has changed from learning one synthetic approach from a knowledgeable individual to learning to synthesize a variety of knowledges from different perspectives and disciplines. Architectural theory is changing from prescription based in historical precedent to critical analysis and explanation deriving in part from the scientific model (Lang 1987). In the process, the discipline seems to have become fractured by the increasingly diverse knowledges it borrows from engineering, art, history, and the social sciences. Additionally, because the majority of the education of architects now takes place within the academy and is also the locus of most of the development of new architectural knowledge, there is a need to define the position of disciplinarity within architecture.

61

This chapter examines architecture as a cultural construct that has come into being through unconscious historical processes but nevertheless now can be subjected to critical appraisal and reconstruction. Instead of analyzing the subfield of sociocultural studies within architecture, I use the sociocultural perspective to critique the field of architecture. Architecture is understood to be an emerging discipline that involves professional practice, research, and teaching. The character and effects of its products—disciplinary knowledge, the forms of disciplinary practices, architectural artifacts—are the responsibility of those within the field. Academics, researchers, and professional practitioners are thus jointly responsible to society and to each other.

Disciplinarity of Architecture

Although the title of this book suggests that the discipline of architecture already exists, and the existence of departments of architecture in universities implies its existence, there is also evidence to suggest that it has a somewhat contingent status relative to other disciplines. Architecture's place in academe in the United States was established in the nineteenth century by the architectural profession as a way to formalize architectural training and grant it expert status. Yet the diversity of its knowledge base has inhibited the development of demarcating boundaries and a unified vision of the field. Architecture's identity is fluid or solid depending on the perspective from which it is viewed. Forces that suggest the discipline is established are (1) the anticipated transformation of architectural education from a predominantly undergraduate degree in the 1960s to a predominantly graduate degree in the near future; (2) the approximately $20 million that supports scholarship and research in North American departments and colleges of architecture;[2] (3) the presence of journals and other venues that support publication of scholarship and research;[3] and (4) the presence of organizations that foster research and scholarship.[4]

The countervailing forces that may suggest a contingent status for architecture[5] in comparison to many other clearly defined disciplines (such as physics or philosophy) are (1) architecture departments are located in inconsistent institutional settings (in institutes of technology, schools of art, professional schools, liberal arts colleges, and within the university in such diverse units as liberal arts, arts and sciences, and design), attesting to the lack of clarity about the essential nature of the field; (2) while faculty generally agree on which subjects need to be taught in architecture departments, they do not agree about the names and organization of these subfields;[6] (3) architectural theory as presently accepted does not incorporate all of the subfields (e.g., computer-aided design, sociocultural factors, acoustic design); (4) while scholarly journals exist, the vast majority of practicing architects read professional journals that regularly publish results of research but primarily feature photographs of built architecture rather than analysis of the buildings; (5) federal agencies that fund research do not specifically designate architecture as a funding category (for example, the National Endowment for the Arts' Design Arts program funds architecture as a design field but not as a technical field, and the National Science Foundation funds architecture through various designations, none of them called architecture); and (6) authors of scholarly work on architecture tend to refer to texts outside the field rather than within, suggesting a lack of confidence in the body of architectural scholarship (see chapter references in this book).

Why does this lack of clarity about the discipline matter? Philippe Boudon, for example, feels that architecture is by nature not a discipline but a set of disciplines, and he proposes that a different subdiscipline called architecturology (like musicology) be established to study the field (1992). But architecture's particular focus on built product, compared to engineering or real estate, requires a synthesis of fundamentally different kinds of knowledges that leads toward unity. Rather than being defined by particular research methodologies as many other fields (e.g., engineering is based on mathematics and laboratory science), architecture is defined by its synthetic practices of representation and design. The need to address the many perspectives of the building requires the ability to layer divergent and sometimes apparently contradictory requirements so that their relationships can be understood and the design choices may be developed. The representation of knowledges to the designer in spatial forms enhances the designer's ability to synthesize knowledge from different fields. The possibility of design integration implies the existence of as-of-yet unarticulated "architectural" questions that if named and described could explicitly frame the identity of the field, link the fractured subject areas, and lead to improved architectural products.

Historical Background

With the apparent exception of ancient Greece,[7] until the eighteenth century, Western architects were trained through an apprentice system. The founding of the Académie Royale d'Architecture in 1671 in France marks the beginning of formal education as the way to convey architectural knowledge (Pérez-Gómez 1983). At that time, formal architectural education supplemented apprenticeship, with a formal curriculum consisting of lectures in mathematical subjects (Pérez-Gómez 1983). In nineteenth-century France, apprenticeship still dominated, although architecture was taught in two academic contexts. At the École Polytechnique, the subjects remained mathematics and drawing, and apprenticeship was oriented to construction science, whereas at the École des Beaux-Arts, the main site of education was the master architect's studio, his place of business, with lectures given at the school on mathematics, drawing, history, and theory (Pérez-Gómez 1983; Broadbent 1995). The contrast between the approach of the École Polytechnique and the École des Beaux-Arts is reflected today in a perceived contradiction between the scientific approach deriving from engineering expressed as architectural technology, and the artistic approach based on an aesthetic understanding expressed as architectural style.

The establishment of architectural schools in universities in the United States during the late nineteenth and early twentieth centuries, and the establishment in Weimar of the Bauhaus school at the beginning of the twentieth century, led to a change in the locus of education from the office studio to the school. The original Bauhaus curriculum in Germany gave students a grounding in the crafts and formal theory. When the Bauhaus moved to Dessau, Hannes Meyer, who succeeded Walter Gropius, developed a two-part curriculum consisting of theory (which included economics, psychology, and sociology) and practical building (which included various technical subjects) (Broadbent 1995). What emerged from these changes is now common practice: apprenticeship is an activity that follows education.

As Bauhaus ideas about architectural instruction spread and replaced the École des Beaux-Arts approach, academic architectural training began to overshadow apprenticeship. But it was only in the 1980s, some two hundred years after the establishment of the first architectural schools, that access to the profession by apprenticeship was eliminated as an avenue to the profession by almost every one of the fifty states (AIA 1994), which now require a professional degree to take the licensing examination. The professional education of the architect now includes instruction in technology (civil and mechanical engineering), history and theory (art history, philosophy, design methods, and social science), communication (studio art and drawing, and computer-aided design), and urban design or planning.

Despite these changes, contemporary educational practices still reflect the master-apprentice relationship in the way the faculty is organized and teaching is done. Some architectural schools in the United States, following the approach taken at the Bauhaus and brought to the United States by Gropius and Ludwig Mies van der Rohe (Saint 1983), are still run by a "master" architect who is also engaged in the practice of architecture. In this system, academics are often perceived to play a role similar to that of consultants in an architectural office, important but not central, while the practicing architects or "studio masters" are accorded more prestige.[8] As the importance of scholarship and research has grown in many academic institutions, however, the balance of power in professional schools has begun to shift toward the tenured full-time academic faculty, leading some schools to pursue various avenues for tenuring architects whose primary responsibility is to their practice.

The tension between scholars and practitioners that results from the changing power relations is aggravated by the forms of architectural instruction. In most architecture schools, instruction is divided between the studio classroom, where design case studies are taught, and the lecture classroom, which houses the university-style subject-based instruction. In extreme cases, this has led to a kind of dichotomy between the "master architects" who "teach real architecture" in the studio setting and the academics who teach the knowledge base that informs the discipline. One consequence has been divergent calls for increased emphasis on research and advanced education (Rapoport 1987), for a reduced emphasis on design in the education of the architect (Gutman 1987), or for eliminating higher education as a requirement for practice (Cuff 1987).

Architectural Knowledges: Engaging the Tacit and the Explicit

These contradictory suggestions for education correspond to two different conceptions of architectural knowledge: (1) the intellectual or explicit knowledge disseminated primarily in academia, and (2) the knowing embedded in the process of making architecture that is essential to design, what Polanyi calls tacit knowledge that is learned by doing and that cannot be critical ([1958] 1962, 264), a conception of knowledge as a way of doing something. Although many architectural scholars and practitioners regard these two forms as competing, the difficult challenge facing the field is how to engage and validate both forms of knowledge.

Among the myriad definitions of knowledge in the *Oxford English Dictionary* (1971) is a section that includes two parts: "the fact or condition of knowing," and "the object of knowing; that which is known or made known." To know both the condition and the object requires both tacit and explicit knowledge. Unlike many other disciplines, architecture's use of apprenticeship and studio teaching to transmit knowledge has primarily emphasized not so much the *conscious* acquisition of (explicit) knowledges as the *unconscious* acquisition (the apprenticeship and studio are, to use Basil Bernstein's term, *contextualized learning*, the doing of design but *recontextualized* from the field [1975, 30]). This method of teaching raises important questions about the nature of architecture as an academic discipline.

Even today it could be argued that a large portion of architectural knowledge is tacit; students learn from observation rather than by being told. The traditional studio instructor, the master architect, holds architectural knowledge in his person and teaches primarily by example and by coaching (Schön 1987). For example, the student may propose three alternative ways to lay out a building entry. An experienced designer can immediately see from looking at the drawings that one is too small and another is in the wrong place. Verbalizing *why* this is so—thus providing an explicit statement of "truth"—is far more complicated than simply being able to recognize this "truth." The awareness of how many people may enter the building, how much space it would take for them to walk past each other into the building, how big an entry needs to be, and where it should be located to symbolically communicate a dignified arrival — these ideas are not simple to explain or justify. Being tacit and contextualized rather than explicit and decontextualized, such knowledge is typically held unconsciously and articulated graphically without a verbal or mathematical description and thus is coded in a way not readily apprehended by outsiders to the field. Because architectural expertise is not evident to those outside the field, some educators believe that the tacit knowledge must be put into an explicit form that can be grasped by students and recognized by the public as valid expertise.

Today it is insufficient to simply assert expertise. Expertise must be backed up by a clearly defined, visible, usually linguistically described, coherent body of knowledge. Lacking this, the profession of architecture has found itself at a disadvantage relative to other fields and with questionable status as a profession, which has led to the development of explicitly *architectural* research (that is, research about architecture, conceived by people in architecture). But the result of the documentation and development of explicit knowledge is an increased emphasis on language as an inherent part of the architectural discipline. Whereas before, the architect was simply trusted to know about building, and his tacit knowledge, embedded in action and transferred through drawings, could result in a building, today's building process requires more. In addition to drawings and other legal documents such as specifications, the architect must provide verbal evidence and justification for decisions in such forms as research studies, planning documents, cost-benefit analysis, and environmental impact analysis.

The existing structure of the knowledge and of theory within architecture, however, does not easily incorporate these new forms of explicit knowledge. Because traditional knowledge was personally held, the architect's expertise, based on trust, needed no justification. Therefore, theories were largely, in Lang's terms, "procedural" (1987) and informal; they described how to make architecture and addressed questions of "form." Because the architect's job was to make built forms, architectural theories focused primarily on the desired physical character of architectural form and space (attributes of styles, arrangement of spaces), secondarily on the best way to create it (geometric systems, construction techniques), and thirdly on the objectives that the form was to meet (articulated within the field as Vitruvius's trinity of firmness, commodity, and delight). Following this formula, the traditional canon consists of buildings that demonstrate innovations in form and space, typically described as architectural styles.

The new knowledge requires theory that is, in Lang's terminology, "substantive." Whether in the area of technology, of history, of social science, or of formal interpretation, the focus of substantive theory is not limited to the form of the architecture but includes as well the ability of that form to achieve specific ends. Whereas procedural theory describes *how* to make architecture, substantive theory explains *why* architecture should be made a certain way. Evaluations of whether and why or why not a form achieves given ends demand not merely the traditional, self-referential procedural theory, which has its authority in historical architectural precedent, but also criteria drawn from outside the traditional discipline, such as how much energy is lost or gained by the use of certain materials, how a building will affect wind patterns or traffic flow, whether a building is perceived to have the appropriate character or to be beautiful, and whether the building supports the desired social agenda.

Procedural architectural theory has a peculiar character. While, like substantive theory, it is written down, it follows the old paradigm of architecture as an art object that only accepts as valid architectural knowledge that which addresses architectural form and space. Conventional architectural theory thereby cannot easily incorporate the discipline's considerable research knowledge that has been developed during the last twenty-five years in such areas as building materials, lighting, thermal design, historic preservation, and sociocultural studies but defines the new substantive knowledge as "outside" the domain of architecture (see Figure 4.1).[9] Perhaps because the resistance of current theory to the authority of explanation is not well understood, ironically, many people who are involved in developing the new knowledge insist on the old definition of architectural knowledge that locates their work as outside the architectural mainstream. Although this may not significantly affect the work of the individual researcher, it severely limits the ability

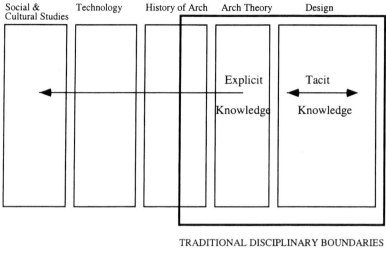

Social & Cultural Studies | Technology | History of Arch | Arch Theory | Design

Explicit Knowledge

Tacit Knowledge

TRADITIONAL DISCIPLINARY BOUNDARIES

Architecture as Art

◀——— Other Issues ———▶◀——— Space & Form ———▶

Figure 4.1. The traditional boundary that limits architectural theory to the making of form and space locates most research-based architectural knowledge outside the boundary of the field.

of students and practitioners to understand the discipline of architecture as a coherent body of knowledge. As a result, they do not engage with research findings in a meaningful way and rarely apply them in practice.

The written body of knowledge that has existed alongside the body of tacit architectural knowledge beginning with Vitruvius in about 100 A.D. was initially limited in scope and served as kind of an optional reference point. Within the modern period, written knowledge has increased almost logarithmically and has taken on a great complexity, incorporating building regulations and codes, including writings on history, art, and engineering, urban design, human behavior, design methods, and theory of architectural form. Accordingly, architecture has borders with as many as twenty-one different disciplines and fields (see Figure 4.2). The knowledge base is broad, and fractured because each subdiscipline exists without reference to the others.[10] Additionally, the explicit knowledges of the subdisciplines are learned in classes largely independent of the tacit knowledge that is learned in the studio, although some faculty are experimenting with more integration.

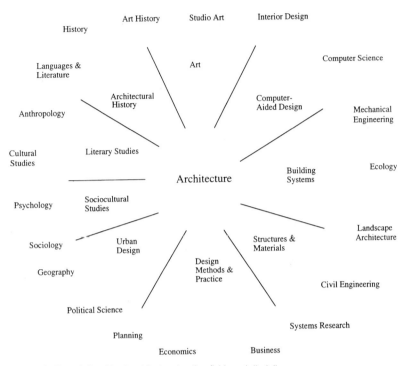

Figure 4.2. The relationship of architecture to other fields and disciplines.

This distinction between tacit design knowledge and the explicit knowledges of the subdisciplines has been assumed to follow the fracture between the scientific approach derived from engineering and the intention-based traditional approach (Pérez-Gómez 1983). The mathematical descriptions of the engineers, while considered useful to know, have been viewed as outside the realm of architectural knowledge. The threat of this disjuncture was not sufficient to challenge the traditional paradigm. But beginning in the 1960s, another fracture emerged that threatens the paradigm: the fracture between the tacit knowledge based in the individual architect, who is assumed to be an expert, and the research, which is concerned with actualization and therefore necessarily involves social issues. But surprisingly, the nature of this second disjuncture has been framed in terms of the old fracture, as the problem of objectivism and the scientific model (Pérez-Gómez 1983), not as the failure of the field to fully incorporate social and political issues (for instance, ecology, diversity).

The traditional explicit procedural knowledge and individually held tacit knowledge are concerned with the relation between the self, the intention, the act, and the generation of the artifact's form. In contrast, the emerging body of substantive explicit knowledge takes a social constructivist approach in addressing the process of making the artifact and analyzing the effects of the completed artifact in the physical and social world.

The new research challenges the traditional paradigm because the concept of architecture as form and space is insufficient to frame the study of the actual functioning of the created environmental artifact, whether in terms of heat loss, social message, or urban context. Architecture examined within its traditional framework is criticized according to the sets of internal criteria for how it is made. The degree to which space and form serve social or political ends is outside the frame, thus not an "architectural" subject. Framing architecture as a socially constructed cultural object, on the other hand, engages humanistic, artistic, and scientific aspects of the field and therefore is a potentially integrating approach. The adoption of such an approach, however, flies in the face of existing ways of understanding and instructing that focus on objectivized form separate from technical outcomes, economics, the human body, and sociocultural experience.

The Discipline of Architecture: Embodying an Out-of-Body Experience

Although constructed architecture is understood by people who inhabit it as a result of a bodily experience, the building that is being designed cannot be actually inhabited. This potential building must be at the same time (1) envisioned as a completed artifact that can be inhabited, and (2) understood as sets of virtual buildings each with different issues and requirements. Because the built environment must stand up, breathe, stay dry, warm, or cool, and serve a series of purposes that entail not just furniture and equipment but psychological ambiance and patterns of activities, the designer is perforce taking different points of view of the artifact depending on the question being addressed. In the design of a city hall, for example, one important perspective involves the user needs: the symbolism of the exterior for the public as an approachable building, the communication of the dignity of the overall function, the requirement of a pleasant and efficient working environment for the city staff, the need for materials than can easily be maintained by the janitorial staff. Another viewpoint is the building as a technological organism: the building can be seen in terms of materials and structure, heating, cooling, and ventilation systems, embedded energy and energy use, and lighting—the character of daylight and artificial light across the day and through the seasons. Yet a third view is the building as an art object, in the play of geometry, the textures, colors, and patterns of the materials, the massing. A fourth view encompasses the building as it fits into the city: its physical appearance relative to the surroundings, the traffic patterns it generates for pedestrians and vehicles, its placement relative to other related buildings. The designer proposes solutions and evaluates them from these and various other perspectives. The building being designed is in a constant state of flux even as the designer seeks to fix it in a single form. The discipline of architecture revolves around the various issues that the built artifact must address and around the means of envisioning and critiquing possible formal propositions through use of representational media.

As mentioned earlier, the discipline of architecture is configured by subfields[11] that have not been definitively described but can be listed as technology (the engineering of structure and material relative to issues of gravity, light, air, moisture, and heat), history and theory (dealing with historical developments, social issues, style, design methods, philosophical issues, urban context), and architectural practice (economics, business practices, regulations, law). In regard to the definition of the discipline, though the boundaries of architecture are unclear, the subdisciplines retain a segregation and integrity defined by the boundaries of their discipline of origin. Integration of the subfields is expected to occur in the process of design, hence design (which answers the question "what ought architecture to be?") is the center of the discipline.

Learning to design involves acquiring knowledge as experience that informs decision making. The transformation of knowledge into experience is a process of embodiment. As mentioned before, to take into account the many different considerations that affect the building design, the designer cannot rely on conscious decision making but must come to know intuitively which choices will be better. The door drawn on the plan must "look" too big or too small without the designer having to measure it. The wall material must "feel" cold or warm without the U-factor being looked up. But the intuition must be held loosely so that it can continually evolve in response to better knowledge. Developing this intuitive ability to make formal decisions based on sound information (tacit knowledge) is the essential goal of present architectural education.

It is paradoxical, however, that the architectural way of thinking has been taught as primarily abstract decision making, what I would call an out-of-body understanding of architecture. Especially in the design studio, despite the hands-on process of generating design proposals, the students often learned to apply abstract formal organizing principles (rules for manipulating geometry, ways of ordering spaces, techniques for putting materials together, systems for light and air, techniques for analyzing site and climate, rules of thumb for location of rooms) without being encouraged to link the principles to existing research or to their own daily experiences. In other words, *the construction of the formal product has been frequently understood in isolation from its effects.* As these rules and principles are repeatedly applied by students, they no longer require conscious thought to use, but the patterns they imply become the basis for developing design alternatives, conventional and innovative.

By almost exclusively emphasizing the geometric and technical formal criteria involved in making the artifact without stressing a parallel empathy with the way it will be experienced, the discipline has repressed the designer's personal knowledge, cultural experience, and ability to imagine actual use of the designed spaces. Ironically, as the students attempted to integrate their different knowledges using the formal design process, their decision-making criteria remained disembodied from daily life, generating the out-of-body designs (designs that look good but are not experienced as good places) that permeate the profession, rather than designs that create desired experiences. Additionally, until recently, there has been no systematic attempt to bring to the architectural design studio the experience of others than the instructor or the student (e.g., people who inhabit the building or clean the building, people who experience the building in unique ways because of physical differences). Even today, the views of these constituencies are not consistently brought to bear on design either by direct feedback or by research on technical issues or issues of diverse sociocultural perspectives. This disembodiment of architecture has profound consequences that are only beginning to be amended.

The focus on formal issues without reference to their impact on society results from seeing the "truth" of architectural formal relationships as having a validity irrespective of, or more important than, its actual performance as a utilitarian object. Despite the widely mimicked statement that "form follows function," generally architects have conceived of function as an abstraction that exists in the designer's mind, about which the client needs to be educated.

In the studio experience and in the acclaimed work of the profession, typically, the documentation of the actual effect of the final architecture (practical or symbolic) is not considered as integral to its design, nor is the personal cultural experience of the designer addressed as a biased but important source of information. The need to assess a constructed artifact in comparison with its design intentions is obvious, as is the need to determine how the artifact performs over time, and how people's uses of it and views of it change. Furthermore it is critical to know how the designer's perception compares to that of others. Architecture that affects us most deeply often does so because of individuals' sensitive understanding of what is important to them and to others. At the same time, as personal perceptions may be exclusively one's own and not shared, the designer's insight must be tempered by a humility to listen to the views of others in the form of personal interaction or reference to written research documentation. Without a critical perspective developed by questioning the effects of architecture and the degree of shared perspective, any evaluation emphasizes formal questions separate from lived experience and is politically naive. Excluding these factors perpetuates the practice of an architecture that avoids confronting the social and cultural issues of the day. As long as architects are only formalists, they do not have to be critical of their clients. When buildings are judged on purely formal terms, the degree to which they consume energy, empower a destructive group, socially stigmatize a population, or in some other way serve an undesirable social goal can be ignored. Furthermore, in ignoring this aspect of architecture, architects disempower themselves, for it is precisely the politics that architecture aids or hinders that make it a powerful medium.

Paradigms and Politics

Even as the student demographics in architecture have greatly changed, the practice and education of architects continues to be dominated by upper-middle-class males of European extraction who design buildings and determine paradigms. The admission to the profession of new groups starting in the 1960s and 1970s (women, members of ethnic and racial minorities, people from working-class backgrounds, as well as people primarily involved in research, theory, and teaching) caused the traditional approaches to be questioned.[12] Although the "apolitical" traditional architectural knowledge continues to provide answers to the issues it has defined for itself and holds the highest scholarly prestige, its framework simply doesn't permit asking basic compelling questions about architectural content (for example, whom architecture serves and how well it does so). If architects are to face the changes in both their own demographics and our increasingly diversified society, excluding sociocultural and political issues from architecture seems to be inadvisable if not impossible.

A critical factor in erasing the sociocultural and political from architecture has been the societal role played by architects. Because in the past the backgrounds of the client and the architect were virtually the same and they therefore shared a value system and worldview, those educated within the field have found it difficult to fully appreciate the degree to which the design of buildings is affected by the relation of architect to client. Those in a society who have the resources to pay for architectural services and to build fundamentally influence the field of architecture. In different historical periods, the introduction of democracy, capitalism, and socialism altered the nature of architectural practice and architectural knowledge because the architectural client changed. Similarly, the emergence of the consumer society has further affected the relation between the client and the consumer or user, challenging existing practices and knowledge. The architect can no longer take for granted that his or her own perspective or that of the paying client can adequately represent the needs of the building's day-to-day users.

The challenges inherent in the design of buildings for people who are unlike either the client or the architect first became fully apparent in the 1960s when the failure of the Pruitt-Igoe housing project in St. Louis, manifested in its destruction, revealed the limitations of relying exclusively on the client and architect to represent the requirements of the building user. The critical questions that Pruitt-Igoe raised about the discipline of architecture could have served to expand its boundaries to include the social, economic, and political issue of understanding the needs of the poor. Instead, the discipline's boundaries remain the same, with such problems defined as outside its primary domain, since they go beyond issues of the professionally defined product: form and space.

Historically, in professional practice, many architects retained their position by servicing powerful clients and accepting their values. When the powerful ignored, misunderstood, or repressed the needs of others in the society, the views of the less powerful did not play a role in the definition of architectural knowledge or practice. Insofar as the traditional perspective is followed, it excludes the powerless, or the "other," and has proved unable to effectively encompass social justice, the politics of diversity, or the politics of empowerment, and these issues remain outside the purview of architecture. Because the views of others, the outsiders, differ, they appear to threaten the existing norms. Involving the user, the ordinary citizen, the public, not only would require more time and energy but would demand substantial changes to existing practices and necessitate difficult challenges to the client's ideas. Including perspectives other than that of the client therefore comes to be seen as "political" in its negative sense and (to the powerful) is usefully defined as outside the boundaries of the profession. By focusing exclusively on form and space, the designer can serve the client without having to question conflicts of interest that may exist.

Clearly a culturally critical position is needed. The inclusion in the field of different kinds of people than are now present, who are not part of mainstream practice, offers one potential source of new cultural visions based on different cultural perspectives than dominate the field at present. This can also be accomplished by using research on attitudes, desires, and habits of groups, as Herman Hertzberger has done relative to such buildings as De Drie Hoven, Home for the Elderly in Amsterdam. Although another approach, participatory design, is not yet a mainstream practice, a number of architects involve community clients and users in projects either typically or occasionally.[13]

The accepted traditional paradigm creates fundamental problems within the discipline; nevertheless, without another to replace it, the various contradictions simply coexist. In Margaret Archer's view, every culture has within it ideas that do not fall within the existing paradigm, and the strength of the paradigm derives from its ability to coexist with these ideas in the light of competing paradigms (1988). While contradictory ideas require a new paradigm, complementary ideas are potentially accommodated within the existing one. Certain key questions in architecture may not have been reconciled precisely because they have been understood to be competing and contradictory to the existing paradigm. Even though the traditional paradigm in architecture is not capable of addressing these apparent contradictions, its proponents see alternative views as threatening to their apparent validity. In truth, the traditional paradigm has value: it is necessary but not sufficient.

A Proposal for an Integrating Paradigm

Examining architecture as a discipline, studying the character of architectural knowledge, reveals a fundamental dichotomy between the past procedural view of architecture as the making of the artifact and the substantive view that incorporates the effects of architecture as well. This effort reengages the social orientation envisioned by the early modernists but rejects their attitudes of Western superiority, universality, simple causality, personal authority and heroism. Developing a substantive approach to architecture that leads to explicit expertise requires extending the view of architecture as an artistic endeavor to include the sociocultural, political, economic, and ecological ramifications of its procedures and products. To maintain a vision of architecture as an exclusively aesthetic artifact would ignore the effects of a building on fuel use, transportation systems, pollution, and so forth, and deny the validity of the experiences of those who are erased by traditional architectural knowledge (people of non-European extraction, females, handicapped peo-

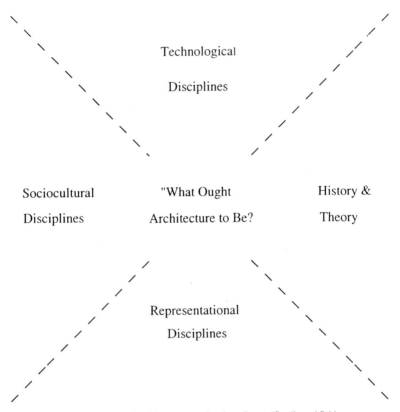

Technological

Disciplines

Sociocultural   "What Ought   History &

Disciplines   Architecture to Be?   Theory

Representational

Disciplines

Figure 4.3. The new paradigm of architecture as cultural medium unifies the subfields.

ple, working-class people, etc.), creating an architecture that is increasingly irrelevant to, and alienated from, the world in which it operates.

If architecture as a built setting is taken as the central focus of the field, however, and its effects on the environment are understood to be as much a part of the discipline as its form and space, then all subdisciplines and perspectives can be seen as essential. To envision them as complementary simply requires a paradigm that engages the tacit and the explicit, the scientific and the mythological, the conceptual and the bodily, the formal and the political.

Such an alternative conception of architecture frames architecture as a cultural medium,[14] deriving from the design question "what ought architecture to be?" It encompasses architecture as it is received and as it functions in the physical and social world (see Figure 4.3); it also includes the procedures that define the field (the design-build process, the attainment of legitimate status). This concept incorporates architecture as art, as technology, as politics, as well as from numerous other perspectives. In an academic context, focusing on a central question ("What ought architecture to be?") rather than on defining boundary conditions (e.g., "It's only architecture if it deals with form and space") frames the discipline so that it is permeable. All of the discipline's present subdisciplines are included, and the possibility exists for including others that also respond to the central question. Moreover, having a single question (or a set of questions; for example, see Leatherbarrow's chapter) also promotes a more integrated understanding of the subdisciplines. Instead of posing contradictory or competing definitions of architecture, it posits that different subfields offer complementary ways to approach a common set of issues.

Furthermore, the cultural approach clarifies the relation between academia and the practicing profession, for it creates complementary roles for the two arenas. Practicing architects respond to the question of what architecture ought to be by creating buildings; academics respond by studying buildings to develop explicit knowledge that guides improved design. The process of education links the two arenas of professional practice and academia. Novice students must learn the explicit knowledge and transform it into the tacit knowledge that allows application, and the experienced professional can learn new explicit knowledges that challenge existing modes of design practice.

To the extent that academics create knowledges that are able to discernibly improve the designed environment or the procedures of the field, the practicing professional will support and value their role. To the extent that the practicing professionals engage with the new knowledge, create better places, and even generate new knowledges themselves, the academics will desire their participation in the educational and scholarly process as important partners.

But the cultural approach also challenges the self-conception of the architect, for authority now resides in the knowledge itself rather than in the person who holds it. If architecture is a cultural artifact, answering the question of what architecture ought to be is no longer the simple prerogative of the architect, but a societal task. Instead the architect becomes responsible for helping develop a process by which answers can be agreed upon. This involves architects (1) participating in research using accepted scientific practices, (2) engaging in more open and participatory design processes, and (3) taking a greater role in public education and political action.[15] Rather than simply being in the responsive mode, architects will have to become proactive, generating a discussion of issues. Involvement in public education will create opportunities for valuing people with a greater variety of backgrounds. By opening up the ranks of the profession to a diverse group of people, the field will be able to respond to the changes that are taking place.

Professional education must provide the student with the tools for a new form of engagement with the world. Other writers in this book mention the increased importance of teamwork, of interdisciplinary approaches to solving problems, of awareness of social and ecological imperatives, of the local and international context. Also important is the locus of authority. As preparation for the new relation to the client and user, the instructor needs to adopt a less authoritarian role. Authority should lie in the knowledge held rather than in the social position. The instructor needs to acknowledge that students come with a valid knowledge of their culture that requires respect (especially for those of cultures different from the instructor), and that their viewpoint does not need to be replaced by an architectural one, but only supplemented by it.

Although the focus of architectural education is likely to remain the design studio, the knowledges and research methods presently conveyed in the so-called support courses will be increasingly important. Studio instruction itself will alter to accommodate the already existing change from a problem-solving approach to that of problem exploration, in which the approach to finding answers is as important as the answers themselves. As also advocated in this book, students must also be exposed to a more scholarly approach to design so that they are prepared to engage with the new knowledges, including the ability to prepare and present logical arguments, to analyze precedent, to cite important texts, and to read critically. But more than this, if architects are to fully participate in a knowledge-based field, their training needs to include sufficient awareness of the parameters of research and scholarship that they can appreciate the limits and potential applications of findings, and so that those practicing architects who wish to can participate in the development of knowledge.

At the same time, it must be acknowledged that in studio learning, as in architectural practice, the explicit knowledges are valuable only insofar as they can be integrated with each other and within the design process itself. As discussed earlier, integrated application occurs when the knowledge is so well understood that it is held in the body of the designer and applied in an unconscious or semiconscious way. Studio instruction must continue to promote this applied understanding while developing the students' critical awareness and questioning of the design actions and products.

In defining architecture as a cultural matter, society can more effectively invest in the field of architecture, thereby empowering architects to effect constructive change. By redefining architecture as a discipline that incorporates not just architectural form but its physical and sociocultural effects, the worlds of academia and practice can become complementary, making architecture the powerful political force it ought to be.

Notes

1. Here, the use of the word *field* or *area* designates the broad arena of architecture including academia and practice, whereas the term *discipline* designates the formalized architectural knowledge base, or knowledges that are produced and disseminated in education, research, and practice.

2. Conservative estimate based on projects reported by key institutions at the Architectural Research Centers annual meeting (Architectural Research Centers Consortium 1993).

3. See, for example, *Journal of Architectural Education, Journal of Architectural and Planning Research, Proceedings of the Environmental Design Research Association, Proceedings of the Association of Collegiate Schools of Architecture.*

4. E.g., the Environmental Design Research Association, the Architectural Research Centers Consortium, and the Association of Computer Aided Designers in America.

5. A powerful argument could be made that these factors simply reflect diversity in the field, but such diversity could also be seen as a lack of clear definition.

6. For example, Jean Wineman's study of doctoral programs ("Comparative Statistics, . . .") shows that the titles of different subject areas are inconsistent. What is History/Theory/Criticism (H/T/C) in one department is History in another and two separate areas called History and Theory in a third. In some departments, the study of design methods is located in H/T/C, in others it is located in its own sub-

ject area, in yet others it is located in Professional Practice. Similarly Environment-Behavior Studies or Sociocultural Factors may be within H/T/C or on its own or not included as a subject.

7. Spiro Kostof notes that Theodorus of Samos, an architect who was instrumental in the construction of the Temple of Athena at Sparta, subsequently ran a private school of architecture in that city (1977a, 16).

8. Bletter (1981, 110–11) notes that before retiring from Columbia in 1933, Dean William A. Boring instituted a system of independent studios headed by "studio masters."

9. Figure 4.1 derives from a diagram made by Simon Beeson in an unpublished paper that was a draft for his master's thesis (1994).

10. The general agreement about the knowledge base is formalized in the United States and Europe through the school accreditation process.

11. Some would argue that architecture is not a discipline but a set of disciplines. Although this may be true to a certain extent at present, this chapter takes the view that defining architecture as a discipline makes it more likely that the connections between what are then subdisciplines will increase in the future, and that consequently architecture will become more cohesive and coherent as a field.

12. There is a great deal of critical material, for example, Anthony 1991; Grant 1991; Davis 1993; Frederickson 1993; and Groat and Ahrentzen 1996.

13. For additional examples, see Sanoff 1990.

14. This position has been implied by a variety of authors such as Rapoport (especially 1982) and Lang (1987) but has specifically been proposed relative to rethinking architectural theory and educational practices by Robinson (1990) and Groat (1993a).

15. For elaboration of this point see Gusevich 1995, as well as Sutton, this volume.

5

Architecture Is Its Own Discipline

David Leatherbarrow

If I had to teach a child geography, I should start with the plan of his garden, it seems to me—as Rousseau did—with the space that his pupil
Emile can embrace, with the horizon that his own eyes can see; then I
should project his curiosity beyond the limit of his vision.

—**André Gide**, *Pretexts*

For architecture to remain significant in our time, it must redefine its
basic subjects. That it is a discipline with its own subject matter can neither
be assumed nor taken for granted because nowadays architecture is often
seen as a practice that borrows methods and concepts from other fields,
whether the natural or the social sciences, engineering, or the fine arts. This
appropriation is neither by accident nor by fraudulent intent; for some
time now, other professionals, engineers, landscape architects, and planners, have performed some of the skills that had traditionally defined
the architect's role, and have done so reliably. It would be naive and
nostalgic to assume that we can return to the way things once were.
Does this state of affairs mean that architects should continue to turn
to other fields for inspiration?

For what is the architect responsible? For what tasks should students
be trained in order that they may act authoritatively in some arena of
cultural work? What skills and subjects are particular to this form of practice and to no other? Are there any? If not, if a distinct role cannot be

identified, should the architect be trained as a "generalist," a "facilitator," or a "coordinator" of the building process, neither its engine nor one of its main gears, but the lubricant that eases its operation? Worse still, has the architect become redundant, a source of friction or wheel spinning, a technology that has become outdated in the accelerated movement of contemporary life?

My aim in the argument that follows is twofold: one, to show that architecture does possess its own subjects and skills, and two, that the neglect of the differences between the practice of architecture and that of related fields, engineering, painting, planning, and so on, should be resisted, for the sake of professional responsibility and intellectual clarity. I want to make this argument by describing what the architect does and what he or she must understand to accomplish specifically architectural work. This means defining a discipline by circumscribing a mode of practice. To say that architecture can be defined in this way is not to claim that this practice is only or essentially a matter of know-how or of technique, for architecture is equally a matter of ethical understanding, as Karsten Harries has recently shown, as have others (Harries 1997).[1] Beyond this, I shall also try to show that the subjects we have inherited in traditional discourse and practice need to be rethought in our time because of changes in the professions and in society. To state it plainly, and with no desire to be sensational, architecture is a discipline in crisis. This crisis is just as apparent in the recent publications that question the relationship between what professors and professionals do as it is in documents such as the Carnegie Report, which testify to the guilty conscience of many educators and their nearly pathological anxiety about the profession's cultural role. Further, new and competing professions continue to emerge and grow, leaving to architecture less and less of its traditional subject matter. Within architecture itself considerable fragmentation of knowledge exists, as do irreconcilable truth-claims, of which three are dominant: technical rationality as the truth of the expert, market experience as the truth of the professional, and creative intuition as the truth of the artist. In this state of affairs, one must endeavor to unmask these "truths" when they become dogmatic and attempt to redefine which aspects of technical rationality, market experience, and creativity are particular to the discipline. Only when this two-part task of critique and reconsideration is accomplished will it be possible to see how authority and responsibility can be restored to architects, and only then will it be apparent how a sense of cultural purpose can be regained in practice. This double task must draw on knowledge of the discipline's tradition of education, reflection, and practice but also propose ways that inheritance can be reshaped because its forms are inadequate to current conditions; hence the need for rethinking or redefining architecture's subjects. But what are the subjects we might take to be basic these days?

The answer from the tradition is clear: in the oldest surviving definition we have, Vitruvius's, we are told that architecture consists of firmness, commodity, and delight. These qualities pertain to buildings, however, not to a discipline; to be seen as the basic premises of a curriculum, they must be viewed as targets of the architect's skill—skill that must be taught, for it is neither "inborn" nor acquired by everyone who matures within a given culture. Shifting the focus from what architecture is to what architects know and do, one could say that for Vitruvius, the architect is that individual who can direct the construction of buildings that exhibit firmness, commodity, and delight.

The paideiatic or educational import of this triad is easier to understand when the Vitruvian categories are translated into the terms of their philosophical antecedents, which are almost certainly Aristotelian and Platonic. To make this comparison is not to say the Roman architect was a careful reader of the classics of ancient Greek philosophy (despite his habit of dropping names); rather, his summary presentation takes for granted a division that had become commonplace in Roman thought, that of Cicero, Varro, and Lucretius, for example. The main source for these Latin thinkers was Aristotle, who distinguished three sorts of human knowledge or virtues of the soul: technical, ethical, and philosophical understanding (Aristotle 1941b, bk. 6).[2] Put differently, three types of activity characterize human life: production, action, and contemplation, which depend on and demonstrate these sorts of knowledge. The goal of each is a specific kind of outcome. The result of production is something made, of action something done, and of contemplation something envisaged or desired. Aristotle and Plato also distinguished these three ontologically, only the first concerns mundane objects, for example. Returning to architecture and stating this division in quasi-Vitruvian terms, one can say that architecture is something made to accommodate human life and to be observed with delight.

As the ingredients of an architect's education, however, these types of knowledge present different challenges, for not one is similarly teachable, precisely because they are different kinds of knowledge. Although Vitruvius was silent on that matter, both Plato and Aristotle thought that of these three types, only technical reason could be taught, either by a tradesman to an apprentice or by a teacher in an academy (Aristotle 1941a, A1; Gadamer 1991, 23–29). All arts or skills are taught as know-how; painting and architecture, for example, also metalworking and sewing, likewise nursing and public speaking. Ethical reason, by contrast, is never taught but is appropriated indirectly, by acculturation, one might say, as a result of maturing and acting within a given society. Further, decisions taken within this horizon affect the individuals who make them and others, not things; yet artifacts preserve traces of these decisions, just as they serve as the physical premises of their accomplishment. Although few individuals become expert in the practice of more than one art, all those who mature in a given cultural context share the same ethical understanding, or they assume that the ethical context of their decisions is the same as that of others. The commonality of ethical understanding is just as true in our time as it was when Aristotle made these distinctions; before students arrive at the steps of the architecture school, they know what patterns of life distinguish a town house from a courthouse, and the ability to make such a distinction evidences their ethical or practical reason, their understanding of the right forms of conduct in the typical circumstances of a particular culture, which is generally a tacit form of understanding. Finally, philosophical reason is not something that can be learned once and for all, or perhaps one should say it must always be unlearned or continually relearned. Ancient thinkers such as Aristotle and modern ones such as Edmund Husserl have described the philosopher as a perpetual beginner whose "progress" has the peculiar habit of returning to its own beginnings. Husserl's last books have titles that begin with phrases like "A First Introduction to . . ." Further, both held that wisdom is what people naturally and continually strive for: "all men desire to know," said Aristotle (1941a) on the first page of his *Metaphysics.*

By analogy, the types of knowledge that define architectural practice are acquired through teaching, acculturation, and questioning. The teachable kinds of knowledge can be called the architect's skills, to distinguish them from the subjects that the architect must grasp in other ways.

Knowing the World by Making Images of It

To begin to identify the skills of an architect, we must answer a question about what it is that an architect makes or produces. Architects do not make buildings these days, even less cities, not even rooms. All of these places result from the arts and crafts of building or construction. This distinction alone is sufficient to establish a clear difference between architecture and the other plastic or performing arts — painting, sculpture, and music, for example — the performance of which is generally, although not always, "solo," meaning that "design" and "production" are concurrent in their development and indistinguishable in their realization, which is very rarely true in architecture, the exceptions being mostly limited to the work of design-build firms and of architects who build their own houses. It is true that individuals other than the artist are often involved in the production of nonarchitectural "works," but almost never is the artist not involved, almost always he or she "handles" the materials of the work, which architects rarely do because they are skilled in design not construction. Architects handle drawings and models, not bricks and boards.

Many architects and critics see artistic creativity as a matter of self-expression. This means that in modern painting or dance, for example, "the artistic work" cannot be fully enjoyed or understood without some understanding of the artist — his or her biographical circumstances and intentions. The reciprocal definition of the designer and the work is assumed by many to be characteristic of contemporary architecture as well; we say the "Gehry building" instead of the Weisman Museum. Robert Klein, in his paper "The Eclipse of the Work of Art," has asked: "What would Brancusi's egg be without its history, and without all of Brancusi?" (1979, 181). No museum or gallery of contemporary art opens an exhibition without labeling each of the "works" on show with the painter's name and the date of the work's execution, even if a title is lacking. A full understanding of a painting depends on knowing the artist's desires and personal history; in fact, this information is so much a part of the work's meaning that sometimes it is taken as its essential subject matter. Put in terms that approximate Martin Heidegger's, the work of art is quite simply what the artist makes—the first defined by the second (Heidegger 1971a, 15–88).

Yet information about "authorship" is never as important in architecture because the drawings of an architect are different in kind from those of a self-expressive painter: while expressive, architectural representations must show more than a designer's style, skill, manner, or biography; these drawings must reveal something otherwise unseen in our world. Paintings, too, have a revealing function. But while pictorial disclosure has no consequences other than those occasioned by its surface, architectural drawing leads to outcomes with entirely different characteristics—I mean those of a full-size, inhabitable enclosure. That these consequences occur gives to the architectural drawing an instrumental function, which is not its only one. The outcome of an architect's skill results in representations of buildings, cities, and rooms, or of their parts at least. "Representation" here is less a mimetic achievement than a prospective one, because in architecture design is always separate from production, envisaging distinct from realizing. Of course, architectural drawings can be viewed the way paintings are seen, but that is neither their only nor their primary purpose. Moreover, seeing architectural drawings as if they were paintings encourages the substitution of a formalist sort of aesthetic judgment for a nonformalist comprehension of broader cultural purposes. Aesthetic appreciation of single images also overlooks the relational or dependent character of architectural drawings. The plans, sections, and details of a building are rarely significant in a pictorial way because they are rarely intelligible individually; unlike paintings, which are almost always "framed" individually (enclosing a world unto itself), the graphic sheets of an architect normally come in sets, each drawing being "cross-referenced" to many others. Architectural understanding means grasping a network, weave, or matrix of figures, each partial but all mutually dependent.

A related distinction is that architectural drawings are different from paintings because they do not show aspects of the world that are outwardly apparent, but rather those that are "hidden" to the nonarchitectural eye. Just as the better digital representations of architecture develop images of what cannot be shown through manual means (such as movement through a setting or the change of lighting in an interior through the course of a whole day), so the traditional media of architectural representation disclose aspects of settings that would be otherwise unseen. A plan drawing, for example, allows one to see all of a building's rooms at the same time. No one can actually view a building in this way, but it is essential in architectural visualization. Likewise, an outline or profile drawing isolates figures from fields for purposes of exact dimensioning. The fabric of the world we inhabit is, by contrast, all of a piece. And finally, sectional drawings show aspects that are hidden from the nonprofessional eye: the interior of a wall or the depth of space behind it. Nothing of the architect's optic is typical of prosaic seeing, nor does it result from ordinary penetration. This is to say that architects, as architects, literally see the world in a unique way, a sort of x-ray detection, but not so mechanical. Architects see rooms, buildings, and streets in this way, but also entire neighborhoods and landscapes. Every design project begins with descriptive drawings, site surveys, which discover aspects of the horizon that are not immediately apparent. These surveys are not "merely" descriptive because they "catch" something essential in a site or region; thus they inaugurate or ignite design projection, whether that involves the elaboration or transformation of existing conditions. Architectural drawings are not only instrumental but interpretative, or biased toward the "hidden" and constitutive depth of the world we inhabit, which is also its potential. The real challenge of teaching drawing is to set up conditions under which students can risk seeing that world anew; seeing it, that is, in ways that allow it to be remade metrically, spatially, and qualitatively.

A third peculiarity to architectural drawings is also important: their fictive character. They are fictive in two ways: depicting something that doesn't yet exist and showing something we would like to have built. Representations in architectural work are intended for two audiences, architects themselves and others who have not been trained in architecture, such as builders, clients, and public officials. These sorts of images are not of buildings that exist; representations of that sort typify the art of premodern painterly description, not architectural drawing.

Distinct from the painter's sort, an architect's images are ones showing situations that have been imagined and settings that could be built. Perhaps an analogy will make this point clear: what the architect's drawing is to the building, the painter's sketch is to the painting: an indication, outline, proposition, or (in the best term I can think of) a *projection.* Further, they show not only what could be built, but what we would like to have built; they combine something imagined with something desired, not the world as it is, but as it should be. In some projects this desire is proposed as an "ought"; in others, it is presented as an obligation, which is why architectural acts must be seen to have ethical and political consequences. To say architectural drawings are fictive is to take advantage of the positive sense of that term, the one commonly used in literature and criticism, not to suggest that drawings of this sort show something impossible or improbable. They do not falsify reality but show how it can be shaped into something the given condition only approximates, something that condition isn't now or hasn't been yet, in much the same way that repressed or concealed passions are actualized when one puts on a mask or, more prosaically, particular kinds of clothes. In these instance of "fabrication," or when so adorned, we accomplish the paradox of becoming someone other than ourselves without ceasing to be ourselves. In 1965 Theodor Adorno opened the Deutscher Werkbund by saying, "Architecture worthy of human beings thinks better of men then they actually are" (Adorno 1979, 38). The function of fictions in art and architecture is to augment reality, which is not to forget nor to repeat it but to enhance it (Ricoeur 1991). Perhaps the clearest way of describing these sorts of figures is to call them anticipatory or approximate, in the sense of getting close to a situation or circumstance we would like to bring into being as the horizon of our lives. Architects always work in the subjunctive, not the nominative, case; each drawing or model is an "as if" (Summers 1991). Architectural representations can be verbal, graphic, three-dimensional, or, in our time, digital; but never are they not representations, which is a shorthand way of saying standing-for or in-the-place-of something that can become real. Making representations of this kind involves abstraction, in which the reduction of some aspects of an artifact allows for concentration on others, those that are taken to be key or essential for architectural purposes, purposes that include the conception, description, and construction of a built work. Yet the instrumental function of architectural representation is neither its only nor its highest purpose. I've identified both hermeneutical and fictive purposes, which are just as important. The other one now apparent is the drawing's rhetorical function. And not only must the client and builder be persuaded, but the architect too.

This last point leads to the greatest impediment to a clear understanding of what is essential in architectural representation: the long-standing and commonly held truism that architectural images display ideas, assuming that ideas precede and guide the development of images, that the conceptual matter (I possess) becomes clear to others when (my) drawings make it visible. Alberti's sense of design as "mental composition of line and angles" has contributed as much to this misunderstanding as has Descartes's description of "clear and distinct ideas." Drawing, as I have come to understand it, is both a public showing and a private disclosure, which is to say a creative articulation of what makes sense to others and to oneself, the demonstration of an idea as well as its advent. Put forcefully: in design, no idea exists until it has appeared in a drawing. Architects think architecture by drawing. Perhaps this dependence of understanding on visualization is similar to what occurs in other forms of articulation: that no idea is understood clearly until it has been voiced or expressed, that understanding does not precede articulation but progresses through it. In contemporary architectural practice, the functions of public showing and private disclosure through drawing are no longer taken to be aspects of one task because we have divided the media of representation into different categories, such as the rendering and the sketch, each having its own practitioners, its own place in the architectural process, and its own "audience." This division is one source of the professional fragmentation to which I referred earlier. The real task of reflection on this architectural subject in the midst of this fragmentation is to redefine and rethink the work of architectural representation as the means whereby several "ways of seeing things" are integrated into one way of knowing the world. Architects know the world through various media and methods of description and projection by showing how it can be made and remade. The instruments and intelligence of this work must be discovered again and described anew.

Architectural Reflection

If the craft of making a certain type of representations is the chief skill of the architect, what are the subjects that individual must understand? The other two parts of the Vitruvian triad, commodity and delight, seem unpromising in the face of this question because these terms have been used so often that they seem used up. I have said already that together with drawing, I want to focus on theory and technology. How do these subjects square with the classical list, with commodity and delight? Let me say immediately that there is no one-to-one correspondence. Nor for that matter is it immediately clear how my topics could be related to Vitruvius's famous *Encyclios disciplina*: "[the architect] should be a man of letters, a skillful draughtsman, a mathematician, familiar with historical studies, a diligent student of philosophy, acquainted with music, not ignorant of medicine, learned in the responses of jurisconsults, familiar with astronomy and astronomical calculations" (Vitruvius 1970, 1.1.3.). This recommendation for a well-rounded or liberal education in architecture follows Cicero's advice to the orator: "No one should be counted an orator who is not thoroughly versed in all those arts which are the mark of a gentleman. Whether or not we make actual use of them in a speech, our knowledge of them or lack of it is immediately obvious" (F. Brown 1963, 100–101). As they did for Cicero, the trivium and quadrivium formed for Vitruvius the basic subjects of architectural education. This list of subjects is longer than the triad to be sure, and few would doubt the value of understanding literature, mathematics, history, music, law, and so on. But in our time, unlike Vitruvius's, these disciplines are broad, highly developed, and diverse. No one honestly assumes comprehension of all that they entail. Thus, from our classical source, we have both poverty and abundance: too little for an architect to strive for, and too much to possibly comprehend.

Perhaps, then, it is time to finally abandon the classical sources and recognize once and for all the unbridgeable gulf between the ancient past and our time. Such recognition would mean dispensing with the classics and the arguments derived from them, thereby breaking the canon of architectural writing. In wider university and academic circles, any mention of a canon these days is often met with wholesale disapproval. Ours is not a promising time for the classics. It seems anachronistic to read the "great books" of Vitruvius, Alberti, Laugier, Ruskin, Semper, Sullivan, and Wright. What do they have to say to us? Many critics have come to see the study of books venerated in the past as a contemporary form of social control "dedicated to the justification of the present by the past" (O'Brien 1986; Weinsheimer 1991).[3] Allegiance to the old books, to those that have been taken as the wealth of our inheritance because they are the ones that have survived through the ages, can now be seen as the uncritical acceptance of what amounts to a repressive tradition. Some literary critics suggest that instead of studying and interpreting classical texts, we should cultivate in ourselves and in our students critical thinking, the capacity to question and to resist this tradition. And the vocabulary of "critical thinking" has been absorbed into architectural discourse: the design practices we want to praise these days are called "critical practices" although few seem willing to explain what that term means. Accordingly, the well-trained student is not the one who is well-read but the one who is always and everywhere capable of critique, which is an act that combines resistance, disbelief, and thoroughgoing questioning. For the not so well trained student, this approach tolerates neglect and indifference.

In the massive shift from conviction to critique, all texts seem open to question,[4] indeed all things in cultural life can be taken as the subject of critical thinking, except perhaps one: the sovereign authority of the questioner himself. Pursued further, this line of thinking would lead to the suggestion that in architecture there exist no "subjects" other than drawing as a form of personal discovery driven by dissatisfaction with inherited culture. This would mean that everything other than self-expression needs to be criticized or deconstructed. On this account, architecture would begin anew in the schools with each first-year class, or with each semester, or with each project, or, again, with each conversation. Take the books out of the studio, eliminate all the "references" from project descriptions, free creativity from the burden of bookishness! Although stunningly unsubtle, this sort of fundamentalist primitivism is commonplace in the twentieth century: it can be found in the heyday of early modernist manifestos, in the postwar period when European émigrés set up shop in North and South America, and more recently in "back to basics" movements. Yet in the turn away from venerable texts, does not the designer, like the progressive literary critic, venerate his or her own discourse? Further, doesn't this turn take creativity itself as a text beyond critique because it answers only to itself, to its own capacity for resistance and independent production? And isn't this entirely uncritical?

There should be no secure place for the veneration of old texts in contemporary architecture. Theory teaching as dutiful citation of ancient doctrine is, indeed, a spent force. For us, authenticity (in understanding as in life) involves self-determination (C. Taylor 1991). Yet are we so dedicated to independence of mind and self-determination that we need to shy away from the reflections of others? We know some texts have sustained critique for long periods of time. Neglecting them may shore up our sense of originality, but they can hardly be ignored when we learn that they treat issues that we find pressing, such as the role of drawing in design, which was in fact considered by each of the architect authors I have listed. Could it be that these texts have survived precisely because they have raised and tried to answer questions that were vitally important to the person questioning them — questions that are still with us? Could they not serve this function in the future? If so, wouldn't these sources be the ones that should properly be called classics? Let me cite Hegel: "[the classic] is essentially a question, an address to the responsive breast, a call to the mind and the spirit" (Hegel 1975, 71).[5] Hegel's definition invites us to see the classic not only as a statement, about which we can agree or disagree, nor only as a stance or position we may want to resist, interrogate, or deconstruct; it may, instead, encourage us to view the classic as articulated wonder, as a discipline of inquiry about a topic we can take up and practice ourselves, having discovered its potential in the example of its author. Understanding on this account would involve an exchange or crossover of questions, what has been formally called a "reciprocity of questioning" (Gadamer 1989, 333–41; Weinsheimer 1991, 129). More simply, it would be the occasion of wonder about themes and issues that have fascinated others, those that architects in the past have taken very seriously. Put broadly, these topics are what architects do, what one should call an architectural work, and who should be called an architect. I think it is fair to say that shared answers to these questions are not self-evident in our time, nor were they in the past. The uncertainty of past authors is apparent in the history of architectural questioning. My suggestion is that the questioning and answering undertaken by others may help us develop our own, and for that reason primarily should be studied. The thesis of reciprocal questioning suggests that the study of classical texts and the subjects to which they pertain takes as its model dialogue, which has always been the foundation for both honest reflection and democratic life. Reflective dialogue with our cultural inheritance is also the way I see teaching the history and theory of architecture, one of the discipline's basic subjects.

The subject matter of reciprocal questioning in architecture is not the history of written assertions, though, nor even of ideas. Teaching architectural reflection is not the same thing as giving a course in the history of architectural ideas. Nor do I think it follows from a history of monuments or exemplary buildings. We must move beyond this way of identifying and instructing in "culture." Neither a table of contents nor a season ticket can be found that would provide direct entry into the vital and vigorous culture that architects must understand. Just because theories and projects arise out of the world in which we live does not mean they are sufficient expressions of it; such an assumption deprives the figures of their ground, as if flames could be understood apart from combustible materials. Although both ideas and buildings do indeed enter into the kind of understanding that is necessary in architecture, the real task of reflection within the discipline is to witness and comprehend the emergence of both ideas and buildings from the cultural context that endows them with vital significance. This context can be named the structure of the life situations that buildings accommodate and symbolize. Situations such as these are not only matters of fact or of personal experience, nor is this structure the same thing as a law, a pattern, or a set of ideal norms. By structure of life situations, I do not mean an arrangement of user needs, client desires, or conventional programs; these factual things are important to know and to acknowledge, but they are insufficient to describe the subject matter of architectural understanding because they take for granted exactly what must be explained: how the various needs, desires, and programs of a given context can be integrated and brought together into a meaningful order. If cultural patterns serve as architecture's prefiguration, the act of designing involves projecting their reconfiguration. Such a prefiguration is not axiomatic or archetypal, though, and statistical study is an insufficient basis for insight into the order of human situations. Thus neither "real" interests documented in surveys nor formal norms grasped in analysis disclose the structure I have in mind; it is both more concrete and more abstract, more like an ensemble of typical incidents, prosaic in its concreteness, and variously institutionalized, but potentially poetic when reconfigured into compact but impermanent unity.

Such a structure of situations is neither already given before an architect begins work nor created from scratch in the process of this work; more accurate would be to say that this structure is the outcome of architectural invention because its disclosure amounts to the articulation of something tacitly known to all of us. How is this possible? How can understanding originate what already exists or bring into awareness what antecedes comprehension? How can something new make sense in the context of the lives we have lived? Can one's faith in what has been be integrated into a vision of what might be under new conditions? The answer to each of these questions is nothing other than the drama of cultural continuity. I call it a drama because its outcome is uncertain and its unfolding is the result of the decisions we make. The "I think" or "so-and-so has thought" of traditional theory must be redirected toward an "I am doing" in conditions such as these. In the continuity of culture, history and tradition have a role but always and only insofar as they can be reshaped creatively into the patterns of "pretheoretical" contemporary life (Gadamer 1989, 267–74; Gadamer 1986, 164).[6]

Theory teaching is more than the citation of texts from our tradition. These sources are useful, and singularly so, when they sustain reflection on problems that are pressing in our time. From what grounds or site do these problems arise? In answer to this question, I have a suggestion that weakens the position of the professor: the real or profound basis for radical reflection on the structure of situations that serves as the subject matter of architecture is every individual's participation in pre-professional or pretheoretical cultural life. Before each student walks up the steps of the architecture school, he or she has already developed the basis for rethinking and renewing architectural content. I have touched on this issue already in my comments on ethical understanding being essential for the architect. Studies of the literature and monuments of architectural history and theory will be renewed and made relevant only when they are reintegrated into the preacademic themes, problems, and patterns of contemporary culture.

Building Architecture in the Modern World

The shaping and reshaping of the patterns of contemporary culture in architecture intend permanence. Writing serves this purpose to a degree but not as well or as vividly as the manifestation of creative thinking that is privileged in architecture; I mean the actual construction of buildings, which results in these patterns receiving shape, durability, and expression. Let me cite August Schmarsow: "Architecture prepares a place for all that is lasting and established in the beliefs of a people and of an age; often, in a period of forceful change, when everything else threatens to sway, will the solemn language of its stones speak of support" (Schmarsow 1994, 295). Architectural construction is the way culture augments the natural and the inherited world, overcoming what in it is fleeting and wanting while enriching it. I have said already, though, that the skills of the builder are not the same as those of the architect; architects make drawings and builders make buildings. Although building technology is not a skill practiced by the architect, it is one of the basic subjects of the discipline, one that we have been too willing to abandon in recent years in pursuit of an architecture of communication that is indifferent to its means of realization. So this subject, like both theory and drawing, needs to be redefined in our time because the conditions under which buildings are produced these days are no longer the same as they once were.

Perhaps the most direct way to indicate the difference between contemporary architectural construction and the building practices of the past is to distinguish between construction as the putting together of materials on the one hand and as the joining together of elements on the other. As ways of assembling things, these two are as different as the things they join. When I say materials are put together in construction, I mean things like bricks, blocks, and boards, which are examples of the types of materials that give a building its palpable presence or physical substance: its color, temperature, size, shape, and "climate." Materials such as these must first be extracted from nature or made, then brought to a construction site where they are assembled together and finally finished. The task of realizing such a construction is the craft of building, not a craft the architect performs but one that he or she is expected to direct. And this is how matters have stood for millennia.

In our time, architects still need to understand these practices in order to direct and oversee them when they occur, but instances of this sort of building are being replaced with increasing frequency by another sort, the assembly of architectural elements that have been made off-site in a workshop or a factory. And these "materials" are not as simple as the former sort; instead of timber and glass from a forest or furnace, ready-made windows, trusses, and partitions come to sites as components, units, or entire systems from factories or warehouses. This is true for construction systems as well as systems of heating and cooling, lighting, furnishing, and all the other components of project realization. The complexity of these elements and systems is often so great that architects do not know how they work, nor how they might be modified, without compromising their "performance." When they come to a site, elements for these purposes are not so much put-together as put-into, not fabricated but installed. This manner of building is a dry not a wet process, less formative than preformed.

Thus, in contemporary building, two different types of procedures exist that require different kinds of understanding on the builder's part, but also the architect's. The first comprehends manual practices, the second industrial production. Vittorio Gregotti has observed, "gothic architects transformed materials into architectural facts, we assemble products" (Gregotti 1996, 52).

The more recent sort of construction can be called "craft" as long as we remember both the two-part history of this assembly or installation process and the external authority of its inception. Correct procedures in contemporary building are often measured against a standard devised apart from any specific project and then applied to each unique case. While on-site adjustments would be cause for praise in traditional building, as examples of ingenuity, in modern practices, alterations or "change orders" are cause for concern because the performance of a modified element can no longer be guaranteed. Perhaps the best way to distinguish between the assembly of materials and of elements is to say that the parts of the first are remade in construction, whereas those for the second are premade before it begins.[7]

Were building technology or design for that matter nothing but the assembly of premade parts according to prescribed procedures, the production of buildings would be like any other form of contemporary mass production, which it is not. Although standardized elements are used in current technologies, building construction is not standardized, despite all the ambitious efforts to make it so and the increasing control of construction managers. Perhaps the standardization of construction remains partial because the unique characteristics of sites, climates, and environments always influence building practices, unlike the stable situation of a factory or workshop interior. Equally significant may be the abilities and habits of builders, as they vary from project to project. Though the overall tendency of the industry is toward rational prescription and standardization, no construction is completed these days without a good measure of on-site adjustment.

For this reason, adjustment, alteration, and modification are the topics of construction that merit attention these days, even though changes of this kind always risk performance failure. These topics should also be part of the subject matter of technology teaching, augmenting traditional topics. The basic question is as follows: on what basis can an architect direct a builder to make adjustments to premade elements? More basically, under what conditions is ingenuity still possible? The answer to this question is a matter of understanding, but also of education. For example, midway through one of their design projects, students could be given a mass-produced element (a standardized window would do) and asked to remake the design or the window to allow for congruity among the different parts of a building and between the building and its site, and in view of the dwelling (the cultural) situation that is envisaged. The imagination necessary for this sort of adjustment or modification is a synthetic sort, the kind that brings together things that had been seen as different or incongruent, a concrete rather than a speculative imagination.

Changes in prescribed procedures or past practices risk performance failure. The singular virtue of technique is repeatability; it is a form of knowledge that enables a practice to be assured of its results: "I have done it once and can do it again." Repetition is true for building technique and for other sorts as well. In archaic Greek myth, humans were given the gift of the arts or techniques by the demigod Prometheus, whose name signifies "knowing beforehand," or envisaging an outcome with the power of foresight, cleverness, or of "sly thought" (Kerényi 1977; Vernant 1983, 237–47; Gehlen 1980, 33; Trimpi 1983, 7). Accordingly, "know-how" is also "knowing before hand." Past procedures become prescribed because they allow for the prediction of outcomes, and in construction practice — especially the market-driven construction practice of our time — predicted outcomes are both valued and safeguarded. Insofar as adjustments, modifications, or alterations prevent prediction, they can be seen to represent a risk not worth taking, and the difficulty of prediction is true in both traditional craft and modern standardized practices.

The reason for taking such a risk, however, is the same now as it has been in the past: to make the project or the practice more perfect in its outcome when the total picture or full schedule of provisions is understood. In the mythical accounts of Prometheus presented by both Plato and Aeschylus, the god who gave humans technology was not admitted into the citadel of Zeus, for he knew nothing of the art of politics, nor of any subjects that concerned the whole of human life (Plato 1991, 320d). A profound lack exists at the heart of technical knowledge, the sense of wholeness, or concern for it. The ways that various contributions participate in the realization of a desired end is what the builder or contemporary technician (as builder or technician) never attempts to understand and what, therefore, the architect (as a representative of the full horizon of expectations) must bring to the process. The adjustment of standards in a building results from an architect's understanding of how all of its aspects, premade or remade, come together to give durable dimension and shape to the patterns of our lives.

Because architects these days can avoid neither craft nor industry they must develop an intuitive grasp of manual procedures and a scientific understanding of the physical world, so that predictions about the performance of elements can be understood. In schools, exercises in full-scale construction, not necessarily of buildings or even parts of buildings but with real materials and different assembly technologies, must be added to studies in statics and mechanics. The first kind of knowing can be called concrete, the second abstract; likewise, they can be called empirical and mathematical, or outwardly apparent and conceptually significant. But while each kind of understanding can be distinguished with these or other terms, no choice should be encouraged. In the terrain called technology, no fork in the road demands a choice between craft and industrial methods; instead of assuming or mapping out a divergence, we must discover and describe a convergence; we need to see how manual and conceptual technologies intersect with one another along the lines of a unified understanding of building production.

The Prosaic Horizon of Architectural Culture

The task of rethinking technology in architecture, like rethinking theory and representation, arises out of dissatisfaction with inherited principles and practices. Because these subjects, like this discipline itself, exist within a context that has changed, they too must change. But this change is not for the sake of conformity or the seamless interweaving of a profession with a society. In my comments on building construction, I implied a yes and a no to the imperatives of contemporary technology. A similar kind of resistance was proposed in view of the excessively autobiographical tendencies of contemporary art. And in my comments on theory, I implied that reflection in architecture should become less theoretical, that it needs to be regrounded within a horizon of typical life situations. In each case, I have advocated a renewed connection between the subjects of architecture and lived culture, some aspects of which will provoke practices of resistance. This connection to concrete existence is decisive in architecture, and in other fields as well. Much of twentieth-century philosophy has argued for a return to the "lived world." The first section of Merleau-Ponty's *Phenomenology of Perception* is called "Traditional Prejudices and the Return to Phenomena." In the same vein and closer to architecture, Karsten Harries (1968) has argued in the concluding sentences to *The Meaning of Modern Art* that modesty and patience will help us see the meanings of the world in which we find ourselves. The ingenuity that I see as the essence of design requires just this interest. Let me again cite Vitruvius (1970): "when therefore account has been taken of the symmetries of the design and the dimensions have been worked out by calculation, it is then the business of [the architect's] skill to have regard to the nature of the site . . . *to produce a proper balance by adjustment,* adding or subtracting from the symmetry of the design so that it may seem to be rightly planned" (6.2.1). The ability to make adjustments of this kind, like the capacity to see similarities where others find them lacking, requires a versatile mind, said Vitruvius, an *ingenio mobili.* Ingenuity cannot be taught, but its occasions can be cultivated by attention to the prosaic circumstances of a given situation and by recognition of what has been "seemly." I understand that care for existing cultural conditions restricts the independent authority of technology, theory, and artistry as they have been practiced in the recent past, but this sort of attention is necessary if architecture is to regain relevance in our society. This shifts one's focus from possible realities to real possibilities.[8] On this basis alone will the subjects of architecture be seen as essential and be redefined in resistance to some of the tendencies of that very same society, those that favor dogmatic indifference to concrete conditions. On this basis, too, the basic subjects of architecture can be discovered again.

Notes

1. I too have treated this issue in Leatherbarrow 1997.

2. For commentary and explication see Gadamer 1975, 278–89; R. Bernstein 1985; Voegelin 1957, 296–303; and Jaeger 1934, 437–51.

3. Weinsheimer (1991, 125) quotes Mary O'Brien (1986, 93) from "Feminism and the Politics of Education." In what follows, I cite and paraphrase Weinsheimer and consulted Eliot 1957; Kermode 1975; Voegelin 1973; and Rykwert 1980.

4. Here I cite the title Paul Ricoeur (1998) has given to a recent set of interviews.

5. I treat this under the heading of topical thinking in Leatherbarrow 1993, 2–6.

6. On page 165 of Gadamer 1986: "It is also easy to see that in the sphere of practice the conclusion is not a proposition but a decision."

7. I owe this "premade-remade" vocabulary to my frequent coauthor Mohsen Mostafavi, although he used it in a slightly different sense.

8. I owe this phrase to Dalibor Vesely.

6

A Dialectics of Determination: Social Truth-Claims in Architectural Writing, 1970–1995

David J. T. Vanderburgh and W. Russell Ellis

Writing, Responsibility, and the Claiming of Truth

> For it is not as a very great philosopher, nor as an eloquent rhetorician, nor as a grammarian trained in the highest principles of his art, that I have striven to write this work, but as an architect who has had only a dip into these studies.
>
> — Vitruvius

A well-known British architect (Duffy 1996) confesses to having been "ruthless" while researching his doctorate, one of the first awarded in a wave of new graduate programs created in the 1970s. Then, as now, research in architecture required frequent cross-disciplinary visits. Such visitors must be ruthless in taking advantage of the host discipline, and ruthless again with themselves to avoid what anthropologists call "going native." In this, they fit the classic image of the architect as using knowledge from many other disciplines without becoming an expert in any of them (Vitruvius 1960, 5–11).

Our epigraph, taken from the oldest surviving architectural text, might thus be read as referring to architecture's multidisciplinarity: architects can be effective using knowledge gained from "only a dip into" domains ranging as widely as physics, city planning, and history. But in the citation we've chosen, Vitruvius specifically limits his responsibility regarding writing: between the lines of his disclaimer is the conviction that his authority comes from outside the disciplines he cites, and even outside writing itself (Patterson 1997). His determination to write "as an architect" initiates a long tradition of treatises and manifestos extending through the Renaissance to the twentieth century (Kruft 1994, 21–40). This was precisely the tradition with which the new architectural researchers of the 1970s sought to break.

Returning from visits to neighboring sciences, these researchers introduced a further sort of ruthlessness by which the architectural author would be constrained to convey only objective new knowledge, not the lively mixture of received ideas, scholarship, and intuition that had characterized the treatises. Now, writing would have to proceed according to strict standards of truth within a carefully narrowed conceptual field, inspired by the epistemologies of the natural and social sciences. But as appealing as such ideas may have been to some architects, particularly those concerned with academic legitimacy, this small revolution could not simply replace treatises with research reports. Instead, at least two ways of "writing architecture" have coexisted uneasily, each claiming some authority over the theoretical basis of the discipline.[1]

This chapter presents an analysis of some of the ideas and events that have marked architectural writing, research, and teaching over the last three decades. We have chosen to look closely at one architectural subfield, which we'll call "social and cultural factors" (SCF). However, this is not so much a review of the literature of SCF as an attempt to relate the fortunes of that literature to broader trends and debates in the discipline at large. Like other research subfields (with names like "building science" and "design methods"), SCF emerged as an answer both to long-term questions regarding architecture and to short-term exigencies in the academy.

Social and cultural factors is a rubric under which teachers, researchers, and practitioners concern themselves with architecture as it affects and is affected by social, cultural, and sometimes political factors. Most departments of architecture now include some teaching, some research, and perhaps a graduate program in the area of SCF. The area has at least two long-standing scholarly societies and is represented in most urban planning and landscape architecture curricula. It also shares literature and faculty with programs in such social-scientific specialties as environmental psychology, organizational behavior, urban sociology, and human geography. In the last twenty-five years, few university-trained architects have received a diploma without being exposed to SCF. Although the founders of the subdiscipline, many of whom are social scientists by training, are retired or nearing retirement, an increasing percentage of current architectural faculty are of the generations of architects who have been educated under curricula that include SCF.

These demographic factors would be enough for one to expect evolution in the field. Mainstream architectural writing has embraced concerns first propagated in SCF; similarly, more recent writing in SCF has moved closer to long-term concerns of architectural theory such as style, precedent, and history (e.g., Franck and Schneekloth 1994; Gaster 1991; Horwitz 1993; Markus 1993; Rapoport 1990). On the other hand, as the "market" — in both financial and intellectual terms — for architectural ideas has changed, SCF has clearly lost some ground among architects. One architectural educator, founder of an SCF journal in the 1980s, recently spoke of his "very mixed success" at drawing architects' attention to the needs of inhabitants (Noschis 1998).

Although we take note of these factors in this discussion, we do not consider them sufficient for an understanding of how SCF and social truth-claims in architecture have evolved. We consider it important to underline some long-term tensions regarding the social mission and legitimacy of architecture — tensions that often emerge in discussions of that particularly vexed category, "social responsibility." Accordingly, we begin with a discussion of the word "social" as an interdisciplinary meeting point, followed by a sketch of some possible lines of argument regarding social aspects of architecture. These two sections introduce a discussion of a kind of epistemological crisis in SCF, and in architectural writing in general, brought on by the incursion of ideas from phenomenology. We end with an example from the fairly recent architectural press, in which one classic debate — between "formalists" and "humanists" — seems to have come to a point of diminishing returns, while some more promising avenues may be opening up.

The geometrical conceit in the succession of our subheadings, from a "point of contact" to "lines of argument," "planes of significance," and "spheres of influence," is intended as slightly more than a structuring device. If, in exploring our question of social truth-claims, the essay follows a roughly chronological schema, one can also view the question as having "dimensional" aspects of varying complexity, present *throughout* the period we discuss. From the terminological "point" to the fuller tableau of conflicting ideological "spheres," each aspect yields different insights.

After all, the exercise of retracing recent history is dangerous enough as it is. Seemingly solid tendencies may reverse themselves suddenly just after one goes to press, and other aspects may show no development whatsoever. Indeed, although we've tried to conclude on an optimistic note, it is possible that the intellectual problems raised here are not any closer to resolution at present than they were at the end of the 1960s; perhaps they are just more clearly posed. The present state may not herald any reduction in the ruthlessness we mentioned at the beginning, but it may indicate that architecture is becoming a home discipline to which its researchers can return more easily from their visits "abroad."

A Point of Contact: The Word "Social"

That a single word can be productive of such alternatives of damnation or involved reserve no doubt says much for the meanings with which it has been endowed. (Rowe 1976, 61)[2]

Innovation within a discipline often involves importing words from elsewhere. These words then become points of contact between two semantic worlds, at once connecting and separating them. Architecture may have more than its share of such points of contact, since its range of relevant interdisciplinary connections is so broad. But the phenomenon shows itself with particular force in the context of architecture's research subfields, where many critical terms are shared with other disciplines. For instance, the terms making up SCF's various labels — "cultural," "behavioral," "social," and so on — all have technical uses, however fluctuating and contested, in the social sciences.

We will limit this analysis to the adjective "social," looking at two roles it has filled in architectural writing. The first, stemming from the historical conditions and palliative mission of social science itself, ties social aspects of architecture to social problem solving. The other is as a polarizing element in recurring debates about how architecture should be made.

The word has a specific history as a technical modifier. Following on Locke's and Rousseau's ideas of the social contract, notions of social problems or social questions quickly came to stand for the nineteenth-century liberal state's concern with public unrest, popular hygiene, and class conflict. As new domains of study began to address these topics in the service of "society," they not only responded to a perceived need for social knowledge but also helped to define the rules and policies on which society operated. In a broad sense, they created the context in which it was possible to speak of a distinct social realm (Rabinow 1989, 168–75).

From the beginning of the term's scientific usage, social theory was unclear as to whose sociality was at issue: was it that of all citizens, or just of those who might inhibit the smooth functioning of the state? The new social sciences took on the implicit mission of social pacification, and the word "social" came to have the class connotations that go with concepts of social housing, social welfare, social policy, and so on. Perhaps because of the high political priority of this mission, "social science" came eventually to stand (in English, at least) for all of the sciences having human beings as their object of study. In arguing for his early and influential conception of social science, Auguste Comte stated this mission clearly: "We have only to complete the hierarchy of the positive sciences by bringing the facts and problems of society within its comprehension. . . . When this has been accomplished, its supremacy will be automatic and will establish order throughout society" (Castell 1963, 226).

Comte's argument contained two assumptions that have remained basic to social science. The first is that the facts and problems of society are accessible to a scientific, or "positive," method of constructing knowledge. The second, about which most contemporary social scientists are more modest than Comte, is that the acceptance of this sort of knowledge will simply follow as a natural consequence of its self-evidence, leading society to take its proper shape. Even if such assumptions are now widely questioned, few would deny their continuing currency. Indeed, it is difficult to justify the existence of social-science knowledge in any other way.

During the second half of the nineteenth century, architecture became a liberal profession in search of legitimacy (see the chapters by

Carol Burns and Julia Robinson in this volume), and architectural writers discovered the usefulness of "service to society" as an element in their rhetorical repertoire. To defend its new turf from builders and engineers, the profession learned to define itself as having special competence in social matters.[3]

As a part of this effort, the discursive direction of architectural writings began to converge with that of social science, both seeking to locate the causes and effects of human events in orderly configurations of space and time. Le Corbusier, in posing his famous choice between "architecture or revolution," gave a stylish turn to a hundred-year-old equation of architecture with social peace (Le Corbusier [1931] 1986, 269).

In the first several decades of the twentieth century, empirical studies of urban neighborhoods, industrial productivity, and housing argued for a kind of sociophysical engineering that would both fight "social contagion" and calm social unrest (Park et al. 1925; Wirth 1969). Such reasoning, about which we will say more, was often adopted by contemporaneous architectural writers, who found it helpful to imagine architecture as a product of objectifiable forces. SCF, emerging several decades later, inherited this mission: "social" referred to a domain consisting of errors to be corrected, instability to be rendered manageable, and social actors to be mollified. Although there were and are programs of fundamental research relating to SCF, it was introduced to architecture mostly as a way of ameliorating the social impact of architectural interventions.

Alongside this carefully defined context — where architecture, now using SCF as its mouthpiece, expressed its commitment to social goals — the word had other connotations that may have carried more weight. "Social connections" are paramount in architecture, both for young architects seeking employment and for mature ones getting commissions. Their importance has long been recognized, perhaps even overemphasized, in art historical studies of architecture, through studies of patronage and stylistic genealogy. But this reading of the word is not the one most often given it in the literature of SCF, just as "culture" has not usually meant the opera, symphony, and museum circuit. The moral and political basis of SCF, especially in the early years, was in meeting "human needs," not studying social climbing. Yet to make a thorough study of social, cultural, or political determinations of architecture, the "high" and "low" connotations would have to be treated together.

Indeed, a number of book-length studies published since the 1980s turn a social-scientific gaze on architects themselves as social actors (Blau 1984; Cuff 1991; Prak 1984; Gutman 1988; Ellis and Cuff 1989). This approach has allowed writers to depict architecture not only as a social *problem* but as a social *practice*. It is, moreover, in line with a contemporary reflexive turn in architecture (see Schön 1983), as witnessed by this book, among others, and an increasing stream of specialized articles (e.g., Varnelis 1999). On the other hand, by abandoning the promise of direct application to architectural projects, studies taking architects as objects would tend to weaken SCF's claim on a central role in the discipline.

Apart from the problem of double meaning, a side effect of giving prominence to the word "social" was to make it available as a pole in older debates of a more general nature. First, as the ideological atmosphere heated up with moral critiques of modernism and architecture-as-art, the so-called social domain — here elided with one understanding of the "functional" — came to be seen as opposed to the tradition of formal invention. We will return to this at the end of the chapter. Second, in the very act of defining fields such as environmental psychology or sociology, environment/behavior studies, and others, the social or "human" factors came to represent whatever was not physical or static in architecture — even if, within the social sciences at large, the understanding of this question was more complex. As Bill Hillier and Julienne Hanson (1984, 11) have pointed out, this formula runs in the well-worn philosophical tracks of mind-matter dualism (see also Latour 1993, 51–55). But in either case, the question of the mutual determination of the social and the architectural was given a particularly difficult cast by the baggage that came with a single word.

Lines of Argument: Positivism and Truth Criteria

It does not follow from the fact that human beings are different from other objects in nature that there is nothing determinate about them. Despite the fact that human beings in their actions show a kind of causation which does not apply to any other objects in nature, namely motivation, it must still be recognized that determinate causal sequences must be assumed to apply to the realm of the social as they do to the physical. (Wirth 1936, xix)

SCF in its founding years promoted a broadly positivist reading of the relation between architectural forms and human beings, making the claim that architecture, properly understood, could and should directly reflect social truths obtained through empirical research. In arguing for the necessity of new research and theory in environmental psychology, one early text claimed that "the decoration of a room, the design of a building, and the choice of a site for a housing project are all based ultimately on decisions about the kinds of behaviors one wishes to foster or discourage" (Proshansky, Ittelson, and Rivlin 1970, 3). This understanding would allow researchers to find lawlike regularities in human behavior that might then inform an instrumentalist architecture designed to produce desirable behaviors.

Although the language was new, the idea was not. Already in the mid–nineteenth century, as Auguste Comte sketched out plans for his positive science of society, critics and theorists such as John Ruskin and Eugène Viollet-le-Duc were searching for invariant formulas in the interactions between ways of life and ways of building. As Louis Wirth wrote the statement we cite earlier, Sigfried Giedion was developing his theses regarding the technological inevitability of the modern movement. Although these writers probably suspected that neither architecture nor human behavior could be wholly determined or determining, the ambient rhetoric of modernity was one of causes and effects. And as social science and architecture met in SCF, the theme of determination was in the foreground.

The critical aspect of positivist determination is its partial nature. Positivism has the great strength of allowing rigorous partial truths, where correlation can stand in for causality, and where tendencies in the data can be assigned degrees of significance and projected into the future using mathematical regression techniques. "With their tools," Albert Mehrabian assured the reader, "environmental psychologists can tell you, for example, whether people who gather to socialize in a given living room will tend to be subdued, stiff, noncommittal, or anxious to leave, or whether they will tend to be outgoing, friendly, relaxed, or eager to remain and have a good time" (1976, 4). In studies of crime in housing projects, one could examine the association of forms with crimes and, while remaining respectful of rules of inference, hope to attack the latter by means of the former. SCF was confident in the early years that it could describe and predict such relationships well enough to be useful, even necessary, to design (Newman 1976).

At the same moment, among architects, a stylistic and ideological rebellion against modern movement orthodoxy was gathering energy, following the emergence of the so-called Team X architects. This group of dissenters from the Le Corbusier–led Congrès International de l'Architecture Moderne (CIAM) included Aldo Van Eyck, Alison and Peter Smithson, Giancarlo De Carlo, and others who rejected large-scale formulaic urbanism in search of a closer relation with the local and historical context. The documentation of this rebellion brought the terminology of participation and neighborhood preservation into anglophone architectural writing, although its effects on North American architectural production were delayed during the postwar boom.

Writers in SCF could now use the positivist framework as a tool for critique of the modern movement. A milestone in this vein was Philippe Boudon's (1969) study of Le Corbusier's Pessac housing project. After forty years of occupation, inhabitants had transformed many of the spare "purist" row houses beyond recognition. In the contemporaneous climate of widespread, violent social activism, no one could miss the irony of this apparent refusal to accept Le Corbusier's exchange of architecture for revolution.[4]

Direct attacks on buildings were not unheard of, as in the case of students' defacing of Paul Rudolph's Art and Architecture building at Yale. Another widely cited illustration of the social failure of modern architecture was the 1972 demolition of the Pruitt-Igoe housing complex in St. Louis.[5] These two anecdotes were recounted with some relish in Peter Blake's *Form Follows Fiasco* (1977, 16–18, 155). Two years later, Brent Brolin sounded a similar note with *The Failure of Modern Architecture* (1976). The latter's provocative title and pointed illustrations did as much as its writing to promote the impression that things had gone wrong in the modern movement. Like A. W. Pugin (1841) more than a century before, Brolin contrasted the faceless, alienating aspect of the architecture of his contemporaries with the craft and specificity of an older way of building. Unlike Pugin, who had defended the Gothic style (and promoted the Neo-Gothic), Brolin suggested a solution not in terms of style and social organization but through the acquisition of more accurate "form-relevant social information" (1976, 110).

SCF's acceptance of a positivist worldview was both a rhetorical asset and an epistemological liability. It allowed writers to recruit architectural practitioners, who found it convincing enough to allow SCF a part in architectural education, and who themselves developed a certain enthusiasm about social and psychological theory and research. But it occasioned persistent problems in making the new knowledge relevant or applicable to the critical situations of particular projects. This was in part, as John Zeisel has suggested, a question of designers' "tacit" versus researchers' "explicit" knowledge (1981, 56–57).

Another way of framing the problem would be in terms of different ways of establishing truth. To demonstrate the truth of a theoretical statement, positivism requires establishing a correspondence between the statement and some set of facts rendered as data. In standard social science methodology, this is often represented by the study of correlations between variables that can be represented quantitatively. This practice, fundamental in social science, constrains the kind of truth that can be legitimately expressed but permits the critical establishment of reliability and validity, two cornerstones of scientific truth assessment. It also permits small or local truths to be assembled together, leading inductively to the possibility of generalization, another central scientific goal.

The correspondence criterion calls for chains of verification, or external validation, that assure a link between theory and a demonstrated reality. For early writers in SCF, then, truth was to be established cumulatively and cautiously. Following this, according to the Comtean thesis of truth's self-evidence, SCF's new social knowledge would naturally work its way into the fabric of architectural production, eventually attaining what Comte had called "supremacy"—a clear determining role. This role is probably what some early SCF writers imagined playing in design, even if their colleagues or their common sense suggested otherwise. On the other hand, architects were used to judging each others' work according to another sort of standard, one that emphasized the synthetic balancing of heterogeneous factors, recognizing the need for compromises, last-minute additions, and withdrawals in the service of overall coherence. For them, as in the Vitruvian limiting of responsibility, no one factor could attain supremacy.

This way of establishing truth, known as coherentism, requires only that the ensemble of theoretical statements be internally consistent. According to Ian Hacking, "a coherence theory is holistic. That is to say, it does not think of truths coming along one by one, each corresponding to its own private fact. Truth, it says, has to do with an entire corpus of sentences, which must be internally consistent, and which is governed chiefly by the tendency of speakers to add or withdraw statements from this corpus in the light of their experiences" (1975, 131).

Coherentism is a peculiar approach to truth, abandoning any responsibility for local explanatory power in the scientific sense. A rational rather than empirical criterion, coherence is a matter of judgment and choice, preferring a flawed but ambitious theory to one that lowers its sights to the strictly attainable. Yet most disciplines use coherence at one stage or another in the process of theory building; indeed, some, like mathematics, must operate primarily on a coherence basis, since there is little chance of establishing correspondence with anything outside their symbolic language.

We're not suggesting that SCF operated on a pure correspondence model and the rest of architecture on pure coherentism. In such a case, architecture would not have become interested in SCF, nor SCF in architecture. Moreover, the goal of a Comtean positive science would be to proceed inductively via correspondence criteria toward a theory that would *also* meet coherence criteria. In the context of SCF's negotiation of territory within architecture, this reasoning could lead eventually to the essentialist claim that all of architecture could be explained and produced in conformity with some sufficiently general social theory. Such arguments are in fact made by some in SCF, for example by Hillier and Hanson, who contend that "environments acquire their form and order as a result of a social process" — in other words, as they assert in *The Social Logic of Space,* any departure from a random distribution of single "cells" must be attributed to social processes (1984, 9–25). Despite their reservations concerning dualism (cited earlier), they maintain a distinction between the physical environment "as a result," on one hand, and the possible reflection of existing environments back on social processes, on the other.

This sort of reduction would be difficult to accept, not only for architects, but for the other subdisciplines of architecture as well, each of which is subject to its own analogous problems regarding determination. Since Vitruvius, we would argue, architecture is and must be interested in other disciplines regarding those aspects of architecture that might be illuminated by their conceptual tools: thus physics, art history, social science, and others are all given a part in architecture. But the implicit bargain struck with the new subdisciplines of the 1970s had to be essentially this: the source discipline would be brought into more direct contact with architectural theory and practice, but it would leave its determinism, as it were, at the door.

Writers in SCF have been attentive to this problem but have tended to limit their concerns to denouncing what Alan Lipman (1974) identified early on as "architectural determinism." Architect and theorist Jon Lang criticizes architecture's "extravagant" claims regarding its social or behavioral effects (Lang 1987, 11). In identifying the problem, however, these writers seem to miss the contradictory implications of their argument. If such effects are in fact weaker than architects think, there would be little justification for a growing research enterprise to study them. Nor have writers in SCF been as concerned about the converse tendency of social scientists to engage in a kind of social determinism of architecture. Stanford Anderson, in his introduction to a volume called *On Streets,* protests against the implicit double bind: "Architects and physical planners are alternately chastised for falsely holding that physical design could have any effect on human thought and action, and then damned for the social irresponsibility of creating the conditions which have led to a worsened urban life. The social critics cannot have it both ways" (Anderson 1978, vii).

Normal scientific practice admits a variety of truth criteria (for example, the criterion of theoretical elegance or parsimony, which is related to coherentism), even though scientists usually insist on the primacy of correspondence. Case studies of scientific research suggest that there are wide variations in the importance of different criteria at different times. This recognition is making it more difficult to distinguish between science and related activities like technological development (e.g., Bijker, Hughes, and Pinch 1987).

Writers in the research subdisciplines of architecture, including SCF, have often made a hard distinction between science and design, claiming that "by definition, design cannot be scientific" (Lang 1987, 19). Yet they generally recognize a need for "quasi-scientific" methods of research that, although not perfectly rigorous, allow less artificial conditions for data gathering. Relinquishing part of positivist rigor may be a start down a slippery slope; indeed, recent studies have begun to question the possibility of building pure correspondence theories at all. According to this growing literature, one might ask whether science *itself* is capable of being scientific in the positivist sense (Stengers and Schlanger 1991).

The variety, complexity, and omnipresence of architecture make it a challenging object for any single mode of inquiry. Despite the evident attraction of a rigorous framework for demonstrating socioarchitectural truths, it is unclear how knowledge gathered in this way could have been compatible with other modes of judgment like coherentism. Moreover, architects' attacks on the modern movement had taken specific aim at its positivist rhetoric.

Nor were architects the only ones to react against positivism; some writers associated with SCF also questioned positivist methods and paradigms. Clare Cooper Marcus (1974), in an important early article, "The House as Symbol of the Self," doubted the adequacy of quantitative methods to capture the meaning of the house, preferring intensive interviewing and analysis based on Jungian archetypes. Christopher Alexander, whose early theory (1964) had been sympathetic to both positivism and SCF, moved quickly to a coherentist position in later work (1979). And Alan Lipman and Howard Harris, in a 1979 conference paper, criticized positivist attempts to treat people as objects on the model of the natural sciences, sidestepping issues of ethics and power.

By the mid- to late 1970s, then, both SCF and architecture were looking for some way of better understanding the lived reality of human beings with respect to architecture. Theorists were disenchanted with the usual truth criteria and the weakness of resulting claims and began to associate this weakness with the apparent failure of modern technocratic culture to meet—or even to understand—people's needs. Architects, smarting from the criticisms leveled at buildings they had once thought of as models, were seeing new possibilities in historic, traditional, and premodern architectures, all of which seemed to possess an authenticity that current work lacked.

Planes of Significance: The Attraction of Phenomenology

Man has always tried to overcome distance. . . . But only modern man has carried this effort so far that with some justice he can liken himself to God, to whom all things are equally close. The full consequences of this attack on distance are still uncertain: while it promises man almost divine power, it also threatens him with a never before known homelessness. . . . When all places count the same we cannot place ourselves and become displaced persons. The ease with which we relocate ourselves and replace our buildings is witness to this displacement. (Harries [1975] 1996, 394)

While Karsten Harries ([1975] 1996), one of the first to bring phenomenology to bear on architecture, criticizes modernity as an "attack on distance," it might be fair to speak of phenomenology as an attack on analytical distance (Nesbitt 1996, 394). From Edmund Husserl's ([1954] 1970) call for a return to "the things themselves" to Martin Heidegger's ([1927] 1996) insistence on immanence and "presencing," this current of twentieth-century thought has made impressive efforts to recover, or at any rate to describe, a sort of primordial closeness to the world in lived experience. It should be noted, however, that phenomenology and its offshoots, including existentialism and phenomenological sociology, must be considered both antimodern and modern. That is, only by acknowledging the modern postulate of a subject-object dichotomy could they attack its inauthenticity. This ambivalent posture runs throughout the literature we discuss hereafter.

Phenomenology, and in particular Heidegger's 1951 lecture "Building, Dwelling, Thinking," which became available in English in 1971, added conceptual weight to the reaction against the modern movement (1971b). Not long afterward, writers in geography, architecture, and landscape architecture began to draw a critical distinction between "space" and "place." The work of Christian Norberg-Schulz, by the early 1970s, evolved away from a "scientific" manner of analysis (1965) toward a more "existential" treatment. In 1974, Kenneth Frampton published an editorial, "On Reading Heidegger," that argued for "place creation" as an alternative to ideas of "autonomous artistic production" then being discussed (Nesbitt 1996, 446). By 1976, Norberg-Schulz was finishing work on *Genius Loci* (1980), which adopted Heideggerian terminology of "gathering" and "dwelling" to speak of architecture as the " 'concretization' of an existential situation." In the same year, geographer Edward Relph (1976) published *Place and Placelessness,* a broader indictment of the modern city. And Alberto Pérez-Gómez, preparing a dissertation that became *Architecture and the Crisis of Modern Science,* was using the work of Husserl to explain the banishment of myth from Enlightenment architectural theory. These diverse writers, having become conscious of the limits of scientific rhetoric and its apparently soulless influence on building, were searching for another means to account for irreducible phenomena like the "sense of place."

For architecture and SCF, phenomenology was like a virus: its terminology infiltrated speech and writing, holding out the promise of expressing the transcendent quality of ordinary places. The word "place" alone came to connote a whole complex of attitudes regarding architecture and its human and natural contexts. Architectural projects began to be evaluated according to their ability to foster a sense of place. By the end of the 1970s, phenomenology was appearing more and more frequently as a reference in SCF's bellwether publication, the proceedings of the Environmental Design Research Association (Wener and Szigeti 1988). As it began to aspire to a distinct status, the phenomenological current in SCF showed a tendency to appropriate into its fold the work of architects and writers who would not necessarily have consented to their nomination as phenomenologists. For one intellectual entrepreneur, any study that showed "sensitive explication of first-hand environmental experiences," "careful observation of places," or "thoughtful examination of literary and artistic texts" could be considered to have "important phenomenological value" (Seamon 1987, 3–27; see also Seamon and Mugerauer 1985).

At its best, the incursion of phenomenological ideas encouraged a useful reassessment of meaning, language, and truth in the context of architecture. One of the clear advantages it proffered was an alternative to the choice between correspondence and coherence models of truth. While these two could be seen, respectively, as requiring either a partial "contact" or none at all between observing subject and observed object, phenomenology required (or implicitly promised) total contact, a relation known as "adequation."

Most phenomenology-inspired critiques of modern architecture, whether identified with SCF or not, took as their central target its "space," a technocratically produced, universalizing, and visually impoverished environment that did not seem to foster a sense of place as did the towns, villages, cabins, castles, and other creations of nonmodern cultures. Whereas modern spaces seemed to be both literally and emotionally empty, these other places appeared crowded with meaningful activity, charged with meaning itself. By visiting, observing, and describing such places, these writers saw the possibility of a more authentic existence. Nonetheless, the rhetorical thrust of their studies — that one kind of architecture, understood necessarily from outside its context, could be taken as a model for their own — reproduced the epistemological situation of positivism.

Despite its appeal for the practice-based discipline of architecture, the phenomenological movement in philosophy had largely concerned itself with unattainable goals. Edmund Husserl, in trying to rewrite the symbolic language of science, had been driven to invent thousands of intermediate terms, sometimes called "noemata," that relentlessly increased the distance between subject and object. Heidegger, even in his early work, had seen immense difficulty in attaining authentic knowledge. For him, "phenomenology" was the name for an exact science of being that could only come after a long process resembling biblical hermeneutics — the interpretation of interpretation. Architectural readers often seized on the quasi-poetic phrasing in his later works, which emphasized the rootedness of both language and practice in tradition; but they tended to avoid a darker, more pessimistic reading that would see "dwelling," or authentic inhabitation, as strictly impossible in the modern condition (Heynen 1993 and 1999; Vidler 1992).

One of phenomenology's important legacies was in the work of continental poststructuralists. These theorists derived from Heidegger and Maurice Merleau-Ponty (1962), among others, a critical energy that led not toward reaffirmation of the grounds of existence but to an assertion of its groundlessness. In the work of Michel Foucault (e.g., 1979), the good intentions of policy makers and intellectuals in social reform of all kinds, which lay at the root of much of SCF, were put into question. And in the work of Jacques Derrida (1967), whose critique of linguistic meaning found it to be radically contingent, writing began to be seen as an activity that could never simply communicate truth, but would participate in a never-ending whirl of sense and countersense. The writing of truth, whether in the Marxian sense of unmasking and denaturalization or in the positivist sense of relaying empirical fact, would not again seem so straightforward.

For architectural writing, then, phenomenology held two virtually incompatible possibilities: choosing the promise held out by an adequationist model of truth could allow a reassertion of ideas and values thought to have been lost under the modern worldview, or embracing the "thrownness," or groundlessness, of being could provide a potentially liberating, if disturbing, example for architectural expression.

The consequences for positivism, with its commitment to partial but powerful truth, were grave. The search for adequation had no need of empirical data, and intimations of groundlessness, like Gödel's "incompleteness" theorem or the more recent chaos theory, seemed to imply that a foothold carved out in reality could melt away in an instant or unleash a hurricane. The appeal for architects of both points of view was clear and immediate. The first allowed some to intensify their search for archetypes and authenticity, and the second allowed others to abandon themselves to a vertiginous formalism. Architects could remain central to their projects, spiraling inward or outward as they chose. But for those who adopted such attitudes, Brolin's "form-relevant social information" was either timeless and available anywhere, or else unobtainable and, in the end, irrelevant.

Spheres of Influence: The Formal and the Social

No longer is architecture a realm that has to relate to a hypothesized "society" in order to be conceived and understood; no longer does "architecture write history" in the sense of particularizing a specific social condition in a specific time or place. The need to speak of function, of social mores—of anything, that is, beyond the nature of architectural form itself—is removed. (Vidler [1976] 1996, 261–62)

The formal and the social have been used as foils for each other in architectural debates for long enough that each pole defines itself with respect to the other. We have already suggested some ways in which ideas and arguments associated with the social have permitted this to take place. Dana Cuff, who has studied what she calls this "recurrent feud" (1989, 64), finds that the words of architects speaking about themselves, their clients, and their practice argue against any "simplistic duality between architecture as an art form and as social responsibility" (1989, 100). Yet the persistent polemics surrounding the two terms, along with a tendency toward extreme claims on both sides, merit further attention.

In such seminal texts as Jane Jacobs's *The Death and Life of Great American Cities* (1961), Constance Perin's *With Man in Mind* (1970), and Robert Sommer's *Personal Space* (1969), authors had explicitly taken up the banner of *le peuple* from the point of view of social science. This argument, which grew rapidly influential throughout the 1970s, held that people, their inner functioning, and their needs were the principal, if not the only, appropriate basis for architectural form. The widespread perception that urban problems were exploding gave an urgency to the enterprise that encouraged writers to see architecture itself as a problem, but also as a potential solution. Moreover, careful analysis of large, structured institutional settings like hospitals (Lindheim 1970), where interventions could be monitored and evaluated systematically, gave credibility to the idea that changes in the physical environment in general should be planned in ways to encourage desired social results. Implicitly or explicitly, the formal domain was defined as having no autonomy with respect to the problems to be solved (cf. Rapoport 1994).

An early and influential publication offered a new understanding of architectural form: Bernard Rudofsky's exhibition catalog *Architecture without Architects,* of 1964, was widely appreciated for its argument against the art historical canon and for the variety and appropriateness of vernacular structures. It was and is often assimilated to an antiformalist (even an implicitly antiarchitect) point of view, particularly one centered around notions of appropriateness and good fit. In part because of the Orientalizing distance introduced, it was easy to suppose that these exotic examples somehow grew out of their contexts in a way that was more authentic than the glass towers of the modern movement. This point of view was soon developed further in other works that emphasized the explanation of "traditional" form by social and cultural factors (e.g., Rapoport 1969; P. Oliver 1975).

But Rudofsky's appreciation of such structures was nonetheless for their formal eloquence as variations within a repertoire of constraints—which is no doubt how the show was perceived by visitors at the Museum of Modern Art. In this, MOMA remained faithful to the avant-garde's long-standing esteem for "primitive" form making. Clearly, it was easier to tolerate a certain tension between social and formal determinism when the objects of study were far removed from the contemporary ideological context.

In terms of the period we consider here, an opening salvo on the formalist side was launched in 1972, when Arthur Drexler ([1972] 1996) prefaced MOMA's *Five Architects* publication (which established the notoriety of Peter Eisenman, John Hejduk, Charles Gwathmey, Michael Graves, and Richard Meier) with the comment that "architecture is the least likely instrument with which to accomplish the [social] revolution" (Nesbitt 1996, 26). The book celebrated a kind of revival of the Corbusian Purist style, but the text marked its distance with respect to Le Corbusier's famous dictum. While "architecture or revolution" had offered one as a way to avoid the other, Drexler dismissed a revolutionary project that might be desirable, but which he considered unrelated to architecture. The uncoupling of form and society was for him a positive objective — a liberation from constraint — but it was expressed negatively as a swipe at the naïveté of "the younger Europeans" of Team X and the like, and those Americans who might feel the same way.

In 1976 Manfredo Tafuri's *Progetto e Utopia* (1973) was published in English by MIT Press as *Architecture and Utopia*. The translation, exchanging "architecture" for *progetto*, "project," sounded a note of calculated irony at just the moment when a number of ironies were being felt in North American architectural production. Using arguments from the Marxian critique of ideology, and in particular Mannheim's *Ideology and Utopia* (1936), whose title he echoed, Tafuri identified a series of historical junctures in the development of the modernist avant-garde, by the last of which he claimed architectural ideology had become enervated, harnessed to a capitalist "politics of things," and consigned to a "utopia of form" (1976, 47–48). What architectural readers particularly retained from Tafuri's book was its distinctly pessimistic assessment of architecture's possible participation in social betterment. He saw architecture as "obliged to return to pure architecture, to form without utopia; in the best cases, to sublime uselessness" (ix). For those in the thick of the SCF project, this proposal was shocking and was taken by some in his own country as revolutionary incitement.

One outgrowth of the appearance of Tafuri's work in translation was the publication of *Architecture Criticism Ideology* (Ockman 1985), the edited proceedings of a colloquium on Marxian "critical theory" and architecture, in the mid-1980s. One of the questions hanging heavily in the air was that already answered negatively by Tafuri: Was it possible for an architect to be politically and socially active as an architect? Or must the two spheres remain separate and "pure," as Tafuri had argued? In the wake of the first large-scale realizations of a so-called postmodern movement, with inflammatory rhetoric both for and against, the volume was notable in its attempt to put things in a broader context. But as the Reagan presidency began to take shape, the lines of debate grew sharper, even while margins of maneuver in architectural practice grew narrower. Following the founding of Physicians for Social Responsibility, a similar organization was founded for architects, designers, and planners. It became more difficult to remain serenely analytical at a time when long-accepted principles of social equity were being put into question.

Thus, while some constituencies in SCF were retreating from the stronger correspondence claims of the 1970s—whether in response to the "pull" of phenomenology or the "push" of postmodernism—the mainstream of architectural writing was becoming more familiar with explicitly social and moral issues such as income redistribution, local autonomy, equality, and ecology. References to feminist or gender theory, Marxian cultural theory, postcolonial theory, and other socially attuned literatures became common if not obligatory in what had once been the relatively detached domain of architectural criticism. Writers such as Kenneth Frampton ([1983] 1996) formulated ideas of an architectural practice that could be inherently critical in its capacity to question dominant cultural values. Architectural projects such as Lars Lerup's "No-family House" (1987) or Diller and Scofidio's "Slow House" (1994a), while identifiably concerned with form in itself, also took up an explicit line of social commentary. In part as a consequence of architecture's characteristically ruthless raids on philosophy, social science, and literary theory, a "social" discourse became thoroughly intertwined with a "formal" one.

In such a context, the hard-line positions in the social versus formal debate began to lose their rhetorical impact. As recently as 1994, Amos Rapoport, one of SCF's most respected spokespersons, published a particularly blunt defense of social or behavioral determinism. Arguing that "a good design may be one the designer personally hates—his tastes are totally irrelevant" (1994, 70), Rapoport came down squarely for a correspondence model of truth, restricting the role of architects' judgment to that of drafting up research results. Although such a position had the merit of being clearly expressed, it could not propose any new elements for the discussion.

In the November 1994 issue of *Progressive Architecture,* Diane Ghirardo, a critic and educator, published a four-page critique of the architect Peter Eisenman, an article as critical of the person as of the work. It denounced Eisenman's opportunism, formalism, and lack of political engagement in strong terms, asserting that his prominence was a result of careful staging that masked a serious lack of content in the work. Eisenman responded (Eisenman et al. 1995) three months later in the same magazine, having demanded equal space and invited texts from friends and colleagues to accompany his own for a densely printed rebuttal. He asked collaborators to propose possible relations between "the formal" and "the political," thus explicitly restating the familiar opposition between artistic liberty and responsibility.

Ghirardo's article had taken a clear position on the matter, comparing Eisenman's apolitical stance with those of two architects, Giuseppe Terragni and Philip Johnson, often criticized as being complicit with fascism. A lack of engagement, according to this reasoning, was little different from an active contribution to oppression. By extension, or perhaps overextension, formalism could be seen as a cover for complicity in crimes against humanity. Such tactics naturally solicited a reference in kind from the other side, comparing the accusations against Eisenman to the charges of "formalism" brought against artists in Soviet show trials of the 1930s (Forster 1995).

Of the contributions to the Ghirardo-Eisenman exchange, the most baldly stated — and weakest — positions were those of the two principal parties. Ghirardo's ad hominem attack strained to link a presumed lack of talent with genocide. Eisenman's own short text, though usefully raising the question of architecture's penchant for moralizing, continued to promote a pure Tafurian uselessness as if twenty years had rendered the argument as incapable of nuance as its opposition.

On the other hand, most of the others entering the debate, whether in Eisenman's defense or in later letters to the magazine, were above all critical of the form-politics opposition sketched out between Ghirardo and Eisenman. One of them stated simply that "both rhetorical positions are unacceptable today" (Wigley 1995), and a number cited the need for questioning formal, social, and political conventions. If such positions are possible even within a scaffolding set up for sterile confrontation, then perhaps architecture is moving closer to a body of theory that can approximate the dialectical complexities of its determination. Rather than a dualist universe in which one factor must dominate or disappear, some contemporary architectural writers are trying to encompass a reality that is richer than that invoked by such polemics. In this respect, Bruno Latour may be correct in his explanation of modernity as a minor episode of dualism on the horizon of history, coming in between long stretches where, rather than choosing between the immanence and transcendence of polar opposites, humans are able to recognize the interdependency of things that modernity has tried to make incommensurable (1993, 132–45).

Conclusions: Dialogue, Not Determinism

Our argument in this chapter can be summarized as follows: the emergence of social and cultural factors (SCF), a relatively distinct body of writing about architecture viewed from a social-scientific perspective, met certain long-term expectations within architecture and also brought out some of that discipline's long-term conflicts or contradictions. The expectations of architects, theorists, and a wider public were that architecture could respond directly, and perhaps exclusively, to a set of conditions marked off as "social." At the same time, in the critical stage of selecting and defining objects, this new domain was limited in the kinds of truths it could expect to demonstrate. Through its acceptance of the positivist epistemological framework of the social sciences, SCF was drawn into a rhetorical position that would prove difficult to hold.

Most writers in SCF were aware from the beginning of the hybrid nature of their enterprise. They were cautious in regarding the issue of determination by or of architecture, even if their admonitions were less often directed at their own than at others' work. But perhaps because of SCF's disciplinary origins in social science, not to mention the envious view of social science toward the so-called hard sciences, they were nonetheless slow to relinquish a first, optimistic understanding of what social truths might be claimed through architecture. Some writers, indeed, have not relinquished that point of view at all. But as the questioning of the stronger claims has taken hold, in part via the influence of phenomenology, the specificity of the field has diminished, as well as its ownership of social and cultural questions.

At the same time, although we do not cover it in detail here, mainstream architectural writing has taken on a distinctly more "social" coloration. With varying degrees of success, such issues as gender, sexuality, class, and family structure have been invoked in conjunction with, rather than in opposition to, possibilities of formal and aesthetic invention in architecture. This must be seen in part as an effect of two decades of work in SCF to get architects to recognize these factors as important. Looking at recent production in architectural history and theory, for example, it would be hard to find a single work that does not refer to social, psychological, psychoanalytical, or cultural theory. Curiously enough, however, the literature cited is almost never from SCF, but directly from the discipline in question. Three recent compendiums of architectural theory, two of which have explicit pretensions to covering the last thirty years, make no reference whatsoever to SCF.[6]

Because we began with observations regarding the ruthlessness and responsibilities of architectural writing, it would be fitting to conclude with a similar theme. Although a great deal of current architectural writing deals with social concerns, very little seems honestly to assess the status of a discipline whose high hopes for its social responsibilities have been so recently and so ruthlessly dashed by a series of internal and external crises. We have tried to evoke the internal crises in the foregoing broad outline; the external ones include the virtual death of public housing in the United States, the runaway development that absorbed many architects' attention during the 1980s, and a cult of "star" architects that shows no sign of relenting. The lessened visibility of SCF is certainly due in part to these crises, as is the recent folding of *Progressive Architecture* after seventy-five years of activity.

Yet in contrast to the situation at the beginning of the 1970s, architecture's place among university-based research disciplines now seems assured. This has been the work of, among others, writers in SCF, who have patiently assembled an academic infrastructure, published, and thus helped assure a certain legitimacy for architecture where it counted. If SCF's truth-claims need revision, the same is true of traditional opposing arguments: SCF has often seemed to see its mission as that of protecting people from architecture, while self-described formalists seem to wish to protect architecture from the people. For once, architecture could come to see that neither of these is really necessary.

Notes

Our thanks to the editors and to three anonymous readers for comments on previous versions of this paper.

1. The possible reasons for this go beyond the scope of this paper, but one possibility is to look at the originary or foundational role assigned to architecture through metaphor by other disciplines, notably philosophy (Karatani 1995; Patterson 1997).

2. Rowe (1953–1954, 61) is referring to the word "composition," but the statement applies to many others as well.

3. For general background, see Larson 1977, 53–63. On architecture, see Jacques 1986, esp. 40–42; Kostof 1977b; Saint 1983.

4. Concerning architecture in the United States, Clare Cooper Marcus's *Easter Hill Village: Some Social Implications of Design* (1975) had a similar message.

5. Roger Montgomery (1989) makes the point that despite its serving widely as a figure for the failure of modern architecture (e.g., in Jencks 1977), the facts of the Pruitt-Igoe demolition are usually misconstrued.

6. Nesbitt 1996; Hays 1998; Leach 1997.

7
Unpacking the Suitcase: Travel as Process and Paradigm in Constructing Architectural Knowledge

Kay Bea Jones

Traveling makes men wiser but less happy. When men of sober age travel, they gather knowledge which they may apply usefully for their country; but they are subject ever after to recollections mixed with regret; their affections are weakened by being extended over more objects; and they learn new habits which cannot be gratified when they return home.
— **Thomas Jefferson,** *Thomas Jefferson's Travels in Europe*

Loving life is easy when you are abroad. When no one knows you and you hold your life in your hands . . . you are more master of yourself than at any other time.
— **Hannah Arendt,** *Between Friends*

I want here to consider the promises and problems of learning through direct site exposure, and to unpack our presumptions as architects, while proposing a revised role for travel in the construction of architectural knowledge. My concern is with "travel pedagogy," by which I mean experientially centered studies dependent on some cultural and geographic shift that radically alters sense perception and challenges visual and spatial cognition. Although learning from experience has pedagogical value among some studio educators, neither the bases for its theoretical grounding nor analyses of trial and error methods have been systematically pursued. Consequently architecture students benefit too little from foreign programs, and experiential means of learning are underdeveloped compared to studio fabrications and representational inventions developed in isolated school environments.

By offering alternative visions to site-based travel pedagogy, my aim is to suggest theoretical and historical grounding for imprecise, experiential inquiry. Opening the field to feminist perspectives requires reconsidering the grand tour tradition for architects and inviting self-constructed knowledge. Writings and drawings of previous sightseers, including ordinary citizens as well as privileged individuals, suggest revisions both of subjects and methods of insightful inquiry. When appropriately engaged, young architects learn to challenge and finally to trust their own eyes and voices.

Relatively recently the advent of computers in the studio has introduced another phase of the false conflict between art and technology in architectural representation. A reevaluation of architecture practices and theories in light of new tools should resituate travel as critical to cultural constructions of architectural knowledge. Ways of seeing are continually enhanced by evolving tools, and although digital media for communication in architecture may be the latest, the need for physical comprehension and reflection brought about by direct experience of urban landscapes is constant. Documentation of personally discovered holistic qualities ought to transcend the desire for the *true* image toward a more complex, if idiosyncratic, understanding.

Travel pedagogy raises concerns for *pace,* the appropriate learning time for information gathered through experience to become knowledge. While at once challenging the full immersion model of studio-based pedagogy, learning abroad depends on the same rigor, focus, critical inquiry, attention to detail, and visualization through creative output as is typical of the design studio. Yet knowing the city as a work of art composed of built artifacts also requires patience to observe fundamental relations of people to places. Hannah Arendt's sense of liberation expressed in response to her direct contact with human values and public realms provides the sublime pleasure of self-knowledge actually and essentially acquired abroad. Self-understanding is unquantifiable, as are links between social practices and cultural spaces, so these topics of learning tend to be peripheral to, if present at all in, engineering-based curricula.

Already my argument gives rise to an inherent conflict between systematic versus imprecise methods, both calling for a charted course with a clear direction and acknowledging the need for free, inventive, non-linear paths. While confronting this paradox, loosening required design studio sequences and charging the students with more responsibility for individual growth can begin to provide the necessary means for successful engagement beyond the bounds of the classroom. Interdisciplinary foundations of knowledge through contact-based methods require a renewed commitment to the time, labor, and resources necessary for a comprehensive sense of architecture's influence on the human condition. Experience-centered research models that require travel depend in part on connecting theories of vision with the development of tools for interrogation and critical site inquiry, especially writing, photography, and drawing.

Yet institutionalized study abroad remains peripheral to architectural academics. First, travel pedagogy is relatively weakly supported by academic institutions, which struggle with cumbersome bureaucracies that confuse curricular interests. Thus students receive too little intellectual and financial encouragement and have too few options for study abroad in architecture. Second, considering Italy-based architecture programs, which have grown in quantity and size during the past thirty years, too few engage the resources of foreign scholars, architects, and local institutions of higher learning. Although some schools have contracted with foreign faculty, few programs offer serious site engagement with the contemporary issues of Italian architecture and public space.[1] Too often, Rome and Florence are treated as museums for historic reliquary instead of vital communities with housing needs in addition to those signification-absorbed monuments. Finally, examination of the products of U.S. and Canadian abroad studies programs in Italy reveals the dilemma of experimental methods and uncertain theoretical foundations for architecture's junior year abroad.[2] The loose connection between field trips, historic analyses, cultural studies, and studio problems and a lack of integration with the home campus curriculum limit the reinforcement of knowledge gained abroad.

The promising evidence that North American universities have recently increased abroad initiatives, including those in non-Western European countries, contributes to the need for more reflection and critical evaluation of alternative site pedagogy. While all experimental models should be encouraged, scholars must evaluate and refine investigative experiential practices. This chapter is aimed at reinforcing and revising the role cultural identity, visual studies, and deep inquiry can play in such scholarship, although it may complicate rather than simplify the means for knowing "great" places. This calls for an integral understanding of cities and landscapes as formal, social, public, and historic montages while accepting that those places must continue to change.

Perhaps by reviewing how architects and scholars have historically gained knowledge through travel, new critical models and tools will emerge. For architects, direct site contact with "foreign" architecture has since antiquity been a source of inspiration and formal ideas from which to build and to write theories of architecture. The history of the grand tour, the rite of passage that for several centuries shaped the education of nobles, philosophers, writers, and architects, offers precedence for contemporary travel as a part of architectural education. Writing from observations made away from home has liberated learning about real places in present time from authoritative dictates and served to inspire future visions. The fertile travel sketchbooks of great modern architects such as Le Corbusier, Alvar Aalto, Gunnar Asplund, and Louis Kahn are still being mined for insights into creative genius. That their education began or was advanced by firsthand experience of buildings and landscapes not native to them must be considered as foundational for the evolution of modern architecture. The avant-garde obsession with novelty and the deletion of history was short-lived, and the view that heroic cultural pioneers were in blind denial as they broke with tradition to usher in a new society is a modern myth. Including previously unheard voices, especially those of minorities, women, and the very inhabitants whose homelands provided the sites visited and depicted by European men can revise the grand tour model. The resulting choruses may introduce unique perceptions and raise useful questions about the diversity of our visions of architecture.

Modernity has not erased the significance of history for the scholar of architecture but has instead both magnified and blurred our vision of the past. Theoretical investigations of modern vision, observers' techniques, and queries about the meaning of mechanical reproduction have challenged the authorities of Western perspectival space. Revolutionary tendencies in art practices brought about when the Bauhaus emerged out of Beaux Arts tradition seem tame when compared to the social implications of television and the urban implications of the automobile but may lead to a deeper understanding of how spatial and cultural apprehension factored the represented image into what we build. These developments merit study to help clarify how, why, and where architects travel. How various sights get seen, felt, and analyzed is tied to the broader cultural construct of Western representation. Architectural depictions from field study abroad continue to serve in the propagation of knowledge. Myriad methods for verbal and visual representation, including, but not limited to, slides in history surveys, textbook graphics, writings of theorists and historians, publications and journals, pop culture's postcards, and tourist snapshots, are all part of architectural culture, and they in turn influence how sights are envisioned. Unpacking and cross-referencing these collected images reveals how various representations communicate architectural ideas at home.

Shifting the focus from the theoretical domain of visual culture to the more quotidian, then, reveals other realities related to contemporary practice, schools of architecture, and economic structures. Most notably, architectural tourism has boomed within the last fifty years. The impact of curious visitors to houses designed by Frank Lloyd Wright in Oak Park has brought some of their owners to post the international slash calling for "no tourism." The desire for privacy among suburban dwellers is in conflict with a mobile, cultured population's longing to see an original. In 1991 *Architectural Record* reported the concerns of John Julius Norwich, chair of the World Monuments Fund and author of *The World Atlas of Architecture,* who suggested that "tourism pollution" raises so serious a threat that access to many sites should be restricted (Masello 1991, 68–69). Norwich, however, makes no suggestion or provision for revenues lost by forgone entry fees, nor does he address issues of democratic access.[3]

Tourism is the subject of much contemporary cultural criticism and interdisciplinary study — as kitsch, as leisure, as marketing, as colonial imperialism, as cultural appropriation and exploitation.[4] In many places, the sacred journey of pilgrimage has been usurped by opportunities for economic advancement. Nostalgia-driven visitors who seek an "authentic" experience while yearning for a past perfected, a revised history, provide us with images of the souvenir-stuffed handbag and the disappointed tourist. Insatiable demands for photographic evidence may force the lens to get between the sight and the sightseer, who feels obliged to gather evidence, proof of his or her being there. Curiosity and observation are overcome by the will to possess. The photographic souvenir reduces the monument to a miniature scale and flattens bodily sensations, diminishing an integrated physical response to a given place or experience.

Yet too little attention has been paid to the intellectual or spiritual quest of the contemporary traveler and the benefits of awe-inspired visions brought home. It is worthwhile in this context to consider the work of architectural educators who have effectively addressed questions about the economics and cult value of tourism. Liz Diller and Ric Scofidio have done so in their creation of two works of art, one built and one published, that reveal inclinations in Western culture's construction of sight-seeing. Their 1991 installation, entitled "SuitCase Studies: The Production of a National Past," includes a collection of depictions of American places framed by narratives, descriptions, informational vignettes, and philosophical considerations.[5] Essentially, "SuitCase Studies" demonstrates what is lost when the reproduction of representative images (the postcard) and words (site description or theoretical text) stands in for the actual experience of a place. Postcards are generic replicas of monuments in miniature, whose reversible front and back allow visitors to personalize a public place. Tourists' frequent use of automatic cameras to duplicate postcard-quality souvenirs is indicative of the desire to satisfy a prescribed expectation, shaped and verified by commercially printed images. For this installation, the architects designed a formation of fifty suspended Samsonite suitcases, each pried open with mirrors positioned to reflect both sides of a single postcard, for simultaneous viewing of the public picture and the personal note. Each piece of luggage was held in tension with a hinged apparatus ready to snap shut. The floating suitcase represented tourists' "baggage," the mute but weighty encumbrances of travel that symbolize the stereotypes and expectations we carry with us and may keep us from seeing the sights we seek. Diller and Scofidio realized the scapegoat that tourism provides in the obfuscation of architectural content. In a subsequent publication, they explain their call for an affirmative look at tourism, one that illu-

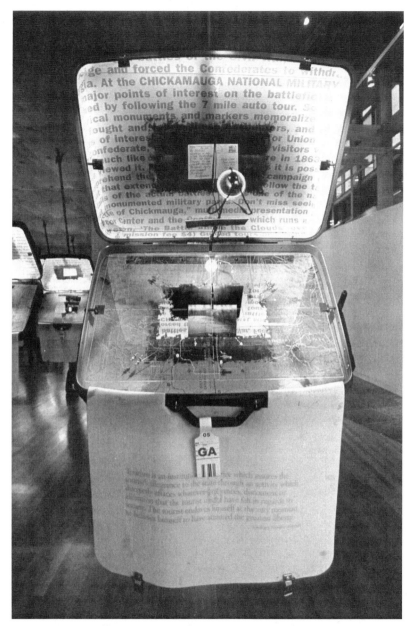

Figure 7.1. Site for *Georgia* in *Tourisms: SuitCase Studies,* an installation by Elizabeth Diller and Ricardo Scofidio. Wexner Center for the Arts, The Ohio State University, Columbus, Ohio, 8 February–22 March 1992. Photograph by Kevin Fitzsimons/Wexner Center for the Arts.

minates the "free play of space-time [and] which thwarts simple, binary distinctions between the real and the counterfeit, ultimately, exposing history as a shifting construct" (1994b, 53).

The viewer is brought to understand that sites that hold value for each culture are in flux. Travel's liberation keeps history alive, not as a fixed tally of facts and tombs, but as habitable places with variable interpretations belonging to the onlooker. Diller and Scofidio's illuminating, if somewhat disparaging, view of American tourism fed my own need to unpack the motivations, stereotypes, and obligations of architects who share a common built culture.

My Point of Departure

I do not question the inherent value of the monuments, cities, and subjects that have constituted traditional in situ scholarship and grand tour routes for generations of architects. I simply find them to be incomplete. Nor do I prescribe a revised itinerary based on a theme to essentialize the right path or identify the specific places we all must know intimately. Instead, I am interested in framing questions about how places are experienced and what knowledge results from locally focused culturally informed architectural studies. Certainly ideas found by observing new and old Rome, Paris, Cairo, Berlin, Chicago, Los Angeles, an Ohio courthouse square, or a rural village differ in content, cultural linkage, and even likely angles of view. It is not the specific sites one travels to see, however, but the restrictions in the methods of studio-based curricula that oppose fieldwork and deserve investigation.[6] Once the process of inquiry has been opened and scholars of architecture find themselves following a conceptual map on unfamiliar ground, new sites present themselves by demonstrating integral relations between appropriate civic forms and the citizens who use them.

In addition to theoretical, historical, and cultural transitions in perception, technical conditions specific to architectural pedagogy require study. Fieldwork strategies depend on at least three processes of representation, verbal descriptions, photographs, and graphic sketches, that allow the observer to establish a personal, immediate, yet unhurried relationship with places explored. Site-specific engagement reveals intrinsic meanings of architectural symbols, and those documentary studies serve in creating images, narratives, and buildings that become rooted in collective memory. Interaction with inhabitants of a place, familiarity with their history, and time to observe changing seasons and daylight facilitate discovery when engagement is active. Lessons so synthesized are better comprehended. Feminist criticism and the perceptions of women as observers have contributed to the archives of our collective memory by providing distinct, complex representations of places. Architects attempting to broaden their understanding of humankind also seek to resituate the art of their craft in the world whose authorities are the use and exchange values of production. If travel is repositioned beyond tourism and among other cultural institutions, especially cinema, theater, the novel, the essay, and the university, it may better serve to illuminate human dwelling:

> Cutting across this art of travel and theater, of history and memory, lie the contaminated intertwinings but distinct classifications of high art and popular entertainment, didactic illustrations and designed commodities, the oppositional aesthetic and the compromised, the pure or pleasural forms of architecture. These are the ways in which we frame the city, visually imagining its form and materially reconstituting its structure: by travel, in theater, at the museum, from the cinema, through its architectural compositions. (M. Boyer 1994, 70)

The act of travel is leave-taking: going sufficiently far to feel a distinct distance from home. Geographic distance matters less than psychological distance, where perceived variations are physical, often unexpected, and affect even daily activities. Consider bank lobbies or transport terminal ticket counters in cultures where people do not tend to queue up. Bus rides in Mediterranean metropolises often provide effective lessons about one's sense of personal space. Olfactory sensations differentiate public markets in Rome from supermarkets in suburban malls. Spatial tolerances, felt before they are acknowledged, identify a realm of consciousness inspired by the heightened sensitivity to everyday life experiences. Although "true voyagers are those who leave / to leave," gain or growth is best measured when the traveler returns home.[7]

Travel has long served as a metaphor for the quest for personal understanding, progress, and knowledge. In Western culture, travel is alternately perceived as a means to pleasure, excitement, entertainment, recreation and rejuvenation, an encounter with the exotic, liberation, discovery, and even conquest. To travel broadens one's horizons. But the voyage also promises danger, conflict, struggle, uncertainty. Classical journeys of Greek tragedy brought self-awareness, but not without costs. Medieval pilgrimage inspired by faith brought sacrifice and travail on the road to salvation, where the destination was more certain than the way. Movement, whether physical or intellectual, and the metaphorical voyage assume a close parallel and imply disturbance; one can lose one's way. Voltaire's *Candide,* in which each character encounters the most brutal and unnerving misfortunes, concludes that it is preferable "to cultivate our gardens" (1930, 144) than to seek fortunes away from home, but such wisdom was gained from direct encounter.

Histories of Travel: The Written Word

Grand tour narratives recorded excursions of the educated classes and the themes of the human condition they investigated. Common topics included consciousness of national identity, domesticity, deliberations about the best vehicles of transport, emotional responses to seeing new sights, personal encounters with others, satisfied or frustrated expectations, and mapping and other devices for recording and orienting the traveler's volatile course. Both Cesare De Seta, author of *L'Italia del Grande Tour: Montaigne da Goethe,* and George Van den Abbeele, in *Travel as Metaphor,* initiate their histories with Montaigne's Italian excursion, begun in 1580. Montaigne's journey offered him political insights and personal developments that appear in the second volume of *Essays,* published in 1588 (Van den Abbeele 1992, 34). One French encyclopedia used his definition for the *voyage* according to three distinct categories, the third of which addressed experiential learning: "*Voyage* (Education.) the great men of antiquity judged that there was no better school for life than that of voyages; a school where one learns about the diversity of so many lives, where one incessantly finds some new lesson in that great book of the world; and where the change of air along with the exercise is of profit to the body and to the mind."[8]

Reaping the benefits of travel is as much a commitment to the intellectual as the physical journey. Montaigne's essay "On Idleness" warns not of immobility but of agitation: "The soul that has no fixed goals loses itself; for as they say, to be everywhere is to be nowhere" (Van den

Abbeele 1992, 14). Montaigne reinterprets the agonies and dangers of travel as advantages, and rather than devote his resources to continuing the construction of the family chateau, he argues by demonstration that the voyage needs no other goal than itself and can take the form of idle wanderings.

The motif of the liberated wanderer recurs but is slowed in the fiction of Rousseau, who preferred to walk (Van den Abbeele 1992, 112).[9] In his opposition between nature and culture, travel is an activity of culture, for which Rousseau both cautions and classifies worthy travelers: "[Voyages] are suitable only to men firm enough in themselves to hear the lessons of error without letting themselves be seduced by them, and to see the example of vice without being dragged into it" (Van den Abbeele 1992, 91). Rousseau's call for only the trained philosopher to embark upon pedagogical journeys sounds curiously like Le Corbusier's warning: "The lesson of Rome is for wise men, for those who know and can appreciate, who can resist and can verify. Rome is the damnation of the half-educated. To send architectural students to Rome is to cripple them for life" (Le Corbusier [1927] 1972, 161).

I have often wondered what to make of Le Corbusier's sharp, ill-articulated advice. Was it his intention to maintain the heroic stature of scopic voyagers and colonizers among the intellectual elite? Perhaps. It also seems to imply that beauty and meaning in the quantities they can be experienced in Rome are like the sirens, so powerful as to paralyze. I choose to read into his concern a prescription for the discipline, responsibility, and will to act on direct encounters with awe-inspiring sights, rather than to be humbled into inactive silence. The travelogue of accumulated experiences from one's journey is not an end in itself but furnishes material for the cognitive voyage between idle wanderings and the recognition of discovery. Writing in situ, and rewriting from recorded experience, is a phased activity of constructing topographical views. For so many grand tour alumni, writing over a lifetime has proven the primary cognitive complement to experiential learning.

Histories of Travel: Graphic Representation

Some early monumental American architecture, often the distant cousin of European models, was imported in whole or in part as a disengaged object. Frequently trained abroad, the architect had access to published treatises, and one is provoked to ponder how much actual exposure produced the imitated objects of that monumental style. Thomas Jefferson, U.S. minister to Paris from 1785 to 1789, was a collector as much of ideas as of artifacts that embodied a sought-after spirit. By assigning democratic principles to neoclassical forms, he founded the American legacy on continental European, rather than English, ideals. He relied heavily on books of lithographic images, many of which he brought home to fill his libraries. Jefferson learned specifically from representations of timeless monuments by way of French interpretations of Roman imperial classicism. For example, he designed Virginia's state capitol building before he ever actually visited the Maison Carrée in Nimes, and he never saw Vicenza, Verona, Venice, or Rome (Shackelford 1995, 103). Because he never visited Palladio's Villa Rotunda, the location of servant space beneath the *piano-nobile* at Monticello may instead have been inspired by the basements of the hillside palazzi he saw in the city of Genoa. His creation of the University of Virginia lawn, a uniquely important evolution representing the liberty of open American thought, grew out of the large, closed *cortile* called for in his study drawings, which appear to have been derived from those he had seen at the Universities of Turin, Milan, and Pavia (Shackelford 1995, 102). Recent historic scholarship of buildings, such as those of Jefferson, privileges the experiential over the purely "academic" (that is, borrowed from publication or graphic reproduction) in attributing credit for formal motifs.

During the next century, better transportation and more leisure time brought increasing numbers of citizens to sites of spectacle. With the growing popularity of travel came greater interest in sharper pictorial images accompanying verbal records of travelers. Christine Boyer traces the history of cities by linking travel with the evolution of representational practices and theories of visual perception: "The nineteenth century displayed a passion for travel as the primary means to learn about history, while simultaneously perceiving travel narratives, history books, historical painting, and architectural ruins to be the modes of vicarious travel through time and space" (1994, 228). Boyer has reviewed the popularity of traveling from the vantage points of pleasure (or escape) and education to argue that less scientific contributions of imagination and memory, in their written forms of travel narratives, are valuable expressions of place-based knowledge. She insists that the evolution of urban form is dependent on a trajectory of visual principles and culture, in which noncodifiable artworks represent a necessary link between travel and architecture.

Boyer identifies "The City as a Work of Art," a grand vision that produced unified, if closed, spatial organization.[10] Renaissance representations of "The Ideal City" stood as reminders that good government was inseparable from public monuments and civic spaces. Today's "City of Spectacle" is perceptually bound to a runaway cycle of undirected image production and consumption. Boyer calls for a rebirth of "experiential knowledge and imaginary musings" to shift the existing preoccupation with reality and "truthful representation."[11] By employing metaphors of travel, actual travel experiences, and allied spectators' representations, good citizens are encouraged to build "The City of Collective Memory," where the shared understanding of, and access to, sites of civic and national pride bring unity to a diverse populace. Visual preoccupations of the nineteenth century inspired travelers to capture images, often in the form of manipulated versions of realist portrayals, to go along with written words in the collections of informed travelers. The earliest Prix-de-Rome fellows who left the École des Beaux-Arts in Paris to reside at the Villa Medici applied their precise watercolor skills to rendering the ancient ruins, however fanciful their reconstructions. In this way they learned the decorum and majestic scale of classical form firsthand with a good amount of fantasy and imagination.[12] Bird's-eye perspectives of urban designs before the advent of commercial flight offered citizens a "real" view they could only otherwise imagine. With the invention of the photographic print, captured views and spectacles could be transported to the stationary traveler. Privatizing the public sight is assumed to be an opportunity afforded by technological advancement, reinforcing the presupposition that science drives culture. Eventually, stereoscopy brought travel's exotic images into the Victorian parlor and relied on binocular vision to produce even more "realistic" effects.

But "modern vision" began to interfere with classical paradigms of visual representation well before chemistry introduced photographic prints. Full development of a theory of modern vision is beyond the scope of this essay, but the role of the observer in the evolution of architectural knowledge is paramount to my thesis of the traveling subject. The camera obscura model of human perception, invoked by Alberti and Kepler and known since antiquity, was cited in the science of optics to explain perception as a reproducible perspective from true vision, determinate and commensurable. The scientific investigation of the mechanics of the eye, its physical surface, internal construction, and physiological function further forced the objectification of the observer as a by-product in technology's effects on perception. Jonathan Crary has studied the psychological viewpoint of the observer to argue that dramatic transitions in sight-seeing preceded and supported the later invention of photography, the formidable device that brought conceptual complexity to visual culture.[13] When the camera obscura, conceived to present objective truth about the physical world since the Renaissance, met science and acquired the power to produce a graven image, photography began to destabilize those same visual principles that depended on a reproducible "true" image. Therein the truth sought by positivists and scientists has been suppressed in light of the knowledge contributed by unique views of poets, artists, and other human subjects.

Taken together, the studies of Crary and Boyer reveal the influence of the spectator on the evolution of visual culture and, thereby, on the creation of art and urban form. The modern traveler required suitable image-making tools to comprehend his or her observations. Means from both ends of the technological spectrum serve in unpacking observational strategies: the *photograph* and the simple *sketch* are distinct processes with dissimilar relations of time and space and are mutually interdependent tools for field observation.

Crary established that the tyranny or merit of evolving techniques for representation, however they may dematerialize images from life, is subordinate to the visions of artists as sightseers. Walter Benjamin made mechanical reproduction in the forms of photography and cinema critical for a progressive response to mass vision by raising questions about the nature of authenticity in artistic production while detaching the work of art from tradition-bound rituals. But photography has also been cited as a violent, reactionary device for the thoughtless appropriation of imagery and "value-free graphics of aesthetic detachment." That the "monuments of Europe are being worn out by Kodaks" appears to result from a quest for authenticity, a response by a culture in search of histories and ideas (Frampton 1986, 41).[14] The expanded audience for architecture created by media that trade in images has directly affected the meaning assigned to what gets built, and in turn determines what gets built. The proliferation of photographic reproduction, which has impacted architectural form, has done more to provoke formal variations and the public's expectations for them and less to clarify the content of civic buildings and spaces.

If it can be instructive to see through the eyes of those modern architects who devoted their creative lives to learning to see by relying on tools of representation while touring, it bears asking how they developed repertoires of forms in the process. Colomina and others have scrutinized Le Corbusier, whose spectatorship as a famous traveler is complex, uncanny, and suspiciously motivated. Historians have documented his tendency to fetishize his objects of interest through visual manipulation, especially those that correspond to the French colonization of Algeria. Yet in letters reflecting on his trips to Vienna, Florence, and Siena, he also describes his awareness of a photograph's inability to do justice to the real thing perceived.

In later years, Le Corbusier abandoned the camera as a "lazy instrument" and relied instead on observational assimilation through his use of the pencil. His travel sketches reveal insights into his creative imagination and process as an observer. A definitive modernist, Le Corbusier worked directly from perceptions of familiar and unfamiliar sites to satisfy his need "to look/observe/see," before he sought to "imagine/invent/create" (Le Corbusier [1927] 1972, 115). His multitude of rapid black-and-white sketches on graph-lined paper of Hadrian's Villa reveals his interest in the organizing plan.[15] By rendering formal sequences and the spaces between objects, he demonstrates his viewpoint from a position within: the interdependency of the landscape and built fragments, and the figure to the ground. His drawing from inside the Parthenon portico looking between column voids across the Acropolis to frame another temple gives scale to the distance between them. Reviewing Le Corbusier's sketchbooks reveals the sublime poetry of well-proportioned, timeless spaces defined by classical decorum and the effort he made to know architecture.

In addition to drawing during his 1907 to 1911 "Voyage d'Italie," Le Corbusier kept a diary with sketchy summaries of his experiences. He followed a course charted by mentors using a Baedeker guidebook and eventually traded his camera for binoculars. He traveled to South America in 1929 and to Algiers again in 1931, trips that mark transitions in his conceptions of architecture and town planning. As a curious spectator, obsessed voyeur, and formal master, Le Corbusier has promoted visual experience in his transformation of classical ideas into contemporary languages. We remain engaged, then, but not surprised by the graphic relationship popularized by Colin Rowe between Villa Stein at Garches, a modern icon of his "five points," and mannerist classicism of Palladio's Villa Malcontenta.[16] Most significantly, Rowe introduced a critical method for understanding modern ideas shaped by wisdom acquired from formal precedence and possibly dependent on experiential knowledge.

The twentieth century's industrial, social, and political revolutions gave rise to the need for architectural innovations of function and symbol. Futurist and constructivist utopians that insisted on a complete break with the past were condemned to erasure by the paradox of their own argument. Unlike them, pioneer modern architects who broke from the neoclassical tradition that schooled them to build new visions shared a direct experiential connection with the foundations of Western culture. The modernized classicism characteristic of the work of Gunnar Asplund originates in his sketches produced while touring Italy and the Mediterranean in 1914 (Ortelli 1991, 22–33).[17] Alvar Aalto's evolution of modern form departs more drastically from the studies of classicism, and his sketches are more expressionistic than those of Asplund. Aalto drew from vernacular structures, landscapes, and monuments with his loose, unifying linework and reductive scrutiny (Schildt 1991, 34–47).[18]

Louis Kahn traveled throughout Italy, England, France, Germany, and Estonia from 1928 to 1929 long after immigrating to America, where he studied architecture (Scully 1991, 48–63).[19] Young Kahn was prepared by Paul Cret to study urbanism and classical decorum and by Viollet-le-Duc's writings to find structuralist principles in historic buildings. Kahn's way of seeing was more informed than his own writing would indicate:

No object is ever completely separate from what surrounds it and it cannot, therefore, be represented in a convincing way as something unto itself: even our individuality can make it seem different from what it looks like to others. . . . We have to learn to see things by ourselves, so as to develop a self-expressive language. In so far as we are concerned, our ability to see derives from the continuous analysis of our reaction to the things we see and to their meaning. The more we look the more we "see." (Gravagnuolo 1987, 13)[20]

During Kahn's second sojourn in Rome while on sabbatical at the American Academy he produced brilliant pastels of Siena and Delphi, of pyramids, hypostyle halls, and Doric colonnades. From so many ruins he discovered the monumental spirit of classical objects that he transformed into modern monuments in New Haven, Exeter, Fort Worth, and Dacca. Kahn witnessed the fact that structures are more than isolated icons; they are anchored in their landscapes or cityscapes, qualified by their material compositions and technologies of construction. The silent power of deep shadows and the solid geometry of Kahn's buildings appear distinct when placed against the background of loud cars and glittery reflections of the transparent modern city.

Alternative Visions

Of course, not only the heroic men of the modern epoch drew to see and traveled to learn, although graphic depictions by women architects who assimilated site experiences abroad may be less accessible and popular than those of their male counterparts not bound to home. Perhaps the most familiar perceptions were provided by a century of photographers, including Berenice Abbott, Margaret Bourke-White, Florence Henri, and Dorothea Lange. Recent artists have provided compelling visualizations that provoke alternatives to what has been considered significant architecture. Mary-Ann Ray's publications (1997a and 1997b) of such diverse subjects as underground Roman constructions and Turkish squatter housing challenge not only the realm of relevant artifacts but also how they are represented and understood. I return now to written evidence prompted by a desire to balance the visions of experientially motivated studies of architecture with curiosity about the perceptions of women abroad.

The editors of collected women's travel writings have identified characteristics that differentiate their narratives from works of comparable men. As remarkable observers of the world they explore, empathetic women travelers become a part of the sites they describe, and demonstrate a constant desire to know the other from within. Early women settlers in this country created detailed descriptions of family and work, adding to the "bare facts" of history ("of wars, political campaigns, agricultural and industrial development" [Christ 1980, 121]) documented by men.[21] Charlotte Perkins Gillman revealed the ironic, controlling twist that appears in the publications of caution that traded on threats of danger as societies attempted to restrict the movements of women. Bonds are often formed between women travelers, especially those who meet on the road, as they confide in one another. Factors of class and race conditioned women's experiences in transit. Journeys to freedom make up the stories of African American women and men after emancipation (Collins 1991, 43). Josephine Baker finds artistic freedom in Paris. Movement as a literary theme serves wandering women protagonists to subvert the depression caused by lack of a physical home. The main character in Toni Morrison's *Tar Baby* reveals with lesser certainty the relative merits of her many migrations. Whether women depart by force or by choice, the distance from home is often essential in the self-identification that inspires a new vision, just as Montaigne discovered. Yet few women writers or architects travel with Montaigne's entourage or stature. As remarkable observers of the world they explore, many women have become a part of the places they describe and while integrating into their new homes have made cultural contributions that have yet to be fully explored.

Within the genre of travel narratives written by or for women, the "quest" theme is distinguishable. The male-motivated quest has been reduced by Joseph Campbell to a mythic voyage in search of a life-validating experience that usually results in winning a bride and earning the voyager his rite of passage to manhood. Women writers have altered the quest theme by internalizing the search for self-development, which often includes an inner spiritual aim that eventually becomes a social quest.[22] For many, this implies connecting their personal history to the history of ideas. Rewriting and re-creating the grand tour is a prerequisite to fully admitting women into the discipline of architecture, its intellectual mechanisms, and its cultural foundations.

Architectural revisionists have discussed feminist influences on the construction of knowledge.[23] Scholars have described "knowing" as a

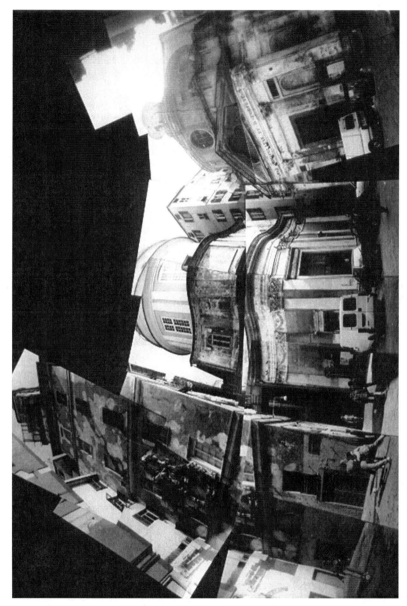

Figure 7.2. Piazza di San Giorgio e San Torpete in Genoa, Italy. Photocollage by author.

creative activity open to subjective, value-driven programs from every-day life that demonstrate female priorities in design proposals. The ways in which travel strategies, written narratives, abroad pedagogy, foreign and collective architectural influences, and women's agency can alter the construction of knowledge in architecture depend on recognizing the value of such knowledge.[24] It is apparent that the move from sub-jective knowledge, in which intuition and personal interpretations from experience provide knowledge, to the "procedural phase," in which the rational, the scientific, and the abstract dominate the composition of information, may place agency at risk (Belenky et al. 1986, 48).

Peggy Deamer has scrutinized theoretical writings and visual fixations from architectural history to identify "evocative criticism," which relies on sense perception as the object-obsessed epistemological position of formalist authorities. According to her critical model, what identifies formalism as the "reductive investigation of compositional 'facts' of the object" (Deamer 1991, 31) in the writings of Heinrich Wölfflin, John Ruskin, and Johann Wincklemann is really hallucination.[25] These men from time to time indulge their eye to invent "abstract entities from perceived configurations." She calls into question their visual descrip-tions and reveals their unconsciously subjective attempts to establish authority by monumentalizing the objects of their gaze. Her challenge to their personal perceptual priorities invites revision, not to eliminate "critical vitality" or subjectivity from judgment, but to more judiciously substantiate the "attraction to the object." One way to counter the fetishized and falsely factualized perceptions attributed to dominant masters is by seeing with one's own eyes and writing to theorize from direct experiences. Deamer's confrontation with "factual authorities" and their methods and objects of research opens the way for intuitive and subjective forms of knowledge that are conscious, well-informed, and contextualized. By observing primary sites, architects can use orig-inal insights built on past knowledge to inform critical new thinking.

I have progressively sought imaginative, willful, and revised ways of knowing drawn from field studies in Italy and other distant sites. As this is a life's work still in progress, a summary would be premature, but at this point I can ascertain that random discoveries have resulted from returning periodically to sites of inspiration. However inefficient or fatiguing, the path to knowledge sometimes involves losing one's

Figure 7.3. Piazza di San Giorgio e San Torpete in Genoa, Italy. Photocollage by author.

way. And by way of self-discovery, those subjects most difficult to diagram as an essential idea have come under the scrutiny of my lens and sketchbook. A persistent subject is monumental Rome, held in a tension established by continuous construction and sequences of urban rooms that change mostly by the quality of daylight, the growth of vertical gardens, and cycles of stripping away airborne grime. Interstitial assemblages, corridors of all dimensions and orientations, scaffolding, with varied patterns of inhabitation are integral parts of the change in scale, materials, and lighting that set up monumental perspectives. Such complex organizations and intersections defy diagrammatic reduction and snapshot framing.

Some lesser-known sites have offered discoveries in the form of idiosyncratic masterpieces interwoven with the networks and patterns that reveal the origins of complex formal ideas. Genoa's densely built industrial waterfront and surrounding hillside palazzi have provided an inexhaustible quarry of ideas both derived from Italy's history of architecture and unique to the physical conditions of too little buildable land. Overlooking the seaport high above the slate-gray capital of the medieval Genoese Republic, one understands the primacy of relationship and context in contemporary Genoa. The integration of the university campus housed in noble palaces and new buildings within the city lends itself to a study of pedestrian passageways as connective tissue. Better living was afforded in the nineteenth century when technology made it possible to build uphill affording better views, fresher air, and more privacy, so transit from housing to shops, offices, and services required vertical pedestrian paths. Public stairs and elevators within condominiums were reintroduced at a larger scale and joined by urban ramps and funiculars. This unique infrastructure renders Genoa enchanting, but impenetrable to the weary, and defines its *genius loci*. All Italian styles of architecture are present, and a few iconic structures symbolize the city, but Genoa is only understood when realizing that all building diagrams are subordinated to a topography that cannot be repressed.

Some architectural subjects require long, slow scrutiny; their mysteries are readily revealed neither to the passing glance nor to the quick sketch. I recently returned to Carlo Scarpa's Castelvecchio museum in Verona after many prior visits. One rainy day I sat to draw in the third of the five entry galleries that open to the castle keep and have fortified

Figure 7.4. Salita della Torretta in Genoa, Italy. Photograph by author.

Figure 7.5. Salita della Torretta in Genoa, Italy. Photograph by author.

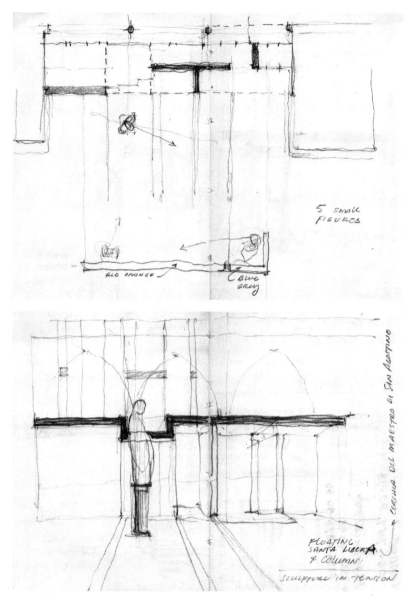

Figure 7.6. Author's sketches of the third gallery in Carlo Scarpa's Castelvecchio Museum, Verona, Italy.

windows to the Adige River. With these drawings, I was finally able to decode one of Scarpa's rooms. Each of the five galleries was designed specifically for its restrained contents of medieval artifacts, including coins, sarcophagi, bas-reliefs, tabernacles, and figurative sculpture. Newly applied surface materials, like the artifacts, are light, neutral tones of stucco, concrete, and travertine, and south daylight is carefully staged to illuminate the axial view down an arched passageway joining the sequence of rooms. The axis is reinforced by paired steel I-beams overhead, a testimony to the modern intervention within medieval walls. Each square gallery room is composed specifically for the interplay between roughly five objects. Flush with the interior southern wall, openings are glazed with nonrhythmic compositions of mullions forcing attention to the superimposition of new and old layers. Rather than frame picturesque views of distant battlements, vertical panes draw attention within the space of the wall. In the second gallery, Scarpa positioned five life-size figures in the full-size room with the back side of his favorite sculpture beckoning visitors. The third gallery lifts three half-scale figures to eye level in a triangular configuration, while two bas-reliefs are hung on opposite walls. The reduced scale of these figures required Scarpa to diminish the scale of the room by positioning an L-shaped screen wall to the river side and thickening the barrier to the courtyard. The L wall is colored with red-orange and blue-gray stucco veneziano and holds two of the three figures.[26] The only floating sculpture, Santa Libera, identified with St. Augustine, focuses the tension of the room and aligns with one of two exterior gothic columns. A folding horizontal plane in the south window wall brings down the scale of the gallery and makes an uninhabitable zone within it. Beneath the thick, black plane is a four-part window composition of alternating solids and voids that are parallel to, but misalign with, a gothic column triptych. Every formal move in the third room can be explained, but not in relation to a single force or form. Each line leads the eye to several related surfaces or nodes, and the whole pays tribute to the art he honors. This square nucleus is a tour de force of control within Scarpa's rambling museum rehab.[27]

I put forth this process of identification, interpretation, representation, and production to constitute "constructed knowledge" in architecture. It can best be accessed by "knowers self-consciously implicated in procedures and sensitive to contexts, careful neither to decontextualize subjects of study nor to disengage from them for the sake of straight-forward inquiries or conclusive results" (Hartman 1991, 21–22). I would expand this access to knowledge associated with women's work to those inquirers willing and able to traverse paths at the disciplinary margins well beyond architecture's definitive core where one may freely wander.

If we accept that constructed knowledge offers an important alternative approach that is uniquely characterized by intuition, cross-disciplinary preferences, collaboration, ambiguity, integration, personal and social values, and historic contingencies, we can then consider observation of everyday life within the agency of travel. Traditional pedagogical practices deserve reconsideration, since travel radically alters the condition of the classroom, the laboratory, and the studio. With physical dislocation comes the potential for change in the nature of examination, interrogation, lecture, representation, and general critique. Teaching methods abroad can substitute techniques of observation and group discussion for typical "objective" examinations of learning. Collaborative inquiry strategically located allows subjects to reveal diverse aspects of themselves. Participants who are then equipped to debate differing interpretations provide a model preferable to the usual subordination to definitive authorities or studio masters.

Graphic, photographic, and journal notes are often sketchy, imprecise, yet spontaneous ways to represent primary sources that aid in discovering their content. The traditional lecture hall or classroom is designed to eliminate distraction, but inside a baroque church in Rome, distraction is beyond control and instead discloses how inhabited architecture works. Buildings, even ruins, are revealed not as ideal, unpopulated, reproduced views but as vital places in their actual condition and usage. Ideas follow discovery, a student-initiated learning process that is active rather than passive.

Walter Benjamin recognized that among all the arts, architecture alone can present a simultaneous collective experience. He challenged notions of authenticity and aura in the valuation of works of art, especially photography and cinema, and as mechanical reproduction was coming of age, he affirmed the representation of those experiences "consummated by a collectivity in a state of distraction" (Benjamin 1968, 239). Above all, he noted the primacy of experience by stating: "Buildings are appropriated in a two-fold manner: by use and by perception — or rather, by touch and by sight. . . . For the tasks which face the human apparatus of perception at the turning points of history cannot be solved by optical means, that is, by contemplation, alone. They are mastered gradually by habit, under the guidance of tactile appropriation" (Benjamin 1968, 240). Photography's role in translating the relationship between the observer and the perceived subject to exchange cult value for exhibition value is evidence that tradition is alive and malleable. In this interpretation, photography has not killed experiences of authentic places, but, like drawing, it is a trace, a tool for interpretation and representation of the content of those built subjects whose roles as shelter and symbol are constant to the physical and spiritual realms of the human condition. Atget's Paris is a complex portrait of an empty, quiet, worn environs with "streets like scenes of a crime" that substantially imprinted Kertez's Paris and Berenice Abbott's way of seeing.[28] Photography and allied means of representation hold unrealized promise for acquiring and interpreting architectural knowledge.

Architects who visit ancient sites will continually discover and define new meanings if the processes of seeing are intentional, insightful, and creative. Hannah Arendt has dealt with the paradox of three coincident conditions of the *vita activa* — *labor, work,* and *action,* recognizing the centrality of labor to the human condition. Yet she cautions against the inordinate value placed on the exchange value cycle of production and consumption in contemporary secular society for elevating the work ethic while diminishing the meaning of the work. During her travels, Arendt discovered and revived the balance afforded by the *vita contemplativa,* where value is replaced in part on observation, liberation, and willful participation in the creative act. In conclusion, if it is true that architecture is fundamentally the result of a profound, creative act, inspirational knowledge sought by architects is of critical value. Broader access to well-paced travel among architectural scholars must be part of that creative process. Observers' insights informed by representational tools of understanding will reground experiential learning within the construction of knowledge in architecture.

Notes

1. For further discussion, see Roberto Einaudi's "American Architectural Schools in Italy" (1987, 141–45).

2. The 1999 ACSA (Association of Collegiate Schools of Architecture) International Meeting held in Rome considered the theme "La Citta' Nuova" (The New City). For the conference, fourteen schools of architecture from North America exhibited current student work produced in their respective Italian abroad studies programs, curated by Davide Vitali. The resulting catalog, subtitled "Looking for the New City/Cercando la Citta' Nuova," was sponsored by AACUPI (Association of American College and University Programs in Italy). Experimentalism is evident as work ranges from Beaux Arts watercolor renderings, to figure and ground urban analysis graphics, to cutting-edge delineations as proposals for historic sites.

3. Herbert Muschamp presented the fund's newest venture, called World Monuments Watch, which is sponsored by American Express and reports on the world's 100 most endangered historic sites. Muschamp recognized the irony of support provided by the same company whose success is rooted in promoting worldwide travel, and he considered the global common bond of preserving cultural "riches" as a new chapter in the history of modern encounters with culturally loaded, if generically chosen, sites. He stated that we are all driven to see everything everywhere, and economic exchange determines use value with little regard for the future (*New York Times,* 31 March 1996).

4. For an excellent discussion of tourism, see Dean MacCannell, *Empty Meeting Grounds: The Tourist Papers* (1992).

5. The original exhibition, called *Tourisms: SuitCase Studies,* opened at the Walker Art Center in 1991 and was exhibited at the List Visual Art Center at MIT and the Wexner Center for the [Visual] Arts at the Ohio State University. *Visite aux armées: Tourismes de guerre* (Diller and Scofidio, 1994b), a collection of essays, was published in French and English for the fiftieth-year anniversary celebrations of the Normandy invasion.

6. Just as methodologies for travel as pedagogy have remained poorly explored, so the selections of sites that hold cultural value have remained limited. Opening the map to barrios, ghettos, villages, and landscapes where postcards are not sold remains an opportunity for design studies. It is currently too easy to destroy the fabric of economically depressed neighborhoods that have not been part of architects' academic exposure or knowledge base. Some studies and appropriate interventions within culturally diverse neighborhoods in the United States are taking place and should enter mainstream scholarship including rural, industrial, and nonphotogenic, landscapes.

7. Charles Baudelaire's adage dangles from the Wisconsin SuitCase in Diller and Scofidio's *SuitCase Studies,* an installation about tourism, and is cited in *Visite aux armées: Tourismes de guerre* (Diller and Scofidio, 1994b, 74).

8. The first two definition categories are Grammar and Commerce. See *Travel as Metaphor* (Van den Abbeele 1992, vii).

9. See "Pedestrian Rousseau" for Rousseau's further justification of his preference for foot travel in northern Italy: "I can conceive of only one means of traveling that is more agreeable than going on horseback, and that is to go on foot. You leave when you want, stop at will, do as much or as little exercise as you want. You see the whole country." Van den Abbeele (1992, 112) establishes relationships between Rousseau's ways of thinking and ways of traveling.

10. Boyer's full development of "The City as a Work of Art" (1994) can be found on pages 33–40.

11. Boyer (1994) cites Baudelaire, who criticized nineteenth-century instrumentalization of perception, on page 22.

12. The French academicians memorialized their own sojourn in the midst of the eternal, if worn, cultural riches of antiquity by having their own portraits painted in the studios of Roman painters. Their ennobling portraits usually included a fictitious arrangement of images of the Coliseum, the Forum, and Piranesi's fantasies, or other selected antiquities, in the background. In this way, they redesigned Rome.

13. For a full development of the history of modern vision as it prioritizes the observer's impact on the culture of science, see Crary's *Techniques of the Observer* (1990).

14. Frampton cites the observation of Abraham Moles (1968) in "The Three Cities."

15. Gresleri (1991, 6–21) publishes thirty-three sketches of Hadrian's Villa, which includes Le Corbusier's own margin notes.

16. See Colin Rowe, "The Mathematics of the Ideal Villa," from 1947, reprinted in Rowe 1976.

17. Asplund's sketches of travels in Italy and Tunisia (twenty-four, reprinted in Ortelli 1991) include heavily noted plan and section diagrams, vistas, material studies in wash, ornamental detail, inhabited streets, and his first attributed sketch in Italy of the eating of "spagetti." The author includes Asplund's travel itinerary.

18. Aalto's forty-eight sketches reproduced include Spanish windmills, landscape and vegetation compositions, and Moroccan fortification walls. Greek monuments are shown in relationship to their sites. A study of a Sicilian stone wall is reminiscent of his later Villa Mairea (Schildt 1991, 34–47).

19. Quality of light and color renditions depicting landscapes in the Mediterranean sun characterize the twenty-eight reproductions of Kahn's sketchbooks in Scully's "Marvelous Fountainheads: Louis I. Kahn: Travel Drawings" (1991, 48–63).

20. Kahn articulated his message in a talk entitled "Value and Aim in Sketching," published in *T-Square Club Journal,* May 1931, cited in "Louis Kahn and Italy" by Benedetto Gravagnuolo in *Metamorphosi* (1987, 13).

21. For additional reading in women's travel narratives, see *Women and the Journey: The Female Travel Experience* (Frederick and McLeod 1993); *With Women's Eyes: Visitors to the New World, 1775–1918* (Tinling 1993); *The House on Via Gombito* (Sprengnether and Truesdale 1991); and *Maiden Voyages: Writings of Women Travelers* (Morris 1993).

22. Carol P. Christ (1980) has identified this work as an important alternative to binary thinking and dualistic notions that have perpetuated in Western thinking. She interprets patterns of the female quest that include a pursuit of "wholeness," a "dark night of the soul," an awakening of new insight, and a new naming of female reality.

23. See Karen A. Franck, who concludes with a statement about her Western, capitalist frame of the subject matter and calls to "overcome opposing dualities" by "discovering both our similarities and differences with women elsewhere in the world" (Berkeley and McQuaid 1989, 201–12).

24. In "Agency" Joan E. Hartman (1991, 48) writes, "we insist on the agency of knowers in order to emphasize our active roles in making and remaking knowledge. We inscribe neither agent-centered explanations that discount social systems in order to endow agents with limitless power, nor to system-centered explanations that neutralize agency as a discursive or institutional effect."

25. Excerpt from Wincklemann's analysis of Greek statuary used in Deamer's demonstration: "Modern works display too many sensuous dimples, while the ancient statuary dimples are used with subtlety and wisdom, reflecting the physical perfection of the Greeks. Often only the trained eye can discover them" (Deamer 1991, 26).

26. Scarpa disguises dual restrooms behind the screen by bifurcating the tapering fortress window.

27. For further documentation and graphics of Carlo Scarpa's Castelvecchio Museum see *Carlo Scarpa: The Complete Works* (Scarpa 1984, 159–63) and *Quaderns,* vol. 158 (1983), pp. 25–51.

28. Benjamin (1968, 226) credits Atget's photographs of deserted Paris streets with subliminal political significance.

8
Environment and Architecture

Donald Watson

When the term "environment" is used in architecture, it refers generally to the surrounding landscape and context of buildings. In both legal and professional architectural practice, "environment" may refer narrowly to health concerns, such as indoor air quality, or broadly to the ecological impacts that building may have on regional air and water quality and ultimately on global climate. Some of these impacts can be measured in terms of human health, energy consumption, and pollution, as well as other environmental indices, including biodiversity of local species and global warming. For the profession of architecture to respond to these issues of environment requires knowledge of building science, human health and biology, and ecology and related environmental sciences.

For many, these issues are outside of the purview of architecture. As architecture is defined in public law as a profession, however, an architect is responsible for the design and specifications of buildings that affect the health, safety, and welfare of building occupants and the public. Additionally, building, planning, and zoning regulations at local and metropolitan levels define the scope of architectural practice to include all impacts of a building design that involve land development and density, and its utility, transportation, and water and sewerage infrastructure. Each and all of these aspects of architecture and planning have environmental consequences.

Environmental concerns in architecture have emerged out of increasing awareness of human and ecological health conditions that result from the way we design and build upon the land. This may be at a small and widely dispersed scale, but with cumulative impact, such as suburban development, or at a large building and urban scale, such as cities and towns. Increasingly, we understand that architectural and planning practices have ecological and climatic consequences that significantly degrade the environment. Such impacts include increased air pollution, depletion and despoliation of local water sources, disruption and permanent loss of the natural landscape, and significant waste of materials during construction and at the end of a too short life cycle of poorly constructed buildings.

Discussion of the environmental consequences of architecture is often set aside and thus marginalized by architectural practitioners and educators. Environmental issues are too frequently seen as "merely" pragmatic or technical issues left for other specialists to worry about. When this is done, the profession misses a great opportunity, if not a responsibility, for renewal of its knowledge base and for reflection on the ethical consequences and values of architectural education and practice, specifically:

- to gain knowledge through research and practice of how architecture and its environmental impacts can be improved significantly by design,

- to respond with architectural design that is inspired by, and thus profoundly responsive to, its ecological role and context,

- to develop paradigms of responsible professional practice, through design of buildings and planning of urban developments, that significantly improve the quality of the environment.

When brought into the worldwide discussion of sustainability — a broadly defined term that challenges us to think and act in terms of long-term and global consequences — architecture has a sharply defined task to respond to environmental concerns. This chapter offers an overview of the issues of environment and the emergent idea of "sustainability," a term that has come to represent a complex of issues around a single basic question: *How do we live upon the planet as responsible citizens in ways that add to, rather than diminish and destroy, the Earth's resources?*

Any proposal for a "discipline of architecture" as the foundation of education and practice must respond to this insistent question.

Issues of human health and of climate-responsive design have been part of architectural discourse since at least the early twentieth century (Conrads 1970). Solar orientation and sun shading informed the work of modernist architects, including Gropius, Breuer, Neutra, Le Corbusier, and Aalto, to mention only a few. In the 1950s, climate, ventilation, and daylighting were inaugural topics at the first established research units at schools of architecture, notably Texas A&M Building Research Station, founded by William Caudill, and University of Michigan Architectural Research Laboratory, founded by Theodore Larson. Beginning in the 1970s, design tools for climate-based energy modeling and simulations, many developed in schools of architecture, became commonly available. In the present decade, issues of human health and the chemical and environmental impacts of building materials are topics of investigation and publications. If one were to sum up this increasingly enlarged scope of "environmental" topics in architecture, it would include:

- *Bioclimate design.* Design of buildings based on local climate, to use microclimate for passive heating, cooling, and daylighting. Often this is highlighted by use of traditional architectural elements.

- *Energy-efficient technologies.* Design of buildings to minimize energy-intensive heating, cooling, and lighting. This is accomplished not only by architectural design but also by the design of mechanical heating, cooling, and lighting systems.

- *Indoor air quality.* Design of buildings to reduce and remove indoor pollution and to create high levels of indoor air quality. This is a function of both natural ventilation and also the mechanical heating and cooling system design.

- *Pollution mitigation.* Planning and design to reduce environmental impacts on the local site, including reduction of air and water pollution. The building and its site and landscape design play a role in how rainfall and groundwater can be cleaned by natural filtration and restored to its aquifer. This also includes attention to reducing construction debris waste, and therefore use of "high recycled content" building materials.

- *Ecological landscape design.* Restoring local sites and landscapes to natural states to strengthen the environmentally healthy role of trees, vegetation, and watercourses. This is often measured by the increase of diversity of plant, bird, and mammal species in the local ecology.

Each of these topics is relatively well defined, with a substantial body of research and publications that constitute a knowledge base for designing energy-efficient and environmentally responsive architecture. Applying lessons from this knowledge base, it is possible to demonstrate reductions in the energy use from one-half to one-tenth of conventional energy consumption in buildings. Reduced environmental impacts follow, since there is direct correlation between energy consumption and air and water pollution (fossil fuel combustion being a major source of carbon dioxide and other noxious gas emissions, and nuclear energy being a common source of thermal pollution of waterways). Further, productivity improvements in buildings can be correlated to improvements in indoor air quality and user controls and choices over indoor comfort and temperature conditions (Loftness and Hartkopf 1997).

This experience and an increasing public concern about environmental issues offer a basis in knowledge and values for defining the discipline of architecture:

1. To strengthen the knowledge base of architecture by recognizing the contribution to the body of knowledge represented by energy and environmental research and practice.

2. To assert the value base of architecture by responding to the ethical and societal critique that the design of buildings should improve the quality of the environment for people and the local ecology in which a building is situated.

3. To vitalize the role of research in architecture so that new and evolving lessons are rapidly adopted in education and in practice.

In this view, research, education, and practice are interrelated endeavors, undertaken out of our professional and ethical responsibility to create buildings and places that renew and sustain the world's cultural inheritance and environmental resources. Research enables the architectural and environmental design professions to build on prior experience through critical evaluation, innovation, and the creation of new knowledge (Watson 1999). A continuously renewed knowledge base is essential to support the ethical and value base of architecture as a discipline, and to develop the expertise and creativity called for to improve the quality of life through the design of inspiring buildings and sustainable communities and environments.

Sustainability: The Roots of a Design Paradigm

As with any paradigmatic idea, the concept of sustainability evolved out of an extended discussion that dates from the 1970s and has precedents paralleling the conservation movement throughout the twentieth century. The term "sustainability" emerged from international agricultural and economic practices. The definition was enlarged to represent an agenda that advocates for comprehensive policies for economic, social, and environmental development. It was essentially an attempt at a "global view," for example, that destruction of rain forests in one part of the world is impelled by industrial (including building) practices in another part.

At the 1992 Earth Summit in Rio de Janeiro, sustainability was defined as "developments that meet the needs of the present without compromising the ability of future generations to meet their own needs" (Munro and Holdgate 1991, 10). The term has been adopted by architects, landscape architects, and urban planners, evident in the AIA/UIA World Congress of Architects June 1993, which declared a professional commitment to principles of sustainability. The concept of sustainability has appeared in urban and regional planning proposals such as the Seattle Comprehensive Plan, where it is defined as a three-legged stool, combining economic opportunity, social equity, and environmental responsibility.

World population growth is the impetus behind dramatic global economic, cultural, and environmental changes but is only one of several factors changing our world and our worldview, which include demographics, environmental resources, technology, and culture. This combination of issues — seen as a global nexus of principles and practices — makes the discussion about "sustainability" new in the evolving history of ideas. At least five issues are joined in the discussion, each with a separate set of antecedents and trajectory:

1. population growth

2. global demographics and politics

3. environments at risk, including disruption of biospheric climatic patterns

4. technology as problem and as solution

5. ideology of human thought and culture

Although architectural and building practices play a part in the technology of production and use of resources, the greatest impact of population growth and changing demographics is in large-scale urban infrastructure, now evident in the problems of megacities throughout the globe. This reinforces the importance of urban design, history, preservation, and planning.

The notion of "sustainability" originates from ecology. Aldo Leopold (1970, 253) helped define the ecological approach to land and landscape, describing the "biotic pyramid . . . [as] not merely soil; it is a fountain of energy flowing through a circuit of soil, plants and animals . . . it is a sustained circuit, like a slowly augmented revolving fund of life." Here Leopold uses the term "sustained" in the sense best given to the word, to emphasize the notion of life regenerative processes in our view of nature and our world. E. F. Schumacher (1973) attempted to bridge economics, technology, natural resources, and (mostly) developing world cultures through the concept of intermediate and appropriate technology. His thinking was seminal, although from his critics' standpoint, utopian. Wes Jackson (1984) is an inheritor of Leopold's land ethic and Schumacher's approach to small-scale economics and technology. These reformers address the conflicting effects of human intervention on the natural environment, attempting to sort out a balance between ecological understanding and the conventional practices and large-scale impacts of industrialized growth and technology.

The term "sustainability" has an evolving "official" definition, first evident when global resource issues gained the attention of progressive world leaders, significant among them Gro Harlem Brundtland, prime minister of Norway. The 1987 Report of the U.N. World Commission on Environment and Development Conference resulted in the Brundtland Commission Report (Lebel and Kane 1989) and developed the definition of "sustainability" later adopted for the 1993 Rio Earth Summit. The effort to apply sustainability to architecture and planning was represented in the United Nations Conference on Human Settlements (II) held in Istanbul in 1996. Its intent and declaration were to stop the deterioration of human settlement conditions and ultimately to improve the living environments of all on a sustainable basis, and to promulgate policies and practices for sustainable human settlements in an urbanizing world and adequate shelter for all.

Whether in the arguments of proponents or critics (see, for example, Rubin 1994 for a critique of mainstream environmentalism), discussions of sustainability seek to combine a global perspective on population, demographics, environmental risk, technology, and ideas about culture.

Population Growth

A number of authors have addressed the population issue, notably Paul R. Ehrlich and Anne H. Ehrlich, who state that "human numbers are on a collision course with massive famines. . . . if humanity fails to act, nature may end the population explosion for us — in very unpleasant ways — well before 10 billion is reached" (1990, 16–17). Meadows, Meadows, and Randers, the authors of the Club of Rome analysis a decade earlier, restate their concern that "unless there are significant reductions in material energy flows, the world faces an uncontrolled decline in per capita food output, energy use, and industrial production" (1992, iii).

The complex intersection of population and environmental factors is offered in reports of the World Resources Institute. Among the critical trends cited are the increasing number of megacities growing apace without any planning or environmental quality mechanisms, increasing rate of tropical deforestation, increasing rate of global toxic emissions in which industrialized countries account for more than half of greenhouse gas emissions worldwide, declining and depleted world fisheries, declining per capita food production, and the widening gap between rich and poor.

Such reports and trends challenge our ability to comprehend, much less to respond with any effective individual action. They seem to be "beyond our imagination," more easily ignored than understood. A balanced overview of our capacity to respond to the exigencies of global population and demographics, and world hunger as a function of environmental and economic development conditions, is attempted by John Bongaarts (1994).

Environments at Risk

Documented by the Worldwatch Institute series State of the World, there is ample evidence of disastrous environmental deterioration worldwide. The combined effects of population growth and resource demand are approaching — in the view of some, are exceeding — the limits of the Earth's capacity to produce food, of oceans to supply fish, of rangelands to support livestock, and, in many countries, of the hydrological cycle to replenish water. A recent State of the World Report (L. Brown 1994) documents the magnitude of per capita declines in fish catches, grain production, viable cropland, and rangelands and a net decrease in forests.

The risks imposed on all living species as a result of human use and misuse of natural resources is argued as an unprecedented threat to biodiversity by E. O. Wilson in *The Diversity of Life*. He restates this case in a 1993 article, "Is Humanity Suicidal? We're Flirting with Extinction of Our Species":

> Humanity is now destroying most of the habitats where evolution can occur.... Even if biologists pulled off the equivalent of the Manhattan Project, sorting and preserving cultures of all the species, they could not then put the community back together again. (1992, 28)

Global Demographics and Politics

Population, environmental degradation, and the resulting impact on demographics are aggravated by uprooted populations fleeing civil strife and environmental devastation.

A prospectus of the political dimension of global population growth and demographics is presented by Paul Kennedy in *Preparing for the Twenty-First Century* (1993), in which he describes the increasing disparity and geopolitical imbalances as a function of environmental resources throughout the world. Kennedy's thesis has gained wide attention, but not universal acceptance, one critique being that he does not account for the capacity of technological innovation to overcome impoverishment. Throughout discussions of sustainability, technology is variously seen as part of the problem or part of the solution. In a recent address at the United Nations, Paul Kennedy responded by noting, essentially, that the technolgy revolution is taking place in one part of the globe while the population explosion is occurring in another. He also noted that some of our new technologies, especially biotechnology, instead of helping the global problem, actually make it worse.

Technology as Problem and as Solution

Discussions of "technology" ultimately direct themselves to business practices and the economy, wherein technological innovation is either advanced or aggrandized by market demand and opportunity. As a result, any "reform of technology" has to be accomplished by reforming conventional economic and business practices. Among the advocates of intelligent use of technology is Amory Lovins, whose book *Soft Energy Paths* (1977) argues that true energy and environmental costs have to be included in market costs and that it is less costly to save energy than to produce it. Lovins's argument is the basis of eco-technology, the approach that design, technology, and science applied creatively can leapfrog current practices with innovations that dramatically reduce energy and environmental costs while improving economic productivity.

Few authors take on as radical a platform for reform of commerce, industry, and "business as usual" as Paul Hawken:

> Living in a civilization that is profoundly and violently at odds with the natural world will not end overnight. But if there is to be an economy of meaning and purpose, it must have two agendas. It must serve and nurture the aspirations of the poor and uneducated, and it must also, as its underlying goal, seek to reconstruct, know, or revive genotypes, species, ecosystems, forests, vernal pools, allelomorphs, subspecies, grasslands, seral stages, reserves, natives, gradients, corridors, and habitat blocks. . . . "Going forward" will someday mean replacing what has been lost, as well as returning what should not have been taken, not only in our forests and grasslands, but in our inner cities and rural backwaters as well. (1993, 214)

Human Thought and Culture

Issues of population, demographics, environment, and technology are ultimately combined in cultural ideas, how we think about ourselves, other peoples, other living species and places. The discussion of sustainability ultimately asks that we reframe and enlarge our sense of responsibility as individuals and as institutions. David W. Orr provides a comprehensive view and advocacy of the role of education. Orr states his premise to rebuild the educational mission to prepare for lifelong and real-world learning: "The shortcomings of education reflect a deeper problem having to do with the way we define knowledge. . . . it is time to ask what we need to know to live humanely, peacefully, and responsibly on the earth and to set [education and] research priorities accordingly" (1993, xi).

The strands of these discussions, however woven, combine in the concept of stewardship as humanity's role and responsibility for sustenance of all living species and systems. In attempting to understand our role individually and collectively in the agenda of stewardship and sustainability, we contend with the limits of our own intelligence and our inability to understand the complexity of life.

We also contend with the limits of our ability to predict the future and the problem of unknowability. Hereafter are citations that illustrate three responses: (1) the techniques of futurism, (2) the inquiry and insights of the social sciences, and (3) the method of critical inquiry and "healthy skepticism."

The futurists. One answer to the "problem of unknowability" is suggested by Peter Schwartz (1991), who argues that in the face of uncertainty, we should sketch out various options, or "scenarios," to gain the advantage of visualizing the range of options—to the extent that human creativity and imagination can project them—making it easier to work toward the perceived improvement. The obvious critiques are that our imaginations may still be insufficient to the task and that the same method can be manipulated to achieve ill-begotten gains as well as noble objectives.

The anthropological perspective. The view of environmentalism as essentially a cultural idea informs the writings of Mary Douglas, professor emeritus at the University of London. Her book *Purity and Danger* (1966) describes how societies, whether tribal or modern, define boundaries that indicate what is "pure" and thus sanctioned, as distinct from dangers including manifest physical threats but also perceived "pollutants." These boundaries — physical, institutional, and ritualistic — create the moral power that defines cultural frameworks. In her article "Environments at Risk," Douglas builds on this idea, describing how contemporary ideas of environment are part of our own cultural reformation:

> Let us compare the ecology movement with others of historical times. An example that springs to mind is the movement for the abolition of slavery of a century ago. The abolitionists succeeded in revolutionizing the image of man. In the same way, the ecology movement will succeed in changing the idea of nature. It will succeed in raising a tide of opinion that will put abuses of the environment under close surveillance. Strong sanctions against particular pollutions will come into force. It will succeed in these necessary changes for the same reasons as the slavery abolition movement, partly by sheer dedication and mostly because the time is ripe. (1970, 1273)

Critical inquiry: what we do when we do not know. Absent a unifying ideology, one looks to methods of discourse and conflict resolution to create consensus. Because our intelligence and imagination are constrained and fallible, one must ask, "What do we do when we do not know?" We cannot predict the future. Moreover, we have great difficulty in reaching consensus within local, regional, and national entities, let alone in developing an international agenda that must be supported by diverse economies and cultures. It becomes a matter of societal or public learning in action: we have to evolve guiding principles and actions — value confirming and way finding — simultaneously.

An approach is provided by the "healthy skepticism" of Thomas Gilovich (1991), who advocates for rational inquiry and the scientific method. One could extend the process of rational debate necessary to ethical judgments advocated in the "discourse ethics" of Jürgen Habermas (1990) and the process of "design as inquiry," in which design alternatives are used as a means of exploring a question, advocated by Donald A. Schön (1983). The combination of rigorous but exploratory questioning and research as part of the design process is suggested in the term "critical practices" applied to architectural education and practice (Watson 1994).

The Impacts on Architecture of the Concepts of Sustainability

Many of these constituent ideas have been impelled by the combined events of population demographics and global industrial practices— including building and urban design—the resulting devastation of resources and diminution and threat to the health and quality of the environment. The role of architecture and environmental design is integral to both the problem of global overdevelopment and its reconstitution through sustainable design. The concept of sustainability as representing environmental concerns is thus central to the agenda of thought and action that might constitute a discipline of architecture.

A number of responses—summarized hereafter as eight ideas that emerge from the concept of sustainability—shape an educational and professional curriculum for sustainable design as it might be advanced in architecture, environmental design, and planning.

Life Cycle and "Cradle-to-Cradle" Materials Reclamation

The "life cycle" or "cradle-to-cradle" concept envisions all materials production as a continuous and sustainable process of use and reuse, essentially the recycling of all materials design and production. Paul Hawken (1993) describes European regulatory standards in Germany and the Netherlands that mandate recycling in manufacturing. The application of life cycle thinking and materials reclamation to building suggests an emphasis on longevity, continuous preservation and renewal of building assets, adaptable systems and replaceable subcomponents, demountability, and reclaimed construction products and systems.

Environmentally Responsible Design and Eco-technology

Energy-efficient and environmentally responsible design has continuously evolved in architecture, evident in the 1930s interest in solar design by early modernists such as the Kech brothers, but also F. L. Wright, Breuer, and Le Corbusier; the 1950s development of bioclimatic design by the Olgyay brothers; the 1970s research into energy-efficient heating, cooling, and daylighting of buildings; and the 1980s and 1990s concerns for human health, air quality, and environmental impact of buildings on the natural landscape. These concerns suggest an enlargement of the role and responsibility of the architect beyond what is conventionally defined as project and client specific to one that addresses the interconnected health of humans and environment in which the building is conceived of as part of an ecological web of nature.

Demand-Side Management of Energy and Resources

Amory Lovins (1977) proposed the approach to energy efficiency via reduced energy demand. He defined the term "negawatt" to represent the quantity of energy saved by reducing demand, in order to dramatize that it is far less expensive and more effective to conserve energy by reducing demand than it is to increase the capacity to produce energy by constructing power plants and energy supply infrastructure. Lovins's seminal work led to the concept of "demand-side management." This approach demonstrates industry-initiated programs (albeit through public regulatory pressure) on a regional and sectorwide basis, a model for similar approaches that can be extended to water, land conservation, and materials recycling.

Sustainable Community Design

Sustainable community design combines architecture, landscape design, and planning, in which towns and communities are conceived of in terms of environmental flows and resources. Design exemplars are described in the publications of Sim Van der Ryn and Peter Calthorpe (1986) and Doug Kelbaugh (1989). In addition to holistic design approaches, community involvement is seen as essential, for which the design charrette and community design clinics provide models, as is emphasis on economic, social, and community involvement and empowerment (Watson 1996).

Metro-regional Planning and Bioregional Design

As an extension beyond the community scale, sustainability design issues can best be addressed by including transportation, land use, and metropolitan-scale environmental impacts of air and water, properly conceived as bioregional planning. This view is not beyond the architectural tradition, evidenced by the contributions to transit-oriented development approaches by Peter Calthorpe and to the town planning by Andreas Duany and Elizabeth Plater-Zyberk. Alongside these, one would cite the ecological planning methodologies pioneered by Ian McHarg (1992) and John Lyle (1994). Water conservation and waste nutrient recovery are also best conceived as regional strategies. Recharging of local aquifer through absorbtive landscaping is a traditional but necessary alternative to conventionally engineered storm water drainage, the neglect for which is evident in floods in overdeveloped sensitive watersheds. Sewer treatment that restores nutrients to topsoil is an economically viable and far more sustainable alternative to conventional disposal, demonstrated in biologically regenerative waste recovery systems at the municipal scale.

Biological Diversity Planning and Conservation

Beyond the enterprise of designing the built environment for human habitation, sustainability gives voice to the biological role of all living species in the web of life, out of the argument for biodiversity argued in the work of Edward O. Wilson (1992), among others. The detrimental impact of building and land use practices is directly correlated to critical biological species decline in North America through habitat reduction, production of toxic chemicals and waste, combustion of fossil fuels, and related agricultural and industrial resource exploitation. Bioregional planning at a continental scale is represented by proposals for the recovery of wilderness to preserve the range of endangered species as an international biological conservation strategy (Noss 1992). Such proposals logically come from an extension of bioregional planning to include biodiversity objectives and values.

Global Development

The discussion of sustainability that emerged from the Earth Summit in Rio has, as discussed, reconfigured the international view away from a geopolitical division of "First, Second, and Third Worlds" to "one world," increasingly interdependent in economic and environmental development. This aspiration has often become embroiled and stalemated in political and ideological debate surrounding economic issues of international aid and obligations of industrialized nations to support the economic development and conservation practices of developing nations. All the while, rapid industrialization continues apace, uninformed by, or negligent of, sustainable design practices. Regardless of these apparent expediencies, the sustainability discussion has given an undeniable perspective of the essential interconnectedness of all economies and environments that must be the framework of future design education and practice.

Design of the Future

Implicit in all these discussions is a commitment and concern for the future well beyond our personal roles and realms — what Robert Gilman, editor of *In Context* magazine, has called "future fairness," offered as a succinct two-word definition of the concept of sustainability. Just as human impact has negative impact on the global environment and thus on future resources, the obverse can also be true, that human impact can have positive benefit through design intention. The caution suggested in the discussion in this chapter still holds, however, that the human mind has proven far from insightful or foresightful in predicting the future, and our capacity for comprehensive actions so necessary to sustainable design has yet to be tested and proved. Nonetheless, the role of stewardship through design conceives of human intelligence and creativity as an integral part of the evolution of life on Earth. The capacity to design — the ability to envision and enact an improved environment — is in this view an ethical instrument and as such is our one best way to prepare for an unpredictable yet more sustainable future.

Although the challenge to understand and sustain the interdependencies of global environmental health and biodiversity appears overwhelming, it need not be dismaying. We do not yet know the upper limit of the human capacity for global education, stewardship, and collective thought and action. This is the single most important premise of the challenge of sustainability, that human creativity, knowledge, and action can regenerate biodiversity and life in all that we do. It would seem to be a fitting question on which to found the discipline of design thought and action called architecture.

9
Reinventing Professional Privilege as Inclusivity: A Proposal for an Enriched Mission of Architecture

Sharon Egretta Sutton

How difficult it is to make audible the voice of oppression in a choir where privilege controls the resources and accepted tonalities of seeing, knowing, and being. Privilege can make choices and assure that these choices are possible within existing institutional frameworks. Privilege is free of the need to constantly improvise and get others to attend to a more inclusive view of history. Oppression, on the other hand, is so consumed by the realities of exclusion that it has little energy left to create its own truth or vision of the future.
— Sutton, "Finding Our Voice in the Dominant Key"

Privilege is having certain rights and benefits such as the capacity to be perceived as valuable, to judge and interpret experience, and to exercise influence over your own fate as well as that of others. It is the psychiatrist who deems a patient insane, the architect who claims the public lacks taste, the sociologist who articulates the pathologies of poverty, the college president who touts knowledge as the wave of the future — each person benefiting from a particular construction of reality. Within the professions, privilege is dispensed via prescribed systems of credentialing in which each person's worth is ranked and rated relative to internally imposed standards. "Through processes of professionalization, practices seek legitimacy and status by developing criteria for the practice and gateways for excluding others from the practice. Most of these efforts are rationalized through the claim of public safety and protection" (Schneekloth and Shibley 1995, 213–14). Over time, ever-increasing standards of performance are implemented to protect the public from incompetence, but these standards also serve "to restrict the number of practitioners, thereby raising their incomes" (Bledstein 1976, 96).

In architecture, where protection of life safety is paramount, a minimum of about nine years is currently required to progress through schooling, internship, and licensure—time that many persons cannot invest, especially because the average income for architects is below that of many other fields with equal or less training.[1] Subsequent to licensure, more capital is needed to continue climbing the ladder of professional success. To be successful, architects must have the economic resources to maintain NCARB certification, belong to the AIA, participate in its mandatory system of continuing education, and submit projects to competitions—all costly endeavors. More limiting is the tacit requirement for a style and habits of mind that are acceptable in inner circles of privilege. Each step of this ladder exacts a higher price, elevating the status of those who have the resources to keep moving up.

Professional privilege came into being in the United States during an era of unrestrained economic growth when the profits of industrialization were magnified by the vast resources of a land-rich country, especially those resources (oil, natural gas, and coal) that could be turned into energy. "Energy is the backbone of the industrial economy. It is what does our work for us, moving our cars, running our machines, bringing water to farm fields and cities, moving the products of industry to markets, as well as being embodied in all the products of the petrochemical industries, the synthetic fabrics, the plastics, and the fertilizers that make our agriculture so productive" (W. Johnson 1985, 24). The economic growth that resulted from such an abundance of energy—and its downside, increased socioeconomic stratification—was essential to the expansion of professional privilege. Architecture, in particular, benefited from the country's vast resources, as well as its expanding urban population. For example, in 1881, Columbia College Trustee Frederick Augustus Schermerhorn succeeded in convincing his fellow trustees to underwrite a course in architecture because "many more architects would be needed to meet the demands for both new buildings and alterations of existing buildings in the suddenly burgeoning urban areas of America" (Bedford 1981, 7–8).

However, constantly increasing standards of living combined with increasing human activity on the Earth have caused the demand for energy to outrun the supply, signaling the end of America's age of unfettered growth and creating an opportunity to dismantle professional privilege. In addition, the increasingly audible voices of oppression are demanding a reconsideration of the exclusionary values that underpin traditional conceptions of professional identity. Although spectacular technological advances have resulted from specialized knowledge, exponential growth in the world's population has led many social and environmental critics to question the sustainability of organizing human experience along the boundaries of specialized, fragmented professions. Even within the professions, persons who promote greater demographic and intellectual diversity point to the loss of talent that comes from narrowly defined ladders of success. Architects have not developed the layers of specialization or scientific clout that other professionals have used to distance themselves from their clients. Yet the field is sharply delimited by professional conceptions and credentialing processes that not only exclude "the other" but render those inside incapable of addressing rapid global changes in demographics, economics, the environment, and communications, among others. Because architecture is so reliant on the energy that is fast disappearing, being able to redefine its professional psyche is crucial to the survival of the field.

How can we transform the professional culture of architecture, which was spawned during the birth of a affluent nation rich in environmental resources, so that it is suited to an age of scarcity? How can we replace exclusionary roles with ones that encompass many different types of knowledge and ways of being? How can our loyalty to the traditions of architecture be enriched by a commitment to address the significant ecological issues that are arising as more of the natural environment is designed, whether by intention or default? In this chapter, I address such questions and generate new conceptions of the profession by examining the fundamental nature of architecture. Such an investigation necessarily involves a historical analysis of the recent past that spawned contemporary professional culture, as well as of the distant past when enduring attitudes were formed toward inhabiting the Earth and using its resources. Feminist historian Gerda Lerner writes: "Women's history is indispensable and essential to the emancipation of women" (1986, 3). I propose that architecture history is equally indispensable and essential to the emancipation of architects—a history that encompasses not just the great buildings studied in history of architecture courses but also the social and political processes through which the Earth was, and continues to be, humanized. Understanding the value systems that shaped the designed environment of Western civilization, and then seeing how this legacy still permeates the architecture profession, can result in the means to unravel the myths that limit our ability to imagine, and participate in patterning, a more just disposition of the Earth's resources.

To begin this investigation, I offer the following six propositions about architecture's inheritance from the distant and near past, as well as its present situation and future prospects:

- The designed environment of Western civilization reflects ancient patriarchal values that sanction the use and abuse of the landscape for private gain.

- These values produced the great monuments of Western civilization, which were constructed at the expense of the less powerful to glorify dominant persons and groups.

- Beginning in the sixteenth century, a scientific worldview emerged that further encouraged disassociation among more and less powerful human beings and between people and nature.

- A culture of professionalism emerged in the United States during the late 1800s that combined ancient patriarchal values with a modern scientific worldview of disassociation, limiting the exercise of specific types of expertise to properly credentialed persons.

- Contemporary architects inherit the patriarchal legacy of using and abusing the landscape for private gain—or monument making—but they have not been so successful in limiting the exercise of architectural expertise.

- To address modern environmental abuses, an enriched mission of architecture would replace its heritage of power over the landscape with place-making processes that are grounded in inclusive values and practices.

In this chapter, I seek to substantiate these six propositions through socially critical analysis. I begin by exploring the interrelated concepts of private property and slavery, which together comprise the traditions of ancient patriarchal society that laid the groundwork for a few persons to exert power over nature and other people. I show how patriarchal values have allowed dominant cultures to mediate between themselves and the "madness of nature" (Vincent Scully's characterization of virgin landscapes), producing the great architecture of the world but also incurring enormous losses to nature and subordinate individuals and groups. I discuss the transformation of ancient values into a modern scientific worldview that created further hierarchies among people and nature—a view that sanctioned unparalleled abuse of natural resources for private gain and ushered in a culture of professionalism in which properly credentialed persons limited access to education and prestigious occupations, as well as to space. I look at the effects of these legacies on contemporary architects, suggesting that although our field is both similar to, and different from, other professions, it cannot respond to problems deriving from centuries of environmental degradation with the values and methods of the distant and near past—that we cannot dismantle the master's house with the master's tools. The chapter ends with a proposal for an enriched mission of architecture that invests in making sustainable, equitable places while also encouraging many persons to contribute their knowledge to the ongoing process of humanizing the Earth. I do not present this mission in a prescriptive manner but rather outline broad values, attitudes, and habits of mind that can transform the psyche of architecture.

A Legacy of Using and Abusing the Landscape

> If I had to answer to following question, "What is slavery?" and if I should respond in one word, "It is murder," my meaning would be understood at once. I should not need a long explanation to show that the power to deprive a man of his thought, his will, and his personality is the power of life and death. So why to this other question, "What is property?" should I not answer in the same way, "It is theft," without fearing to be misunderstood, since the second proposition is only a transformation of the first? (Proudhon 1994, 13)

Our anthropocentric worldview makes it practically impossible to understand social critic Pierre-Joseph Proudhon's linking of private property and slavery. The concept of being above nature rather than with it—having the power to define and use it for human purposes—is so basic to the modern mind that it seems absurd to propose that the ownership of land and people are equivalent. Yet the unwritten pages of history do link private property and slavery as the first institutionalized forms of human dominance, since slavery derived from the need to have sufficient labor to cultivate land and establish permanent places of residency. Owning land and owning labor were two sides of the same coin. The invention of private property initiated a class-stratified society in which stronger villages engaged in intertribal warfare to expand their holdings; slavery was invented when the women who resided on these conquered lands were taken into captivity.[2] Just as the concept of private property paved the way for one group to "steal" the lands of another, so the oppression of women created a mind-set that allowed some individuals to "kill" the humanity residing in enslaved persons, thus conferring permanent slave status on them and their offspring. These interrelated social constructions—private property (with its correlative, war to defend property) and women's subordination (with its correlative, slavery)—"were largely derived from Mesopotamian and, later, from Hebrew sources" (Lerner 1986, 11). They comprise the major metaphors that define Western patriarchal society. But how did these social constructions evolve, how did they affect the designed environment, and what is their continuing role in the architecture profession?

Because no written histories exist for this period, opinions differ on how some men got control over other men, all women, and specified portions of the landscape. However, "from the available data, it appears that the most egalitarian societies are to be found among hunting/gathering tribes, which are characterized by economic interdependency" (Lerner 1986, 29). Traditional societies do not perceive the social hierarchies that exist in the modern mind, but rather women and men are accorded equally important roles in relation to nature, which is experienced as a living, nurturing organism. During the Paleolithic and early Neolithic periods some 15,000 years ago, the social roles of women and men in Mesopotamia began to be more asymmetrical as tools and weaponry allowed increasing control over nature. Women, who spent most of their thirty- to forty-year life spans in pregnancy and nursing, came to be associated with the Earth and its magical powers of nurturance; men, instead, began to be more occupied with the violence of large-scale hunting and warfare.

Structural anthropologist Claude Lévi-Strauss (1969) hypothesized that the transformation from a hunter-gatherer society to a patriarchal one came about as agricultural production and animal husbandry became paramount. The elder males of one tribe began to procure women from other tribes for their reproductive capacities, intermarriages consolidating their ability to guarantee the possession of certain cultivated areas from one generation to the next. According to Gerda Lerner, market economies resulted as scattered Neolithic villages became agricultural communities, then urban centers, and finally states. Concentration of populations and specialization of labor increased commodity production and trade of goods with distant lands. As propertied classes consolidated their power through militarism and the institutionalization of slavery, extended tribal relationships evolved into patriarchal families in which women (and their children) were subordinate (Lerner 1986, 54). Land, women, children, and slaves were reified as the property of powerful men who also exerted control over the public affairs of state, undertaking immense construction projects and keeping the written records that constitute history.

Although the sequence of events is debatable, clearly a concept of property emerged over time that conferred on special males the quintessential right to appropriate the human and nonhuman world for personal gain. Indeed, "Roman law defined property—*jus utendi et abutendi re sua, quatenus juris ratio patitur*—as the right to use and abuse a thing within the limits of the law" (Proudhon 1994, 35). That is, owners were empowered by law to use and dispose of their property as they saw fit. Although legally owning women, children, and slaves has been abolished in modern Western society, the concept of owning land continues to be a pivotal institution that comprises the primary means for accumulating wealth. "Paramount in value for many societies . . . is lineage. Its prestige lies in its effectiveness in guaranteeing an individual's and a people's immortality. Lineage signifies permanence rather than fields that can be overrun by wilderness, houses that can rot, and cities that can be razed to the ground" (Tuan 1989, 69). Property is fundamental to lineage, because ownership is preserved from one generation to the next along with "the right to let, to lease, to lend at interest, to

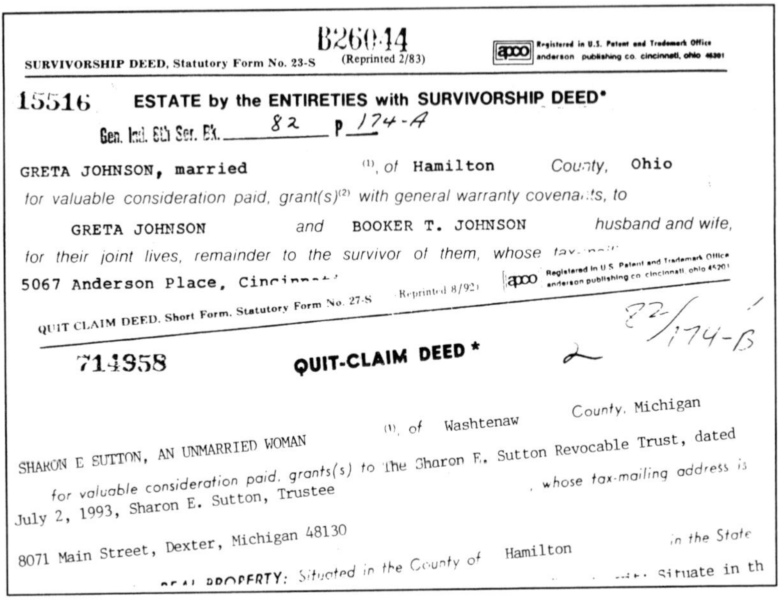

Figure 9.1. Photocopies of typical deeds indicating the marital status of the property owner.

exchange for profit, to invest in annuities, and to levy a tax on a field"
(Proudhon 1994, 63). This concept of land ownership is the basis for
current differences in the income of workers, who derive most of their
income from salaries, and affluent persons, who derive a large portion
of their income from landholdings (Bowles and Gintis 1976, 197). As
evidence that property is still an expression of these early notions of
patriarchal privilege, consider the wording of a standard deed, in which
the marital status of the owner(s) is specified. I can think of no other
purchase that requires the public disclosure of such information.

The monuments of Western architecture, from the ancient castles
and churches of Europe to the corporate structures that shape the contemporary landscape, express permanence on the Earth, making concrete the lineage and immortality of powerful individuals and groups.
These monuments appear wherever there is a concentration of the economic resources that enable the ownership (or theft, in Proudhon's terms)
of land. Thus the production of the most magnificent architecture is
made possible by the power asymmetries of patriarchal society. I propose that the link between male privilege and the production of architecture has contributed to architects' reputation for being elitist while

greatly limiting their ability to influence those privileged persons who have granted themselves the legal right to exert power over the landscape for private gain. I return to this point later, but first I look more closely at how patriarchal values have shaped the designed environment by considering the processes through which nature has been increasingly humanized.

A Power-Over Process of Humanizing the Earth

The designed environment — its roads and buildings, its farmlands and gardens — is a cultural artifact, as are the sociopolitical systems that make its invention possible. Both the designed environment and its corresponding organizational framework are edifices of the human imagination and, as such, are expressions of a society's dominant moral vision. Geographer Yi-fu Tuan (1989) has looked across several Western and non-Western cultures to explore the ethical dilemmas that arise as societies attempt to order the world through their constructions. According to Tuan, "When cultivators clear the bush to create a landscape of fields and houses, they do so in answer to the needs of survival, but that cannot be all: the humanized world, existing visibly and tangibly before them, gives shape to their lives and serves at the same time as a flattering and reinforcing mirror of their humanity" (68).

Viewed against modern anthropocentric standards of living, the so-called barbarians of hunter-gatherer societies were destitute — without education, unable to alleviate disease or access the basic necessities that make a wholesome existence possible. However, such standards were an invention of Neolithic societies, who were the first to fear death and conceive life as a linear evolution toward greater and greater control over human frailties and nature. As the legends of many early civilizations suggest, pre-Neolithic societies conceived the world differently, associating the humanizing of nature with a loss of simplicity and fundamental decline in the quality of life. For example, the Taoists of sixth-century China believed that all of nature had once been tame. In an original Eden, the ancient Chinese could tread on serpents, grasp the tails of tigers, and entrust their children to be nurtured by birds in their nests. As their culture evolved to include hunting, fishing, and other forms of environmental control, nature became cruel and unaccommodating. Consequently, people had to work far harder to survive and lost their sense of unity with the world around them. Likewise the Greeks envisioned a Golden Age in their distant past in which nature surrendered her fruits unasked. According to this fable, the Greeks lost their innocence and the protection of the Olympian gods as their culture evolved and people learned to slaughter animals for consumption (Tuan 1989, 70–80).

These Chinese and Greek myths parallel the Judeo-Christian view of creation in which it is said that God gave Adam and Eve "dominion over the fish of the sea, and over the fowl of the air, and to every thing that creepth upon the Earth." God placed them in a planted garden that contained "every tree that was pleasant to sight, and good for food, including a tree of life as well as a tree of knowledge of good and evil." Adam and Eve were enjoined "to dress and to keep" their garden, and to eat freely of its trees except for the tree of knowledge of good and evil, but Eve allowed a serpent to convince her that she could possess this tree and its knowledge. Such human audacity resulted in a fall from Grace — the serpent condemned to crawl in the dust, the man to till the soil, the woman to bear children and obey the man (Genesis 1–3).

As the fables of early cultures suggest, the history of civilized life reveals an ever expanding control over nature through increased knowledge and more complex social systems, yet it also reveals a lust for power that can result in human suffering, economic injustice, social unrest, and war. Western civilization's advances in technology — especially irrigation — provided greater control over the production and storage of crops and increased the amount of land that could be farmed. Such technology enabled the hoarding of surplus goods and concentration of populations in the elaborate temple-towns of the fourth and third millennia B.C. Upper-class male rulers (as well as their wives and daughters, who themselves frequently occupied subordinate positions of power as rulers of conquered territories) oversaw the construction of huge temple complexes and centralized irrigation projects. "The financing of such vast enterprises, the maintenance of labor squads paid in rations, and the investment of surpluses in the mass production of certain craft products for export, all led to the consolidation of power and the specialization of function in the hands of a temple bureaucracy" (Lerner 1986, 56).

The construction of empires on conquered territories, the subordination of women, and slavery became visible expressions of male power. The more lavish the architecture, the more voluptuous the harem, the more numerous the slaves, the more worthy the man. As historian Calvin Luther Martin explains:

> Invariably we witness these budding civilizations, or city-states, launching themselves on ambitious building programs, constructing spectacular, even flamboyant, typically colossal temples, pyramids, and plazas, for the glory and pleasure of the heavenly pantheon with whom these potent priest-kings conferred and consorted. Such structures were built as well, no doubt, to overawe the populace.... The temples, pyramids, palaces, statues, stelae, and other such monumental artifacts constituted tangible expressions of history: they left something human, something connected with the activities of a special individual, on the sacred landscape. (1992, 60–61)

These monuments of domination, which make up a typical history of ancient architecture curriculum, represent spectacular feats in design and engineering. Created by countless slaves and workers who lost their lives mining the Earth's resources on behalf of their overseers, they are an expression of values that allow special individuals to exert control over the human and nonhuman environment. The hidden curriculum of such courses tells students that social and environmental injustices are an accepted aspect of the creation of beautiful spaces, but what has been the history of place making in more recent times?

A Modern Scientific Worldview of Dissociation Emerges

> The critical characteristics of the modern scientific world view are separation and dissociation. Cartesian logic laid the foundation for the scientific paradigm by differentiating mind and body, subject and object, value and fact, spirit and matter.... Most importantly, Cartesian duality set human beings apart from and over nature, thus opening the way for a relationship that is primarily exploitative and manipulative. (Stirling 1990, 78)

In the sixteenth century, the encroachment of powerful persons on "the other" was heightened by an expanding market economy that arose in the city-states of Renaissance Italy and quickly spread to northern Europe.

European discovery and exploitation of the Americas alongside the increasing use of money fueled the growth of cities as centers of trade and handicraft production. A capitalist economy emerged that "was based on nonrenewable energy — coal — and the inorganic metals — iron, copper, silver, gold, tin, and mercury — the refining and processing of which ultimately depended on and further depleted the forests" (Merchant 1992, 45). During the sixteenth and seventeen centuries, forests were denuded, cleared lands were turned into pastures, swamps were drained, and mines were dug as the emerging field of experimental science furthered the domination of nature for human benefit.

The social relationships surrounding the making of cultural artifacts were also evolving. By the eighteenth century, the status of artisans had been elevated from that of workshop-trained craftspersons to that of "fine artists" who received technical and practical instruction in state-supported academies such as l'École des Beaux-Arts. However, before the Enlightenment, these artists still executed the religious, political, and social visions of the nobility. "The patrons decided what was to be done and who was to do it. When these choices were inspired, as they were in some of the greatest monuments in the history of Western art — the Parthenon, the Abbey of Saint-Denis, the Sistine Chapel — the fusion of a patron's vision with an artist's gifts led to crucial creative breakthroughs" (Strauss 1984, 181).

After the bourgeoisie-led revolutions of the late eighteenth and early nineteenth centuries in the United States, France, England, South America, and elsewhere, artists no longer enjoyed a clear relationship to monarchs whose authority derived from their royalty. Less confident in their artistic sensibilities, the bourgeoisie "preferred the reworking of formulas from the past to new responses to the vast social changes of the present" (Strauss 1984, 181). Having lost their clearly defined connection to nobility, artists began to position themselves as "geniuses" who possessed superior gifts, an idea that was not confined to the arts. In what was perhaps an effort to replace the social hierarchies created by royalty with a differentiation among the bourgeoisie, an English scientist, Sir Francis Galton, originated in 1869 what came to be known as the "Great Man Theory." According to Galton and his disciples, "leaders possessed universal characteristics that made them leaders. These characteristics were seen to be fixed, largely inborn, and applicable across situations" (Hollander and Offermann 1993, 63). This theory of inborn specialness resulted in a new class of avant-garde artists who took a deliberately adversarial stance toward the general public.

Whereas these avant-garde artists laid the foundation for architects' disassociation from the political and public arenas, the activities of city planner Baron Georges Eugène Haussmann foretold the fragility of their relationships with venture capitalists. In 1853, Napoleon III designated Haussmann prefect of the Seine, giving him a charge to restructure Paris to serve the needs of Napoleon's upper-middle-class constituency. "Between 1853 and 1879, Haussmann changed this bustling core of the old city—containing a score of churches and monasteries, some 14,000 inhabitants, and a tight network of dozens of streets, alleys, and quays crowded between the cathedral and the old royal palace—into an institutional center" (Saalman 1971, 17). Haussmann's monumental boulevards with their expensive facades for the teeming inner quarters of the city allowed investors in new construction or renovation to predict the future growth of an area. "The big real estate operators . . . were quick to buy up all available property alongside the newly created boulevards, correctly anticipating the enormous rise in these properties' value as the new streets became the prime sites for fashionable residences and commerce" (22–23). Haussmann used his administrative skills to increase the profits of France's bourgeoisie, segmenting the city into social molecules that resembled the growing division of labor in industry (Sennett 1976). Backed by an authoritarian president, Haussmann had enormous prestige until his demise due to the deficit financing of this vast undertaking, predicting the fragile position of the architect-as-servant for venture capitalists in current times.

These trends — an emerging mind-set that conceived the world via objective rules of disassociation, an expanding market economy controlled by self-made predatory capitalists, and an unparalleled "utendi et abutendi" of resources for the benefit of those capitalists — underpin the paradigm of professionalism that was exported to the New World.

The U.S. Culture of Professionalism and Knowledge Making

In the United States, a culture of professionalism arose between 1870 and 1920 that reflected both ancient patriarchal values and a modern scientific worldview of dissociation. As a nascent industrial economy ushered in an unmatched era of affluence, immense increases were taking place in such indicators of prosperity as the magnitude of the gross national product, miles of railroad and telephone and telegraph wire, number and size of cities, life expectancies and availability of life insurance policies, number of new books and newspapers, and amount of postal activity (Bledstein 1976, 46–48). During this period some of the nation's most magnificent architecture was being built. While many cities, like Pittsburgh, were absorbing the pollution created by manufacturing, industrial profits were also financing such architectural treasures as Chicago's Palmer House Hotel, New York's Old Metropolitan Opera House, and San Francisco's Nob Hill, to name just a few. Yet unemployment was on the upswing as the profits of industrialization intensified sociogeographic stratification. Well-to-do white Americans were physically distancing themselves from poor, ethnic-minority, and so-called deviant persons through the creation of specialized spaces, for example, estates, tenements, boarding schools, and insane asylums (Bledstein 1976, 46–48).

It was in this Gilded Age of spectacular economic success that professional privilege took shape, a culture that "over the years has established the thoughts, habits, and responses most modern Americans have taken for granted" (Bledstein 1976, 80). Jargon and technical formalities acquired through strenuous rites of passage reinforced the legitimacy of certain types of knowledge that in turn increased professional status "for those who have the power to validate their own models of the world can validate their own power in the process" (Spender 1981, 1). As symbols of professional authority were institutionalized, the public's dependence on that authority increased. In historian Burton Bledstein's words, "It was within the power of the professional person to define issues and crises — threats to life and security — perhaps real and perhaps unreal. And it was within the power of the professional to justify his actions, including the use of socially sanctioned violence, by appealing to a special knowledge called scientific fact. No metaphysical authority more effectively humbled the average person" (1976, 105).

In the United States, the rise of the professions coincided with the appearance of the middle class. "Through professionalization, the middle class sought to carve out an occupational niche that would be closed both to the poor and to those who were merely rich" (Ehrenreich 1990, 78), and higher education emerged to protect the boundaries of professional knowledge. "By building up its higher schools and drawing upon the graduates for positions of leadership, the middle class hoped to dominate all the institutional services Americans were increasingly requiring" (Bledstein 1976, 121). A distinctive aspect of this period was the division of life into specialized sectors, which reflected the bureaucratic hierarchies of industry and a growing segregation of land uses and specialized building types. By the 1880s, medicine had fractured into specialties in almost every region of the body (which yielded higher fees and more prestige than general practice), and the subdivision of scholarly disciplines had resulted in almost two hundred learned societies. The knowledge explosion of the twentieth century saw the distinction of the applied and theoretical research aspects of a particular field, which led to further fragmentation and specialization. "Particularly powerful in molding our contemporary sense of things has been the division between the various 'tracks' to achievement laid out in schools, corporations, government, and the professions" (Bellah et al. 1985, 43). These achievement tracks mirrored categories of space, regulating the environmental experiences of individuals and groups according to their social status. As evidence of the persisting link between access to socioeconomic position and access to the designed environment, consider the communal spaces of secretaries versus the private offices of executives, the disenfranchisement of ethnic neighborhoods versus the heavy mortgaging of white ones, and the quality of bus terminals versus that of airports.

At the beginning of the twentieth century, women and persons of color were openly denied access to education and employment and thus to the privileged spaces of society. The existence of institutionalized sexism and racism — and the different socioeconomic conditions for advancement that resulted — is apparent in the labor statistics of the era. Consider that in 1900, males accounted for 51.1 percent of the population, females accounted for 48.9 percent, and Negroes for 11.6 percent (Bureau of the Census 1904a). Yet females and Negroes made up a minuscule proportion of the more elite professions. Civil engineering and surveying was one of the more restricted fields, numbering a total of 43,535 persons with only 84 (0.2 percent) women and 120 (0.3 percent) Negroes, including one woman. Architects, designers, and draftpersons numbered 29,560 with only 1,042 (3.5 percent) women and 52 (0.2 percent) Negroes, all men. Medicine was among the most inclusive of the elite professions; physicians and surgeons numbered 132,235, with 7,399 (5.6 percent) women and 1,734 (1.3 percent) Negroes, including 160 women (Bureau of the Census 1904b).

Thus the U.S. culture of professionalism was shaped by the interests of powerful white males who used a process of credentialing to socially and spatially keep "the other" out while intimidating the public into acquiescing to their authority, which derived from their proven command of certain areas of esoteric knowledge. Rituals such as taking standardized examinations; awarding degrees, honors, and prizes; using jargon, formalisms, and technical devices; and wearing and displaying symbols of status emerged as objective proof of this professional authority.[3] Higher education became a gateway for accredited individuals who, it was claimed, had earned their privileges through objectively measured talent, merit, and achievement. Over the years, the expanding professionalization of many everyday tasks has increased people's reliance on professional expertise while decreasing their sense of personal efficacy (Illich 1977). Persons who cannot pay for services, whose worldview is out of sync with patriarchal concerns, or who do not have the political clout to resist professional privilege are likely to suffer the most from making daily survival tasks into services that are regulated by law and provided by licensed persons.

The Differing Legacies of Contemporary Architects

The progress of architecture was both similar to, and different from, other professions, a similarity being the stance of superiority it established toward the public. This characteristic was nurtured, in part, at the Bauhaus in Weimar, Germany, where Walter Gropius designed a curriculum that was in sharp contrast to the regimented training of l'École des Beaux-Arts and other traditional academies. Gropius challenged the prevailing association of art with historicism and state authority, seeking to establish the individuality and autonomy of the artist while creating explicit links between art and new manufacturing processes. The Bauhaus was a center of controversy, being established amid the uncertainty of the postwar years, having an uneasy relationship with the government that supported it, and pursuing the contradictory goals of emphasizing creativity while requiring conformity through a guild system of training and examination (Naylor 1985, 50–56). Reflecting the parameters of modern science, the Bauhaus articulated so-called objective formal laws that gave validity to specific esthetic qualities, thus setting up a Cartesian duality between good design and bad taste. Through its curriculum, the Bauhaus laid the groundwork for an "us and them" relationship with clients by sanctifying the great individual (and typically white male) designer, characterizing the public as unsophisticated and incapable of recognizing creativity, and framing esoteric stylistic preferences as objective criteria for good design.

Although architecture adopted the mainstream culture of professionalism in its disassociation from clients, it seemed to resist the extreme differentiation that occurred in other fields. Instead, specialties in varied aspects of the physical environment turned into other disconnected and competing fields — planning, engineering, landscape architecture, interior design, environmental design, construction management — so that architecture remained a generalist profession. Even though the first doctoral degree was conferred at the University of Michigan as early as 1959, even though "more than a quarter of the approximately 100 accredited schools of architecture in this country offer either a doctoral program or a post-professional masters program, or both" (Groat 1991, 1), with additional advanced degrees coming on line each year, even though the field boasts several scholarly publications and organizations, even though schools and colleges of architecture receive about $25 million in research funding, the image of a generalist practitioner as exemplified by the fictional character Howard Roark still prevails. Research and specialization have not become part of architects' psyche.

As evidence, consider a special report by the Carnegie Foundation for the Advancement of Teaching on architecture education and practice. The outcome of a thirty-month study, the report is based on an extensive review of the literature, as well as the accreditation reports of approximately fifty professional degree programs in architecture; visits to two dozen architecture firms and fifteen accredited programs; interviews with eminent practitioners and scholars; attendance at professional meetings and symposia; and surveys of architecture students, faculty, and administrators (E. Boyer and Mitgang 1996). Despite this in-depth methodology, the report confined its entire discussion to the first professional degree, rendering invisible the doctoral and postprofessional degrees that also make up architecture education. Thus, one of the most puzzling questions in the field—namely, how research-oriented activity can best complement building-oriented activity—was not even framed.

Most likely, this oversight occurred because research and scholarship were not broached as a significant aspect of architecture by the broad range of persons who participated in the study.[4] As Boyer and Mitgang (1996) themselves acknowledge, "The field has become increasingly varied, yet there remains fixed in the minds of many a single image of the architect that may well be an antique" (12). Because of this unitary image, architecture remains remarkably cohesive, comprising characteristics of personal style and individuality, but also historical principles and personalities that define every young person's socialization into—or exclusion from—the field. Julie Thompson Klein (1993) has suggested that such cohesiveness tends to result in a more exclusionary field than those that fragment into numerous specialties.

Architecture also differed from other professions in that its membership did not gain the power to unilaterally "prescribe" solutions for their clients' needs. Ivan Illich characterized this role, explaining that "professional power is a specialized form of the privilege to prescribe.... Merchants sell you the goods they stock. Guildsmen guarantee quality. Some craftspeople tailor their product to your measure or fancy. Professionals tell you what you need and claim their power to prescribe. They not only recommend what is good, but actually ordain what is right" (1977, 17).

Despite the establishment of an arduous education and certification process, as well as legislation controlling the practice of architecture, architects were unable to secure such legitimacy. Given the historical and contemporary connection of private property to the consolidation and exercise of power, it seems unlikely that architects could possibly have established the right to independently prescribe the landscape as other professions have done in their areas of expertise; the right to prescribe buildings would have interfered with another right, namely, the right to accumulate wealth through one's landholdings. Or perhaps the lack of legitimacy is due to our preferred connection to the arts rather than engineering, a field with more scientific authority, and our resistance to architecture as scholarship and research.

Finally, architecture differed from other fields in maintaining a large measure of intuitive, one-on-one teaching. Contemporary pedagogy connects to "architectural principles that have been transmitted from one generation of architects to another for thousands of years. . . . Despite the logic inherent in these ordering systems, the manner of their transmission from one generation of architects to another has been more akin to folk art than to the studied and systematic teaching of science" (Polshek 1981, 3). Many critics, this author included, have pointed out the disadvantages "of a medieval guild culture where each person learns at the side of another person, thus perpetuating all the intellectual limitations and cultural biases of the mentor" (Sutton 1992, 67). However, I believe that these weaknesses in architecture's professional armor—lack of specialization, inability to prescribe, and one-on-one mentoring—also offer clues for developing a modus operandi more suited to an emerging era of scarcity. I return to these issues at the end of the chapter, but first I consider the nature of that era and its environmental challenges—challenges a newly conceived profession of architecture must address.

Modern-Day Use and Abuse of the Landscape

Consider just a few of the most troubling facts related to population explosion and environmental degradation:

- Almost 100,000 people are added to the Earth's population every year with the total increase over the next ten years equaling the current populations of North America, Western Europe, and the former Soviet Union combined.

- Affluent persons in the United States reap eleven times the income of the poor, giving this country one of the highest contrasts in the distribution of economic resources in the industrialized world—a skewed distribution that almost matches India's.

- With only 4 percent of the global population, the United States consumes 30 percent of the world's resources and contributes 50 percent of its waste, or fifty times more pollution per capita than an undeveloped country.

- Suburban and exurban households are major sources of pollution, averaging ten automobile trips a day at a cost of forty to seventy cents per mile, much of it federally subsidized.

- Every twenty-four hours the number of new drivers and new cars increases by ten thousand; in the same period, twelve square miles of farmland are converted into low-density, auto-dependent development.

- Energy usage has doubled since 1960 owing to increased use of electrical appliances, cars, and other items once considered to be luxuries.

This excessive humanizing of the Earth "brings into question the adequacy of Western culture and the assumptions upon which it rests. Of particular concern are the cultural assumptions underlying the belief systems of the developed countries whose technologies and patterns of consumer-oriented living are depleting the world's energy resources at an alarming rate" (Bowers 1993, 3). These cultural assumptions include fundamental socioeconomic inequities, use and abuse of the landscape for profit, emphasis on individualism over community, and elevation of so-called objective technical knowledge over other forms of knowing. The scale of human activity on the Earth is making the many voices of oppression more audible, compelling many leaders to rethink Western society's destructive and exclusionary belief systems. A worldview that was created from a position of privilege to protect its own power cannot be responsive to rapid global changes in demographics, economics, the environment, and communications, among other contemporary challenges.

The capacity to accommodate the planetary shifts that are in progress — shifts that call for radically different professional values and practices — is critical to architecture, which deals with the disposition of human and physical resources through a process of place making. "Place-making is the way all of us as human beings transform the places in which we find ourselves into places in which we live. It includes building and tearing buildings down, cultivating the land and planting gardens, cleaning the kitchen and rearranging the office, making neighborhoods and mowing lawns, taking over buildings and understanding cities" (Schneekloth and Shibley 1995, 1).

However, during the last century, local place-making processes have been usurped by national and international venture capitalists and their hired professional place makers — planners, urban designers, architects and landscape architects, engineers, interior designers, construction managers — greatly reducing the knowledge about specific locales that necessarily comes from their users. Although professional place makers have an indispensable role in development (especially in tempering a particular client's concerns with the broader public interest), the ongoing process of creating what environmentalist Wendell Berry refers to as a "beloved country" requires local knowledge and commitment on the part of individuals who see themselves as a collective. The allocation of this work to external sources not only disempowers laypersons by denying them the opportunity to take control over circumstances that affect their lives but also puts economic interests ahead of the value of community. "Of virtually all this land it may be said that the national economy has prescribed ways of use but not ways of care. . . . The economy, as it now is, prescribes plunder of the landowners and abuse of the land" (1990, 110).

Economically driven place making results in the abandonment of older buildings, bulldozing of entire neighborhoods for tourism, stripping of forests, and polluting of streams — the common denominator of all forms of environmental degradation being that the most well-to-do persons reap private profits at the expense of persons with the fewest resources. As in Haussmann's Paris, those with economic and political power determine the nature and direction of growth to serve their best interests. The use of land for profits has resulted in uneven development in many cities throughout the world in which some areas of the landscape are extremely overbuilt while others are left to decay. Wealthy corporate investors (who own an increasing percentage of the landscape) influence zoning laws, specify the nature and distribution of the country's infrastructure, and determine where the biggest industries with the best jobs are located. Because their frame of reference is based on economic rather than quality-of-life concerns, any area deemed unprofitable can simply be discarded as capital is shifted from central city to suburbia and on to rural areas where farmers are being simultaneously squeezed out by agribusiness and development.

As an example, consider southeast Michigan, where I used to live. Detroit was abandoned beginning in the late 1960s as suburban sprawl began consuming proportionally greater amounts of land. Although

Figure 9.2. Beginning in the 1980s, the once elegant architectural fabric of Detroit began to be decimated as the city's more well-to-do residents left in search of a suburban or rural lifestyle. Photograph by the author.

the density of older cities in this area is about five-and-a-half dwelling units per acre, newer subdivisions are being constructed at one-and-a-half dwelling units or less per acre with more exclusive homes occupying five to ten acres each (SEMCOG 1991). As new subdivisions go in, the tax base increases to support more infrastructure, which encourages more development, thereby consuming the open space that attracted people to the area in the first place.

In southeast Michigan, the population is expected to increase just 5 percent over the next thirty years, but the natural landscape is expected to decrease by 40 percent (SEMCOG 1991). Because an individualistic, car-oriented, socially homogeneous lifestyle is preferable to the higher density and diversity of a city, almost the same population is consuming increasing amounts of virgin land, while Detroit is left to those without choice. Such sprawling development implies more traffic congestion, longer commuting, and much higher levels of pollution, since the single-use subdivisions that are currently being built require every adult to drive to all their daily activities including working, shopping, recreating, and caring for children or the elderly. Because residential property in this area receives $1.40 in public services for each $1.00 it con-

Figure 9.3. In newer suburban and exurban subdivisions, fewer people occupy bigger homes on larger lots, but the quality of construction is typically lower than that found in older housing. Photograph by the author.

Figure 9.4. Retail shops in Detroit struggle to attract customers, leaving abandoned an environment that would be characterized as "new urbanism" in a more affluent area. Photograph by the author.

Figure 9.5. The strip malls that spring up to serve new subdivisions not only lack architectural quality but risk economic failure as other competing strip malls are built in the cycle of development and abandonment. Photograph by the author.

tributes (Poulson 1996), continued sprawl will not only result in increased pollution, loss of agriculture, and environmental degradation but also create a long-term drain on the economy.

Current land use policies sacrifice the integrity of human relationships and the landscape in favor of real estate profiteering. These materialistic development policies encourage monotonous megascale projects that eliminate distinctive, pedestrian-oriented communities. They isolate poor people in urban areas without a socially acceptable means of earning a living. And they ruin the countryside, which is ruthlessly mined for its resources and then turned into more unplanned development. Wherever land is less expensive, tax rates lower, environmental controls fewer, or planning officials less sophisticated is where opportunistic leapfrog development can occur unimpeded.

Although there are elaborate legal structures to protect individual rights, laws exist that actually encourage vandalism of everyone's collective right to the physical environment. The single-use residential enclaves that are being built all over the countryside ravage the natural environment, privatize public life, suck the vitality out of denser urban areas, and fail to consider the means through which communities can sustain themselves economically. In most instances, new housing is far

Figure 9.6. As subdivisions are built, taxes increase, and farmers, unable to make these higher payments, exchange a way of life for lucrative cash payments—some willingly, others with such sorrow as to result in deep depression or even suicide. Photograph by the author.

Figure 9.7. In less affluent areas of the world, the natural landscape is clear-cut to produce the construction materials for our more affluent way of life. Photograph by the author.

more expensive and less sound architecturally than what was devaluated in older areas. Such pillaging of human, physical, and economic resources is particularly disturbing in light of the exponential growth of the world's population, especially outside the United States.

Until recently the costs of supervaluating and devaluating land were borne by less-powerful persons; as resources are depleted, the costs of unchecked sprawl and increasing reliance on the automobile are more broadly borne by businesses, the government, and middle-class families. As the circle of effect widens, an opportunity is created for innovation, since every weakening in the economy that derives from a legacy of exclusionary values provides an opening for achieving more inclusive, sustainable ones. "The sustainable economy... assumes that technological advance will not be adequate to sustain the world as we know it, and that the future will inevitably require more use of human muscles, simpler tools and machines, less transportation, and a simpler material standard of living, but with compensations in terms of a way of life that is on a more human scale, richer in cooperation and community, and less dependent on a fragile and declining industrial economy" (W. Johnson 1985, 12).

In the last section, I outline the thoughts, habits, and responses that architectural scholars, researchers, and practitioners must engender if they are to contribute their expertise to the creation of a more interdependent, balanced future.

A Proposal for an Enriched Mission of Architecture

The field of architecture has inherited an ancient legacy of patriarchal values that give powerful venture capitalists the right to use the landscape for personal gain at the expense of many less powerful persons. Architecture also inherits a modern worldview of dissociation that allows us to distance ourselves from murky environmental problems. We continue to sanctify "star" architects, characterize the general public as being deficient in its aesthetic sensibilities, and use the stylistic preferences of a particular era as surrogate criteria for good design — habits of mind that can be found in all the professions. Yet architecture is also distinct from the other professions in that it lacks specialization, has inadequate prowess to "prescribe" the landscape, and still transmits design expertise through one-on-one instruction. Although these characteristics might be seen as deficiencies, they also might serve as a springboard to a more enriched field — a field that can contribute in a more meaningful manner to the challenges of the twenty-first century.

To turn our deficiencies into assets, architects would need to adopt less hierarchical, more inclusive approaches, not only toward humanizing the landscape but also toward the social construction of knowledge about that landscape. Rather than being individualistic monument makers, we would need to engage in place making with communities. We would need to expose students of architecture to a socially critical history of architecture and build the inner courage to challenge the notion of private property for personal gain. We would need to encompass research and scholarship as well as practice while replacing esoteric design criteria with the social, environmental, and economic qualities of space that enhance human and nonhuman life. We would need to expand disciplinary boundaries to include all persons who affect the built environment. And we would need to create a community of inquiry through which to explore the challenges of the twenty-first century. The chapter ends by outlining these seven overlapping areas of proposed change in architecture's psyche.

Conceiving a Sustainable Approach to Humanizing the Earth

1. *Developing Informed, Socially Just Values and Practices.* An enriched mission of architecture requires a reconceptualization of the legacy of monument making so that place making better reflects the social and environmental conditions of our time. Whereas monument making is primarily product-oriented, place making is process oriented as well. By maximizing human capital, appropriate place making can minimize the ups and downs of world trade, depleted oil fields, dry wildcat wells, and high-priced foreign oil that elevate construction costs. Because it emphasizes relationships, appropriate place making can minimize unemployment, underemployment, and all the social pathologies accompanying those conditions. It can diminish the spatial segregation that leaves impoverished neighborhoods without jobs, social capital, financial investment, and a sufficient tax base for essential services.

To facilitate such informed and inclusive place-making processes, architects can build on the visioning skills they already possess to engage the public in conceiving alternative, more socially just, futures. For example, they should be able to help children and adults imagine the benefits of slower-paced lifestyles, less pollution and toxic wastes, simpler technologies and renewable resources, and using human hands and ingenuity to work together toward a common purpose. Just as physicians were able to link cigarette smoking and cancer, architects should be able to demonstrate the negative outcomes of continued construction of competing convention centers, hotels, retail malls, cineplexes, amusement parks, and gambling casinos. Just as social activists were able to convince the public of the advantages of mainstreaming disabled populations, architects should be able to convince them of the benefits of living in socioeconomically integrated, self-sufficient communities in which poor and affluent people can walk to their jobs, stores, schools, and entertainment while still being connected to those same things globally via telecommunications.

Such informed visioning requires not only the ability to engage in empirical research and theoretical scholarship but also the interpersonal skills of facilitation, dialogue, and persuasion—of intellectual leadership. More important, such visioning requires that architects see the world through a lens of social justice. Currently, most architects are not exposed to such skills and values. They are primarily product oriented, are deficient in their analytical capabilities, and only recently have begun to value interpersonal skills though with an almost total lack of social consciousness. An enriched mission of architecture would emphasize process, embrace and build on its emerging intellectual foundations (discussed in greater detail hereafter), and draw from other disciplines that have been working to develop the values and practices of a socially just, multicultural society.

2. *Creating a Socially Critical History of Architecture.* Lerner describes the human and nonhuman possessions of ancient rulers, the meaning of which is most often disregarded in history of art and architecture courses. As she explains: "The queen's body was found on a bier; she had been buried with her fancy head-dress of gold, lapis lazuli, and carnelian, an exquisite gold cup in her hand. Two female attendants were crouched against her bier, which was surrounded by burial offerings of splendid metal and stone work. . . . Against the wall there were nine bodies of women adorned in fine jewelry; in all there were sixty-three men and women buried with the king" (Lerner 1986, 60).

Unfortunately, most architecture students learn to methodically ignore such conspicuous waste of expensive materials, as well as the reality that slavery produced some of the greatest architectural monuments of the world. For example, I vividly recall a registration exam preparation course in which an instructor explained the correct answer for a particular multiple choice question relating to an Egyptian pyramid. We were not, he told the class, to select the choice that referred to its construction by slaves but rather to mark the one referring to its formal characteristics—the so-called objective, universally acknowledged parameters of design, systematized at the Bauhaus, that rise above messy political, social, economic, and cultural conditions. Given such indoctrination, small wonder that most aspiring architects learn to discount the broader context of place making or to consider it as a constraint to their creativity. Learning to ignore social inequities not only makes students' privileged position invisible but also renders them ineffectual in addressing those inequities. If architects are to help "affect the configuration of the landscape that was etched by racism, as well as by real estate and automobile tycoons for whom we created facades of success" (Sutton 1993, 79), they should themselves understand how social relations are reflected in the designed environment. For an enriched mission of architecture to evolve, our professional knowledge base should encompass active engagement in socially critical inquiry, especially with respect to history, which forms the basis of all social awareness. A socially critical history of ancient and modern architecture is essential to the emancipation of architects.

3. *Taking On the Issue of Property.* Most persons would agree that slavery is morally wrong; few would concur that property is dishonorable, especially not those middle- and upper-class persons whose superior social status requires its existence. For architects to launch a debate against the very social institution that sustains them would be dangerous—dangerous but necessary. As the rate of humanizing of the Earth intensifies, it will become increasingly fraudulent for architects to claim that they are protecting the public's health, welfare, and safety while cities decay, farmland is paved over, and energy resources are depleted. Property was not such an egregious theft in the days of Cicero (when the concept was written into law) because people were less mobile and property was *possessed*—or physically occupied by local owners—as opposed to being *appropriated* by multinational venture capitalists.[5] In this time of global economics, multinational corporations do not possess but rather appropriate property, determining from afar and on a massive scale the fate of persons whom their wealthy chief executive officers do not even know.

This situation is unacceptable if individuals and communities are to be empowered to determine their own sustainable futures. To advocate the right for self- and community determination, an enriched mission of architecture would necessarily tackle the dishonorability of appropriating property.

An Inclusive Approach to Knowledge Making

4. *Uniting the Practice and Discipline of Architecture.* As Julia Robinson points out elsewhere in this volume, most people think of architecture exclusively as a professional practice, concerned with executing specific

building commissions. Certainly, professional education in architecture has traditionally been conceived as having a generalist core drawn from knowledge in the arts and humanities, as well as the social and physical sciences. In the recent past, undergraduate and graduate professional education were minimally distinguished by the time required to earn a degree. Now that this requirement has been eliminated as a condition of accreditation, no clear distinction remains between a bachelor's and master's degree, confirming the unitary image of an architect, no matter what her or his intellectual preparation. However, during the last century, architecture has evolved from a practice that is informed by other disciplines into a discipline in its own right and with a distinct body of specialized knowledge. This knowledge, while unique to architecture, is not constrained by particular commissions or the limits of current practice.

As I have argued elsewhere, "it is the discipline that offers the greatest possibility for leadership for it is in this mode that we can anticipate a future need or goal in a way that we cannot as practitioners" (Sutton 1992, 66). Marching all students through the same generalist core not only minimizes their leadership potential but also works against intellectual, practical, and demographic diversity. An enriched mission of architecture would offer multiple routes through professional education by encompassing the production of knowledge, as well as its application — to buildings and to a whole variety of place-making processes. These multiple routes would open the door to an array of careers in academia, government, industry, and politics while encouraging a solid intellectual foundation for practice — and one that develops independent of the current limitations.

5. *Sharing the Privilege to Determine Ways of Knowing.* Rather than mourn the inability to prescribe — a role that will come under increasing attack as the postmodern condition of relativity replaces the idea of a single truth — architects should be able to engage the public in making its own informed prescriptions. Instead of defending stylistic preferences and demeaning the public's inability to comprehend those preferences, architects should promote "good design [as] a breadth of view that leads people to ask how human artifacts and purposes 'fit' within the immediate locality and within the region" (Orr 1994, 106). In an era where faith in government is lagging and the sense of community is disap-

pearing in the face of greed and narrow self-interests, the making of places poses an unsurpassed occasion for contributing to the ongoing process of making a democracy. In ecologist David Orr's view,

> The process of design and construction is an opportunity for a community to deliberate over the ideas and ideals it wishes to express and how these are rendered into architectural form. What do we want our buildings to say about us? What will they say about our ecological prospects? To what large issues and causes do they direct our attention? What problems do they resolve? What kind of human relationships do they encourage? These are not technical details but first and foremost issues of common concern that should be decided by the entire... community. When they are addressed as such, the design of buildings fosters civic competence and extends the idea of citizenship. (1994, 114)

To articulate realities that benefit many persons rather than just a privileged few, an enriched mission of architecture would draw from expert as well as vernacular knowledge, professional as well as self-help practices, and from broadly based evaluation and assessment procedures. Expert knowledge and practices should be free of the jargon and technical formalities that are intended to raise the prestige (and salaries) of professionals. Rather, the most complex concepts should be made accessible, even to young children, and vernacular knowledge — the knowledge that people have about a particular place — should be valued as essential to the ongoing processes of environmental change and management.

Professionals engaged in an enriched mission of architecture would not be prescribers but rather supporters of dialogue, "enabling and facilitating others in the various acts of place-making even while offering expertise in such discrete acts as planning, design, scientific inquiry, representation, construction, destruction, and maintenance" (Schneekloth and Shibley 1995, 5). Philosopher Michael Polanyi ([1958] 1962) referred to *personal knowledge* to describe a much wider range of human perceptions, feelings, and intellectual powers than what is considered as *objective knowledge*. Because experience of the physical environment includes not only its concrete features but also the symbolic meaning those features have for various individuals, architects should be able to draw out the personal knowledge of citizens, using it to generate a fully informed dialogue on place making.

6. *Expanding Disciplinary Boundaries.* Problems in society are not neatly divided up according to disciplines, and yet most professionals are consumed by establishing boundaries around themselves that determine who can legitimately engage in a particular craft. Likewise education is conveniently pigeonholed by disciplines with knowledge being divided into smaller and smaller categories as information expands. As two activist practitioners noted, "there is an ongoing attempt to create boundaries that separate and differentiate the [practice of place making] on many levels, revealing a world more concerned with distinction and division than with connection and relationship. Professors and professionals collectively differentiate themselves from 'laypeople,' even as professors and practitioners seek to differentiate themselves from each other into separate academic and practice domains" (Schneekloth and Shibley 1995, 194). Such boundary definition, including the distinction between theory building and practice, is counterproductive to making communities that are aesthetically sound, economically viable, ecologically sustainable, and spiritually enriching.

"Ecological design requires the ability to comprehend patterns that connect, which means getting beyond the boxes we call disciplines to see things in their ecological context" (Orr 1994, 108). It requires a recognition that the discipline-centric problem solving that industrialized the Earth cannot repair the damage caused by industrialization. Architecture has tended to remain a generalist field, but it has also suffered from insufficient knowledge (and socially critical awareness) to contribute to the significant environmental issues of the modern era. An enriched mission of architecture would address both these issues, embracing all the subdisciplines, as well as "the many persons who are needed to achieve truly humanistic environments — policy specialists, human relations experts, building materials researchers, community development advocates, and so forth" (Sutton 1993, 79). In this way, professional knowledge would be specialized while being integrated theoretically across various other disciplines in its application to specific problems. When combined with vernacular knowledge, this expanded intellectual base would reflect the richness of specific places, events, and people.

206 — Sharon Egretta Sutton

7. Transforming Values via a Community of Inquiry.

When Moses led the Jews out of Egypt, he and his followers spent forty years in the desert. The modern Israelis have proven in a number of recent wars that the Sinai is easily crossed, and even for the primitive transport of Moses's time, forty years of travel seems outlandish. Why did Moses and his followers take so long to cross this modest desert? It seems that the personal and social transitions from the fleshpots of Egypt to freedom in the Promised Land required a change of perceptions, and the human mind is not easily transformed. It was essential to give up the slave-like ways that had been learned in Egypt. By the time the Jews reached their homeland, all but two persons who remembered Egypt had died off, so that the new people, readied in the desert for the Promised Land, completed the journey and entered upon their inheritance reborn. (Duhl 1990, 7)

Lacking a period of isolation such as Moses had to relinquish the paternalistic legacy on which their careers are built, how can architects begin to give up their slavelike ways and envision a Promised Land? Should they even try such a Herculean task? Many social justice advocates talk about the joy of struggle as an end in itself—a sense of satisfaction despite the awareness that true equality is probably unachievable. "We believe in fulfillment—some might call it salvation—through struggle. We reject any philosophy that insists on measuring life's success on the achieving of specific goals—overlooking the process of living. More affirmatively and as a matter of faith, we believe that despite the lack of linear progress, there is satisfaction in the struggle itself" (Bell 1992, 98).

Instead of ruling out the broader social issues that surround the making of places as "not architectural," architects can expand or (as it is currently popular to say) "add value" to their work by embracing and making visible the sociocultural dimensions of the physical environment. Being part of a group of persons engaged in critical debate—a community of inquiry—is essential to seeking fulfillment through the struggle for justice. In asking the question "What is the nature of architectural knowledge?" hopefully this volume takes a step toward creating such a community.

Notes

1. Comparing salaries in architecture to those in other high-status professions is difficult because of the dearth of information on architects and variations in the way labor statistics are kept. However, a compilation of data from 1994 by Helen S. Fisher (1997) suggests that the annual earnings of mid-level architects ranged from a low in North Dakota of $34,877 to a high in Anchorage of $57,283. In comparison, the annual national average for entry-level civil engineers is $31,987. And the annual national averages for mid-level professionals in other fields are $68,271 for attorneys working for the federal government, $125,000 for family physicians, and $156,000 to $200,000 for surgeons.

2. History suggests that the kinship relations that evolved between women and men were a prelude to slavery in that "men had certain rights in women, which women did not have in men. Women's sexuality and reproductive potential became a commodity to be exchanged or acquired for the service of families" (Lerner 1986, 77). Female enslavement was a logical progression from the practice of marital exchange, which confirmed women's greater physical vulnerability. Males, on the other hand, were typically slaughtered because they were seen as a bigger threat. The final act of male dominance was the rape and impregnation of female captives.

3. In architecture, these rituals include design studio charrettes and juries, architectural licensing exam, architect's license and seal, AIA and FAIA lapel pins, and various medals of honor, among other devices that assure one's worthiness and position within the profession.

4. Architecture's failure to encompass its research and scholarship dimensions is also evidenced by the makeup of the five collateral organizations that comprise the field. Each of these independent organizations represents a different aspect of the field—practice, education, student status, licensure, and accreditation. Each has a CEO, executive officers, and board of directors who regularly exchange ideas within and across organizations on current trends in the field. The first three sponsor events and give awards that allow their constituents to gain recognition. Research and scholarship are nowhere represented in this institutional structure but have typically been dealt with via short-lived committees that depend on the largesse of the other organizations.

5. Proudhon refers to Cicero in talking about the difference between the possession and appropriation of place. The Earth, according to Cicero, is like a vast theater that is common to all and in which each person can only possess one place. The notion of private property allows people to appropriate places they do not actually occupy.

10
Thinking "Indian" Architecture

A. G. Krishna Menon

Foreword

Thinking the "Indian" in Indian architecture is the subject of this chapter. The architecture of India is probably on the periphery of concerns informing other contributions to this book, yet I suggest that there are many disciplinary affinities and areas of overlapping interest between them that could profitably be mined and examined, especially in an era of globalizing professional practice.

I would like to make two prefatory comments to place my views in context. The first concerns the postcolonial perspective that informs my discussion, and the second, the need to take into account the experience of globalization at the postcolonial site both as a strategy and as a framework for discussion. In the West, the discipline accommodates the contemporary architecture of India as a regional variation of universal modernism (Frampton 1992). Even in India, that view is hardly disputed: this is the crux of the matter. My analysis challenges these perceptions by bringing to the forefront of concern the interconnection of issues of nation, empire, migration, and ethnicity, on the one hand, and nature, culture, and economic development, on the other, with the production of architecture in India.

The materiality of buildings and the very process of realizing the architectural project—which includes clients, engineers, buildings contractors, the regulatory authorities, and, of course, architects—inflects all theoretical discussions on the subject. It also rescues such discussions from being mere academic exercises, evading engagement with the real politics of the postcolonial predicament.[1] Thus what I say is importantly determined by my location as an architect practicing and teaching in India. In this sense, the architecture of India may be *talked* about and *written* about in the metropolis, but it can only be *experienced* at the postcolonial site. I base my discussion on this ingenuous experiential reality.

The shift in focus to the locus is also strategic because it de-centers the disciplinary discussion from the metropolitan sites to the sites of experience, thereby providing a different, a subaltern, perspective to the process of globalization. This is necessary because it makes for a legitimate means of organizing resistance to the emergent forces of neocolonialism that have begun to define the relationship between the First and Third Worlds, both in academics and business. These forces are vitiating the possibility of equitable dialogue between the two sites. I suggest that this aspect of globalization should be examined critically so that these neocolonial formations can be identified and challenged; doing so would be an exemplary objective in the discipline of architecture.

There is no singular meaning to the phenomenon of globalization: it is an omnibus term. It refers, on the one hand, to the dramatic expansion of trade and commerce over the oceans and airspace, beyond traditional alliances that were restricted by old political spheres of influence, particularly in the era of colonialism and the barriers of the Cold War. International trade and commerce are as old as history, recognized as one of the catalysts in the evolution of past civilizations. Increasingly, in modern times, however, it is becoming more aggressive and intrusive, the tail that wags the dog: to facilitate international trade and commerce, it is becoming necessary to ensure (or impose) a new world order.[2] This putative world order has brought us closer to the idealistic (and ideological) concept of the frontierless "one world" on the one hand, but it has also brought in its wake the homogenization of cultures on the other. At another level altogether, new hybrid cultural developments are occurring. This process is transforming many old and underdeveloped civilizations in a manner that may not always be desirable.

Discussions in the discipline of architecture accommodate both meanings of the term "globalization," as trade and culture. As trade, the global reach of professional practice is forcing a new perspective on the traditional practice of architecture by requiring new deployments of knowledge, skills, and resources; as culture, the "flattening of the cultural landscape" and the emergence of new hybrid cultural formations are the theoretical thresholds in a discipline that valorizes the avant-garde. Architecture is no longer tightly territorialized, spatially bounded, historically unself-conscious, or culturally homogeneous — not in the Third World, and certainly not in the First. As Homi Bhabha put it, "all forms of culture are continually in a process of hybridity" (1990, 211). However, the problem is that the changes brought on by globalization are interpreted differently by different societies, depending on their location and level of economic development, and these perceptions are sometimes so opposed to one another that, indeed, sometimes one man's meat may well be another man's poison. Thus societies that steer the process of globalization see it as a wonderful opportunity whereas those at the receiving end experience it as a threat, a juggernaut careening out of control. In either case, globalization is forcing the issue at both sites. My focus is on those at the receiving end in the second site, and my proposition is that without the help of those steering, it is not possible to bring the juggernaut under control.

The central problem in my discussion is the need to present the ethical dimensions of the issue of globalization by introducing the concept of accountability. This challenges the ingrained presumption of both the authority of the Western experience and the usefulness of models derived from that experience. Contesting this tendency becomes the sine qua non of my analytic methodology. Such explicit exclusions, however, are problematic, and I am mindful of the caveat eschewing the dichotomies of "us" and "them" in postcolonial analysis. Nevertheless I recognize the usefulness of this framework in reading the events of the (past and) present. It helps displace the hegemony of Western scholarship in matters relating to the Third World, and to provide, perhaps, a more appropriate strategy for dealing with the problems of globalization.

Displacing the hegemony of Western scholarship is easier said than done. The fact is, most of what we know about the architecture of India has emanated from the outside: either from the privileged position of academic institutions in the West or by scholars trained by, or intellectually committed to, such institutions. "Knowledge" of Indian architecture was thus constructed by the West.[3] Institutions there form the core, or hub, of the globalization phenomenon and by virtue of their strategic position develop a vested interest in maintaining their dominance in the production of knowledge on postcolonial sites. The sheer volume of literature they have produced on the subject constitutes a formidable and unassailable corpus of texts and preempts the possibility of developing other terms of reference at other locales. The situation is not unlike the one expressed by the women's movement, questioning the privileged position of the white, male gynecologist in the production of knowledge about women's bodies.[4] At the risk of adopting what may appear to be merely a bellicose academic strategy, a combative stance is almost called for in the task of thinking about the "Indian" in Indian architecture.

The hermetic and self-referential nature of the discussion on architectural theory in the discipline in Western institutions needs to be countered, particularly in the context of globalization.[5] It is also my hope that based on an analysis of "Indian" architecture, a more humanist approach could be developed within the discipline — East and West — to confront the challenge of globalization.

The "Indian" Identity

Defining the "Indian" identity has plagued intellectuals in India for a long time, particularly since the rise of nationalist consciousness in the nineteenth century. Nationalists responded to the often provocative parochialism of the colonizer by presenting evidence of a common Indian culture, identifiable through Brahmanic and non-Brahmanic sources; in epics, myths, and folk stories; in the familial resemblance in the art and architecture of the subcontinent; in common customs and mores, all testifying to a civilizational bond that bestowed a certain unified coherence on the peoples of the subcontinent.[6] It is not surprising that with the attainment of independence (in 1947), the *idea* of a unified and homogeneous nation became an ineluctable reality. It manifested itself in many forms of artistic expression, not least in the field of architecture. The imperative to modernize, the urgency to "catch up," reinforced this idea. The use of the English language, too, is complicit in the collusion of a modern artistic expression and the idea of the newly independent nation-state. Thus it became common to refer to "Indian architecture," "Indian art," "Indian music," and "Indian culture," when, in fact, one was referring to an astonishing variety of architecture, art, music, and culture within a political entity called India.

We can now see these identity constructions for what they were, and continue to be: semiotic packages reflecting the desire to find continuity with an idealized past and as a bridge to an idealized future. The problem with such packaging is not that it reflects such a desire but that it flattens out and simplifies a complex reality of architecture-in-the-making. These idealizations are being contested in several academic disciplines (Niranjaha et al. 1993), but not surprisingly, in architecture, where, in fact, the issue of identity is central to the process of form making and place making.

The truth of the matter is that major developments in the contemporary architecture of India have had their origins in the colonial period. This reality is often ignored when architects in India try to achieve "Indian-ness" in their works, without pausing to consider the ontological significance of their quest; even when they reject it, their position is still rife with their indifference to the urgent ideological and philosophical issues of contemporary cultural formations. We can see in this conundrum how the colonial and the colonized mind-sets coexist: the once colonial imperative remains unchanged in the ways of thinking Indian architecture today.[7]

Indian architects have not considered this conundrum an issue and have thus failed to develop the colonial legacy into transformative architecture in the fifty years since independence. There are several historical reasons for this failure, but the two of immediate significance are the absence of theory in the pedagogy of architectural education, and its absence in architectural writing.

Contemporary architectural education evolved from the art and technical schools established by the colonial government in the 1850s. They supplanted the traditional system of building by master craftsmen, who had passed their knowledge down from one generation to another for millennia. Unlike the situation in Europe, where industrialization transformed traditional skills and knowledge systems over time, in India, the jump-start introduction to modern architecture by the colonial government made for a decisive break with the past. No attempt was made to transform the traditional system of building; indeed, it was purposively bypassed by colonial builders.

The art schools trained native draftsmen to assist British military engineers employed to construct civil and military buildings for the empire. The objectives of the technical schools were also limited, providing rudimentary knowledge in order to produce functionally competent surveyors, storekeepers, and junior engineers. Even this minimal education was coveted because it offered the prospect of a secure, white-collar job in government service. Slowly the correlation between architectural education, such as it was at the time, and secure government employment became ingrained in public and professional consciousness. To the colonized, the objective of going to school was to obtain a job, not knowledge. Schools adjusted their pedagogy accordingly, with no attempt made at replicating the kind of architectural education that existed in England — at least not in the beginning.

In the early part of the twentieth century — when architectural schools as we know them today were established — the educational ideology that evolved in the early art and technical schools prevailed. The academic content addressed vocational objectives, and the pedagogy became examination oriented. The curricula in the first schools attempted to mimic courses conducted in England but did so without re-creating the spirit or milieu that existed in classrooms there (Lang et al. 1997). This instruction has now become formulaic in nature, and with the establishment of more and more schools, particularly in the last decade (there are more than a hundred schools in India today), the crisis in architectural education has become acute. Not surprisingly, therefore, one finds that in most architectural schools, architectural design is purged of any theoretical underpinnings. Evaluation of the students' design projects also reflects the lingering influence of the early technical schools: they are more appropriate for evaluating knowledge-based technical subjects rather than open-ended design projects. Mechanical skills and competence at a pragmatic level are valued over innovation and experimentation. However, during the colonial period, this education did enable Indian graduates to obtain their professional registration in England, so it must have ensured a certain degree of competence and conformity with standards there. The problem is that educational objectives have ossified, and this stagnation is the source of complaint.

The origins of the profession in the colonial period also cast it as an engineering discipline. The introduction of new building materials such as concrete and iron during the latter part of the nineteenth century consolidated this bias, and it continues to characterize the thinking in architecture and architectural education. For example, the qualifying requirement for *all* architecture applicants is proficiency in science subjects; those with a social science or humanities background are not eligible. In fact, in many universities, architecture is offered as one option among several engineering disciplines, and many students enroll in architecture only after they fail to gain admission to a preferred engineering course.

This bias toward technical education is reflected in the established hierarchy in the Public Works Department of the government, a large employer of architects. The hegemony of the engineers in architectural matters is complete and has continued since the department was instituted 150 years ago. Recently, after highlighting the devaluation over decades of the role of architects in the department, an architect has been appointed as its head, but the old mind-set continues. This positional breakthrough is seen as a token exception rather than the rule. Consequently architects in government service have remained low-level functionaries in the decision-making hierarchy. Even during the latter part of the nineteenth century when British architects began to distinguish themselves from their engineering colleagues, they did so in matters relating to the appropriateness of aesthetic style rather than other, broader disciplinary considerations. In any case, their limited initiative did not diminish the importance of the engineers in deciding architectural matters. These historical circumstances are the background to the widespread public impression that architects, by and large, only add to the cost of buildings and are dispensable; engineers, on the other hand, are essential to realizing the architectural project. Such impressions have eroded the credibility of the profession. This does not provide the most fertile ground in which to cultivate the issue of architectural identity. The technicalization of the profession has resulted in evading the substantial problems of form making and place making in Indian architecture. Consequently, when confronted with these issues, the architect very easily translates them in technical, nuts-and-bolts terms.

Because of the limited nature of education, the architect is only able to manipulate available stylistic expressions in an arbitrary manner without the foundational support of disciplinary theory. The explicit objective of achieving architectural identity is addressed by merely attempting more and more exotic architectural expressions, within the limited means available for realizing them. Thus architects in India had been practicing PoMo kitsch long before it became popular in the West! The issue of the limited means itself is seldom foregrounded in education or practice.

It would not be an exaggeration to claim that these failures of the profession can be attributed to the educational agendas defined and initiated by Thomas Babington Macaulay's (in)famous "Minute on Education" of 1834,[8] which paved the way for the alienation we note between the profession and society at large. It also provided the broad rationale for colonial governance that India inherited at independence. As Rukmini Bhaya Nair points out, modern educational and administrative institutions that were established by the colonial government show up as "postcolonial poetics" in

> the attribute of "fatalism" among the mass poor; it construes itself as apathy among the upwardly mobile middle class; and finally stands revealed as bland and total unconcern among those who hold positions of awesome political and/or bureaucratic power. (1999, 8)[9]

"Postcolonial poetics," as Nair describes it, begins to explain why architects either are unable to come to grips with the deep structural problems of the profession or are indifferent to them. The profession was established to service the needs of the empire but is now expected to tackle the complex dynamics of contemporary Indian society. It seems to have given up on this effort. The educational system ensures that in architectural terms, we are clones of the West, appropriating their heroes, models, methods, and devices. Naturally, students find it easier and more satisfying to study in a Western university and then stay on, to find their niche in that society; it certainly takes less effort. The profession in India has been "genetically" encoded through Macaulay's Minute to service the needs of Western society and believe in the transformative potential of the globalization process initiated by the West by adopting Western techniques and technology to achieve the objectives of development. Contemporary education does not equip the student to consider alternatives, or critically mediate the complex issues involved in imparting their creations with an Indian identity.

Outside the schools, the opportunity to redress academic inadequacies are few and far between. Professional debate is desultory. There are few books on architectural issues that could help create awareness among practicing architects, and in any case, it is an acknowledged truism that "architects do not read." But the problem is compounded, because what little is available is invariably cast in what Edward Said has trenchantly described as the "Orientalist" mold.[10] In colonial times, this hierarchy was understandable in political terms; today the positional superiority of Western centers of learning becomes an issue because it perpetuates the hierarchy and, thereby, the Orientalist agenda. Consequently, the critical issues facing the profession in India, of who builds, and why and how they build, has not been polemicized — not by the West, whose gaze focuses on "high architecture," not by the profession in India, whose gaze mimics that of the West.

In the last fifty years, there have been very few attempts to understand — let alone analyze — the architectural scene in the country. If one discounts occasional articles of interest in popular and professional journals, one finds that the earliest attempts at a comprehensive analysis of contemporary architecture date only from the 1980s, when two exhibitions on the architecture of India were organized by the government. These exhibitions were undertaken not in response to professional demand but because the government commissioned them for extended publicity purposes as part of the Festival of India exhibitions in France, the former Soviet Union, and other countries.

Although these exhibitions were produced for *external* public relations, they served a similar domestic purpose as well. Policy makers in the early eighties were concerned at the negative image of India in the wake of political militancy, the collapse of the command economy, and the incipient intrusion of globalism in all aspects of national life. It was therefore thought that a feel-good exercise highlighting the cultural strengths of the country would invigorate flaccid nationalist ideals. These influential architectural exhibitions, along with their explanatory texts, must therefore be viewed in the light of the overall objectives of the festivals. Not surprisingly, one finds that their well-meaning authors were predisposed to identify and present the "good" face of the architecture of India. This is not to say that one would have expected them to show the "bad" face, but that their predisposition colluded with the Orientalist characterization of Indian architecture. In the process, it reinforced the need for external validation so precious to the self-esteem of Indian architects.

The first exhibition was put together in 1985 for the Festival of India in France and was curated by the Delhi architects Raj Rewal and Ram Sharma (1985). This exhibition surveyed the variety of historic precedents and models in one section (Raj Rewal), and the diversity of contemporary architectural practices in another (Ram Sharma and Malay Chatterjee). Tradition and modernity were counterpoised within the overarching framework of "Indian architecture" for consumption by an intended audience in the West: the wonder that was, on the one hand, and our "Indian" brand of modernism, on the other. All this was set off against the backdrop of a third section of the exhibition, on the works of Le Corbusier in India (curated by Jean-Louis Vèret). In hindsight, one wonders whether placing the great "rational" architect of the West on the same platform as the architecture of the "exotic" East did not strike the organizers of the exhibition as somewhat ironic, tailor-made to pander to the intellectual predilections of their French hosts. Then again, how could it? The bristling polemic issues were never recognized as such while the exhibition was being organized, and they continue to be beyond the ken or concern of the vast majority of Indian architects today.

The second exhibition was made for the Festival of India in the former Soviet Union in 1986, made up largely of the work of architects in Mumbai (formerly Bombay), and was curated by a team lead by Charles Correa.[11] It was titled "Vistara," and it probed the architectural elements and devices that constitute the "essence" of the architecture of India. The underlying agenda was to reformulate the history of architecture in India from an "Indianized" perspective. It presented the various epochs of Indian history as a succession of myths: the myth of the Vedic period, the myth of the Islamic period, and the myth of the modern period, presenting a historical narrative about Indian architecture that was neither progressivist nor historicist. There was a separate category for nonformal architecture devoted to housing and settlements.

The curators of the exhibition imbued their message with a grand vision of Indian architecture as the stuff of myths and legends. One must
recall that the search for an internal principle of unity to the past was a
recurrent theme with nationalist intellectuals smarting at colonial cultural slights. "Vistara" can be seen as the architectural stream of this intellectual tradition. The theme reflected the commonly held perception
among the architectural elite; backed by the hype of an international
event, it served a heady brew for the majority. It struck the jingoist chord
in a profession that was low in public and self-esteem, but as Ritu Bhatt
and Sonit Bafna pointed out in a critical appraisal, this was a familiar
trait:

> Its agenda of playing the cultural counterpart to the West are illustrated
> through images of symbols, myths and magic diagrams and conform rather
> well to the stereotypical Western "orientalist" mindset. On that front, the
> exhibition seems merely to have helped reinforce the stereotypical western
> understanding of the architecture of India which mediates between conti-
> nuity and change, tradition and modern, regional and international, and
> handicraft and technology, and so forth. (Bhatt and Bafna 1997, 51–52)

The messages projected by these exhibitions were influential within
the profession in India because for the first time and in a comprehensive manner, they enabled local architects to view the grand themes of
the architecture of the country. It also established the characteristics of
Indian-ness: the spatial morphology of the desert town of Jaisalmer,
the typology of the north Indian *haveli,* the strategy of low-rise high-
density housing development, and the geometry of the interlocking public spaces of Fatehpur Sikri; in short, the compelling architectural features of the hot and dry regions of the country. This architecture was
valorized to the exclusion of other equally authentic and compelling
categories available in the other regions of this climatically and geograph-
ically diverse country. While issues of tradition and modernity were being resolved in different ways in different parts of the country, their
manifestation in the Chandigarh-Delhi-Ahmedabad-Mumbai axis was
identified as being exemplary. After the exhibitions, anyone with the
slightest interest in the subject from outside India had only to walk in
to find a receptive audience for appreciative books on Indian architecture — and many did.

The exhibitions mined a rich lode of research material, and biographies on Indian architects and architecture followed these initiatives. It should be noted, however, that these books were written almost exclusively by foreign authors. Except for G. H. R. Tillotson's *The Tradition of Indian Architecture* (1989) — which in any case was not a biography — none broke new ground in the understanding of Indian architecture. Tillotson's book was an exception, and it focused on a willfully neglected area of architectural development — the colonial period.[12] In doing so, he challenged several perceptions shared by architects producing "high architecture," including the one that held the colonial period to be an unfortunate interregnum in the development of architecture in India. Tillotson provided a nuanced reading of the contentious colonial legacy and showed what postcolonial theorists in other disciplines have identified as the "ambivalent prehistory of postcolonialism" (Gandhi 1999, 4), in the development of contemporary Indian architecture. This is the actual complicity of the colonizer and the colonized, revealing the "transactive/transcultural aspects of colonialism" (125).

Tillotson's perspective could have paved the way for a revisionary postcolonial emphasis on a shared cultural experience, but few grasped its significance. He had convincingly demonstrated the contemporary relevance of at least two architectural formations that took place during the colonial period, one within the Princely States, and the other in British architecture in India. He argued that the methods and devices used to resolve architectural controversies in both cases were being played out in the development of contemporary architecture in India. He pointed out that the postcolonial architecture of India was no different — rhetorics notwithstanding — than its colonial antecedents. These arguments naturally went against the grain of local professional perceptions, which were in any case inflated by the grand themes of the exhibitions, and some even thought that his thesis was "fatuous" (Grover 1990).

The foreign authors who were commissioned by publishers to write biographies of Indian architects were doing so with an eye on the market abroad. They produced attractive monographs on important Indian architects, each stressing the Indian-ness in their works: Sherban Cantacuzino (1984) and Hussein-Uddin Khan (1987) on Charles Correa; William Curtis (1988) on Balakrishna Doshi; Brian Brace Taylor (1992) on Raj Rewal; and Stephen White (1993) on Joseph Allen Stein. Given the nature of the publications, it is not surprising that these monographs were hagiographic coffee-table items. The book on Stein, however, is an exception: it too is hagiographic but is noteworthy in its passionate advocacy of the architectural ideas of Stein, an American architect settled in India. It was clearly written with a U.S. constituency in mind, but White provides a remarkable analysis of Stein's works in India, shorn of the obligatory hype on Indian-ness that such biographies were expected to purvey.

The substance of my objection to these books is not that the authors or the intended markets were foreign but that the nature of scholarship they produced was suspect. Foreign authors writing on Indian subjects found themselves in the same conundrum as Indian architects addressing a foreign audience: both colluded in perpetuating the Orientalist project and failed to come to grips with the complex reality of architecture-in-the-making.

Other than the book by Tillotson and the monographs, there have been only two other serious attempts at critical writing on the contemporary architecture of India that merit consideration (I am discounting here several books that were merely catalogs, and the Raj-inspired nostalgia on Indian urbanism and architectural themes). The first was by Vikram Bhatt and Peter Scriver, *After the Masters: Contemporary Indian Architecture* (1990). It has become an influential text among students largely on account of the paucity of books on Indian architecture, but critically speaking, it did not accomplish anything more than to catalog fifty-two projects, once again primarily within the already identified "architectural belt," and under the rubric of four, by now tired categories: Roots and Modernity; Alternatives for a Developing India; Architecture and the Marketplace; and Emerging Architecture. Also familiar is the target audience:

> It is our conviction that [the assessment of Indian Architecture] would do much to renew the passion for the act and art of building with which the current Architecture of Europe and North America has lost touch in its present state of complexity and confusion. In more recent buildings of comparable scale and power, technical and economic limitations combine with a clear sense of purpose in the face of real needs to produce an architecture

that has managed to elude the malaise and impotence of much current design in the West. It would be a mistake to confine an appraisal of this architecture within an exclusive Third World perspective.... Our explanation
for the present lies in a more accurate appreciation of both historical and
temporal context global rather than an ethno-centric reality. (Bhatt and
Scriver 1990, 7–10)

What needs to be highlighted in this statement of intent is how explicitly these authors discount "ethnocentric reality" in their assessment
of the architecture of India: this is the characteristic of Orientalist historiography. Seen through the filter of postcolonial analysis, the historical
and positional superiority of the West is further perpetuated by adopting this perspective and becomes a matter of concern. But these colonial imperatives have escaped the attention of the discipline in India,
and consequently, no architect found *this* book "fatuous."

The second is a recent publication, *Architecture and Independence,* by
Jon Lang, Madhavi Desai, and Miki Desai (1997). It is perhaps the first
serious attempt at understanding the development of contemporary architecture in India and has had a muted impact because of the weighti-
ness of its contents. Going by the subject matter, it has all the ingredients
for success: depth of coverage, a focus on Indian identity, and a reas-
suring confirmation of conventional expectations about the architecture of India. Its great value, however, is in the encyclopedic survey of
the architecture of India it has undertaken to identify the general principles that describe and explain the use of buildings to convey specific
meaning, and to have illustrated them with the diversity of regional
examples. But once again, one notes the two recurrent characteristics
of writing on the architecture of India — first, the obsession with pan-
Indian categories and themes and, second, addressing their text to an
external audience. Explaining their method, the authors state, "These
decisions reflect our desire to present an argument which is intelligible
to a broad range of students and scholars across the world rather than
to write strictly for an Indian market" (Lang et al. 1997, xvii).

Who, then, will "write strictly for an Indian market"? And why
should that perspective not be of interest to "scholars across the world"?
Indeed, will a focus on the "Indian market" make a difference to the
way one conceptualizes architecture in India?

The problem inherent in the construction of pan-Indian themes of Indian architecture, both past and present, is the elision of the many regional narratives in the country. Attempting to "write strictly for an Indian market" may avoid this pernicious trap. The "regional" needs to be critically examined by scholars in India, in the manner that it has been examined in other disciplines. In literature, for example, recent scholarship has conducted thoughtful discussions on nationalist redeployments of the Indian past needing to assert antiquity, authenticity, and an unruptured continuity of Indian culture.[13] Such a discussion in the field of architecture may have an equally salutary effect on thinking architecture, and on the architects' propensity to pursue Orientalist agendas in their works.

Critics who present architects and the architecture of India (particularly to a foreign audience) almost invariably cast aside the "ethnocentric reality" and turn to Orientalist categories. This propensity is now being reinforced by the process of globalization. Although there is no doubt that a "deep structure" (Ameen 1997) unites the diverse forms of ethnocentric artistic expressions, it has not been plumbed by the gratuitous definitions of Indian architecture. Architects and critics in India need to view their past and their present as being continuously mediated in diverse ways by the many regional forces of contemporary development (Menon 1989).

What is also to be noted in the construction of the "Indian" is that it has only viewed a select few practitioners from the architectural belt of the country. Their works have been valorized as interpreting the national zeitgeist. The critic, East or West, has not felt compelled to explain their meaning, or the theoretical principles governing the works of these architects. For the architects themselves, perhaps, it is not necessary that they explain them, but to those who interpret, teach, write, and reflect on architecture, it is important that they do so. What has been attempted so far is in the nature of information and opinion, leaving the ground open for incisive criticism.

It is not my intent here to devalue the few efforts at writing about the contemporary architecture of India, but it is necessary to point out that there are historically rooted issues to consider in order to understand the manner in which these writers have gone about trying to define pan-Indian themes: this is the task for postcolonial analysis. The unifying rubric "Indian architecture" is rooted in colonial imperatives and does not do justice to this contemporary reality. In addition, it "precludes the possibility of seeing tradition as constantly in the making, as strenuously contested and redefined by different communities" (Niranjana et al. 1993). It also runs the danger of distorting facts, by either investing a regional architecture with characteristics it does not possess or co-opting more interpenetrative cultural formations. Neither culture nor architecture is coterminous with a national identity: they only share the same postcolonial political space. Fifty years after independence, architects in India need to absorb this insight, both in their practice and in thinking about architecture. However, here one needs to introduce a word of caution: among society at large, this insight is being hijacked by nativists and cultural chauvinists; the discipline needs to recognize that traditions need to be *transformed* to meet contemporary exigencies, not merely identified and reproduced as a foil against globalization.

Under the circumstances, the response in the profession should be not to evade the issues but to recognize that there is clearly a need to reconsider the prevalent strategy and methodology of architectural theorizing—from its focus on pan-Indian themes to examining more carefully regional, context-specific architectures of India.[14] From such a process of accumulating diverse empirical data from the regions, it may be possible to understand and define the synoptic essence of contemporary Indian architecture that has thus far eluded the critics.

Afterwords

The prognosis for attempting a revisionist strategy in thinking is not encouraging. After fifty years, it does not seem likely that architects in India, or their mentors in the West, will abandon their Orientalist predilections in the near future: their respective agendas dovetail with each other much too comfortably. The pedagogy in architectural schools in India has also ossified, and it does not appear to recognize the importance of postcolonial theorizing and questioning its colonial-rooted logocentricism. The colonial government introduced modernity into the country but in doing so privileged the imperatives of order and stability over change and the ability to reflexively interrogate the status quo. This colonial mind-set is now deeply rooted and has found fertile ground in a society where the deep structure has valorized obedience and conformity for millennia (Roland 1988). In this sense, the postcolonial present is, in Edward Said's words, a "uniquely punishing destiny."[15]

The ontological significance of modernism established through colonial imperatives has not been questioned by the mainstream of the profession. The intellectual consequence of this neglect has been that the West continues to construct the master narratives of development, leaving us to "Indianize" it to suit our circumstances. It is ironic that while the West is deconstructing the concept of the master narrative, in India we continue to abide by it. Nevertheless, although there does not appear to be any possibility of dismantling the text, there still remains, as Derrida once put it, the possibility "to reconstitute them in another way" (Merquior 1986, 222): this is the objective of my analysis in this conclusion.

To begin, it must be recognized that the ability to reconstitute the postcolonial present in another way is being severely constrained by the overwhelming forces of globalization. To the West, this hegemonic process (in business and academics) is an opportunity, the new frontier.[16] Their intention may be honorable and altruistic in academic terms, but in terms of how the process unfolds in the Third World, it is markedly destructive. It therefore needs to be taken into account in any discussion on the subject within the discipline of architecture. What becomes apparent is the unholy congruence between the characteristics of contemporary globalization and the incursion of the East India Company into India almost three hundred years ago. To illustrate my point, I quote from a letter I received from an Indian expatriate working in a large North American consultancy firm with extensive practices in China and Southeast Asia, initiating a dialogue to establish his firm's business interest in India. Having studied in India and being familiar with its endemic problems, he naturally recognized the strength of the opening gambit, offering access to sophisticated high-tech architectural and engineering services for developing "mega-building projects" in India. His initial survey, he wrote, had revealed that there were no "typically high-rise, steel-frame and glass shell/envelope" buildings in India. He observed:

I did not see a single building over 20 stories when I visited Delhi and Bombay in April 1997. I did not see cranes at construction sites. Chains of manual laborers appear to be doing the work that is done by construction machinery in the U.S. Cities like Bombay (where land prices are higher than downtown Chicago) need high rise buildings. . . . There is therefore a potential for creating self-contained satellite mini-cities near old cities. . . . There has to be a highway system connecting the old and new cities and to the airport. This has to be worked out with politicians and law enforcement agencies since one of the problems will be control over access to such areas. You cannot have slums being set up next to such buildings. I think foreign investors will expect this. . . . Modern high-rise, high-tech buildings need specialized and trained people . . . [so his firm] must get involved in developing trained personnel in all aspects of design, construction and operation.

How does one even begin to explain to such well-wishers that the solution they offer will cause as much anxiety as the problem? These so-called solutions address the problem of paucity of work in North American architectural offices, *not* the need for high-rise buildings in India. Their objective is primarily to shore up their bottom line by servicing the needs of foreign personnel and multinational companies now in India to manage the West's globalization projects. The real problems of the country escape them. They have only a tangential interest in the condition of architecture or the needs of local inhabitants. The tragedy is compounded by the clearly unethical values that guide these ventures in the Third World, something that would never be considered back home. Thus my expatriate colleague went on to propose the need to establish offices in India and affiliate local commercial and industrial conglomerates who are

familiar with Indian conditions to deal with corruption and bureaucracy . . . [and] obtain guarantees and assurances from Central and State Governments in India to protect Indian and foreign investments. Assurances are required to prevent slums on the property and to prevent access to and misuse of the complex. For example, there may have to be admission charges to shopping malls to prevent homeless people from living or squatting on the premises.

That offer is straight from the horse's mouth. I have quoted at length to give the authentic flavor of the process of architectural globalization in practice. Nevertheless, this process is irresistible. Within two years of that letter there was ample evidence that the visions contained in that offer — sleek, glass-enveloped office buildings — were in common sight, each with its own system of utilities and services (since the provision of these services by the local authorities is usually inadequate and unreliable), expressways to airports, and new luxurious, gated residential enclaves (to avoid slums and other unaesthetic local sights and experiences). It is with these developments in mind that I noted that the prognosis for a revisionist architectural strategy is not encouraging.

How, then, can these forces be contested or "reconstituted another way"? For one, there cannot be a common strategy for the entire country. The conditions are too diverse, and in addition each region is undergoing differential structural changes and population shifts. A variety of hybrid cultural formations are developing, each with different needs and priorities. For another, whatever policies emerge, they will have to address three broad areas of concern that are ignored in the process of globalization: first, issues relating to sustainability in both the ecological and human systems in conditions of initial poverty and scarcity of resources; second, the conservation of the built and natural heritage, both of which are degrading at an alarming rate; and third, the issue of how to deal with emerging technologies and their implications for architectural design and education. The last will determine whether the emerging technologies will be inimical or not to the general well-being of society.

Any policy to reconstitute architectural agency in a country like India must also take into account the endemic rural-urban divide. Even as we attempt to de-center the postcolonial discussion from the metropolis to the "site," the new sites are invariably the metropolises of the Third World. As Gayatri Spivak pointed out:

> Let us not artificially exclude the rural from Indian urbanism: let us look at them as the locus of hard core economic resistance, where the binary opposition between economy and culture is broken down every day. Where initiatives for local self-government immediately confront the global . . . that rural is the new dynamic front against exploitative globalization. (1997, 13)

The position that local architects take on such issues is clearly divided. Some have reason to be wary, but others welcome the changes brought about by globalization — for equally good reasons. In any event, there will always be a strong internal desire to access the goods and services offered by global trade: this is inevitable in a webbed world. There is a First World in every Third World (and indeed a Third World in every First, but that raises different disciplinary problems). It is too late to militate against international exchange, whatever one's reasons, because we are all acutely aware of the dangers of isolationist policies. What is necessary is to mitigate the impact. Paul Ricoeur, in his 1961 essay *Universal Civilization and National Cultures,* distinguished between civilization and culture and equated universal civilization with universal technology, which he saw as being inseparable from the long-term liberative aims of modernization, and defined national cultures as the historically evolved genius of any particular society that was under threat in the process of modernization. He pointed out that no developing country is able to forgo the benefits of universal civilization for long; however, he questioned the necessity of jettisoning the old cultural past to get on the road to modernizations.

The problem with Ricoeur's thesis is that it puts the pressure to resist the universalization of culture on the "victims" of universal civilization. The desperate need to modernize and obtain the benefits of economic development gives primacy to the role of foreign capital and multinational corporations in state policy. This is the obverse of globalization. When it takes place in the era of scaling down the role of the state in the name of liberalization and efficiency, the interests of the broad mass of people are compromised.[17] This follows the trickle-down theory in economics and effectively blocks progress toward economic — or architectural — self-reliance. This is already a part of the Indian experience of the last decade and is dragging the country into neocolonial dependency. The letter I received from my expatriate colleague illustrates the process at work in architectural matters. This is the logic of "development" typically perpetrated on the Third World by the West. Rather than leave the victims to their own devices, I suggest that it is necessary to work *together* toward a mutually empowering agenda for architecture, one that would encourage plurality while avoiding the propensity for introducing neocolonialism as a model for globalization or the exchange of ideas. Others in the West have explored this concept, but I present here a view from the bottom up, as it were.

Colonialism from my point of view is not a thing of the past but an ever present reality. Gunboat diplomacy may be dead (although in this unipolar world even that proposition may require reconsideration), but equally unrelenting forces of co-option are at work in the global marketplace. These forces of domination and subordination emanate from, and are perpetuated by, multinational corporate organizations and educational institutions, both East and West. We must begin to see the connection between knowledge and politics by conceiving architecture as "willed human work—not mere unconditioned ratiocination" (Said 1979, 15). Is it possible to develop a new architectural paradigm for the third millennium by applying the imperatives of "willed human work"?

I believe that clues to developing such a new paradigm can be found in other disciplines, in particular the women's and environmental movements. Both movements have formed alliances at the international, national, and local levels without losing sight of the specific realities of domination. Both movements have radically altered the way the world is viewed, and I believe for the better, in general and in the particular. I also believe that it is possible—and increasingly necessary—to conduct discussions about architecture with a vision similar to those that guided the women's and environmental movements in the recent past.

Architecture in the West, at least since the advent of modernism, has focused on the avant-garde. The pursuit of the avant-garde dovetails with the imperatives of consumerism, first within the boundaries of a local market, and later in the global market. Thinking architecture in a world of growing "permissiveness and speed" (Meiss 1995) forces architects to retreat in a laissez-faire acceptance of conditions as they are. Few question its implications either for themselves or for others, or the pernicious proclivity to cast the West in the universal mode. Few in the West need to. This must be resisted both from within and from without. To begin with, one can learn lessons from the experience of the Third World, currently at the periphery of the Western field of vision. The periphery needs to be brought into focus in the manner that Kenneth Frampton has attempted in formulating his concept of Critical Regionalism (Frampton 1992). Not that I am holding Frampton out as an ideal, but he at least engages with the issues with which I am concerned.

What can the West learn from the Third World? For one, how to deal with deprivation and scarcity. The resources of this planet are finite, and if the Third World were to emulate the First (as is being suggested by multinational business interests through the process of globalization) and adopt architectural models promoted by architects addressing their business interest, then the consequences would be disastrous. It is better by far that the best practices in the Third World become more universalized, not only in other parts of the Third World, as is being suggested by international aid agencies, but in the First World as well. For another, some of the finest cultural resources of the world exist in the Third World as *living* traditions. Ironically, this situation exists because these countries are still "underdeveloped," but traditional crafts and ways of life are still in practice: this is an asset, not a liability as it is made out by the managers of global development. The nations of the First World have lost much of theirs through industrialization and wars, and a similar prospect confronts the Third World. Again, some of the finest examples of conservation-oriented development practices exist in the Third World: one has only to see the documentation and research produced by the Aga Khan Foundation to appreciate the strength in this proposition. Suffice it to say that equitable exchange and genuine dialogue are possible and can become a constructive agenda for the discipline of architecture in the third millennium. These and other questions should find their way into the agenda of education in India if we view architectural education as a discipline and not merely as vocational training. But they are equally relevant to educational institutions in the West, particularly the United States, where there is an old and cherished tradition of academic innovation.[18]

I earlier mentioned the possibility of providing legitimate means of organizing resistance to neocolonialism through a de-centered reading of Indian architecture. While keeping this objective in mind, two kinds of resistance must be distinguished. The first stems from a fear of change assaulting us from the outside. Here the attempt is to safeguard ingrained beliefs and practices by invoking the sanctity and inviolability of local traditions. Tradition is used as a shield against many things that cannot and ought not to be resisted. The second is more discriminating: it does not accept change unconditionally but attempts to negotiate its consequences to keep it in consonance with what exists or was received from the past. Thinking in the discipline of architecture must be directed toward the latter kind of resistance.

It has been said that one must first "change the imaginary in order to be able to act on the real" (Spivak 1987, 145). This process must be viewed as a shared agenda in the discipline of architecture. Changing the imaginary requires the construction of an appropriate model to define Indian identity, one that is relevant to the times; acting on the real requires the will to act on this new understanding in order to effect change. A de-centered view of the profession brings into focus many acts of resistance and attempts "to reconstitute them another way." These are the models we should develop.

What I have said so far is based on my experience teaching and pursuing a professional practice in India, but similar concerns have been expressed elsewhere by others in other cultures. Everywhere, and particularly in the Third World, the range of architectural knowledge is expanded through pressures arising from the tendency to globalization, the imposition of Western values, and the pressing need for quick solutions. This process interacts with traditional cultures, local identity, and community. The disciplinary concern that emerges under the circumstances is the importance of reconstituting the new knowledge within the historical and development framework of particular architectural cultures and heritages. Although architectural knowledge contributes to a universal discipline, its applications must be governed by local and regional specificities: local needs demand local solutions.[19]

We have seen that the recurrent problem with earlier models used to define "Indian" have privileged the past, implying, axiomatically, that the present and the future are another's terrain. We have also seen that it is not possible to sustain such definitions, as they invariably fall apart when confronted by the hybrid nature of globalization. The aspiration to retain the local in the global context persists. In development studies, for example, it has been suggested that this could be accomplished by telescoping global and local to make a blend — "glocal," or the process noun, "glocalization" (Teymur 1992, 39–48). This is taking place, often in an unself-conscious manner in various parts of the country, but it does not receive the attention it deserves in the din created by the votaries of Indian identity. These are the models to which I am referring to reconstitute the architectural paradigm. Postcolonial theorists have identified and valorized this process of hybrid cultural formations (Bhabha 1994), but their insights have not influenced architectural criticism.

Below the clouds enveloping the Olympian heights of the metropolitan discourse on Indian identity, a different architectural scene is unfolding. The view from the ground shows a profession in great ferment. A half century after independence, it is apparent that the rationale for imbuing architecture with an Indian identity is wearing thin; only a few among the older generation of architects tread that turf. My paper has tried to deal with their predicament. There is evidence of both complicity and resistance to the forces of globalization that are set to transform the country. Traditional architectural practices have not, in fact, been wiped out, in spite of two centuries of concerted modernization.[20] On the one hand there is a resurgence of interest in the *vastu shastras*,[21] the ancient treatises on (Hindu) architecture, and on the other, greater reliance on vernacular architectural practices rendered invisible by the colonial gaze. The persistence of these traditional practices provides the rationale for the de-centered postcolonial gaze and makes visible — and possible — the many small and big acts of resistance that are beginning to characterize the contemporary architecture of India (Bhatia 1991). The interstices between the imperatives of the architectural program and praxis, both in academics and in the field, are beginning to be occupied by activists who are rewriting the architectural narrative.[22] Even the government is in on the act: the Housing and Urban Development Corporation has set up a network of Building Centers across the country to encourage local vernacular building practices as a strategy to house the millions.

Why, then, my pessimism regarding the prognosis for change? Herein lies the paradox: the uniqueness of the postcolonial circumstance prevailing in India is that the modernization project is at the cusp: it is still possible to teach the West a lesson or two in the discipline of architecture in the process of defining local, regional, and national architectural identity. However, the same imperatives are the cause for the violence of cultural regionalism and religious nationalism that has made it difficult to utter anything constructive about indigenous architectural identity. This is one cause for pessimism. But it is still possible in India to take the road less traveled — and here and there, that is making a difference. Diverse forms of architecture are blossoming. As Ranajit Guha pointed out in the debate over what is, or is not, an appropriate or "proper" mode of analysis of the colonial history of India: "There is no one way of investigating this problematic. Let a hundred flowers bloom and we don't mind even the weeds" (Moore-Gilbert 1997, 203). This inclusive view describes the postcolonial architectural scene in India. But who — in the East or West — is listening? This is the other cause for pessimism.

Notes

1. See, for example, Aijaz Ahmad. In the introduction to *Theory: Classes, Nations, Literatures,* Ahmad makes the point that Western cultural criticism in general has become detached from any concrete connection with popular political struggle, and the material forms of activism are replaced by a textual engagement that sees *"reading* as the appropriate form of politics" (1992, 3).

2. Consider Article 301 and Super 301 of the General Agreement on Trade and Tariff worked out by the World Trade Organization to bring noncooperative nations into the fold.

3. See Tillotson's *The Traditions of Indian Architecture* (1989). This is an important book in the genre of "constructing the knowledge" of Indian architecture. Almost 80 percent of the books listed in its bibliography are by foreign authors and sources.

4. See Ehrenreich and English's *Complaints and Disorders: The Sexual Politics of Sickness* (1973). The authors analyze the biomedical rationale, developed primarily by male doctors, used to justify wholesale gender discrimination and assert the need for a new substance and style of medical practice as it relates to women.

5. See, for example, Kate Nesbitt's *Theorizing a New Agenda for Architecture: An Anthology of Architectural Theory, 1965–1995* (1996). *All* contributions to this anthology focus on the architecture and architectural writing in the United States and Europe. One cannot fail to notice the shift in architectural discourse from the production of architecture to the production of discourses about architecture. The contribution by Kenneth Frampton entitled "Prospects for a Critical Regionalism" (468–82) is the only one that recognizes the potential of another architectural culture, another politics in place creation. William McDonough, in "Design, Ecology, Ethics, and the Making of Things" (400–407), writes about "dealing equitably (not imperialistically) with our immediate neighbours and with Third World countries." There is no other evidence of the new agenda for architecture recognizing the non-Eurocentric and non-American perspective brought into focus by globalization or the role of architecture in global hegemonic cultural formations.

6. See "Introduction" (1–3) and "Who Is an Indian?" (150–95) in Khilnani 1997.

7. See "Independence and Dependence" (Tillotson 1989, 127–47).

8. Thomas Babington Macaulay was a powerful member of the Supreme Council of India from 1834 to 1838 and wrote the "Minute on Education" for the

benefit of the Committee on Public Instruction, of which he was president. This is the seed from which the modern educational system in India has grown. The contempt that Macaulay showed for Indian civilization shaped British educational policy, and in consequence, Indian attitudes toward Indian civilization. Macaulay's declared aim was to raise "a class of persons, Indian in blood and color, but English in taste, in opinions, in morals and in intellect." One is still trying to come to terms with this legacy. See Tillotson 1989, 29–33.

9. "Postcoloniality and the Matrix of Indifference" (Nair 1999, 8) will be extracted in the forthcoming publication *Lying on the Postcolonial Couch: The Sacralization of Bureaucratic Space and the Poetics of Indifference*.

10. According to Said (1979), Western scholars "discovered" and explained the Orient in terms that were familiar to the West. In this manner, the East was appropriated at the intellectual level as it was simultaneously being appropriated politically. Contemporary scholars, both East and West, who perpetuate this tradition are termed "orientalist."

11. A brochure was produced for the exhibition but is now not easily accessible. An article briefly explained the exhibition in the *Journal of the Indian Institute of Architects* 51, no. 4 (October–December 1986): 26–33.

12. To understand the preoccupations with "roots" in contemporary Indian architecture, see Balkrishna Doshi, "Social Institutions and Sense of Place" (13–24), and Raj Rewal, "The Use of Traditions in Architecture and Urban Form" (52–63), in Ameen 1997.

13. See introduction to *Women Writing in India: 600 B.C. to Present* (Tharu and Lalitha 1991) for discussion on nationalist redeployment of the Indian past.

14. I attempted this from 1997 to 1998 at the TVB School of Habitat Studies, New Delhi, by undertaking a critical study, "Architecture of Delhi from 1947–1997." Exhibition material was produced but left incomplete for lack of funds. However, a CD-ROM of the exhibition material is available for reference. Several insights in this paper owe their genesis to that study project.

15. See *Orientalism*. Said (1979, 27) was of course referring to the web of racism, cultural stereotypes, political imperialism, and dehumanizing ideology surrounding the Palestinian.

16. See, for example, *Losing Control? Sovereignty in an Age of Globalization* (Sassen 1996) and *Globalization and Its Discontents* (Sassen 1998).

17. See, for example, *Spectres of Capitalism: A Critique of Current Intellectual Fashions* (Amin 1998). Amin draws attention to the aspirations of the have-nots of the post–Cold War era and the process of globalization.

18. See, for example, *Open the Social Sciences: Report of the Gulbenkian Commission on Restructuring of the Social Sciences*. In its conclusion, the report says: "The United States has had a long history of structural experimentions in the university systems — the invention of graduate schools in the late nineteenth century... the invention of the systems of free electives by students... the invention of social science research councils after the First World War, the invention of 'core

234 — A. G. Krishna Menon

course' requirements...invention of area studies...perhaps the U.S. social science community can once again come up with imaginative solutions to the very real organizational problems we have been describing" (Wallerstein [1996] 1997, 99–100).

19. See William O'Reilly 1999, Proceedings of the Fifth Colloquium in Architecture and Behaviour held at Monte Verita, Ascona, 6–8 April 1998 in the theme "Architectural Knowledge and Cultural Diversity." These colloquiums are an offshoot of the now defunct journal *Architecture et Comportement/Architecture and Behaviour,* published by the Federal Institute of Technology, Lausanne. The journal during its fifteen years of existence from 1981 focused on cultural diversity as expressed by building users and design. As a challenge for function and form, the journal valorized the particular against the universal.

20. The Vastu-Shilpa Foundation was set up by Balkrishna Doshi in 1978 in Ahmedabad with the aim to initiate research, studies, and investigations relevant to the study and practice of architecture and planning in the Indian context. Their major emphasis has been on the importance of relationship between tradition, culture, and lifestyle of people with architecture and planning They have accumulated a large corpus of publications and research data on the living habitat that persists in India.

21. See, for example, *The Penguin Guide to Vaastu* (Amin 1998). Also, Sthapati, *The Journal on Traditional Indian Architecture,* published by the Vastuvidyapratisthanam, 1/3780 Amulyam, Bilathikulam, Calicut, Kerala 673006, India.

22. See note 14. The exhibition identified the works of several younger architects working and teaching in Delhi. Their works are rooted in three broad disciplinary concerns, which are (1) relevance and use of vernacular architectural practices, (2) reducing the cost of buildings through innovative technology and alternate building materials, and (3) climate as the major determinant of architecture. Overall, the study revealed little evidence of a self-conscious search for "Indian" identity.

11
Interdisciplinary Visions of Architectural Education: The Perspectives of Faculty Women

Linda N. Groat and Sherry Ahrentzen

Architects frequently take great pride in pointing to architecture as the most interdisciplinary of professional pursuits. Indeed, for many, one of the great attractions of the field is its inherently interdisciplinary quality, the necessity of integrating widely divergent concerns—aesthetic choices, social implications, the highly technical issues of structural and mechanical calculations, as well as matters treated in other professional fields such as interior design and landscape architecture. In this respect, architecture might be characterized as "inherently interdisciplinary," in the way that others have characterized academic fields such as geography, or professional fields such as public health (J. Klein 1990).

Paradoxically, however, architecture programs within the academy are often criticized for their highly insular character (e.g., E. Boyer and Mitgang 1996). Serious intellectual dialogue with allied fields is all too often constrained and inhibited. One significant reason may be the studio system of architectural education as it is presently constituted at most schools (Ahrentzen and Groat 1992). Although not integral to the studio pedagogy per se, in common practice both students and faculty are frequently enveloped in this all-consuming environment. At most schools, not only do studios meet at least three full afternoons, but the design work of the studio commonly takes place in evenings, on weekends, and especially during the round-the-clock marathons just before deadlines, commonly referred to as the "charrette." Indeed, many students express concern about having to adopt a social and academic schedule that separates them from family, friends, and the life of the larger university (Groat and Ahrentzen 1996).

Now in the face of massive cultural, technological, and economic changes, the profession of architecture may actually be forced to reconceptualize and transform itself. To accomplish this, architectural education will have to be at the forefront of such a transformation, and this, we believe, will necessitate adopting a more *fundamentally* interdisciplinary mode.

It is the thesis of this chapter that faculty women in architecture are in a special position to advance the agenda of an interdisciplinary perspective of the field. To date, women in architectural education have typically been viewed as less influential than even the modest demographic statistics suggest, a consequence of faculty women's apparent tendency to teach either in speciality areas outside the studio setting or in beginning — meaning "less professionally relevant" — design classes (Landecker 1991). Yet, as in other male-dominated fields such as science and engineering, the argument can be made that creative advances in the field may depend on the substantive contributions of nontraditional academics who can challenge and explore the boundaries of the discipline (e.g., Jenkins 1995; Duderstadt 1995). Indeed, some have even taken this argument a step further to claim that the most significant work in a field can be uncovered "simply by walking along its boundaries" (Dogan and Pahre 1990, 1).

Evidence to support this argument as it pertains to the discipline of architecture is drawn from the authors' ongoing research on women in architectural education and primarily from the analysis of in-depth interviews with a sample of forty faculty women in architecture.[1] Before advancing the details of this argument, however, it is important to elaborate the current state of architecture, in general, and women's role in architectural education, in particular.

The Present and Future in Architectural Education

Architectural education finds itself challenged to rethink its basic premises as a result of the confluence of at least two trends: (1) fundamental changes within the architectural profession, especially in terms of its role in the sociocultural context, and (2) challenges to existing assumptions about the university's role in society.

With respect to the first point, any number of authors have recently called for reassessments of the fundamental principles of the profession. For example, in a recent lead article in *Progressive Architecture,* editor Thomas Fisher posed the question "Can This Profession Be Saved?" (T. Fisher 1994). He then identified three key trends that threaten the traditional base of architectural practice: an eroding client base; the loss of professional turf to allied fields such as interior design, construction management, and engineering; and the waning of professionalism in general. Other authors (e.g., Groat 1993b) have identified broader trends that have affected the role of traditionally organized architectural firms, including the flattening of management pyramids, the rise of an electronically based rather than a place-based economy, and the role of knowledge workers in the global economy.

These significant changes are also forcing the formal reassessment of the nature of professional education in architecture. In the United States, the American Institute of Architects (AIA) and the Association of Collegiate Schools of Architecture (ACSA) joined with the accrediting and registration boards and the student associations to sponsor a major study of architectural education and practice; this study was conducted by the Carnegie Foundation, and its report was released in May 1996 (E. Boyer and Mitgang). The Carnegie study sought to generate informed conversation among interested parties (rather than to advocate prescriptive modifications), a goal that seems to have been achieved through commentaries in architectural media and through various conferences and meetings. Meanwhile in Britain, the architectural profession barely survived the effort to strip it of its legal exclusivity, that is, its status as a licensed profession. In response to such challenges, the Royal Institute of British Architects (1993) recently published its *Strategic Study of the Profession,* which includes a segment titled "Expectation versus Reality in Architectural Education." Clearly, although many or most architecture schools in this country have not yet attempted a fundamental transformation, there will be significant changes in the near future.

Second, and more briefly, spiraling tuition costs, declining state budgets, and the resulting public outcry demonstrate that many universities are themselves struggling to reinvent their institutional premises and frameworks. For example, universities increasingly feel the need to justify the public's investment by demonstrating that the faculty's service and research output yields significant benefits to the public. In this regard, many architecture programs can gain stature from highlighting outreach activities that influence the local built environment for the better.

Even more fundamentally, however, many critics both in and beyond academia now question the viability of the disciplinary framework of our current university system. As one noted academic leader has put it: "The 'interdisciplinary moment' is not a fad, but a fundamental and long-term restructuring of the nature of scholarly activity" (Duderstadt 1995, 5). To the extent that architecture programs choose to remain disconnected from allied disciplines, their role in the university is likely to be called into question. Moreover, the combination of both the diminished role for traditional architectural practice and the decline in enrollment base (experienced by at least some schools) suggests that architecture schools will be in an increasingly weak position in many university contexts. In such an environment, architecture programs will have to envision a compelling mission beyond mere preparatory training for a traditional and increasingly constrained professional role.

Given these trends, architectural education *must* reconsider its basic premises, and this includes one of its most hallowed traditions: the design-as-centerpoint model of architectural education (Ahrentzen and Groat 1992). Typically, that model assumes that the design activity is central and other forms of knowledge dissemination (i.e., the lectures and seminars that usually provide input from the related disciplines) simply provide a support structure for that centerpoint. In practical and operational terms, the centrality of design studio is reinforced by the intensive time commitment it entails for both students and faculty. Although this pedagogical format is often praised for being the fulcrum of "the discovery, application, and integration of knowledge," many architectural programs have not made the most of its potential (E. Boyer and Mitgang 1996). Not least, when design is defined in very narrow terms, the intellectual context for that design activity (as represented

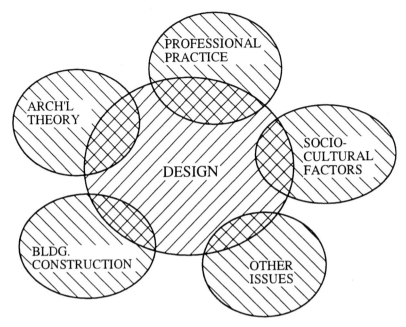

Figure 11.1. The design-as-centerpoint model of architectural education.

by either nonstudio architecture coursework or by courses in other disciplines) is often relegated to marginal status.[2]

The Status of Women in Architecture

Over the last twenty-five years, women have made significant inroads into what has traditionally been a male-dominated profession. As of the 1994 to 1995 academic year, women constituted roughly 31 percent of the enrollment at accredited architecture schools (E. Boyer and Mitgang 1996, 98), almost 20 percent of the professional ranks in architecture (U.S. Department of Commerce 1996), yet still only approximately 10 percent of the membership of the AIA (E. Boyer and Mitgang 1996, 98). Although this is clearly an advance over earlier years, these figures are disappointing when compared to the statistics for other previously male fields such as computer science, pharmacology, accounting, and medicine (Ahrentzen and Groat 1992).

In architectural education, specifically, women have made steady but slow progress in increasing their numbers. During the 1995 to 1996 academic year, women constituted only 19.4 percent of all architecture faculty, an increase of approximately 3 percent over the 1991 to 1992 academic year. Unfortunately, tenured women faculty represented only 3.5 percent of the total faculty, whereas tenured male faculty constituted 28.1 percent of the total faculty. Whereas these figures are in and of themselves disappointing, of more significant concern is the extent to which the roles of faculty women are seen to be marginal, particularly when viewed through the lens of the design-as-centerpoint model. Reflecting this perspective is a recent article in the professional magazine *Architecture* (Landecker 1991) that implicitly accepts the design-as-centerpoint model. Indeed, the article notes that most tenured women faculty teach history, planning, or social factors rather than design; and when they do teach design, they are most likely to teach first-year studios, which many departments view as support for the "real" work of upper-level studios. In other words, women faculty are seen as peripheral to the central task of advanced studio teaching.

In sharp contrast to this perspective, we believe that the "marginal" roles traditionally assumed by women faculty may actually be fundamental to the inevitable transformation of architectural education. As

Table 11.1. A Comparison of Men and Women Faculty's
Presence in Architectural Education

	1991–92	%	1995–96	%
All Faculty				
Total Women	568	16.4%	767	19.4%
Total Men	2888	83.6%	3177	80.6%
Total	3456	100%	3944	100%
Tenured Faculty				
Tenured Women	91	7.6%	137	10.9%
Tenured Men	1101	92.4%	1110	89.1%
Total Tenured	1192	100%	1247	100%
Tenured as % of Total Faculty				
Tenured Women		2.6%		3.5%
Tenured Men		31.8%		28.1%

Note: Data derived from statistics published in the newsletter of the Association of Collegiate Schools of Architecture, November 1996. Reprinted by permission from the *ACSA News*, published by the Association of Collegiate Schools of Architecture.

we mentioned earlier, many noted scholars have observed that women's contributions in a variety of male-dominated fields have not only challenged established orthodoxies but enlarged the subtantive domain of inquiry in creative and fundamental ways (e.g., Jenkins 1995; Duderstadt 1995). And in a more explicitly political vein, the scholar bell hooks notes that "marginality" does not simply represent distance from the powerful center; marginality is an enabling "site of radical possibility, a space for resistance" (hooks 1990). In the case of architectural education, women faculty may be deprived of input and influence, but in very important ways, this distancing from the center enables them not only to see the inherent contradictions and inequities at the center but also to claim the "space" from which important alternatives may be launched.

We are arguing that architecture, as a field, is indeed in such a moment when transformation and radical possibility are required. We do *not,* however, mean to suggest that it is only women faculty who would play such a role; rather, we suggest that the particular perspectives on the scope and content of architectural education that we found to be common among many faculty women will necessarily be important for all who wish to transform the discipline. This means that women faculty, joined by men, could and should play pivotal roles in such a transformation.

To substantiate this argument, we will draw extensively from research on women in architectural education that we have been conducting for several years, particularly our study of faculty women. This research was based on intensive interviews with approximately forty faculty women in architecture and entailed three broad themes: attractions to architecture as a career, career experiences, and visions of architectural education. Our goal was to maximize the variety and range of perspectives rather than to reflect the proportion of women with such characteristics in the total faculty population. For this reason, our sample of faculty women was a *stratified* rather than *random* sample. Thus the faculty women were selected for interviews based on a combination of criteria, including level of appointment, teaching area, level of perceived equity at their institution (derived from a previous survey), and the number of faculty women in the department. As a consequence, our sample is heavily weighted to tenured women, who constitute 55 percent of the sample but only 18 percent of all faculty women. Yet because these are precisely the women who are most likely to exert influence within the academy, their perspectives merit serious consideration.

Women at the Crossroads: Reconceptualizing the Domain of Architecture

There are at least four specific ways in which the perspectives of faculty women might transform architecture into a more truly interdisciplinary endeavor. Each facet of transformation will be discussed in terms of recommendations from the Carnegie report, specifically those concerning the scope and content of the curriculum (E. Boyer and Mitgang 1996).[3] Significantly, although the major points of our argument were developed well before the Carnegie report was released,[4] we concluded, once the report was published, that the significance of our argument could be illuminated more fully by demonstrating the correspondence between our analyses of the faculty women's perspectives and the Carnegie report's recommendations. To demonstrate how each point of transformation actually reflects the faculty women's perspectives, extensive commentaries and analyses will be drawn from the in-depth interviews we conducted.[5]

Equally important, we must emphasize that the reasons many faculty women have been drawn to an interdisciplinary perspective are complex and varied. Not least, many of the women have encountered significant constraints at various points in their careers, in the form of prejudicial advising, hiring practices, teaching assignments, and so on.[6] In other words, it is the social construction of the field, rather than an innate disposition of women to either interdisciplinary work or any particular specialism, that is primarily implicated here (Ahrentzen 1996). As we discuss each point of transformation, then, we will also indicate some of the forces that seem to draw women to these interdisciplinary roles.

Championing the Ideals of a Liberal Education

One of the most commonly stated claims about architectural education is that it represents, in and of itself, a model for "liberal" education. This argument is based in large measure on the assumption that, because architecture is inherently interdisciplinary—touching as it does on a broad range of technical, social, and artistic issues—it naturally incorporates the disciplinary range that constitutes a liberal education.[7]

These disciplines are frequently engaged in a very limited manner, however, framed primarily by their application or relevance to architecture. Such an instrumental view of other disciplines runs counter to the very principles of a liberal education. The political philospher Michael Oakeshott, one of the most quoted authorities on the subject, has characterized liberal education as an "adventure in human understanding" that is "liberated from the distracting business of satisfying contingent wants" (Fuller 1989, 27–28).

Significantly, architecture's claim to being a model of liberal education is substantially challenged by the Carnegie report. Although the Carnegie authors do acknowledge the multiple ways in which architectural programs support the goals of a liberal education (e.g., through foreign studies programs), they also unequivocally point out the limits to such a claim: "Visiting a variety of architecture programs, we found questionable the oft-stated claim that architecture education is, per se, a 'liberal education.' One of the most sobering moments of our campus visits occurred when we asked a fourth-year student to describe the school's humanities courses. He replied: 'What are humanities?'" (E. Boyer and Mitgang 1996, 78). Moreover, as they point out, despite accreditation criteria requiring at least 20 percent of a professional degree program to be allocated to liberal studies, many architecture programs do not in fact meet either the spirit or the letter of these standards.

As many architects and educators recognize, however, the profession of architecture will not remain vital unless future architects can frame the design problems they encounter in terms that go well beyond the confines of their own field (E. Boyer and Mitgang 1996, 77). This necessitates an education that encourages making connections at both a profound level (i.e., understanding ethical choices in the broadest terms possible) and a much more practical level (i.e., being able to communicate orally and in written form with both colleagues and laypeople).

Interestingly, we found in our interviews of faculty women in architecture that their own educational backgrounds predispose many of them to emphasize the value of a liberal education and, more importantly, to use this foundation to make connections between architecture and many other disciplines. At the most basic level, the demographic statistics on the women we interviewed reveal that nearly half of them (eighteen out of forty) had received a bachelor's degree in another discipline. In part, this may reflect a common pattern in the career trajectories of women who came of age prior to the time when women entered architectural schools in dramatically increased numbers. As a survey conducted by *Progressive Architecture* magazine indicated, a substantially larger proportion of women architects — as compared to men — entered the field *after* they had either begun or finished college (T. Fisher 1987).

At a more substantive level, when asked about what they considered to be the most positive or negative aspects of architectural education, many women commented on architecture's relation to a "liberal" education. To be sure, a few of our interviewees did argue that architectural education, in and of itself, did constitute a liberal education. As one adjunct studio instructor stated: "Architecture is almost the supreme version of a liberal arts education . . . because it does an incredible job of training people in terms of thinking things through."

Far more common, however, was the women's sense of frustration that most required architectural curricula do not incorporate the liberal arts in a serious way. As the Carnegie report noted, some programs mandate such tightly packed course schedules that they virtually preclude the possibility of students seriously engaging other disciplines. One faculty member at a state institution in the Midwest put it this way: "The students that . . . come in at the age of 18 [get] into a curriculum that's very structured, [and they] don't really get a lot of history, a lot of English, or a lot of other subjects outside of the field. . . . I think that can be very restrictive."

But the most consistent and most serious concern that emerges from the women's commentaries is that sense that the pedagogical milieu of their programs — despite course requirements to the contrary — is unsupportive, even antithetical, to the values of a liberal education. This feeling seems to result from faculty women's belief that liberal education is not simply learning about a few other subject areas but rather entails both critical thinking and a deeper, more profound level of discourse. For example, one junior faculty woman at a small, private program put it this way:

> I believe in some kind of a liberal education basis, . . . but I don't really see that happening. I don't really see much understanding of what liberal education is and what it could contribute to a program. I hear lip service to it and I think there are very good intentions, but I'm not sure it's really understood what it's about.

A tenured respondent in an administrative position at her school was considerably more blunt in her assessment of some of her colleagues' attitudes:

> They expect [students] to know some things about science and the humanities, but they don't want to deal with that or integrate it into the educational process. . . . they're very narrow. . . . Since the time I was first involved in architectural education [in the late 1960s], . . . I have seen this narrowing and narrowing and cutting off of these other, I would say, enriching the educational process.

Perhaps even more disturbing is the sense among quite a few women that even when students are encouraged to pursue interests and linkages to nonarchitectural disciplines, such pursuits are treated in a less-than-substantial manner. Indeed, a number of our respondents applied the word "superficial" to such extra-architectural endeavors. One senior faculty woman at a public institution even suggested that the very complexity of the architectural field may work against the values of a liberal education:

> Architectural education is hard and it requires students to be familiar with a whole lot of different disciplinary pursuits. And because of that, students have to learn to be superficial, and that to me is negative. . . . So it's very difficult to get them to something more deep and substantial about a [particular] question, when they're accustomed to think that superficiality is the correct way to go.

In sum, many of these faculty women expressed their keen disappointment that architectural education all too frequently does not live up to its idealized potential for being inherently sympathetic to the goals of a liberal education.

Forging Interdisciplinary Connections

A second frequently cited benefit of architectural education is that its inherent interdisciplinarity fosters a natural meeting ground with its allied disciplines. But while acknowledging this potential, the authors of the Carnegie report question whether this potential is sufficiently realized in many architectural programs. In fact, they argue: "Making the connections, both within the architecture curriculum and between architecture and other disciplines on campus, is, *we believe, the single most important challenge confronting architectural programs*" (E. Boyer and Mitgang 1996, 85; emphasis ours). The Carnegie report's discussion of how such connections might be made includes examples of at least two types of initiatives: more flexibly organized curricula that enable students to pursue architectural specialties such as environmental sustainability, environment and behavior, or computer visualization; and secondly, substantive connections with experts in allied disciplines, including ecologists, engineers, historians, real estate experts, and landscape architects.

We would contend that for many architectural programs, an effective resource in achieving this interdisciplinary goal may be their own faculty women. To put it another way, because many faculty women have established expertise in the various specialty areas of architecture, they may be able to serve as the points of linkage to allied disciplines. In our sample of interviewees, we find that thirty-two (a full 80 percent) of the women have significant responsibilities for teaching in nondesign areas of the curriculum. And in a similar vein, thirty of the women have done academic degree work in another field either as undergraduates or in other nonarchitecture graduate degree programs; sixteen have Ph.D. degrees, and nineteen have master's degrees in another field. This formal training in other disciplines does not mean, however, that the majority of our respondents have little or no educational background in architecture itself. Indeed, a majority (twenty-two out of forty) have degrees in both architecture and another field. (Equal numbers have either degrees only in architecture [nine] or degrees only in another discipline [nine].) Although we don't have a comparable set of data for male faculty, this degree of experience and involvement with allied fields and subspecialties of architecture appears extraordinarily high.

Several complementary and overlapping hypotheses may explain these demographic data. First, in line with the conventional wisdom that women have to be "better" than men to be considered "equal," it appears that one route for successful women is to prove competence in a specialty teaching area by doing advanced degree work. This seems particularly true for the "first wave" of women who joined architectural faculties when it was still rare to find women in the field. Second, some women may have chosen to pursue advanced degrees outside of architecture because other disciplines were more receptive to women (i.e., art history, psychology, landscape architecture, etc.). Third, women who find themselves on the periphery of their field (especially given the pervasive allegiance to the design-as-centerpoint model) might be more likely to seek collaborations with colleagues in more sympathetic fields or at the margins of their own fields. Fourth, some women approaching the tenure "hurdle" may have found it advantageous to work in aspects of the field where the more clearly defined standards of academic achievement can be measured and fulfilled. Thus the preponderance of women in nondesign specialties may be the result of a combination of their strategic choice to "slant" their work in that direction and a screening process whereby women with a primary specialty in design may have been filtered out through the tenure process. Finally, since these subspecialties are generally less valued than "design," there would likely be less contentious debate about letting outsiders (i.e., women) teach them.

Although the specific contextual factors affecting the gendering of teaching specialities in architecture may be unique, comparable dynamics can be identified — to a greater or lesser degree — in other academic fields. For example, Ellen Messer-Davidow's (1999) analysis of physics, sociology, art history, and literary studies has identified a number of common trends that conspire to situate women at the edges of their disciplines, including filtering practices, subfield segregation, faculty stratification, and the shunting of women into supporting roles. Similarly, Aisenberg and Harrington (1988) have found that academic women from a variety of fields have been drawn to (or perhaps pushed into) scholarly pursuits that make connections among various disciplines and apparently distinct subfields. In their own sample of faculty women from a cross section of academic disciplines, approximately 70 percent chose to pursue nonmainstream areas of scholarship that challenge existing orthodoxies.

In our analyses of the interview material — particularly in the segments regarding attractions to and visions of architectural education — we find that the faculty women voice considerable support for the interdisciplinary character and potential of the field. To be sure, few (if any) offered a precise definition of the term "interdisciplinary," but many did explicitly mention the necessity for, and their commitment to, integrating knowledge from artistic, social, and technical fields. In her recent book *Interdisciplinarity*, Julie Klein (1990) cites the model of schools of public administration and public health where students are trained in the various contributing disciplines of the field; similarly, many architecture schools are modeled in the same way, with experts from a variety of disciplines contributing to a broad range of courses.

In this light, more than 80 percent of the women raised the issue of interdisciplinarity, either in reference to architecture's most positive attributes *or* as an unrealized ideal; most frequently they mentioned both. At a basic level, a few of our respondents simply acknowledged the interdisciplinary scope of the field as a positive attribute. For example, one tenured faculty member mentioned interdisciplinarity as a major attraction of the field: "Through architecture I could get involved in things that range from construction to politics." Another senior woman elaborated this same theme:

> An architect has to be sensitive to many, many issues and many, many disciplines. . . . In addition to architecture and design and all the construction parts and the technical aspects, there [are] — and I think they're geared mainly for the architect — special courses in the social sciences that deal with psychology of color, psychology of people, sociology, even economics. You have to know all these things in order to create a place or a building.

Far more typical, however, were the faculty women who noted architecture's interdisciplinary character as something very positive but also voiced grave concern about how this benefit is seriously constrained or eroded in the programs they know best. For example, one tenured woman, who was otherwise quite positive about many aspects of her program, wished its interdisciplinary potential could be better realized:

I want to really enhance the more complex nature of the profession and be more open to . . . new modes of collaboration. [We've] got to get the planners and architects talking to each other . . . we need the engineers as part of the team.

A tenured faculty member at a technologically oriented school voices a similar sentiment but concludes on a more discouraging note:

I think the positive characteristic is that it could be interdisciplinary. You learn a lot about other fields. But . . . we have a tendency to teach those courses outside the department by ourselves. I teach an engineering course. I happen to be an engineer. It would be great if we could find an engineer who had a vision [and] could be teaching . . . and you set up this dichotomy. There are the possibilities of a true interdisciplinary education in architecture. . . . But we have a tendency to think that we do everything best and I think that's the problem. In the end, the positive turns into a negative.

The respondent's observation that as architects we tend "to think we do everything best" is a sentiment that is raised forcefully by a number of other faculty women. In the view of some respondents, this tendency leads to, and is expressed in, a lack of respect for others' expertise. As one program administrator put it:

The architect knows everything. He knows how to design, he's a sociologist, anthropologist. He's just an "expert" on everything. He's an engineer, . . . a geologist. And so there's no room for anybody else in that process.

Similarly, a junior faculty woman at a small, private institution expressed her concern that all too frequently, attempts to use interdiciplinary linkages to other fields are not handled in a serious way, thereby reflecting a lack of respect for substantive expertise in other disciplines:

I think it's insulating, . . . and other fields might have discovered what we're discovering today, a long time ago. We still stay with our preconceptions; we don't read enough in other fields. Another [thing] is this pillaging of other fields where you just pick up a book on postmodernism and all of a sudden you teach a course. . . . I think historians are more serious towards their own discipline. They respect the work and the expertise of other people.

In sum, the vast majority of our respondents noted architecture's interdisciplinary potential as a positive value, yet nearly all of these respondents also felt that this potential was seriously eroded by an academic milieu that either did not take full advantage of it, or worse, undermined it by treating allied disciplines and specialties superficially and without due respect.

Integrating the Disciplines in the Studio: A Role Circumscribed, Discouraged, or Denied

Not surprisingly, the authors of the Carnegie report — like most architectural educators — believe that the studio offers great potential for integrating interdisciplinary perspectives. As they put it: "The good news is that architecture, by nature and tradition, holds vast potential as a model for the integration and application of learning, largely because of its most distinctive feature — the design studio" (E. Boyer and Mitgang 1996, 85). Their enthusiasm for its potential and some notable examplars at various schools is, however, tempered by the fact that they also found many studios that do not live up to these possibilities. In other words, the wonderfully integrative potential of studio is all too frequently stunted by relying on "a narrow base of architectural knowledge" (88).

A similar sense of frustration also runs through the extensive commentaries of many of the faculty women with whom we talked. Many of them believe that they — as well as others either in specialty areas of architecture or in allied disciplines — could make significant, even essential, contributions to the integrative potential of studio. All too frequently, however, they are made to feel marginal, irrelevant, or worse, inadequate to the task. We believe that in many cases, this process of marginalization is the result of a fundamentally different view of the scope of "design"; the vast majority of the faculty women we interviewed are inclined to view the task of studio work to be broad in scope — as opposed to a model that relies on a "narrow base of knowledge," as it was characterized by the Carnegie report.

Even some faculty women who consider themselves to be primarily studio faculty are made to feel their contribution is less worthy than that of their male colleagues. For example, despite having a specialty in design technology, a junior faculty member noted that one of her regular studio courses was dismissed by other faculty as "women's work." As she put it: "We mostly did housing and service buildings for public housing residents, and somehow that was looked on as not real architecture. It's not like designing museums and the things that men do."

Other women, even if they teach in studio on a reasonably regular basis, are seen as peripheral because their primary responsibility is in a nonstudio area. As one junior faculty woman told us: "I think as an architectural historian, I'm ... in a secondary position." Later she elaborated:

> I think an ideal program would include integration of the studio with other disciplines. We tried an experiment having bridge courses, that would connect a lecture course with a studio course. But it was not handled well administratively and thus failed.... Opening up the juries to ... include clients, as well as architects, and maybe politicians, ... a more diverse range of people [would be useful].

Others, trained in and hired with the expectation of teaching studio, are then discouraged from it. One senior woman, who arrived at her school with avid interest and expertise in design teaching, was actively discouraged from studio teaching and subsequently channeled only into lecture courses on a specialty area in which she had little background. In her view, the school's curriculum is framed this way: "There's design and then everything else is support for those.... And so [her specialty] is seen as a very marginal activity."

Given the dynamics that we have just described, it is no wonder that a significant gender gap in studio teaching emerges from an analysis by Professor Michael Kaplan of University of Tennessee (1993). Using data from the 1992 ACSA Faculty Directory, he concluded that 61 percent of tenured male faculty teach in design studios, whereas only 41 percent of tenured women faculty teach studio. However, when we compared the directory's listings with the teaching descriptions of our interviewees, we found an interesting discrepancy. In this comparison, thirty of the complete set of forty interviewees (75 percent) reported that they participated in studio, whereas the directory data indicated that only twenty-five of the women taught in studio. What accounts for this discrepancy? In four of the five instances, the details of the individuals' situations suggest an interpretive bias in the schools' reporting to ACSA; in the remaining instance there is no apparent explanation for the discrepancy.[8] To be more specific, we find that two women whose primary

Table 11.2. A Comparison of Men and Women Faculty
Participating in Design Studios

Number of schools that have tenured women *design* faculty	40	
Total tenured faculty in the 108 schools that grant tenure	1,590	
Total tenured men	1,453	91.4%
Tenured men teaching design	890	61.0%
Total tenured women	137	8.6%
Tenured women teaching design	56	41.0%
Number of tenured women teaching history/theory	25	
Number of tenured women teaching in other areas	56	
Total tenured design faculty in the 108 schools that grant tenure	946	
Number of tenured women teaching design	56	5.9%

Note: Data derived from statistics developed by Prof. Michael Kaplan and published in the newsletter of the Association of Collegiate Schools of Architecture, September 1993. Reprinted by permission from the *ACSA News,* published by the Association of Collegiate Schools of Architecture.

specialty is architectural history are listed as teaching only that specialty even though they also teach studio. In the third case, the faculty member had taught studio at a previous institution but had recently been hired by another institution to teach history as her primary assignment; in the fourth case, the faculty member had taught and intended to teach studio in the future but had recently been diverted into technical courses and temporarily sidelined with maternity leave.

Moreover, a number of women who were not now teaching in studio described their frequently thwarted efforts to teach their specialty material in studio formats. For example, one expert in historic preservation felt she was intentionally discouraged from teaching studio courses she had hoped to be part of. As she put it: "They probably feel, since I don't practice in the traditional manner, . . . I should not be involved in those architectural design courses." Similarly, another respondent was finally able to teach a studio related to her specialty after much lobbying on her part. But in the end she felt her effort was hopelessly compromised. As she puts it: "It was team-taught, and they wouldn't let me take the leadership role, [and] the whole point of my teaching [the specialty] was diluted because I didn't have control over what was being taught."

Based on the analyses of faculty women's commentaries, we strongly believe that the underrepresentation of women in studio teaching is not simply a reflection of their proportionately fewer numbers in the field in architectural education. In fact, there appears to be a consistent pattern by which the integrative contribution they are eager to make is minimized, ignored, or denied. Although many of the women clearly consider this exclusion from studio teaching a personal disappointment, it represents an even greater loss for the students, and the field as a whole.

Teaching Beginning Design as a Connection to Other Disciplines

In most academic fields, teaching advanced courses is considered more prestigious than teaching beginning classes, and architecture is no exception to this pattern. Moreover, to the extent that advanced studio teaching is seen as more "professional" and beginning studio is seen as "nurturing," these roles tend to be framed as a gendered dichotomy. Taking an avowedly feminist stance, the educational theorist Bruce Wilshire observes: "In the professionalized university, the messy work of caring for students and 'staying at home with them' [is] construed as 'women's work'" (1990, 271–72).

Despite the unwholesome tendency toward gender bias that appears to be woven into the denigration of teaching beginning students, we would like to pose a more hopeful perspective on women faculty's role in teaching early design. As we have mentioned, a variety of socioeconomic changes are forcing a reexamination of the field of architecture that will soon have a major impact on architectural education. Already, in the face of employment and academic pressures, some architecture schools have moved toward an increased emphasis on introductory architecture courses for liberal arts majors and students who wish to study architecture in preparation for careers in allied fields. For example, the University of Kansas recently modified its curriculum to make it more amenable to undergraduate liberal arts students who have an interest in architecture as a disciplinary major, but not necessarily as preparation for a career as a licensed architect (Domer and Spreckelmeyer 1990). Thus faculty responsibility for general, beginning design courses may in fact come to play a pivotal role in transforming architecture programs, and perhaps even the university as a whole.

In a complementary vein, proponents of the studio model of architectural pedagogy have argued that the model of "reflective" practice (as found in the studio) is an appropriate antidote to the emphasis on "technical rationality" that pervades many disciplines (e.g., Schön 1987). Since the publication of Schön's work, other scholars have incorporated and elaborated Schön's analyses in their discussions of pedagogical models for a variety of professional fields (Curry et al. 1993). More recently, the authors of the Carnegie report have argued that "core elements of architectural education," many of which are embedded in the studio model, might well have much broader relevance for other educational settings and disciplines (Mitgang 1996). In this light, then, the teaching of beginning design and the introduction of studio practices to nonarchitectural majors may well be the site of important innovations for the university as whole.

Indeed, political and economic forces — such as spiraling tuition costs and declining state budgets — are leading many universities to reaffirm their commitment to undergraduate education. Significant in this trend is the acknowledged need to reinvigorate the pedagogical foundations for higher education. Particularly at major research universities, the traditional disciplinary territories, staffed by faculty researchers and advanced students, are being challenged by a vision of an undergraduate-centered, interdisciplinary, and holistic learning environment. As one noted university administrator puts it: "Instead of offering extremely specialized undergraduate majors, perhaps we should design an undergraduate education that would prepare a graduate to move in many directions (Duderstadt 1995).

These converging trends suggest that faculty women who teach in the early design studios might be at the forefront of transformations in higher education. On a purely demographic level, the data from our interview sample do in fact tend to support the conventional wisdom that women are more likely to teach in the early years of design studio. Of the twenty-three women who specified the level of their studio teaching, eighteen (78.3 percent) teach in beginning studio, and eleven (47.8 percent) teach advanced studio.[9] However, because we don't have comparable figures on male faculty, the precise degree of gender bias is unclear.

What we can conclude, based on the commentaries of faculty women, is that the tendency to place women faculty in beginning studio courses is less a function of their lack of seniority than a function of the gendered conventions described by Wilshire.[10] Even some of the senior women, well seasoned in studio teaching, described long-term patterns of course assignments that effectively denied them both advanced studio assignments and leadership roles. For example, one senior woman (who is now a high-level administrator) told us at the time of her interview that she had never been allowed to teach in the final-year studio. Unfortunately, many of these women then internalize this biased decision making as if it were a criticism of their teaching capabilities; as this same senior woman noted: "There's just something about me that's not fifth-year material." But, in fact, her experience is part of a pattern that other women have noted at their own schools.

Given the continuing male dominance of the field, the gendering of studio assignments is particularly pernicious — not only for faculty women's self-esteem and career development but also for the message such a practice conveys to the students. One junior faculty woman explained that she had recently worked hard to be assigned studio in the final two years of the program. She described her motivation this way:

> One of the reasons why I keep pushing it is to have . . . [a] female up there because we've never had any females teach any upper level courses, anything higher than third year, and I think it's important for the students, both male and female, to see a female up there teaching.

Perhaps not surprisingly, then, few faculty women recognized the potential opportunity to reconfigure the beginning studio in light of the emerging interdisciplinary trends in architectural education and, more broadly, undergraduate education. One senior women who has primarily taught in first-year studios, however, expressed her concern about the double-edged sword that her teaching assignment represents:

> I realize I fell into two kinds of stereotypes of women being in a way more nurturing and . . . better able in a way to deal with first-year students. I myself always thought it was the most critical and sensitive year. . . . I feel that it's not sufficiently appreciated, . . . [there are] a variety of condescending attitudes towards teaching beginning students. When faculty colleagues come in [to serve on studio juries] it's . . . disappointing [because of] their behavior with beginning students.

Moreover, one of her colleagues dismissed the role of first-year studio teaching as something anyone could do!

An Alternative Model of Architectural Pedagogy: A Tapestry of Cultural Invention

To summarize, we believe that at least two trends will necessitate a transformation of architectural education: the changing realities of architectural practice, and the changing role and context for higher education more generally. To flourish — even simply to survive — architecture programs will need to embrace a more fundamentally interdisciplinary perspective. As we have argued throughout this chapter, our in-depth interviews suggest that as a group, faculty women can and should play a central role in this transformation. By virtue of their educational background and teaching roles, many faculty women are already committed to, and actively working toward, such an interdisciplinary mode.

To reiterate, we have identified four specific ways in which the perspectives of faculty women are consistent with the recommendations of the recent Carnegie report: (1) by maintaining and promoting the ideals of a liberal education; (2) by forging interdisciplinary connections, both within architecture and among allied disciplines; (3) by seeking to integrate such interdisciplinary connections in the studio experience; and (4) by emphasizing the role of beginning design instruction, thereby providing a potential site for engaging individual students outside architecture, as well as the larger university context more generally. Although not all of our respondents were committed to, or engaged in, *all* four of these activities, the vast majority were actively pursuing a more interdisciplinary agenda for architectural education.

In the end, we believe that such a transformation will mean that the long-hallowed design-as-centerpoint model of architectural education is no longer viable; in its place, we would propose the model of a *tapestry* that comes to life through its diverse and interwoven threads. Whereas the centerpoint model implies that "design" is hierarchically central as compared to the peripheral "support" courses, the tapestry model suggests that the "thread" of design, while integral to the overall pattern, is neither a discrete entity nor hierarchically ordered (Ahrentzen

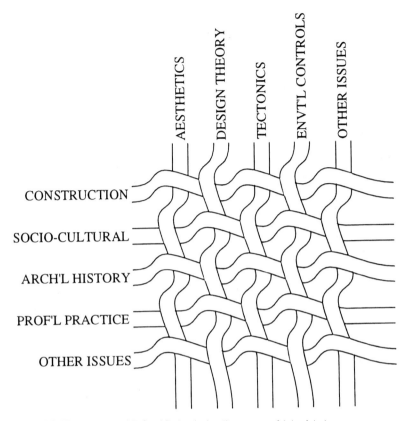

Figure 11.2. The tapestry model of architectural education: a woven fabric of design.

and Groat 1992). Because the tapestry model incorporates the notion of diverse threads and patterns that come together in an integrative pattern, we believe that this metaphor is very much in the spirit of the Carnegie study's conclusions. As Boyer and Mitgang put it: "To the perennial question, then 'does design studio take up too much student time?' our answer is this: at schools which offer studio sequences that allow students to leave school with a narrow base of architecture knowledge, there is too much studio. At schools which use the studio to guide students *through a gradually more complex and integrated exploration of architecture in its many dimensions—aesthetic, cultural, historic, practical, and technical—*there can hardly be too much" (E. Boyer and Mitgang 1996, 88; italics ours). It is our hope that conceiving of architectural education in terms of the tapestry metaphor will not only expand the potential of architecture for our current and future students but also ensure that the profession's role in society will remain a viable one.

Notes

First and foremost, we wish to acknowledge the willingness, even eagerness, of the more than forty faculty women, who shall remain anonymous, to participate in this study. We were assisted by a number of people in the course of this project. Wendy Meister, Dina Battisto, and Patricia McGirr worked tirelessly to code mountains of interview transcripts; Wendy Meister was also invaluable in conducting most of the phone interviews and helping to identify major themes. Ellen Messer-Davidow provided very useful and thought-provoking comments on an earlier version of this chapter.

In addition to the support of the Graham Foundation for Advanced Studies in the Arts, we are also grateful for additional support from both the Office of the Vice President for Research and the Horace Rackham Graduate School at the University of Michigan.

1. The Graham Foundation for Advanced Studies in the Arts generously provided the major support for this project, titled "Myth, Reality, and Alternative Visions of Architectural Education." The interviews were conducted in 1992 and constituted a follow-up to a survey of faculty women published by ACSA (Association of Collegiate Schools of Architecture) and conducted by Ahrentzen and Groat (1990).

2. For example, a broad-based studio project on the design of a school might entail discovering student, teacher, and parent needs through interviews and the like (with potential input from an education department or public schools), applying existing materials research for specific climatic conditions, and integrating both issues with traditional formal and aesthetic concerns. A more narrowly focused studio might emphasize formal manipulation either without or with minimal attention to the other issues.

3. The scope and content of architectural curricula are specifically addressed in "Chapter 4: A Connected Curriculum."

4. The core of this chapter's argument was presented at a conference titled "Knowledges: Production, Distribution, Revision" at the University of Minnesota, April 1994. In 1997 a substantially expanded and theoretically reframed version of the current chapter, titled "Voices for Change in Architectural Education: Seven Facets of Transformation from the Perspectives of Faculty Women," was published in the May issue of *Journal of Architectural Education* (Groat and Ahrentzen 1997).

5. Many other thematic areas—besides those relating to the scope and structure of the discipline—were explored in these interviews, and these will serve as the basis for publications in other contexts.

6. Well-known architect Denise Scott Brown was quoted regarding just this point in a recent article for *U.S. News and World Report* by J. Sieder (1996, 66–68).

7. For an extended discussion of this view of liberal education, see D. Domer and K. Spreckelmeyer 1990, 35–37.

8. ACSA directory information is solicited from all member schools using a standardized format. Each school is responsible for compiling faculty data, including the designation of teaching specialties according to ACSA's standardized coding terms. Although there is nothing that precludes a school's soliciting faculty input, many schools choose to have a single administrator or staff person assemble the data. As a result, the number and type of teaching specialties listed may or may not reflect an individual faculty member's view of his or her teaching contributions.

9. The two percentage figures total more than 100 because some faculty teach at both levels.

10. As one reviewer pointed out, seniority itself is a gendered artifact. In a sexist academic context, male seniority maintains gendered practices in hiring, promotion, curricular design, and so forth. However, our data demonstrate that gender segregation in studio teaching entails other, perhaps more pernicious, aspects of gendering.

12

A Framework for Aligning Professional Education and Practice in Architecture

Carol Burns

During the past thirty years, the relationship between architectural education and architectural practice has provoked recurrent anxiety. The discussion has become especially animated since the mid-1990s. Schools, professional organizations, and publications have all devoted great attention to analyzing and commenting on the disjunction between education and practice.

Two factors animate this concern. First is the dynamic state of the profession. Architectural practices, after emerging from a devastating recession in the early 1990s, have been undergoing significant changes. Practitioners today must be highly inventive merely to survive, and many are experimenting with new types of practice, new partnerships, and new methods of delivering services and projects. "Practice" is not now as easily defined as it was even five years ago, and so it is harder to educate future architects about it.

Second, the state of professional schools is in flux. The relationship between professional schools and the university is based increasingly on common values and procedures; professional schools are now accommodating themselves to standards and processes that have long dominated the traditional disciplines — the natural sciences, mathematics, and humanities. To acquire and maintain status in the university, professional school faculties must observe comparable standards of intellectual rigor, theoretical consistency, and publication.

These changes within practice and education are adaptive, and they might have productive outcomes. Together, however, they are problematic. On the one hand, those within schools of architecture often view the profession as confused, with too many practitioners of dismaying conservatism, mediocrity, and even incompetence; therefore schools question what to teach students who will more often than not enter traditional practice. On the other hand, practitioners often view new graduates as untrained for employment and lacking a working comprehension of fundamentals — such as drawing conventions — and of the complex demands on the profession.

Schools of architecture *should* stand apart, I believe, from the everyday demands of the profession and marketplace. Education and practice each has its own particular limitations and allowances; all that is distinctive about one in relation to the other should be maintained and valued. Education provides the student with ways to approach architecture, as both discipline and profession. Andrew Saint asks, "How far can that divergence [between education and practice] go before the link between school and the profession becomes dangerously tenuous, and the implicit guarantee that the school prepares the student for the world of work verges on dishonesty?" (Saint 1996, 16). I would like to answer the question not by measuring the appropriate distance for separation but by establishing alignments to connect these related yet disjunct realms.

The Culture of Professionalism

The argument is situated in a discussion of the historical formation of the culture of professionalism and the relationships between the professions and the university. The term "profession" dates to the sixteenth century. The first to require university training were the "learned" professions of law, medicine, the clergy, and, to some extent, the military. Architecture became an established profession soon after in Europe; the formalization of the principal professions, including architecture, occurred in the United States during the mid–nineteenth century. These disciplines, with their university connections, were originally in the domain of the elite. Clients and patrons of professional services came from the ruling classes. The combination of learned expertise and aristocratic patronage conferred special status on all the professions.

In this country, the establishment of a formalized profession of architecture was intended, in part, to remedy the lack of control of design services. Large-scale public works projects after the Civil War required specific expertise. The formation of the profession had support from leading architects (e.g., those trained at the Ecole des Beaux-Arts in France, including Richard Morris Hunt and H. H. Richardson) and from the public.

In the second half of the nineteenth century in the United States, a "culture of professionalism" emerged (Weber 1987, x). After the Civil War, vigorous economic growth produced wealth most striking for the inequality of its distribution. Traditional local communities were declining; urbanization intensified. Industrialization and modernization entailed an extension of commodity relations to all sectors of social life. A system of beliefs, habits, and practices for anticipating, ordering, and responding to these challenges was needed, and developments in "science" and "rationality" were its key elements. The culture of professionalism developed in this highly conflicted field of forces.

A set of learned values and habitual responses, this culture represents the collective effort of the middle classes to attain status, standing, and control in the face of economic and social change (Weber 1987; Bledstein 1976). Its defining features are (1) professionals are certified as competent in a specialized field, having undergone a lengthy period of training in an accredited institution; (2) professional competence assumes mastery of a particular discipline — an esoteric body of useful knowledge linked to general principles and systematic theory; (3) professionals "render a service" rather than provide an "ordinary commodity"; and (4) only professionals can render such a service. Together these features confer on practitioners their special authority and status.

Specialization alone does not explain the complex ethos that arose with, and has distinguished, professionalism. Studies of professionalism, even the most descriptive and functionalist, identify certain characteristics that differentiate the professions from specialized vocations in general, the most important being the professionals' claim of autonomy within a field. This autonomy derives not simply from their specialized skills; the services rendered by a doctor, lawyer, or architect are not only specialized — as are those of an auto mechanic — but, in a crucial sense, *incommensurable*. Through the idea of incommensurable services rendered (not merely sold), the professional seeks to distinguish learned activities from commodity relations; professional services have a value irreducible to the market value. This claim has decisively shaped techniques, attitudes, and forms of professionalism.

The professional commands a body of methodical recondite knowledge, inaccessible to the layperson and yet in itself coherent, self-contained, and based on founding principles. Such principles provide the intellectual basis for the laws, rules, and techniques that constitute a discipline and a praxis requiring lengthy training and initiation. Moreover, professional knowledge is, ideally, objective; such objectivity confers authority, allowing the professional to rise above the self-interest of business relations. Professional services attain value not from the standard exchange procedures of the market but rather from the fulfillment of specific social needs. Although professionals sell, as do all possessors of commodities, they profess concern for the general good, the necessities of public health, safety, and welfare. In short, professional services have use value, not exchange value. It is precisely in the effort to be distinct from the businessperson, on the one hand, and from the worker, on the other, that the professional finds it necessary to cultivate a professional ethos and culture.

Present-day views about the status of the professions diverge. Arguing for maintaining professional territory, Carl Sapers stresses the professional's fiduciary responsibility (1996, 89). In the collaborative making of complex things, someone, I believe, must be responsible for creating a shared idea; in making a building, this person is the architect. At the same time, I among others question the status of the professional based on a monopoly of knowledge and the power of exclusion. A social construct based on historical conditions that no longer obtain should rightfully be subject to examination. If we admit the impossibility of returning to a mid-nineteenth-century notion of the professional, the adaptive evolution of the professions requires examination and alteration of their structures.

Professionalism and the University

Returning to the historical analysis, the rise of the culture of professions is linked to university education. In the latter half of the nineteenth century, the university became the institutional expression of the culture of professionalism. An attack on all forms of monopolistic privilege in the eighteenth and early nineteenth centuries led to a relative shift in the balance of power toward academic institutions and against professional bodies (see Boorstin 1958, chap. 7). As a result, American professional bodies have overseen accreditation of university-based educational programs rather than directly qualifying members through their own systems of training and examination, as had been the case in England (T. Johnson 1972). The acknowledged vehicle for achieving professionalization, the university offered the means to establish and maintain the professional claim to a monopoly of competence. Thus neither the professions nor the university can be fully comprehended apart from the other or from the social processes that shaped them jointly.

Universities, having grown in number and size by the turn of the century, offered to a rapidly growing number of teachers a refuge from the business world. Salaried university employment allowed faculty to pursue research and teaching relatively free from the pressures of the client or the marketplace. Teachers in professional schools could promote a "purer" brand of professionalism than their practicing colleagues while working to develop the cognitive and technical basis of their disciplines. Academic independence was solidified by the ideology of freedom of inquiry and the tenure system. In response to expansion, the university adopted a managerial model taken chiefly from the industrial corporation. Ironically, the creation of the academic career path had sprung from the efforts of "pure" researchers on behalf of research, most of whom shunned utilitarian concern with practical vocational pursuits. Nevertheless, the university began to evolve into an increasingly bureaucratic configuration. The notion that the university model is "different" persists, despite its imposition of bureaucratic management systems on its own academic operations and its convergence with the corporate sector and the state apparatus.

Thus the culture of professionalization pertains to the academic milieu as well as to the professions per se. Itself divided into more or less isolated, self-contained departments, the university embodies the kind of compartmentalized universality that characterizes the cognitive model of professionalism. Areas of training and research, once instituted as specialisms or subfields, increasingly ignore the founding principles of individual disciplines. The notion of academic "seriousness" discourages reflection on the historical processes by which individual disciplines established their boundaries. Specialization increasingly implies that one "field" cannot reflect on another. The insulation and isolation of American academia from other segments of society are the negative prerequisite of the isolation that marks the professional perspective generally. The detachment of the university professor is characterized by the status of tenure and its assignation "without limits of time."

With the ethos of professionalism, utilitarianism and standardization infuse the organization of the university. The university, the main center for the "production of professional producers," supports both a bureaucratic notion of career and the traditional professional pattern of "fee for service" consultation. These two models coexist, the latter available as an "entrepreneurial" option.

The state of mind resulting for both professionals and professors is described by Alfred North Whitehead:

> Effective knowledge is professionalised knowledge, supported by a restricted acquaintance with useful subjects subservient to it. This situation has its dangers. It produces minds in a groove. Each profession makes progress, but it is progress in its own groove. Now to be mentally in a groove is to live in contemplating a given set of abstractions. The groove prevents straying across country, and the abstraction abstracts from something to which no further attention is paid. But there is no groove of abstractions which is adequate for the comprehension of human life. (1959, 282–83)

Whitehead's appeal to a holistic, organic reflection that might compensate for the limits of professionalism has been largely ineffective, because it — like all traditional philosophical attempts to transcend specialized knowledge — places itself over and above what it seeks to transcend (Weber 1987, 32).

In the thirty years since Whitehead wrote, many "grooves" have become finer and deeper, most notably in the professionalization of academia. Today a vast institutionalized form enables, constrains, and informs the production of effective knowledge. Its institutional divisions are embodied in the specialization and exclusion of intellectual practices.

Professional Education in Architecture

Within the professional schools of architecture over the past fifteen or so years, the discipline has established a discourse separate from the discourse of practice. Theory has become a freestanding enterprise, independent of particular forms of practice, and "theory specialists" are working hard to emerge as a distinct class of academicians. The increasing emphasis on the production of scholars, rather than the production of professionals, creates a disconnection from notions of how architects and architecture exist outside the academy. Students bear the brunt of confusion about this disconnection.

What architecture schools expect from students and expect to offer students is not clear. It is difficult to devise provisional answers—or even to communicate the questions—but too few efforts are made. Students in school are asked to do things they will never be asked to do as architects, and they can be misled by this. Professional firms are not harmed by such educational practices; the firms train those who can think critically. But individual students can be hurt, and are. Schools proffer a model for practice that is not reflected in practice—the single individual acting autonomously. This model creates desires to set up immediately on one's own without time enough to complete the legal and practical requirements of training that only professional experience can provide. The disconnection between school and practice leads to doubts about the schools' stance toward the profession as well as to distress among recent graduates, many of whom confront practice with wrenching dismay.

How can schools address this disconnection? Academic courses in architectural theory, design, and professional practice can address issues inherent to architecture. Professional practice curricula can attain rich intellectual depth, rather than offer primer-level pragmatics. The very concept of architectural practice demands substantial expansion, not only concerning architectural services, but also critically addressing the sociocultural role of architecture. The conceptual models and language framing these matters should become more sophisticated. Outmoded concepts of professional life obscure present and potential actuality.

Architectural theory can develop methodologies that pertain to the discipline rather than repeatedly adopting methodologies "from the outside," as it has, first from the social sciences and then from the humanities. The discourse of practice clearly has its intellectual and theoretical side. However, this discourse is being developed not within the architecture schools but rather in management, sociology, anthropology, and psychology programs. This discourse explores the professional service and the culture industries (either of which can encompass architecture), their future, how the global economy will change them, and the supply of professionals in relation to the demand for their services. As Robert Gutman says, "These subjects may be as decisive for the future of architecture and the profession as the theories under discussion in schools of architecture" (1995, 11).

Substantive improvement of conceptual and analytical frameworks for architectural practice could support sharper definition of issues and aims. For example, contemporary theoretical pragmatics could be employed to analyze the various disciplines from the "inside." This analysis could show concretely, in each case, that the demarking of the field through exclusionary limits effectively organizes a discipline but nonetheless diverges from the self-consciousness of the practitioners. Both of these outcomes issue from the ethos of professionalism. Another avenue for exploring such limitations would be a poststructuralist analysis of professional discourses. This analysis could precisely demonstrate how the apparently objective, denotative language of individual disciplines entails, necessarily but implicitly, a precise series of prescriptive speech acts, involving injunctions and commands constitutive to the professional ethos in general. Making those prescriptive systems explicit and revealing the strategic nature of apparently constantive discourse would contribute to both the discipline and the profession.

Alignment

More immediately, I would like to advance a conceptual framework that aligns the shared interests of school and profession. The education of a professional should not be formulated in terms of the boundaries between academia and the profession. A broader model should be envisioned—a series of alignments that go across and link these interrelated distinct realms. I would like to describe several.

- This chapter offers an example-in-action of a "bull's-eye model of alignment." It aims simultaneously to target information, knowledge, and theory inherent to architecture. Particular facts are construed as an argument, a framework of knowledge, in a critical theoretical context. The bull's-eye model requires cutting across multiple disciplines, or "going cross country," and it calls for future work. It allows the professional and professorial outlooks to stand apart but at the same time acknowledges multiple historical and strategic connections between them. Advancing discourses that contribute to both the discipline and the profession, it seeks to develop theories that have practicable and ethical application in the field.

• An "alignment of disjunction" admits that schools are focused and "bracketed." The model is explicit about how academic activities relate to practice, admitting, for example, that a majority of academic studio courses devote their time to a portion of activities within what is professionally characterized as the schematic design phase. This model can nevertheless convey a sense of what lies outside, beyond the brackets of school, by sponsoring contact with worlds of activity that, while no more "real" than that of school, have different allowances and limitations. The model encourages students to "look around" past school in field trips, work experience, and sponsored summer internships. During schooling, it embodies experientially the premise that architecture joins disjunct realms. It is fostered tacitly and explicitly by faculty who teach as well as practice, in some way, more than "paper architecture."

• A "multiline alignment" allows that there are multiple paths through education and through architecture, leading to multiple outcomes. One segment of this line exists within professional schools that offer focused curricula for students. At Harvard University Graduate School of Design, new "pilot programs" allow extended study of particular topics as a means to develop a specialty within the professional degree program. The programs exist according to interest in them. Initiated by the faculty, they have addressed such topics as computer-aided manufacturing and Chinese cities; in response, students have initiated a self-guided pilot program on American cities. Another segment of the multiline model is composed of architecture courses for nonmajors. These can have great impact on a broader informed appreciation of design and its importance in the physical environment. Vincent Scully taught architectural history to generations of Yale undergraduates who never became architects but became inspired by architecture and later worked with architects in their own capacities.

- A "point-to-point alignment" connects directly from academic to professional experience. This is the aim of internship programs, such as at University of Cincinnati or Waterloo University, as well as externship programs, as at Rice University or University of Virginia. "Mentor offices" that establish direct connections between practitioners and students can provide advice, contacts, familiarity, self-guided decision making, "testing" of interests, and appreciation of school experience.

- An "alignment with gaps" allows architecture students to take academic courses for a semester with no design studio. Perhaps a controversial idea, this curricular component allows students to focus on academic studies free of the overriding pressure of studio commitment. It is an option presently available in two of seven semesters at Harvard Graduate School of Design, including a research-based thesis project.

- A "line segment" offers immediate connection to the craft of making. Building projects, like those at Yale and the University of Texas at Austin, connect directly from school to construction sites. The use of excellent shop facilities does this similarly in everyday practice at schools such as Cooper Union or the offices of Kevin Roche or Cesar Pelli. Developing such an obvious and almost commonplace resource as the woodshop contributes immeasurably to the culture of material making.

- "Parallel lines" question the traditional academic tenure path by supporting faculty committed to professional practice. A historical example includes adjunct academic appointments without tenure. The status of "professor in practice" invented at Harvard Graduate School of Design admits the institutional importance of tenure but effectively allows half-time tenure positions, with annual teaching loads negotiated to balance with professional commitments.

- A "vector" is a line of education that includes "continuing," "professional," or "lifelong" education. Continuing education may offer the most substantive structure for long-term connections between education and practice. The AIA has recently made professional education mandatory for membership.

- A "line that terminates" entails regular review of architectural licenses, legislating that professional status ought not to be passively held for life. Professional status should be used or renewed to remain in effect. State licensing boards and NCARB could be more directly concerned with the sunsetting of licenses in relation to requirements for continuing education.

These examples describe a few of the possible alignments between professional education and professional practice. I am arguing for them, others that doubtless can be cited, and the creation of many more. The diagram of the relationship begins with schooling and practice as two disjunct realms that are overlaid and cross-connected with many layers of different types of lines. The crossing should be easy, often, rich, fueling, and integrative. Education and practice should inform each other at the scale of a lifetime in the same way that research and design inform each other at the scale of a project. I argue for many types of lines, for strong ongoing connections between the contemporary profession and schools of architecture.

Conclusion

Professions and universities have been structured in close relation to each other, both founded on ideas of technical rationality in the late nineteenth and early twentieth centuries. Within technical rationality, the dominant method for research and practice is problem solving. Problems are solved through a process of elimination, selecting from available means the one best suited to established ends.

The process of elimination leads to a correct — or at least defensible — answer, but only if given consensus about what the ends should be. The importance of phenomena that defy the model of technical rationality deserves increased recognition. Occurrences such as uniqueness, complexity, uncertainty, value conflict, and instability demand better understanding.

The discipline of architecture is messy because it is inclusive; it is a formal and material undertaking in the context of ever-shifting social, political, and economic conditions. Complex conditions today present unexpected opportunities to architects and architectural education. Through the studio and jury system, architecture teaches not problem solving but problem setting, the process of defining the decisions to be made, the ends to be achieved, and the means that may be chosen. Making sense of an uncertain situation that initially makes no sense requires broadening the questions to connect seemingly unrelated things and to consider answers and ideas not yet explored. This process leads not just to answers but to optimal solutions that address the largest number of concerns in the most elegant way. Architects and professors of architecture willing to conceive of themselves not just as specialized building designers but as people able to structure complex human problems and to engage in dialogue and action within the social physical world will contribute to both education and practice.

13

Reduction and Transformation of Architecture in Las Vegas

Garth Rockcastle

This chapter focuses on how the efforts to bring a public library and art museum project into being exposed several cultural realities and disciplinary limitations I still find discouraging. For nearly twenty years prior to this project, I took for granted what I thought were several of architecture's central functions. First, its core cultural function was to structure, edify, and reveal the enlightened aspirations of humanity. Second, its central political function was to advance and realize broader public interests over private interests. And third, its primary aesthetic function was to develop the artistic, poetic, and experiential potential of its spatial and material nature. All of these disciplinary objectives were called into question during the process of realizing this project.

This chapter is based on my professional experience with the design of the new Sahara West Library and Art Museum in Las Vegas from 1990 to 1997 by our firm, Meyer, Scherer and Rockcastle, Ltd. My partner, Jeffrey Scherer, and I shared responsibilities for the project; he, the library portion, and I, the art museum, site design, and public art portions. This library and art museum project, the last of the library district's three keystone, dual-purpose projects, was also the city's first public art museum. Although several affinity groups (a watercolor society, a few private galleries, and the UNLV University of Nevada, Las Vegas, art department) had modest spaces to host occasional exhibitions, the visual arts (especially contemporary art) had no public home in Las Vegas.

It can be argued that Las Vegas is fueled by a rare cultural program (gambling) and has thereby become an unusual place. Drawing meaningful inferences from it about the future of the profession or discipline may have real limitations. I wish to argue, however, that Las Vegas's "unique" qualities are becoming less so, and understanding what is happening there is more critical for us. For almost three decades, Las Vegas (and the cultural ethos that propels it) has been prescient. It has given birth to new cultural developments and corresponding transformations of the roles of architecture.[1] As gambling has become "gaming," so too have most casinos become mixed-use entertainment centers. For most developers, city officials, and even citizens today, the economic vitality of the commercial sectors of a city is a far more important measure of civic health than is the life of the arts or the quality of public space. Even the words used to characterize the expressive qualities of new architecture — "sensational," "spectacular," and "fantastic" — are more fitting than words like "sublime," "subtle," "intrinsic," or "integral" used to judge aesthetic value earlier in this century. Although this is especially true for the function and quality of commercial architecture, the cultural facilities we were charged to design were affected by these same social and political mores. It is on this basis that I believe this project and this city are fertile topics to reflect on the following:

1. the profound role cultural mores play in shaping and directing the development of the discipline;

2. emerging requisites for knowledge, skill, and ethical reasoning to meet new professional and disciplinary challenges;

3. odd distinctions people make (and the biases they hold) about related creative disciplines; and

4. some implications for the future of our discipline.

But first, a bit more about the city of Las Vegas, the project, and its background.

The City

For most of us, Las Vegas is one of the least likely places to find a progressive, publicly sponsored experiment in architecture and culture such as the one it has embarked on for nearly two decades. The city is known around the world as being a cultural antithesis to what public libraries and museums typically connote — the value of the life of the mind. But as the fastest growing city in America from the 1970s through the 1990s, more than tripling in population (from 310,000 to just over 1,250,000 by mid-1999), other interpretations of what the city is about are possible. This growth stressed the metropolitan infrastructure — its streets, utilities, and services such as public schools and libraries — bringing about a climate of urgency. Such stress may have opened local minds to alternative ideas and ways of doing things. In addition, the significant contributions the "gaming industry" provided through special taxation and a hungry job market gave the city and Clark County plump public coffers and the ability to bond ambitious building programs. It appeared initially to us as though the public ability and will to risk and explore were considerable.

The economic success the city experienced soon spawned a virtual national revolution in reorienting municipal and state economic development. What started as liberal gambling laws in Las Vegas and Reno, Nevada, became special gambling districts in other municipalities across the country. Additionally, state tax relief through legalization and sponsorship of lotteries and the approval of tribal enterprise by legalizing the development of casinos on Native lands spread like a prairie fire across the country. This revolution has even been referred to as the "Vegas" contribution to a new paradigm for American civic life:[2] a model that views gaming and related entertainment as necessary replacements for the traditional, more outdated urban cultural venues of public life (cultural facilities and retail districts). Vegas became the epitome of a new type of American city, the kind Baudrillard variously refers to as a "newly materialized, . . . cinematic, . . . erotic, . . . self-publicizing, . . . mobile, . . . utopian, . . . free enterprise, . . . parody museum" (1988a, 46, 56, 77, 79, 88, 103). In this way, Las Vegas is a prophetic civic laboratory for exploring the potential of the evolving American culture and metropolis — a place where we might see most clearly the values, political processes, institutional identities, and civic boundaries of the twenty-first century.

The Project and Its Background

In the late 1970s the Las Vegas–Clark County (LVCC) Library District embarked on an ambitious initiative to develop and significantly transform the role and character of its public library system for metropolitan Las Vegas. In the early seventies it was one of the nation's smallest and weakest library systems, per capita, in the country.[3] In 1972 the district hired a visionary and aggressive new director, Charles Hunsberger, from Columbus, Indiana. What he envisioned was to build a progressive library system that would rival any in the country in terms of collection size, media diversity, and innovative service.

Several factors made this accomplishment possible. First, Hunsberger's pursuit of the vision was unwavering. Second, a core group of cultural supporters and activists (many of Mormon persuasion) worked for this civic initiative within and outside the library system. They offset, in some modest way, the city's national reputation as a capital of vice and hedonistic behavior and, by implication, as a cultural wasteland. Third, explosive population growth and the city's omnipresent development of the city to accommodate it created an optimism and sense of adventure that translated to broad public support of the library district's early visions and dreams.

The prospect of building as many as fifteen new public libraries to serve the city's explosive growth soon led Hunsberger to realize that a facility's design could also promote, by architectural example, important civic values and leadership. His belief may be of no surprise to those readers who, familiar with twentieth-century American architecture, will recall that Columbus, Indiana (Hunsberger's first home), distinguished itself nationally for having one of the largest collections of "name-brand" modern works of architecture. In Las Vegas, Hunsberger reckoned, a similar potential existed if there was sufficient political and cultural will to support such a program. In his master plan for this civic expansion, he called for a dispersed network of satellite, or branch, libraries that were conceived as neighborhood catalysts for diverse public services. The district used a selection process for hiring nationally recognized designers for the three largest facilities, which would combine branch library functions with (1) a children's museum, (2) a performing arts center, and (3) an art museum.

By the early nineties the LVCC library system had become one of the most generously supported, dynamic, and experimental in the country.[4] However, since 1992 these initiatives were more vigorously criticized by several commentators and politicians in the local media for "losing sight of its primary public responsibility and charge, the collecting and making available to the public, books."[5] Central to this local criticism was the district's development of its three highest-profile libraries, those multipurpose facilities linked with the development of other new cultural facilities. The district was criticized for taking on the role of metropolitan cultural developer under the guise of library expansion. Ironically, at the same time, the national library community was praising the LVCC initiatives and accomplishments and citing the district as "innovative leaders, a model for the future role of libraries in this country."[6]

The idea of an art museum in the city, the controversial part of the project program, was not a sudden or capricious one. In the mid-1970s, the LVCC Library District began its sponsored exhibition program by permitting library hallways to be used for hanging photographs by local photographers. By the time the Sahara West Library and Art Museum opened in January 1997, fifteen satellite galleries were in full-time operation and managed by a full-time district gallery manager. The district manager had initiated several successful programs and managed many different arts programs. The district had exhibited more than 150 local and 30 national artists over the past fifteen years, and the permanent collection of art grew from nothing to just over 350 works and twenty-five site-specific commissions. This is, of course, above and beyond the sponsorship of several hundred K–12 student exhibitions in local libraries.

With all of the enthusiasm and anticipation I had felt from the client and arts-oriented public from 1991 to 1993, I was caught by surprise when in 1993 the project became the target of a divisive and almost debilitating public controversy. The administration and board of the library district, various municipal political constituencies, the arts community, and the local media became embroiled in a nasty struggle over the fate of the museum component of the project. The arguments for and against the art museum made me reflect on numerous cultural, political, and disciplinary implications revealed by the controversy. Although the struggle never focused on the project's formal design, two aspects of the project fueled the public debate. First, and most fundamental, was the inclusion of an art museum in the project. Most detractors believed that the district should not be underwriting the construction or operating costs of an art museum with library funds. Some even thought there was no need for an art museum in a city like Las Vegas. Second, the inclusion of commissioned "public art" in this project was seen as a waste of public funds, and as such "should not be used to buy art."[7]

The controversy was so disruptive to the library district that it contributed significantly to the ousting of the original director, Charles Hunsberger, led to the removal of several board members, and eventually eliminated most of the intrinsic or public art contracted for our project. It almost succeeded in removing the museum from the project, The nearly completed museum space came dangerously close in 1996 to being leased for other "income-producing" uses. Uses seriously discussed included a synagogue, a roller skating rink, a café, and a storage warehouse. However, the art museum did open in January 1997, as an art museum, close to what was originally envisioned.

The opportunity to design a unique cultural facility is a rare occasion for an architect. Although many libraries have some gallery or exhibit functions within, we knew of no precedent that combined in one building a fully functioning art museum with a full-service public library. Our building design was developed both to bring clarity to the subtle but important distinctions between the two cultural missions and to simultaneously unify them into a dynamic whole (see Figure 13.1). We believed it was important to cast the building and its landscape as an active agent of cultural and public sensibilities. This was accomplished by contrasting it with the surrounding built fabric by designing strong, clear, abstract forms, disposed of in compound, active, sculptural ways.

The project design was also influenced by several external phenomena including a unique regional history, a harsh climate, and the city's architectural and site planning conventions. In opposition to the city's front-parking-lot norm for commercial property, we hollowed a segmented, radiating lot out of the rear of the site to help camouflage the sea of cars and hide views of some of the adjacent properties (see Figures 13.2 and 13.3). This allowed us to create entry spaces that participate with the interior courtyard in a dynamic spiral around a central but radiating building mass. The front, or West Sahara Boulevard side, of the site uses a raised plinth to present public sculpture and the building itself (see Figure 13.4).

The central mass in the heart of the courtyard houses a soaring children's story hour room on the upper floor (reached by a bridge from the library) and a dark, cool, contemplative "grotto" on the first floor

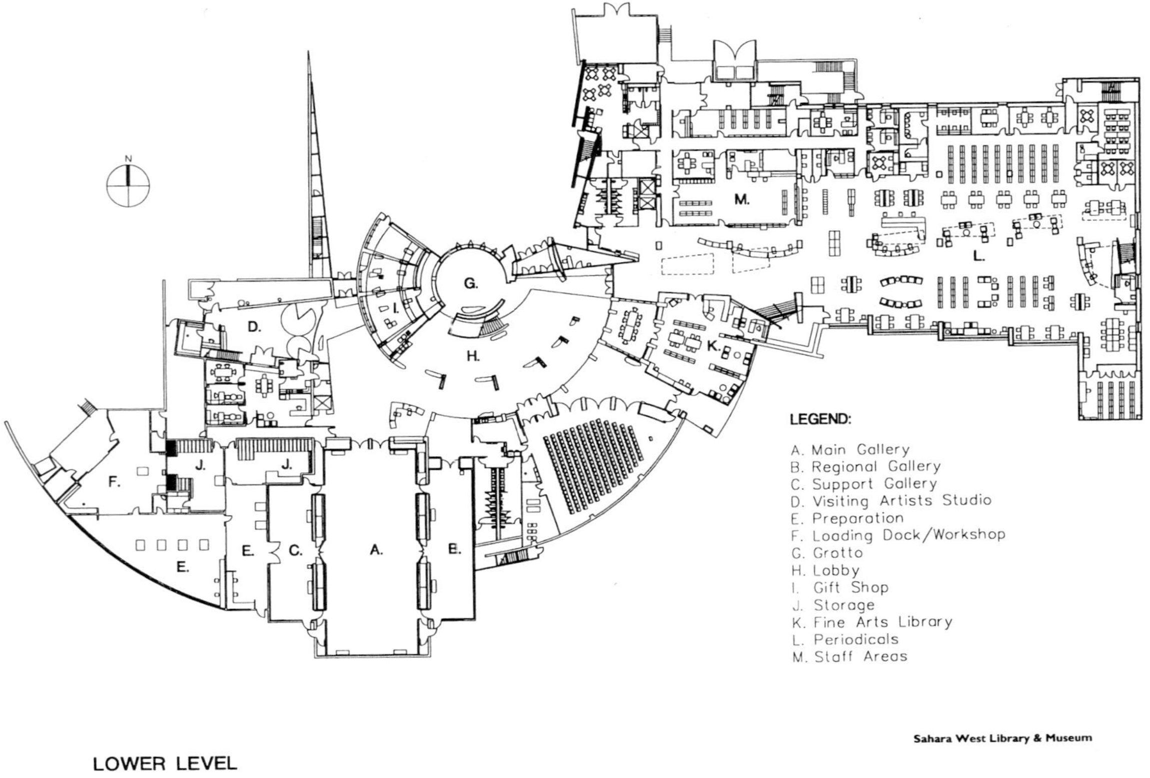

LOWER LEVEL

Figure 13.1. Main floor plan. Courtesy of Meyer, Scherer and Rockcastle.

N

LEGEND:

A. Main Gallery
B. Regional Gallery
C. Support Gallery
D. Visiting Artists Studio
E. Preparation
F. Loading Dock/Workshop
G. Grotto
H. Lobby
I. Gift Shop
J. Storage
K. Fine Arts Library
L. Periodicals
M. Staff Areas

Sahara West Library & Museum

Figure 13.2. Site plan. Courtesy of Meyer, Scherer and Rockcastle.

(see Figure 13.5). Public, shared functions (museum store, assembly hall, etc.) all gather around this center (see Figure 13.6). The two institutions (museum and library), each designed to embody its distinct cultural function, radiate outward from this center.

The library is essentially a two-story box holding gridded stacks of books with animated features (vaulted common reading room, private clipped-on study carrels, and a radiating young people's library) embedded in or attached to it. Its spatial crown is a telescoping vault aiming east toward the world-famous gaming "strip" and locally significant sunrise mountain. An arched "celestial wall" at its end marks seasonal, mythic, and celestial events (see Figure 13.7). Harsh southern sunlight is shielded by broad overhanging screens to protect the south-facing windows and skylights from excessive heat gain while scattering and driving reflected light through and across the library. The resultant daylight is gentle and even throughout the library.

The main museum gallery is conceived of as a large, mute container that easily transforms its spaces and mounting surfaces to accommodate shifting curatorial objectives. It is flanked by two smaller, less dy-

Figure 13.3. East face of building. Courtesy of Timothy Hursley.

Figure 13.4. Front side (south) facing West Sahara Boulevard. Courtesy of Timothy Hursley.

Figure 13.5. Interior common atrium. Courtesy of Timothy Hursley.

namic galleries. The main gallery is incised by a full-length operable light monitor permitting, diffusing, or excluding daylight as exhibits warrant. Custom cabinet and wall segments and an adjustable hung ceiling and lighting system permit the arrangement of variously shaped display spaces.

Materials in their natural state (black granite, clear seal hardwoods, clear anodized aluminum, and cement gray stucco) contrast with the highly animated and colorful surfaces typical of Las Vegas's commercial architecture. They complement the building's strong abstract forms and serve as a more neutral background for the dynamic, programmatic life of the building.

The design evolved in two phases: the first from August 1990 to June 1991, before a public referendum for the bonding request in the fall of 1991 to raise taxes for the project; and the second from the spring of 1993 to winter of 1994. The project was on hold for almost two years, we were told, to gain public approval of it, and later to allow five other branch libraries of higher priority in the pipeline to be completed first. Over that two-year period, several board members were replaced by new political constituencies. When we were asked to resume developing the project's design and work toward completing the project, a new sense

Figure 13.6. Interior common atrium. Courtesy of Timothy Hursley.

of urgency had surfaced. Upon presenting the final design to the board in a public meeting in late fall 1993, we felt an undertow of political and cultural conflict brewing in the community and between the district's board and its administration. We soon learned of the vulnerability of Charles Hunsberger's directorship and discovered a well-organized effort to kill (or maim) the Sahara West library and museum project and to remove him from leadership.

Figure 13.7. Exterior view of celestial wall. Courtesy of Timothy Hursley.

At the heart of the controversy were two issues that related directly to our project; one, the relevance of library funds used to support art museum functions, and two, whether site or intrinsic building art was an appropriate use of library funds. The first ultimately led to a retreat by the district in providing the leadership to raise private funds to support the art museum's operation. The second led to the removal, renaming, and treatment of planned site art as "design features." On the surface, these accommodations seemed like a small price to pay to keep the project intact and moving forward, but as it turned out, the new climate was a mere indication of a dark and more deeply problematic cloud of sinister agendas.

Reactions and Comments

We were called on by the arts advocates to provide some background research on the issues surrounding the conflict. We cited relevant national precedents and helped formulate arguments to defend the cultural initiatives embodied in both our project and the others throughout the district. The cultural implications surrounding the conflict seemed to expand at every turn in the debate. The broadening spectrum of issues raised, the claims made against the project, and the objections to the mission of the district during public hearings and in editorials in the local newspaper included:[8]

The public bonding for our libraries was for books and "responsible" facilities to house them, not for art, and museums to house it in.

The Library District Board and Charles Hunsberger defrauded the public because there was no real mention on the state bonding referendum of an art museum. [Although there actually was.]

The art museum, as it is conceived of here, is an invasion of the old elitist concepts of art and a threat to our western way of life. It represents just what many in Las Vegas came to escape: oppressive traditions, academic and intellectual dictations of culture, and a public obligation to support it.

We don't need that kind of art in this community. We have some of the best public art in the world on the strip. People come from around the world to see it.

In Las Vegas one has the freedom to make or acquire one's own utopia in whatever form one wishes. Any effort to regulate or impose on others the terms or conditions of anyone else's utopia is an affront to this essential freedom.

These assertions were often met with alternative official and other community testimony:[9]

> It simply is not true that the public was misled. The programs, architectural plans, and models were all available for public viewing at the central library and covered completely in the newspaper.

> I didn't come to escape the cultural trappings of older cities in this country. I came to retire in an exciting community and growing economy. I have fond and life-transforming childhood memories of visiting a real art museum. Why deprive ourselves and our children of this?

> The promise of a legitimate, or critically curated art museum is like a dream come true for the many artists of this community. It is a well-kept secret that this is a thriving community of artists, because secondary income producing jobs are plenty and the dry, warm climate is ideal. Regrettably, their galleries, and the real art community, remain five hours to the west, in Los Angeles.

> The proposed leasehold conditions (market rate rent, limited term lease, and no cooperation for fundraising) are an insult to the local arts community. If this space goes to alternative uses because of these conditions, the public shame will be on your shoulders, and the historic view of this will not be very flattering of you.

> It is a fallacy to assume that the well-being of this community is well served by not having an appropriate facility for the public presentation of the visual arts. There is no comparably sized city in the world without such a facility. We need it to meet the needs of the 90's and carry Las Vegas proudly into the next millennium.

Although the controversy was never really "resolved," having surfaced the way it did left a residue of cultural conflict and disciplinary confusion in its wake. A local nonprofit arts initiative "The Las Vegas Art Museum" is leasing the museum for the first three years while the district searches for a long-term tenant. All but one of the scheduled public art installations were eliminated because they looked too much like "art." The one realized was unceremoniously removed two weeks after the artist completed it.

Disciplinary Insights

So what can be learned about our discipline from all this? I found myself drawn to the questions raised about the widening gaps between public and professional expectations for the role and nature of architecture and art in American (or at least Southwestern American) culture. These gaps seem to be made wider and more treacherous by the apparent desire of the public (officials, clients, and construction industry and lay constituencies) to contract the disciplinary domain of architecture, whereas its agents (architects, educators, theoreticians, and researchers) seek to expand its boundaries, influences, and agency. However, most current practitioners of the architectural discipline do not appear well prepared or inclined to meet the new political challenges that our (d)evolving American culture is posing for it. In addition, advocates for distinguishing the discipline of architecture too much from more popular cultural and disciplinary discourses contribute to widening such gaps and deepening what I often think of as a symmetry of ignorance.

I agree with Stanford Anderson's vision, mentioned elsewhere in this volume, of the discipline of architecture as an "open and liberating environment." I also agree with his characterization of the discipline of architecture and the profession of architecture as "partially but not wholly coincident." However, the increasing separation of the disciplinary discourses from practice is a deepening problem. I believe that

1. the academic and critical stewards of the discipline need to expand and better ground their endeavors in real and contemporary exigencies, and

2. the professional practice of architecture needs to advance its role as a critically engaged means for disciplinary experimentation, advocacy, and education.

In essence, I am advocating that each become (or do) more of what the other is (or does). I feel an increased urgency both to better ground our discipline and to more critically charge its modes of practice. Just as the disciplinary discourses have shown us that disciplines are far more than the subjects that occupy them, a vigorous professional practice needs to be far more than the service it provides or traditions it upholds, raising the following questions:

1. What does our discipline define as the essence of a "library" or a "museum" (or any other building type), and what are the dangers and opportunities of crossing their established boundaries?

2. What is or should be the cultural boundaries between libraries, museums, or subsets of the arts? Should they be changing to meet the times, or should they be stable cultural anchors in some cultures and cities?

3. Is the cultural malaise in Las Vegas an aberrant, local phenomenon or a larger, growing cultural reality in America, or even throughout the contemporary world?

4. Does the emerging American cultural ethos I encountered in Las Vegas hold any real cultural promise or potential for the future, or are my pessimism and subjectivity interfering with my ability to see that potential?

5. What does my (our) ill preparedness for this conflict and debate imply about the deficiencies of professional education, continuing education, or disciplinary discourses and the needs or realities of future practice?

6. What kind of unexamined disciplinary assumptions do I (or any of us) bring to my (our) professional work, and how can I become more aware of them in order to overcome them?

7. How can we improve the likelihood that challenging cultural buildings and landscapes, ones that aspire to critically revealing the limits or contradictions of our social or aesthetic values, might avoid becoming political "lightning rods," or should they be?

8. Does professionally (or institutionally) acting "otherwise" in the face of such local conflict really serve local interests, or is it the same self-serving, egocentric delusion to which architects often find themselves turning?

9. What responsibilities or rights do various public constituencies have? How do we know what is for the public good, especially when there are arts publics, library publics, and taxpaying publics as constituencies?

These questions beg numerous disciplinary and professional issues left largely unclear by current discourses and formulations of our profession, its role, and its history. Although comprehensive answers to these are impossible here, I believe it useful to share some of my disciplinary and cultural views that have grown out of the experiences with this project.

First, because many of the ingredients of contemporary life are undergoing profound change, I believe that our discipline needs to broaden and deepen our examination of, and experimentation with, alternative paradigms for how architecture serves society. Recent revolutions in the electronic and computing, communications, and environmental fields will likely have profound impacts on the materiality, scale, density, and representations of architecture. In addition, new lifestyles and values are emerging with these changes, which will further propel change in the very purposes architecture serves. Many critical questions need to be addressed. What new or altered roles will buildings play? What new spatial relationships will emerge? What new conceptual boundaries will be crossed? What alternative roles will architects play?

Second, I am now convinced that new and insidious challenges are emerging to undermine the livelihood of cultural facilities and public amenities in cities today—especially in the rapidly growing newer cities or younger (suburban) portions of older cities. Public life, space, and infrastructure are diminishing in importance and in substance as many Americans retreat from the perceived hostility and irrelevance of traditional cultural mores and venues. The immediacy and allure of cable TV, computer games, and videos, and near universal access to the world via the Internet keep us in the warmth and security of our homes. At the same time, recent conservative political and economic forces have succeeded in diminishing public support for public infrastructure (parks, education, and various arts programs), leaving much of it weakened, neglected, and even undeveloped. I believe we (as practicing architects and academic stewards of our discipline) need to understand, debate, and critically engage these forces in our culture to ensure that in fact, we make conscious decisions with full awareness of their consequences. It wouldn't be the first time in human history for a culture to discover afterward that it had been lured into "progress" that it regretted. The far-reaching, rarefied, and fragile nature of what cultural enterprise provides a society cannot simply be converted into the goods, services, and amusements of a marketplace economy.

Third, healthy cities and civilizations are well served by the diverse and critical agency of the arts. The arts (performing, visual, literary, media, and design) should publicly and openly reflect, reveal, develop, and challenge the myths and conventions of the societies they serve and those who sponsor and sustain them. The arts are distinct from any other form of human exchange in that they rely on the principles of "gift" exchange (Hyde 1983). Unlike the motivation to sell or acquire goods and services (economic exchange) or to court and gain political influence (power exchange), gift exchange asks us to cultivate and prepare ourselves for the making, offering, and appreciation of aesthetic value, intellectual power, spiritual insight, sensual pleasure, and emotional gravity (Rockcastle 1987). It is simply impossible for a culture to thrive if there is no place or custom of gift exchange.

Many communities are confused today about the important distinctions between the role of art and the role of entertainment, and this confusion is undermining the very integrity of public life. In communities like Las Vegas, the belief that the entertainment value of the "strip," with its attendant visual and experiential amusements, is tantamount to the cultural benefits of art is both mistaken and frightening. The magnitude of gaming-related development as a means to urban revitalization and public life cries out for critical appraisal, discussion, and debate.

Fourth, I want to emphasize the important distinctions between what we should expect from the architecture of cultural buildings and landscapes and what we should expect from the architecture of commercial, residential, and industrial uses. Cultural facilities have a greater responsibility to reflect, invite, or foretell the more obscure and ambiguous qualities of places and ideas. Although all buildings fulfill needs and catalyze interpretation, some buildings are expected to do one more vigorously than the other. Factories and department stores, for example, are more often valued by how efficiently they function, or support function, than by how they might symbolize or challenge. Churches and museums, on the other hand, are more often valued for how their meanings live and how they evoke reflection and interpretation. There are also important subtle distinctions between various types of cultural facilities. Because cultural experience and value can be found in several experiential spheres (spiritual, aesthetic, sensual, intellectual, emotional, etc.), building types have evolved to cater to each differently (churches, museums, spas, schools, theaters, etc.). The urban fabric of any city is an embodiment of both *constructed purpose* (use, make profit from, signify beliefs, regulate behavior, etc.) and *discovered interpretation* (by way of instruction, interest, imagination, make-believe, accident, etc.). However, cultural facilities, when they are at their best, imply the less tangible or foretell the possible through metaphorically manifested story and uncommon experience.

Fifth, I regard reflective architectural practice as more than just using one's professional knowledge or just caring for others (clients and users). When critically cultivated and engaged, practice contributes not only to the development and transformation of the project and the project's constituencies but to the very development of the discipline. By discovering, exploring, and advancing difficult and sensitive issues and ideas, with appropriate balance between confidence and humility, practice probes and exposes deep disciplinary phenomena. For me, practice makes apparent the greatest limitations and possibilities of the discipline. Architecture is always an imperfect embodiment, and its practice is often a messy process. However, when reflected on and shared openly with others, its fertility for providing disciplinary insight and development is most significant.

Final Thoughts

It is reasonable that public entities and professional endeavors that experiment with alternative cultural facilities and programs should expect to encounter political and philosophical challenge. Our disciplinary discourses and our education and training for practice need to better prepare us for the challenges of our times with more insightful and innovative procedural and political savvy. Further programming and design experimentation must continue with new cultural facilities, and critical appraisal and debate should lead to further theoretical exploration.

To some extent because Las Vegas is such a simple or literal cultural landscape and political system, it is an ideal context for seeing what are likely to be more subtle patterns in other communities. Though the unique cultural and political environment of Las Vegas was frustrating and often depressing to work in, I always perceived our responsibility at a minimum to be "coexperimenters," if not critical cultural conspirators or subversives. We were aware that being given an opportunity to design a progressive facility that supports a challenging cultural program is a rare opportunity for architects. There were, at the same time, several mitigating factors that made this ambitious systemwide initiative challenging if not destined for contentious political confrontation in the community.

Provincialism and fear of the unknown remain impediments to cultural and community adventure and growth. Both professional communities (too often with strong self-interest that seeks to block "importing" of outside professional services) and public constituencies need to see how such experiments have the potential to improve local and national cultural health. As well, the practitioners and intellectual stewards of the discipline need to more fully address the how and why of these conflicts to better serve the development of the discipline and the culture it serves. Case studies like this project offer numerous possibilities for broad rigorous analysis and critical appraisal. The health and well-being of our discipline and how it is practiced depend on it.

Notes

1. These issues and this critical discourse stem from the landmark book *Learning from Las Vegas,* by Robert Venturi, Denise Scott Brown, and Steven Izenour (1972). The large body of critical, theoretical contributions of many who have written about the role of semiotics in architecture since that time has also contributed to this evolving disciplinary discourse.

2. From references in the "Virtual Unreality: A New Paradigm or the Theming of Our Cities" Conference held in September 1996.

3. From information provided to me by the LVCC Library District.

4. From LVCC Library District "per capita" statistics.

5. From undated local newspaper citations provided to me.

6. From American Library Association personal testimonials.

7. From both public testimony I witnessed and undated newspaper citations provided to me by the CCLV gallery manager.

8. From various newspaper reports of public meetings, public testimony I heard and took notes from, and published editorials.

9. From newspaper and public testimony comments I read, or from official responses provided to me by the library district.

14

The Profession and Discipline of Architecture: Practice and Education

Stanford Anderson

Academic disciplines may be charged with irrelevance, as occupying "ivory towers." Then again, these disciplines may project themselves into worldly affairs, courting criticism either for their inconsequence or for the corruption of their ideals. In the academy today, one encounters a mistrust of disciplinarity as laying false claims to authority. There is also often a curious absence of the notion of "profession" — perhaps because both critics and supporters emphasize academic disciplines rather than those disciplines, such as medicine and law, that are recognized to prepare professionals. Disciplines merit critical examination, but I conceive the discipline of architecture as providing an open and liberating environment. This chapter looks at architecture but may also be considered as an exploration of how a "discipline" may be articulated when it is part of a field that also incorporates a "profession."

In recognizing both the profession and the discipline of architecture, I do not intend an invidious distinction but rather intend simply to acknowledge different responsibilities and practices in these two modes of attention to a field. To launch this consideration of the profession and the discipline of architecture, I find it necessary to consider these distinctions in the context of architectural education.

Recognition as a school of architecture is to be a *professional* school of architecture. In many countries, schools hold this status by a license from the state; in the United States, schools are accredited by an organization, the National Architectural Accrediting Board, which is partially controlled by the national professional organization, the American Institute of Architects. Recognition as a professional school implies an important responsibility to society — preparing people to enter the practice of architecture. To this end, we have professional degree programs (indeed, it is the degree program, not the school, that is accredited). In most if not all instances, our schools of architecture conceive of this professional degree program as the centerpiece of the school; I imagine few have any quarrel with that focus. Increasingly, however, our schools of architecture incorporate other degree programs: advanced research degrees, including doctoral degrees. What new relations are then established between architecture and education, and among degree programs?

To explore these issues, I distinguish between the profession of architecture and the discipline of architecture. We might imagine a diagram in which the profession of architecture extends horizontally and is intersected, vertically, by the discipline of architecture. Thus the two realms of activity intersect; they are partially but not wholly coincident.

The profession is centrally concerned with the current structure of practice in order that it may fulfill commissions to the highest standards. Its concerns are mainly synchronic and synthetic. Admittedly, the profession does have a temporal dimension that possesses both invention and memory, but these are synchronically structured. That is to say, within the profession, memory and tradition survive operationally (currently, for example, modern architecture and critical debate about it). Other aspects of the tradition survive in the discipline but are not professionally operative (the guild systems of medieval builders, for example, and even their architectural forms and technologies).[1] The profession is also inherently projective — it brings something into being. Yet it cannot be so exploratory that its projections are outside the resources and time scale of its client needs. On the other hand, numerous conditions or activities that are necessary to a successful practice, and thus deserving of attention within the profession (examples might be public relations, office management, and the state of the economy), are rarely central to the conception and understanding of architecture in a stricter sense. Thus, from the point of view of the profession, we see an appropriate inclusion of concerns that are not intrinsically those of architecture while certain forms of architectural knowledge are strategically excluded.

We may also look at this situation from the vantage point of the discipline of architecture. By the "discipline of architecture" I mean a collective body of knowledge that is unique to architecture and, though it grows over time, is not delimited in time or space. Trabeated (post and beam) systems and wall and vault construction appeared early in the history of architecture and are still studied in purely technical terms; even when viewed purely technically, such systems are necessary to architecture. When, however, these systems are understood to create opportunities and constraints for the definition of space, the control of circulation, and the play of light, these are issues of the discipline of architecture. To distinguish the surface of a wall from the wall itself and to find in this distinction the opportunity for representation are propositions within the discipline of architecture.

The nature of a "proposition within the discipline of architecture" may be clarified through a short exposition of Le Corbusier's "Five Points" (1946, 1:128–29). With the development of reinforced concrete, the rigidity and many of the technical limits of trabeated structures were swept away. The possible span of a beam relative to its support increased greatly. Cantilevers could be much more extensive and, thanks to the continuity of the reinforcing rods, could diminish the forces in a neighboring bay of the structure. These traits were recognized in the technical development of architecture, in the engineering aspect of architecture. Le Corbusier, however, developed a series of related "points" for architecture that were made possible by this new technology. As shown in his diagram of the Five Points (see Figure 14.1) and in an exemplary work based on those principles (see Figures 14.2 and 14.3), Le Corbusier asserted that (1) the building could be carried on a sparse array of columns *(pilotis)* and could thus leave the ground plane open; (2) the closure between inside and outside and from room to room (or better, now, space to space) could be independent of the structure, thus allowing a "free plan" relative to the structure and, independently, from floor to floor; (3) and (4) the independence of the exterior surface from supporting structure allowed a free development of the facade, which Le Corbusier showed in the relatively constrained version of the long horizontal (what we call "strip") window; and (5) the flat roof slab permitted a roof garden. Even individually, but especially collectively, these points recognized new, inherently architectural potentials beyond the strict technical capacity of a new structural medium. The Five Points offer an example of the growth of architectural knowledge: new architectural opportunities, made possible by a new technology but nonetheless intrinsically architectural. Le Corbusier wrongly propagandized his invention as one possessed of a temporal necessity, but his forceful invention did require that henceforth architects had to choose to work with these principles or not. Le Corbusier here made a contribution to architectural practice, but more fundamentally to the discipline of architecture.[2]

The structure of knowledge within the discipline is such as to preserve the memory, indeed to continue to study, of that which is external to the range of current practice. Similarly, from a disciplinary base, one can make speculative projections about what might be, unconstrained by the need for a synthesis within the time frame of a client. Historically, we may see this in Piranesi's *Carceri,* Ledoux's "revolutionary" projects, Frank Lloyd Wright's "Broadacre City," and Constant's visions of "New Babylon." Today we see it in visions of the environment of our prophesied cybernetic future. These last comments point to a distinction in the products of the profession and the discipline. The physical artifact, typically a building, as the product of the profession absolutely requires a synthesis whether well or badly performed; the products of the discipline take many forms and possess their own integrity but emphasize a given aspect of architecture, establishing resources for an architectural synthesis rather than taking that step.

If we now turn back to schools and degree programs, I think the implications of my line of argument are clear. The professional degree programs have come into being, and assume their form and responsibilities, in relation to the profession. The discipline of architecture, including its transcultural aspects and its anachronisms and speculations, is primarily the domain of the research degree programs. The less-than-full congruence of the domain of the profession and that of the discipline entails the presence, within a school of architecture, of persons, types of inquiry, and subjects that do not always address one another directly — indeed, they may quite properly, within the current time frame, be irrelevant to one another. Beyond the condition of current utility, the range and structure of the discipline deserve to be explored in their own right, but also because what appears irrelevant today may yet prove otherwise.

Jusqu'au béton armé et au fer, pour bâtir une maison de pierre, on creusait de larges rigoles dans la terre et l'on allait chercher le bon sol pour établir la fondation.

On constituait ainsi les caves, locaux médiocres, humides généralement.

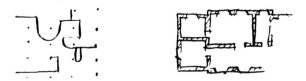

Puis on montait les murs de pierre. On établissait un premier plancher posé sur les murs, puis un second, un troisième: on ouvrait des fenêtres.

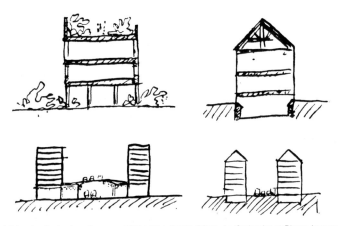

Figure 14.1a. Le Corbusier, diagram of "The Five Points," from *Le Corbusier et Pierre Jeanneret: Oeuvre complète de 1910–1929*, 4th ed. (Zurich: Erlenbach, 1946), 129. Copyright 2000 Artists Rights Society (ARS), New York/ADAGP, Paris/FLC.

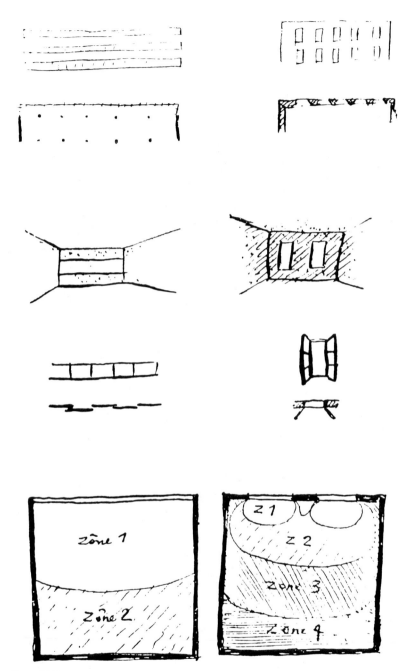

Figure 14.1b

Figure 14.2. Le Corbusier, Villa Savoye, Poissy, France. Exterior view. Courtesy of the Rotch Library Visual Collections, Massachusetts Institute of Technology.

Of course, it would be a pity if these two enterprises did not recognize their significant relations as well. The diagram I evoked at the outset included an intersection of the profession and the discipline. Within this intersection important transactions are initiated from both sides. Le Corbusier was a passionate practitioner, yet he is so frequently cited because both his ideas and his works contributed to the growth of the discipline. Both Viollet-le-Duc (Viollet-le-Duc [1854–1868] 1979, 1987; Summerson [1949] 1963; Hearn 1990) and Gottfried Semper (Semper [1851] 1989, [1860–1863] 1977; Herrmann 1984) are remembered primarily for their theoretical contributions within the discipline of architecture, yet numerous architectural works could not have taken the form they did without such theories. The intersection of the profession and the discipline deserves careful attention. Indeed, precisely this aspect of the profession must be emphasized in schools, while other aspects of a student's professional development await immersion in the architectural office. From this intersection, the professional-degree student ventures into the more esoteric aspects of the discipline, both for an understanding of its past and to revel in imagining a practice that does not yet exist. Put somewhat differently, the intersection of the profession and the

Figure 14.3. Le Corbusier, Villa Savoye. View from terrace to salon. From Collection Lucien Hervé from T. Benton, *The Villas of Le Corbusier, 1920–1930* (New Haven: Yale University Press, 1987), 207. Copyright 2000 Artists Rights Society (ARS), New York/ADAGP, Paris/FLC.

discipline, whether in schools or more generally, should not be emphasized to the extent of, on the one hand, undermining the synthetic activities of the profession that must reach outside the discipline, or, on the other, honoring the discipline only if it is of immediate or proximate utility.

We want the discipline to grow and become more articulate. We want professional practice to reach its highest standards. As researchers or professionals, we want to make our own contributions to these enterprises. As educators we want to prepare the next generation to make their contributions in each of these areas. Degree programs exist only to serve these ends; to maintain the fruitful distinction between professional and research degrees is fundamental.

This last statement is under challenge. In February 1996 the European Association of Architectural Educators held a meeting at the Technical University in Delft on the topic "Doctorates in Design + Architecture." The impetus for the meeting was pressure within the European Community nations to move toward an architectural professional degree termed a doctorate. An as yet small but increasingly vocal number of advocates for the same policy exists in the United States. As a matter solely of terminological change, this would be merely an unfortunate example of degree inflation. But at least in some quarters in Europe, the change in title is accompanied by a change in the agenda of professional architectural education — moving it into the realm of a research degree. At first glance, a higher degree title may appear to be a positive step toward a more rigorous architectural education and in step with changes in architectural production. However, to date, professional education in architecture has been a course of long duration that, nevertheless, few would argue overqualifies its graduates. Put more positively, architecture students begin with little specialized preparation from secondary or undergraduate education and, encountering a rather complex, certainly broad, field, need the current extended-degree programs to emerge as promising architects. It seems implausible either that all of these students want or need an additional research component or that even the best of them would excel on two fronts simultaneously. Actually, the matter is more complex than this, and I have overstated my case. In my own school, professional students are increasingly introduced to research techniques; professional and research degree students in architecture and other fields share in studios and workshops; and some professional students participate in faculty research projects. Professional students do increasingly engage research agendas, but we would not think to demand an independent advanced (let alone doctoral) research thesis at the same time that a student is culminating a professional education. If terming a professional degree (in the United States, historically a bachelor of architecture and for some decades increasingly known as a master of architecture; in Europe often known simply as a "diploma") a doctorate is not just a misnomer, it both endangers the professional degree agenda and devalues the traditional doctoral degree. Such a move would, under its most positive construction, insist on a highly developed thesis in the intersection of the profession and the discipline of architecture. This demand seems too much to ask too early of these students. Furthermore, the new demand would be made in a context where professional and disciplinary studies are diffused into one another at an early stage of education, potentially weakening these two domains within which the intersection is recognized.

Before concluding, I would like to open some areas of discussion that assume the continuing presence of distinct professional and research degree programs.

The Distinctiveness of the Discipline of Architecture; or, Limits to Inclusiveness of the Discipline of Architecture; or, Architecture Schools Should Be Schools of Architecture

A school of architecture that incorporates a research component should recognize that both the profession and the discipline of architecture possess a degree of autonomy. Even though architecture stands in significant relationship to many other areas of knowledge, and even though schools of architecture include faculty with expertise in other areas of knowledge (typically artists, engineers, historians, and social scientists), architecture does not reduce to some composite of those other areas. We need, for example, structural engineers who are fully competent technically, but within a school of architecture we can expect that researchers, and the people who are the recipients of research degrees in architecture, should conceive and interpret that technique more broadly, as it is integrated to the (evolving) discipline and profession of architecture. I seek to sustain this view from a respect for the field of architecture as distinct from other activities; schools of architecture have a responsibility to sustain and advance this distinction. It is a criterion that, under a condition of limited resources, might serve to limit and direct the types of inquiry to be included within schools of architecture and their degree programs. If the research is solely technical or, to take another example, is a general historical inquiry, or is otherwise disengaged from the profession or the discipline of architecture, does it have priority in this place?

Recognizing and Stimulating the Contributions of the Profession to the Discipline (and Vice Versa)

The profession of architecture and the professional degree programs should be concerned to contribute to the discipline of architecture. In teaching, perhaps even more than in practice, designers should be chosen for their ability to entertain and advance the more general level of discourse about architecture that contributes simultaneously to the profession and the discipline. This capacity of design professionals should be respected and encouraged. When possible it should also be incorporated into the research degree programs.

In terms of background, orientation, and time, however, it may well be exceptional that design professors can also conduct or direct research in a form that is appropriate for the Ph.D. degree. Perhaps advanced disciplinary research is the realm for a professional doctoral degree in architecture, though I am skeptical. I think, rather, that the exploration of this intersection of the profession and the discipline can continue in two familiar ways: (1) through projective formulations of designers presented in essays, diagrams, models, and architectural works, as well as through the less formalized demands of the professional and advanced masters degrees; and (2) through the advanced research conducted by those who have completed both professional architectural degrees and traditional doctorates in correlated fields (e.g., engineering, history, social sciences). Such double graduate education is demanding, yet increasingly common among well-qualified candidates.

Relative to the modes of research just mentioned in the realm of architectural designers, a rarer mode for such contributions would be the development, from a disciplinary base, of true architectural research on the intersection of the discipline with practice. Such research would include analysis of the nature of current practice, seen from the more general disciplinary view. It would also include the speculative projection of either new or neglected architectural knowledge into current practice.

I have sought to articulate a range of research and teaching activities that should be complementary to one another while providing for the growth of the discipline and the enhancement of the profession. Such activities have long existed; that is why we already have the profession and the discipline of architecture. The promise of advanced academic research is both to accelerate and deepen these inquiries and the related projections. Intrinsically, I don't see any great problem in encouraging this work within our research universities (or other private or governmental research institutes). But I don't wish to end without recognizing two practical problems.

The first is the question of the willingness of the research institutions to fund research that maintains a commitment to the discipline of architecture—as contrasted to research in technical matters that support, surround, or intersect architecture. Even funding for significant technical areas such as energy, sustainability, and air quality is scarce; intrinsically architectural research is typically deemed too esoteric for funding. Yet the discipline of architecture does intersect with the professional, and together they shape our physical environment, which is too often rightly subject to both aesthetic and environmental criticism. We need a more open view of how disciplinary research can contribute to improving our knowledge and our environment.

My second problem is more serious than that of funding; within the field of architecture itself, it sets limits to the development and effectiveness of research (and thus also contributes to the funding problem). If we are to have a larger number of advanced research people in architecture, more outlets must exist than just additional teaching positions. Is the profession prepared to support research in those vital areas where it intersects with the discipline of architecture, or even in the more rarefied aspects of the discipline, and thus to receive advanced research into its practice?

I conclude with some observations about my understanding of a "discipline" in contrast to other usages in this book and elsewhere. In the conference that launched this book, Julia Robinson began her précis with the following sentence: "The field of architecture is in the process of evolving from what has been a practice, informed by other disciplines, into a discipline with its own body of knowledge." And later: "This paper will explore the history of the field and the seeds that have been laid for creating a discipline out of the practice of architecture." For me, these statements too little recognize the body of knowledge that has long since built up within the discipline of architecture. They appear also to minimize what I think must remain an important distinction: architectural knowledge versus knowledge (of other kinds) applied to architecture. Robinson raised this matter as a question: "Are there 'architectural' questions, or are there simply a variety of questions that can be asked of architecture?"[3] I say there are both (consider again the Le Corbusier example offered earlier); both are important, and it is important not to take one for the other.

Whatever our differences, both Julia Robinson and I have used the term "discipline" in a positive sense. We both see the discipline as a key vehicle in the production of knowledge and the advancement of the field. At least in my case, I see the discipline as an open and liberating environment: the place where what appears anachronistic or visionary, currently inappropriate or unrealizable, can be thought, preserved, advocated. I see the discipline as that which fosters participation in the field by nonprofessionals: preservationists, local historians, visionary engineers, builders, advocacy groups, and citizens, to name a few. This view stands in contrast to the not uncommon suspicion of "disciplines." Of course, many such doubts or questions are legitimate and must also be applied to the construct I have called a discipline. The question remains for me: Is some of the difference from my construction to those who are more skeptical about disciplines owing to the absence of the concept of "profession" and the encouragement of a broader framing discourse that it entails?

Notes

This chapter derived from the author's contribution to the University of Michigan symposium on Ph.D. Education in Architecture, 11–12 November 1988.

1. This is not to say that the profession does not leap back over time to embrace once again aspects of the architectural tradition that had become dormant. Classical revivals have been several in the history of architecture. The Bauhaus, famed for its role in the development of modern architecture, began with a favorable reassessment of the practices of medieval guilds. Indeed, as I will argue, the discipline of architecture maintains a record and an awareness of the architectural tradition that is then used selectively—by imitation, but also critically and inventively—in the profession.

2. I would like at least to note the challenge as to the ontological status of the work of the architect as opposed to that of the contributors to the discipline (even if architects working in a different mode). Yes, a building should keep rain off our heads whereas a theory does not. Since the Renaissance the product of the architect has increasingly been the documents by which a building is constructed rather than the building itself; however, I do not choose here to emphasize this convergence of architectural with other forms of intellectual work. Rather, I prefer to emphasize that buildings, like sculptures, paintings, diagrams, and texts, are objective documents of human thought even if they must also be differentiated in many ways. New architectural conceptions may first appear in a built work. Certainly in examining prehistoric and ancient architecture we develop our disciplinary knowledge from the works themselves (with, in a few cases, some limited support of drawings or texts). While there is something that we can term *synthesis*

in every form of production, I particularly emphasize synthesis in the architect's professional work because a building will at least imply answers to numerous issues that may deliberately and correctly be omitted from theoretical or historical discourse about buildings.

3. These quotes by Robinson were taken from a lecture presented at the conference "Knowledges: Production, Distribution, Revision." For conference details, see note 1 in the introduction.

Works Cited

ACSA. 1993. *ACSA Newsletter* (September). Washington, D.C: Association of Collegiate Schools of Architecture.

———. 1996. *ACSA Newsletter* (November). Washington, D.C.: Association of Collegiate Schools of Architecture.

Adorno, Theodor W. 1979. "Functionalism Today." *Oppositions* 17 (summer): 31–44.

Ahmad, Aijaz. 1992. *In Theory: Classes, Nations, Literatures.* London: Verso.

Ahrentzen, Sherry B. 1996. "The F Word in Architecture: Feminist Analyses in/of/for Architecture." In *Reconstructing Architecture: Critical Discourses and Social Practices,* edited by Thomas A. Dutton and Lian Hurst Mann, 71–118. Minneapolis: University of Minnesota Press.

Ahrentzen, Sherry B., and Linda N. Groat. 1990. *Status of Faculty Women in Architecture Schools: Survey Results and Recommendations.* Washington, D.C.: Association of Collegiate Schools of Architecture.

———. 1992. "Rethinking Architectural Education: Patriarchal Conventions and Alternative Visions from the Perspectives of Women Faculty." *Journal of Architectural and Planning Research* 9, no. 2 (summer): 95–111.

AIA. 1994. *The Architect's Handbook of Professional Practice.* 12th ed. Edited by David Haviland. Washington, D.C.: American Institute of Architects Press.

Aisenberg, Nadya, and Mona Harrington. 1988. *Women of Academe: Outsiders in the Sacred Grove.* Amherst: University of Massachusetts Press.

Alexander, Christopher. 1964. *Notes on the Synthesis of Form.* Cambridge: Harvard University Press.

———. 1979. *The Timeless Way of Building.* New York: Oxford University Press.

Ameen, Farooq, ed. 1997. *Contemporary Architecture and City Form: The South Asian Paradigm*. Mumbai, India: Marg Publications.

Amin, Samir. 1998. *Spectres of Capitalism: A Critique of Current Intellectual Fashions*. Translated by Shane Henry Mage. New York: Monthly Review Press.

Ananth, Sashikala. 1998. *The Penguin Guide to Vaastu: The Classical Indian Science of Architecture and Design*. New Delhi: Viking.

Anderson, Stanford. 1978. Introduction to *On Streets*, edited by Stanford Anderson. Cambridge: MIT Press.

Anthony, Kathryn H. 1991. *Design Juries on Trial: The Renaissance of the Design Studio*. New York: Van Nostrand Reinhold.

Archer, Margaret. 1988. *Culture and Agency: The Place of Culture in Social Theory*. Cambridge: Cambridge University Press.

Architectural Research Centers Consortium. 1993, "Schools Report." Minutes from the annual meeting, November.

Arendt, Hannah. 1958. *The Human Condition*. Chicago: University of Chicago Press.

Aristotle. 1941a. *Metaphysics*. In *The Basic Works of Aristotle*. 9th ed. New York: Random House.

———. 1941b. *Nicomachean Ethics*. In *The Basic Works of Aristotle*. 9th ed. New York: Random House.

———. 1984. *The Complete Works of Aristotle: The Revised Oxford Translation*. Revised by Jonathan Barnes. Princeton, N.J.: Princeton University Press.

Banham, Reyner. 1960. *Theory and Design in the First Machine Age*. New York: Praeger.

Baudrillard, Jean. 1988a. *America*. Translated by Chris Turner. London: Verso.

———. 1988b. *The Ecstasy of Communication*. Edited by Sylvere Lotringer, translated by Bernard and Caroline Schutze. Brooklyn: Semiotext(e) series, Autonomedia.

———. 1988c. *Selected Writings*. Edited by Mark Poster. Stanford: Stanford University Press.

———. 1994. *The Illusion of the End*. Translated by Chris Turner. Stanford: Stanford University Press.

———. 1999. "Truth or Radicality? The Future of Architecture." *Blueprint* 157 (January): 30–35.

Bedford, S. M. 1981. "History I: The Founding of the School." In R. Oliver 1981, 5–12.

Beeson, Simon. 1994. "Consideration of the Work of Sian Armajani." Unpublished paper for the Department of Architecture, University of Minnesota.

Belenky, Mary Field, Blythe McVicker Clinchy, Nancy Rule Goldberger, and Jill Mattuck Tarule. 1986. *Women's Ways of Knowing: The Development of Self, Voice, and Mind*. New York: Basic Books of Harper Collins.

Bell, Derrick A. 1992. *Faces at the Bottom of the Well: The Permanence of Racism.* New York: Basic Books.

Bellah, Robert N., R. Madsen, W. M. Sullivan, A. Swidler, and S. M. Tipton. 1985. *Habits of the Heart: Individualism and Commitment in American Life.* Berkeley: University of California Press.

Benjamin, Walter. 1968. "Work of Art in the Age of Mechanical Reproduction." In *Illuminations, Essays, and Reflections,* edited by Hannah Arendt, translated by Harry Zohn, 217–51. New York: Schocken Books.

Bennett, Tony. 1988. "The Exhibitionary Complex." *New Formations* 4 (spring): 73–102.

Berkeley, Ellen Perry, and Matilda McQuaid, eds. 1989. *Architecture: A Place for Women.* Washington D.C.: Smithsonian Institution Press.

Bernstein, Basil. 1975. *Class, Codes, and Control.* Vol. 3, *Towards a Theory of Educational Transmissions.* London: Routledge and Kegan Paul.

Bernstein, Richard. 1985. "From Hermeneutics to Praxis." In *Hermeneutics and Praxis,* edited by Robert Hollinger, 272–76. Notre Dame, Ind.: University of Notre Dame Press.

Berry, Wendell. 1990. *What Are People For?* San Francisco: North Point Press.

Bhabha, Homi K. 1990. "The Third Space." In *Identity: Community, Culture, Difference,* edited by Jonathan Rutherford. London: Lawrence and Wishart.

———. 1992. "Postcolonial Criticism." In *Redrawing the Boundaries: The Transformation of English and American Literary Studies,* edited by Stephen Greenblatt and Giles Gunn, 437–65. New York: Modern Language Association of America.

———. 1994. *The Location of Culture.* London: Routledge.

Bhatia, Gautam. 1991. *Laurie Baker: Life, Work, Writings.* New Delhi: Viking.

Bhatt, Ritu, and Sonit Bafna. 1997. "Vistara: A Critical Appraisal." In *Proceedings of the Theaters of Decolonization Conference, Chandigarh, January 6–10, 1995,* edited by Vikramaditya Prakash. Seattle, Wash.: Office of the Dean, College of Architecture and Urban Planning, University of Washington.

Bhatt, Vikram, and Peter Scriver. 1990. *After the Masters: Contemporary Indian Architecture.* Ahmedabad: Mapin Publishing; Middletown, N.J.: Grantha Corporation.

Bijker, Wiebe E., Thomas P. Hughes, and Trevor J. Pinch, eds. 1987. *The Social Construction of Technological Systems: New Directions in the Sociology and History of Technology.* Cambridge: MIT Press.

Blake, Peter. 1977. *Form Follows Fiasco: Why Modern Architecture Hasn't Worked.* Boston: Atlantic-Little, Brown.

Blau, Judith R. 1984. *Architects and Firms: A Sociological Perspective on Architectural Practice.* Cambridge: MIT Press.

Bledstein, Burton J. 1976. *The Culture of Professionalism: The Middle Class and the Development of Higher Education in America*. New York: W. W. Norton.

Bletter, Rosemarie Haag. 1981. "Modernism Rears Its Head: The Twenties and Thirties." In R. Oliver 1981.

Bongaarts, John. 1994. "Can the Growing Human Population Feed Itself?" *Scientific American* 270, no. 3 (March): 36–37.

Bonta, Juan Pablo. 1979. *Architecture and Its Interpretation: A Study of Expressive Systems in Architecture*. New York: Rizzoli.

Boorstin, Daniel. 1958. *The Colonial Experience*. Vol. 1, *The Americans*. New York: Random House.

Boudon, Philippe. 1969. *Lived-In Architecture: Le Corbusier's "Pessac" Revisited*. Cambridge: MIT Press.

———. 1992. *Introduction à l'Architecturologie*. Paris: Dunod.

Bourdieu, Pierre. 1994. "Doxa and the Common Life." Interview with Terry Eagleton. In Žižek 1994.

Bowers, C. A. 1993. *Critical Essays on Education, Modernity, and the Recovery of the Ecological Imperative*. New York: Teachers College Press.

Bowles, Samuel, and Herbert Gintis. 1976. *Schooling in Capitalist America: Educational Reform and the Contradictions of Economic Life*. New York: Basic Books.

Boyer, Ernest L., and Lee D. Mitgang. 1996. *Building Community: A New Future for Architecture Education and Practice*. Princeton, N.J.: Carnegie Foundation for the Advancement of Teaching.

Boyer, M. Christine. 1994. *The City of Collective Memory: Its Historical Imagery and Architectural Entertainments*. Cambridge: MIT Press.

Brightman, Carol, ed. 1995. *Between Friends: The Correspondences of Hannah Arendt and Mary McCarthy, 1949–1975*. New York: Harcourt Brace.

Broadbent, Geoffrey. 1977. "A Plain Man's Guide to the Theory of Signs in Architecture." *Architectural Design* 47 (July–August): 474–82.

———. 1995. "Architectural Education." In *Educating Architects*, edited by Martin Pearce and Maggie Toy. London: Academy Editions.

Brolin, Brent C. 1976. *The Failure of Modern Architecture*. New York: Van Nostrand Reinhold.

Brown, Frank. 1963. "Vitruvius and the Liberal Art of Architecture." *Bucknell Review*, 99–107.

Brown, Lester, et al. 1994. *State of the World 1994: A Worldwatch Institute Report on Progress Toward a Sustainable Society*. New York: W. W. Norton.

Bureau of the Census. 1904a. *Abstract of the Twelfth Census of the United States 1900*. 3d ed. Washington, D.C.: Government Printing Office.

———. 1904b. *Occupations at the Twelfth Census*. Washington, D.C.: Government Printing Office.

Cantacazino, Sherban. 1984. *Charles Correa*. Singapore: Concept Media.

Castell, Alburey. 1963. *An Introduction to Modern Philosophy in Seven Philosophical Problems.* 2d ed. New York: Macmillan.

Christ, Carol P. 1980. *Diving Deep and Surfacing: Women Writers on Spiritual Quest.* Boston: Beacon Press.

Collins, Patricia Hill. 1991. "Learning from the Outsider Within: The Sociological Significance of Black Feminist Thought." In Hartman 1991.

Colomina, Beatriz. 1994. *Privacy and Publicity: Modern Architecture as Mass Media.* Cambridge: MIT Press.

Colquhoun, Alan. 1981. "Typology and Design Method." In *Essays in Architectural Criticism: Modern Architecture and Historical Change.* Cambridge: MIT Press.

Conrads, Ulrich, ed. 1970. *Programs and Manifestoes on 20th-Century Architecture.* Translated by Michael Bullock. Cambridge: MIT Press.

Cooper, Clare. See Marcus, Clare Cooper.

Crary, Jonathan. 1990. *Techniques of the Observer: On Vision and Modernity in the Nineteenth Century.* Cambridge: MIT Press.

Crosbie, Michael. 1995. "The Schools: How They're Failing the Profession." *Progressive Architecture* 76, no. 9 (September): 47–51, 94, 96.

Cuff, Dana. 1987. "The Optional Academy." *Journal of Architectural Education* 40, no. 2 (Jubilee): 13–14.

———. 1989. "Through the Looking Glass: Seven New York Architects and Their People." In Ellis and Cuff 1989, 64 and 100.

———. 1991. *Architecture: The Story of Practice.* Cambridge: MIT Press.

Curry, Lynn, and Jon F. Wergin and Associates, eds. 1993. *Educating Professionals: Responding to New Expectations for Competence and Accountability.* San Francisco: Jossey-Bass.

Curtis, William. 1988. *Balkrishna Doshi: An Architecture for India.* New York: Rizzoli.

Davis, Regina. 1993. "Writing Multiculturalism into Architectural Curricula." *Journal of Architectural Education* 47, no. 1 (September): 30–37.

Deamer, Peggy. 1991. "Subject/Object/Text." In *Drawing/Building/Text: Essays in Architectural Theory,* edited by Andrea Kahn. New York: Princeton Architectural Press.

de Certeau, Michel. 1984. *The Practice of Everyday Life.* Translated by Steven Rendall. Berkeley: University of California Press.

Deleuze, Gilles. 1993. *The Fold: Leibniz and the Baroque.* Translated by Tom Conley. Minneapolis: University of Minnesota Press.

Derrida, Jacques. 1967. *L'Écriture et la Différence.* Paris: Editions du Seuil.

Diderot, Denis. 1978. *Encyclopedie: The Complete Illustrations, 1762–1777.* New York: Abrams.

Diller, Elizabeth, and Ricardo Scofidio. 1994a. *Flesh: Architectural Probes.* New York: Princeton Architectural Press.

———. 1994b. *Visite aux armées: Tourismes de guerre* (Back to the front: Tourisms of War). Basse-Normandie: FRAC.

Dogan, Mattei, and Robert Pahre. 1990. *Creative Marginality: Innovation at the Intersections of Social Sciences.* Boulder, Colo.: Westview.

Domer, Dennis, and Kent F. Spreckelmeyer. 1990. *The Liberal Education of Architects.* Lawrence: University of Kansas School of Architecture and Urban Design.

Douglas, Mary. 1966. *Purity and Danger: An Analysis of Concepts of Pollution and Taboo.* New York: Praeger.

———. 1970. "Environments at Risk." *Times Literary Supplement,* 30 October, 1273.

Douglas, Mary, and Aaron Wildavsky. 1982. *Risk and Culture: An Essay on the Selection of Technical and Environmental Dangers.* Berkeley: University of California Press.

Draper, Joan. 1977. "The École des Beaux-Arts and the Architectural Profession in the United States: The Case of John Galen Howard." In Kostof 1977b, 209–37.

Drexler, Arthur. [1972] 1996. Preface to *Five Architects: Eisenman, Graves, Gwathmey, Hejduk, Meier.* New York: Oxford University Press. Quoted in Nesbitt 1996, 26.

Duderstadt, J. 1995. *Intellectual Transformation at the University of Michigan.* Ann Arbor: University of Michigan Press.

Duffy, Francis. 1996. "The Value of a Doctorate in Architectural Practice." In *Doctorates in Design and Architecture—Proceedings,* edited by Jan Brouwer et al., 9–18. European Association of Architectural Education/Publikatieburo Bouwkunde, Delft University of Technology.

Duhl, Leonard J. 1990. *The Social Entrepreneurship of Change.* New York: Pace University Press.

Eco, Umberto. 1980. "Function and Sign: The Semiotics of Architecture." In *Signs, Symbols, and Architecture,* edited by Geoffrey Broadbent, Richard Bunt, and Charles Tenely, 11–69. New York: John Wiley and Sons.

Ehrenreich, Barbara. 1990. *Fear of Falling: The Inner Life of the Middle Class.* New York: HarperPerennial.

Ehrenreich, Barbara, and Dierdre English. 1973. *Complaints and Disorders: The Sexual Politics of Sickness.* New York: Feminist Press.

Ehrlich, Paul R., and Anne H. Ehrlich. 1990. *The Population Explosion.* New York: Simon and Schuster.

Einaudi, Roberto. 1987. *Metamorphosi 6–7.* Rome: Roberto De Nicola Editore.

Eisenman, Peter, et al. 1995. "Eisenman (and Company) Respond." *Progressive Architecture* 76, no. 2 (February): 70–73.

Eliot, T. S. 1957. *On Poetry and Poets.* London: Farrar, Straus and Cudahy.

Ellis, William Russell, and Dana Cuff, eds. 1989. *Architects' People.* New York: Oxford University Press.

Fisher, Helen S. 1997. *American Salaries and Wages Survey.* 5th ed. Detroit: Gale Research.

Fisher, Thomas. 1987. "P/A Reader Poll: Career Satisfaction." *Progressive Architecture* 68, no. 2 (February): 15–16, 20.

———. 1994. "Can This Profession Be Saved?" *Progressive Architecture,* 75, no. 2 (February): 44–49, 84.

———. 1996. "Three Models for the Future of Practice." In Saunders and Rowe 1996.

———. 2000. *In the Scheme of Things: Alternative Thinking on the Practice of Arhitecture.* Minneapolis: University of Minnesota Press.

Forster, Kurt W. 1995. [Untitled contribution]. In Eisenman et al. 1995, 91.

Foster, Hal. 1985. "The Expressive Fallacy." In *Recodings: Art, Spectacle, Cultural Politics,* 59–78. Port Townsend, Wash.: Bay Press.

———, ed. 1987. "Of Bodies and Technologies." In *Discussions in Contemporary Culture.* Seattle: Bay Press.

Foucault, Michel. 1970. *The Order of Things: An Archeology of Human Sciences.* New York: Random House.

———. 1972. *The Archaeology of Knowledge and the Discourse on Language.* Translated by A. M. Sheridan Smith. New York: Pantheon.

———. 1979. *Discipline and Punish: The Birth of the Prison.* Translated by Alan Sheridan. New York: Random House.

Frampton, Kenneth. [1974] 1996. "On Reading Heidegger." Originally published in *Oppositions* 4 (October): n.p. Reprinted in Nesbitt 1996, 442–46.

———. [1983] 1996. "Prospects for a Critical Regionalism." *Perspecta* 20: 147–62. Reprinted in Nesbitt 1996, 470–82.

———. 1986. "Photography and Its Influence on Architecture." *Perspecta* 22: 38–41.

———. 1992. *Modern Architecture: A Critical History.* 3d ed. London: Thames and Hudson.

Franck, Karen A., and Lynda H. Schneekloth, eds. 1994. *Ordering Space: Types in Architecture and Design.* New York: Van Nostrand Reinhold.

Frederick, Bonnie, and Susan H. McLeod, eds. 1993. *Women and the Journey: The Female Travel Experience.* Pullman: Washington State University Press.

Frederickson, Mark Paul. 1993. "Gender and Racial Bias in Design Juries." *Journal of Architectural Education* 47, no. 1 (September): 38–48.

Fuller, Timothy, ed. 1989. *The Voice of Liberal Learning: Michael Oakeshott on Education.* New Haven, Conn.: Yale University Press.

Gadamer, Hans-Georg. 1975. *Truth and Method.* New York: Crossroad.

———. 1986. *The Idea of the Good in Platonic-Aristotelian Philosophy.* Translated by P. Christopher Smith. New Haven: Yale University Press.

———. 1991. *Plato's Dialectical Ethics: Phenomenological Interpretations Relating to the Philebus.* Translated by Robert M. Wallace. New Haven: Yale University Press.

Gandhi, Leela. 1999. *Postcolonial Theory: A Critical Introduction.* Delhi: Oxford University Press.

Gaster, Sanford. 1991. "History for Environmental Social Scientists." In Person-Environment Theory Series of Working Papers PETS-009. Berkeley, Calif.: Center for Environmental Design Research.

Gehlen, Arnold. 1980. *Man in the Age of Technology.* Translated by Patricia Lipscomb. New York: Columbia University Press.

Ghirardo, Diane. 1994. "Eisenman's Bogus Avant-Garde." *Progressive Architecture* 75 no. 11 (November): 70–73.

Gide, André. 1959. "The Future of Europe." In *Pretexts: Reflections on Literature and Morality.* New York: Meridan Books.

Gilovitch, Thomas. 1991. *How We Know What Isn't So: The Fallibility of Human Reason in Everyday Life.* New York: Free Press.

Grant, Brad. 1991. "Cultural Invisibility: The African American Experience in Architectural Education." In *Voices in Architectural Education: Cultural Politics and Pedagogy,* edited by Thomas A. Dutton, 149–64. New York: Bergin and Garvey.

Gravagnuolo, Benedetto. 1987. *Metamorphosi 6–7.* Rome: Roberto De Nicola Editore.

Gregotti, Vittorio. 1996. *Inside Architecture.* Translated by Peter Wong and Francesca Zaccheo. Cambridge: MIT Press.

Gresleri, Giuliano. 1991. "From Diary to Project: Le Corbusier's Carnets 1–6." *Lotus International* 68: 6–21.

Groat, Linda N. 1993a. "Architecture's Resistance to Diversity: A Matter of Theory as Much as Practice." *Journal of Architectural Education* 47, no. 1 (September): 3–10.

———. 1993b. "Reconceptualizing Architectural Education: The Necessity for a Culturalist Paradigm." In *Architecture + Culture: Proceedings of the International Research Symposium,* edited by Tim Donais, Trevor Boddy, and Enn Kayari. Ottawa, Canada: Carleton University.

———, ed. 1991. "Introduction to the Monograph." In *Post-professional and Doctoral Education in Architecture: A Monograph.* Ann Arbor: University of Michigan College of Architecture and Urban Planning.

Groat, Linda N., and Sherry Ahrentzen. 1996. "Reconceptualizing Architectural Education for a More Diverse Future: Perceptions and Visions of Architectural Students." *Journal of Architectural Education* 49, no. 3 (February): 166–83.

————. 1997. "Voices for Change in Architectural Education: Seven Facets of Transformation from the Perspectives of Faculty Women." *Journal of Architectural Education* 50, no. 4 (May): 271–85.

Grover, Satish. 1990. "Review of G. H. R. Tillotson *Traditions of Indian Architecture.*" *Architecture + Design* (New Delhi)7, no. 6 (November-December): 104–6.

Gusevich, Miriam. 1995. "Architecture and Its Dis-contexts." In *Architecture and—Legitimacy,* edited by Hans van Dijk and Liesbeth Janson, translated by D'Laine Camp and Donna de Vries-Hermansader. Rotterdam: Nai Publishers.

Gutman, Robert. 1987. "Education and the World of Practice." *Journal of Architectural Education* 40, no. 2 (Jubilee): 24–25.

————. 1988. *Architectural Practice: A Critical View.* Princeton, N.J.: Princeton Architectural Press.

————. 1995. "Two Discourses of Architectural Education." In *Practices* (Center for the Study of the Practice of Architecture, University of Cincinnati) 3–4 (spring): 10–19.

Haacke, Hans. 1995. Exhibition pamphlet from "Obra Social" show at the Fundació Antoni Tàpies, Barcelona, 21 July–3 September.

Habermas, Jürgen. 1990. *Moral Consciousness and Communicative Action.* Translated by Christian Lenhardt and Shierry Weber. Cambridge: MIT Press.

Hacking, Ian. 1975. *Why Does Language Matter to Philosophy?* London and New York: Cambridge University Press.

Harries, Karsten. 1968. *The Meaning of Modern Art: A Philosophical Interpretation.* Evanston, Ill.: Northwestern University Press.

————. [1975] 1996. "The Ethical Function of Architecture." *Journal of Architectural Education* 29, no. 1 (September): 14–15. Reprinted in Nesbitt 1996, 394–96.

————. 1997. *The Ethical Function of Architecture.* Cambridge: MIT Press.

Hartman, Joan E. 1991. "Agency." In *(En)gendering Knowledge: Feminists in Academe,* written with Ellen Messer-Davidow. Knoxville: University of Tennessee Press.

Hawken, Paul. 1993. *The Ecology of Commerce: A Declaration of Sustainability.* New York: HarperCollins.

Hays, K. Michael, ed. 1998. *Architecture Theory since 1968.* Cambridge: MIT Press.

Hearn, M. F., ed. 1990. *The Architectural Theory of Viollet-le-Duc: Readings and Commentary.* Cambridge: MIT Press.

Hegel, Georg Wilhelm Friedrich. 1975. *Aesthetics: Lectures on Fine Art.* Vol. 1. Translated by T. M. Knox. Oxford: Clarendon Press.

Heidegger, Martin. [1927] 1996. *Being and Time.* Translated by Joan Stambaugh. Albany: State University of New York Press.

————. 1971a. "The Origin of the Work of Art." In Heidegger 1971b, 17–87

————. 1971b. *Poetry, Language, Thought.* Translated by Albert Hofstadter. New York: Harper and Row.

Herrmann, Wolfgang. 1984. *Gottfried Semper: In Search of Architecture.* Cambridge: MIT Press.

Hesse, Eva. 1969. Artist's statement. In *Art in Process IV.* New York: Finch College Museum of Art.

Heynen, Hilde. 1993. "Worthy of Question: Heidegger's Role in Architectural Theory." *Archis* 12 (December): 42–49.

————. 1999. *Architecture and Modernity: A Critique.* Cambridge: MIT Press.

Hickey, Dave. 1993. *The Invisible Dragon: Four Essays on Beauty.* Los Angeles: Art Issues Press.

Hillier, Bill, and Julienne Hanson. 1984. *The Social Logic of Space.* Cambridge and New York: Cambridge University Press.

Hollander, E. P., and L. R. Offermann. 1993. "Power and Leadership in Organizations." In *Contemporary Issues in Leadership,* edited by William E. Rosenbach and Robert L. Taylor. 3d ed. San Francisco: Westview Press.

Hollier, Denis. 1989. *Against Architecture: The Writings of Georges Bataille.* Translated by Betsy Wing. Cambridge: MIT Press.

hooks, bell. 1990. "Marginality as Site of Resistance." In *Out There: Marginalization and Contemporary Cultures,* edited by Russell Ferguson, M. Gever, T. Minh-ha, and C. West, 341–43. Cambridge: MIT Press.

Horwitz, Jamie. 1993. "Picturing Privacy." Person-Environment Theory Series of Working Papers PETS-015. Berkeley, Calif.: Center for Environmental Design Research.

Hoskins, Keith W. 1993. "Education and the Genesis of Disciplinarity: The Unexpected Reversal." In Messer et al. 1993a, 271–304.

Husserl, Edmund. [1954] 1970. *The Crisis of European Sciences and Transcendental Phenomenology: An Introduction to Phenomenological Philosophy.* Translated by David Carr. Evanston, Ill.: Northwestern University Press.

Hyde, Lewis. 1983. *The Gift: Imagination and the Erotic Life of Property.* New York: Random House.

Illich, Ivan. 1977. "Disabling Professions." In *Disabling Professions: Ideas in Progress,* edited by Zola, McKnight, Caplan, and Shaiken. Salem, N.H.: Marion Boyars.

Ingraham, Catherine. 1992. "Architecture: The Lament for Power and the Power of Lament." *Harvard Architecture Review* 8: 50–65.

Jackson, Wes, Wendell Berry, and Bruce Colman, eds. 1984. *Meeting the Expectations of the Land: Essays in Sustainable Agriculture and Stewardship.* San Francisco: North Point Press.

Jacobs, Jane. 1961. *The Death and Life of Great American Cities.* New York: Random House.

Jacobson, Roman. 1960. "Closing Statement: Linguistics and Poetics." In *Style in Language,* edited by Thomas A. Sebeok, 350–77. Cambridge: MIT Press.

Jacques, Annie. 1986. *La carrière de l'architecte au XIXe siècle.* Paris: Musèe d'Orsay.

Jaeger, Werner Wilhelm. 1934. *Aristotle: Fundamentals of the History of His Development.* Oxford: Clarendon Press.

Jameson, Fredric. 1991. *Postmodernism: or, The Cultural Logic of Late Capitalism.* Durham, N.C.: Duke University Press.

Jencks, Charles E. 1977. *The Language of Post-modern Architecture.* Rev. and enlarged ed. New York: Rizzoli.

Jenkins, D. 1995. "Changing the Culture for Women in Science and Engineering." *Women in Higher Education* 4, no. 6 (June): 8.

Johnson, Terence. 1972. *Professions and Power.* London: Macmillan Press.

Johnson, Warren A. 1985. *The Future Is Not What It Used to Be: Returning to Traditional Values in an Age of Scarcity.* New York: Dodd, Mead.

Kaplan, Michael. 1993. "Statistics on Tenured Faculty." *ACSA Newsletter* (September): 28. Washington, D.C.: Association of Collegiate Schools of Architecture.

Karatani, Kojin. 1995. *Architecture as Metaphor: Language, Number, Money.* Translated by Sabu Kohso. Writing Architecture series, edited by Michael Speaks. Cambridge: MIT Press.

Kelbaugh, Douglas, et al., eds. 1989. *Pedestrian Pocket Book: A New Suburban Design Strategy.* New York: Princeton Architectural Press.

Kennedy, Paul M. 1993. *Preparing for the Twenty-First Century.* New York: Random House.

Kerényi, Karl. 1977. *Prometheus: Archetypal Image of Human Existence.* Translated by Ralph Manheim. Princeton, N.J.: Princeton University Press.

Kermode, Frank. 1975. *The Classic: Literary Images of Permanence and Change.* New York: Viking Press.

Khan, Hussein-Uddin, ed. 1987. *Charles Correa: Architect in India.* London: Butterworth Architecture.

Khilnani, Sunil. 1997. *The Idea of India.* London: H. Hamilton.

Kimball, Roger. 1998. *Tenured Radicals: How Politics Has Corrupted Our Higher Education.* Rev. ed. Chicago: Elephant Paperbacks.

Klein, Julie Thompson. 1990. *Interdisciplinarity: History, Theory, and Practice.* Detroit, Mich.: Wayne State University Press.

———. 1993. "Blurring, Cracking, and Crossing: Permeation and the Fracturing of Discipline." In Messer et al. 1993a, 185–211.

Klein, Robert. 1979. *Form and Meaning: Essays on the Renaissance and Modern Art.* Translated by Madeline Jay and Leon Wieseltier. New York: Viking Press.

Koolhaas, Rem. 1993. "Rem Koolhaas: Why I Wrote Delirious New York and Other Textual Strategies." Edited by Cynthia Davidson. *ANY* 1 (May–June): 42–43.

Kostof, Spiro. 1977a. "The Practice of Architecture in the Ancient World: Egypt and Greece." In Kostof 1977b.

———, ed. 1977b. *The Architect: Chapters in the History of the Profession.* New York: Oxford University Press.

Krause, Elliott A. 1996. *The Death of Guilds: Professions, States and the Advance of Capitalism, 1930 to the Present.* New Haven, Conn.: Yale University Press.

Kroloff, Reed. 1996. "How the Profession Is Failing the Schools." *Architecture* 85, no. 8 (August): 92–93.

Kruft, Hanno Walter. 1994. *A History of Architectural Theory: From Vitruvius to the Present.* Translated by Ronald Taylor, Elsie Callander, and Antony Wood. New York: Princeton Architectural Press.

Kruger, B., and P. Mariani, eds. 1989. "Black Culture and Postmodernism." In *Remaking History.* Port Townsend, Wash.: Dia-Bay Press.

Lacan, Jacques. 1980. *Écrits: A Selection.* Translated by Alan Sheridan. London: Tavistock Publications.

Landecker, Heidi. 1991. "Why Aren't More Women Teaching Architecture?" *Architecture* 80, no. 10 (October): 23–25.

Lang, Jon T. 1987. *Creating Architectural Theory: The Role of the Behavioral Sciences in Environmental Design.* New York: Van Nostrand Reinhold.

Lang, Jon T., Charles Burnette, Walter Moleski, and David Vachon, eds. 1974. *Designing for Human Behavior: Architecture and the Behavioral Sciences.* Stroudsburg, Pa.: Dowden, Hutchinson and Ross.

Lang, Jon T., Madhavi Desai, and Miki Desai. 1997. *Architecture and Independence: The Search for Identity—India 1880 to 1980.* Delhi: Oxford University Press.

Larson, Magali Sarfati. 1977. *The Rise of Professionalism: A Sociological Analysis.* Berkeley: University of California Press.

Latour, Bruno. 1993. *We Have Never Been Modern.* Cambridge: Harvard University Press.

Leach, Neil. 1997. *Rethinking Architecture: A Reader in Cultural Theory.* New York: Routledge.

Leatherbarrow, David. 1993. *Roots of Architectural Invention: Site, Enclosure, and Materials.* Cambridge: Cambridge University Press.

———. 1997. "The Conscience of Design: Adjusting Architectural Premises." *Practices* 5–6: 174–84.

Lebel, Gregory G., and Hal Kane. 1989. *Sustainable Development: A Guide to Our Common Future.* Report of the World Commission on Environment and Development. Washington, D.C.: Global Tomorrow Coalition.

Le Corbusier. [1927] 1972. *Vers une architecture.* Translated from the French by Frederick Etchells as *Towards a New Architecture.* New York: Praeger Publications.

———. [1931] 1986. *Towards a New Architecture.* Translated by Frederick Etchells. New York: Dover. Originally published by John Rodker, London, as translated from the 13th French edition.

———. 1946. *Le Corbusier et Pierre Jeanneret: Oeuvre complète de 1910–1929.* 4th ed. Edited by Willy Boesiger and Oscar Stonorov. Zurich: Éditions d'architecture.

———. 1964. *Le Corbusier et Pierre Jeanneret: Oeuvre complète de 1929–34.* 7th ed. Edited by Willy Boesiger and Oscar Stonorov. Zurich: Éditions d'architecture.

Lefebvre, Henri. 1991. *The Production of Space.* Translated by Donald Nicholson-Smith. Oxford, U.K., and Cambridge, Mass.: Blackwell.

Leopold, Aldo. 1970. *A Sand County Almanac: With Essays on Conservation from Round River.* New York: Ballantine.

Lerner, Gerda. 1986. *The Creation of Patriarchy.* New York: Oxford University Press.

Lerup, Lars. 1987. *Planned Assaults: The Nofamily House, Love/House, Texas Zero.* Montreal: Canadian Centre for Architecture; Cambridge: MIT Press.

Lévi-Strauss, Claude. 1969. *The Elementary Structures of Kinship.* Translated by James Harle Bell, John Richard von Sturmer, and Rodney Needham, editor. Rev. ed. Boston: Beacon Press.

Lindheim, Roslyn. 1970. "Factors Which Determine Hospital Design." In Proshansky, Ittelson, and Rivlin 1970, 573–79.

Lipman, Alan. 1974. "The Architectural Belief System and Social Behavior." In Lang et al. 1974, 23–30.

Lipman, Alan, and Howard Harris. 1979. "Environmental Psychology: A Sterile Research Enterprise?" In *Expériences conflictuelles de l'espace/ Conflicting Experiences of Space,* Proceedings of the 4th International Architectural Psychology Conference, edited by J. G. Simon, vol. 1, 457–75. Louvain-la-Neuve, Belgium: Universitè Catholique de Louvain.

Loftness, Vivian, and Volker Hartkopf. 1997. "Flexible Infrastructure." In *Time-Saver Standards for Architectural Design Data: The Reference of Architectural Fundamentals.* Edited by Donald Watson. 7th ed. New York: McGraw-Hill.

Lovins, Amory B. 1977. *Soft Energy Paths: Toward a Durable Peace.* Cambridge: Ballinger.

Lyle, John T. 1994. *Regenerative Design for Sustainable Development.* New York: John Wiley.

Lyotard, Jean-François. 1984. *The Post-modern Condition: A Report on Knowledge.* Translated by Geoffrey Bennington and Brian Massumi. Minneapolis: University of Minnesota Press.

———. 1991. *The Inhuman: Reflections on Time.* Translated by Geoffrey Bennington and Rachel Bowlby. Stanford: Stanford University Press.

MacCannell, Dean. 1992. *Empty Meeting Grounds: The Tourist Papers.* New York: Routledge.

Mannheim, Karl. 1936. *Ideology and Utopia: An Introduction to the Sociology of Knowledge.* Translated by Louis Wirth and Edward Shils. New York: Harcourt, Brace and World.

[Marcus], Clare Cooper. 1974. "The House as Symbol of the Self." In Lang et al. 1974, 130–46.

Marcus, Clare Cooper. 1975. *Easter Hill Village: Some Social Implications of Design.* New York: Free Press.

Markus, Thomas A. 1993. *Buildings and Power: Freedom and Control in the Origin of Modern Building Types.* London: Routledge.

Martin, Calvin Luther. 1992. *In the Spirit of the Earth: Rethinking History and Time.* Baltimore: John Hopkins University Press.

Masello, David. 1991. "Ban the Boom?" *Architectural Record* 179, no. 3 (March): 68–69.

McGuire, Christine. 1993. "Socio-cultural Changes Affecting Professions and Professionals." In *Educating Professionals,* edited by Lynn Curry and Jon F. Wergin. San Francisco: Jossey Bass.

McHarg, Ian L. 1992. *Design with Nature.* New York: John Wiley.

Meadows, Donella H., Dennis L. Meadows, and Jørgen Randers. 1992. *Beyond the Limits: Confronting Global Collapse, Envisioning a Sustainable Future.* Post Mills, Vt.: Chelsea Green.

Mehrabian, Albert. 1976. *Public Places and Private Spaces: The Psychology of Work, Play, and Living Environments.* New York: Basic Books.

Meiss, Pierre von. 1995. "Design in a World of Permissiveness and Speed." In *Educating Architects,* edited by Martin Pearce and Maggie Toy, 110–15. London: Academy Editions.

Menon, A. G. Krishna. 1989. "Conservation in India: A Search for Direction." *Architecture + Design* 6, no. 1 (November–December): 22–27.

Merchant, Carolyn. 1992. *Radical Ecology: The Search for a Livable World.* New York: Routledge.

Merleau-Ponty, Maurice. 1962. *The Phenomenology of Perception.* Translated from the French by Colin Smith. New York: Humanities Press.

Merquior, Jose G. 1986. *From Prague to Paris: A Critique of Structuralist and Post-structuralist Thought.* London: Verso.

Messer-Davidow, Ellen. 1999. *Disciplining Feminism: Episodes in the Discursive Production of Social Change.* Durham, N.C.: Duke University Press.

Messer-Davidow, Ellen, David R. Shumway, and David J. Sylvan, eds. 1993a. *Knowledges: Historical and Critical Studies in Disciplinarity.* Charlottesville: University Press of Virginia.

————, eds. 1993b. "Introduction: Disciplinary Ways of Knowing." In Messer et al. 1993a, 1–21.

Mitgang, Lee. 1996. "Could Design Education Save Our Schools?" *AIArchitect* (September): 21. Washington, D.C.: American Institute of Architects.

Moles, Abraham. 1968. "The Three Cities." In *DATA: Directions in Art, Theory, and Aesthetics; an Anthology,* edited by Anthony Hill. Greenwich, Conn.: New York Graphic Society.

Montgomery, Roger. 1989. "Architecture Invents New People." In Ellis and Cuff 1989, 260–61.

Moore-Gilbert, Bart J. 1997. *Postcolonial Theory, Contexts, Practices, Politics.* London: Verso.

Morris, Mary, ed. 1993. *Maiden Voyages: Writings of Women Travelers.* New York: Vintage Books.

Munro, David A., and Martin W. Holdgate, eds. 1991. *Caring for the Earth: A Strategy for Sustainable Living. A Report of the Second World Conservation Strategy Project.* Gland, Switzerland: published in partnership by IUCN (World Conservation Union), UNEP (United Nations Environmental Programme), and WWF (World Wide Fund for Nature).

Nair, Rukmini Bhaya. 1999. "Postcoloniality and the Matrix of Indifference." *India International Center Quarterly* (Delhi) 26, no. 2 (summer): 8.

Naylor, Gillian. 1985. *The Bauhaus Reassessed: Sources and Design Theory.* London: Herbert Press.

Nesbitt, Kate, ed. 1996. *Theorizing a New Agenda for Architecture: An Anthology of Architectural Theory, 1965–1995.* New York: Princeton Architectural Press.

Newman, Oscar. 1976. *Design Guidelines for Creating Defensible Space.* Washington, D.C.: U.S. Government Printing Office.

Niranjana, Tejaswini, P. Sudhir, and Vivek Dhareshwar, eds. 1993. *Interrogating Modernity: Culture and Colonialism in India.* Calcutta: Seagull Books.

Norberg-Schultz, Christian. 1965. *Intentions in Architecture.* Cambridge: MIT Press.

————. 1980. *Genius Loci: Towards a Phenomenology of Architecture.* New York: Rizzoli.

Noschis, Kaj. 1998. "Let's Not Forget the User." In *Architecture and Teaching: Epistemological Foundations,* edited by H. Dunin-Wyseth and Kaj Noschis, 103–10. Lausanne, Switzerland: Comportements.

Noss, Reed F. 1992. "The Wildlands Project: Land Conservation Strategy." *Wild Earth Magazine* (Canton, N.Y.).

O'Brien, Mary. 1986. "Feminism and the Politics of Education." *Interchange* 17, no. 2: 91–110.

Ockman, Joan, ed. 1985. *Architecture, Criticism, Ideology.* Princeton, N.J.: Princeton Architectural Press.

Oliver, Paul, ed. 1975. *Shelter, Sign, and Symbol.* Woodstock, N.Y.: Overlook Press.

Oliver, Richard, ed. 1981. *The Making of an Architect, 1881–1981: Columbia University in the City of New York.* New York: Rizzoli.

O'Reilly, William, ed. 1999. *Architectural Knowledge and Cultural Diversity.* Lausanne, Switzerland: Comportements.

Orr, David W. 1993. *Ecological Literacy: Education and the Transition to a Postmodern World.* Albany: State University of New York Press.

———. 1994. *Earth in Mind: On Education, Environment, and the Human Prospect.* Washington, D.C.: Island Press.

Ortelli, Luca. 1991. "Heading South: Asplund's Impressions." *Lotus International* 68: 22–33.

Oxford English Dictionary: The Compact Edition. 1971. 1st ed. Oxford: Oxford University Press.

Özkan, Suha. 1999. "The Dilemma of History: Theory and Education in Architecture." In O'Reilly 1999, 145–54.

Park, Robert Ezra, Ernest Watson Burgess, and Roderick Duncan McKenzie, eds. 1925. *The City.* Chicago: University of Chicago Press.

Patterson, Richard. 1997. "What Vitruvius Said." *Journal of Architecture* 2, no. 4 (winter): 355–73.

Pérez-Gómez, Alberto. 1983. *Architecture and the Crisis of Modern Science.* Cambridge: MIT Press.

Perin, Constance. 1970. *With Man in Mind: An Interdisciplinary Prospectus for Environmental Design.* Cambridge: MIT Press.

Plato. 1924. *The Dialogues of Plato.* Oxford: Oxford University Press.

———. 1991. *Protagoras.* Translated by C. C. W. Taylor. Rev. ed. Oxford: Clarendon Press; New York: Oxford University Press.

Polanyi, Michael. [1958] 1962. *Personal Knowledge: Towards a Post-critical Philosophy.* London: Routledge and Kegan Paul.

Polshek, James S. 1981. "Introduction." In R. Oliver 1981, 1–4.

Poulson, D. 1996. "Sprawl Creates Environmental Woes for State." *Ann Arbor News,* 29 April, A1–8

Prak, Niels L. 1984. *Architects: The Noted and the Ignored.* New York: Wiley.

Proshansky, Harold M., William H. Ittelson, and Leanne G. Rivlin, eds. 1970. *Environmental Psychology: Man and His Physical Setting.* New York: Holt, Rinehart and Winston.

Proudhon, Pierre-Joseph. 1994. *What Is Property? An Enquiry into the Principle of Right and of Government.* Translated by Donald R. Kelley and Bonnie G. Smith. New York: Cambridge University Press.

Pugin, Augustus Welby Northmore. 1841. *Contrasts: Or, A Parallel between the Noble Edifices of the Middle Ages, and Corresponding Buildings of the Present Day, Shewing the Present Decay of Taste.* London.

Quaderns D'Arquitectura I Urbanisme. 1983. Vol. 158 (July–September).

Rabinow, Paul. 1989. *French Modern: Norms and Forms of the Social Environment.* Cambridge: MIT Press.

Rapoport, Amos. 1969. *House Form and Culture.* Englewood Cliffs, N.J.: Prentice-Hall.

———. 1982. *The Meaning of the Built Environment.* Beverly Hills, Calif.: Sage.

———. 1987. "Statement for the ACSA 75th Anniversary Jubilee Issue of *JAE.*" *Journal of Architectural Education* 40, no. 2 (Jubilee): 65–66.

———. 1990. *History and Precedent in Environmental Design.* New York: Plenum Press.

———. 1994. "On 'The Invisible in Architecture': An Environment-Behavior Studies Perspective." In *The Invisible in Architecture,* edited by Ole Bouman and Roemer van Toorn, 66–73. London: Academy Editions.

Ray, Mary-Ann. 1997a. "Gecekondu." In *Architecture of the Everyday,* edited by Deborah Burke and Stephen Harris, 153–65. New York: Princeton Architectural Press.

———. 1997b. "Seven Partly Underground Rooms and Buildings for Water, Ice, and Midgets." In *Pamphlet Architecture,* no. 20. New York: Princeton Architectural Press.

Relph, Edward C. 1976. *Place and Placelessness.* London: Pion.

Rewal, Raj, and Ram Sharma. 1985. *Architecture of India.* Paris: Electa Moniter.

Ricoeur, Paul. 1991. "The Function of Fiction in Shaping Reality." In *A Ricoeur Reader: Reflection and Imagination,* edited by Mario Valdés. London and New York: Harvester Wheatsheaf.

———. 1998. *Critique and Conviction: Conversations with François Axouvi and Marc de Launay.* Translated by Kathleen Blamey. New York: Columbia University Press.

Robinson, Julia W. 1990. "Architectural Research: Incorporating Myth and Science." *Journal of Architectural Education* 44, no. 1 (November): 20–32.

Rockcastle, Garth. 1987. "Myth, Poetry, and Gift in Architecture." In *Midgård: Journal of Architectural Theory and Criticism* (Minneapolis: School of Architecture and Landscape Architecture) 1, no. 1: 159–67.

Roland, Alan. 1988. *In Search of Self in India and Japan: Toward a Cross-Cultural Psychology.* Princeton, N.J.: Princeton University Press.

Rorty, Richard. 1994. "Feminism, Ideology, and Deconstruction: A Pragmatist View." In Žižek 1994, 226.

Rossi, Aldo. 1981. *A Scientific Autobiography.* Translated by Lawrence Venuti. Cambridge: MIT Press.

———. 1982. *The Architecture of the City.* Translated by Diane Ghirardo and Joan Ockman. Cambridge: MIT Press.

Rowe, Colin, 1953–1954. "Character and Composition." Reprinted in Rowe 1976.

———. 1976. *The Mathematics of the Ideal Villa and Other Essays.* Cambridge: MIT Press.

Royal Institute of British Architects. 1993. *Strategic Study of the Profession.* London: Royal Institute of British Architects.

Rubin, Charles T. 1994. *The Green Crusade: Rethinking the Roots of Environmentalism.* New York: Free Press.

Rudofsky, Bernard. 1964. *Architecture without Architects: A Short Introduction to Non-pedigreed Architecture.* Garden City, N.Y.: Doubleday.

Rykwert, Joseph. 1980. "Classic and Neoclassic." *The First Moderns: The Architects of the Eighteenth Century.* Cambridge: MIT Press.

Saalman, Howard. 1971. *Haussmann: Paris Transformed.* New York: George Braziller.

Said, Edward W. 1979. *Orientalism.* New York: Random House. London: Routledge and Kegan Paul.

———. 1994. *Culture and Imperialism.* New York: Random House.

Saint, Andrew. 1983. *The Image of the Architect.* New Haven, Conn.: Yale University Press.

———. 1996. "Architecture as Image: Can We Rein in This New Beast?" In Saunders and Rowe 1996.

Sanoff, Henry, ed. 1990. "Participatory Design in Focus." In *Participatory Design: Theory and Techniques.* Raleigh: North Carolina State University.

Sapers, Carl. 1996. "Losing and Regaining Ground: A Jeremiad on the Future of the Profession." In Saunders and Rowe 1996.

Sassen, Saskia. 1996. *Losing Control? Sovereignty in an Age of Globalization.* New York: Columbia University Press.

———. 1998. *Globalization and Its Discontents: Essays on the New Mobility of People and Money.* New York: New Press.

Saunders, William S., and Peter G. Rowe, eds. 1996. *Reflections on Architectural Practices in the Nineties.* New York: Princeton Architectural Press.

Scarpa, Carlo. 1984. *Carlo Scarpa: The Complete Works.* Translated by Richard Sadleir. New York: Rizzoli.

Schildt, Göran. 1991. "The Travels of Alvar Aalto: Notebook Sketches." *Lotus International* 68: 34–47.

Schmarsow, August. 1994. "The Essence of Architectural Creation." In *Empathy, Form, and Space: Problems in German Aesthetics, 1873–1893,* edited by Robert Vischer, translated by Harry F. Mallgrave and Eleftherios Ikonomou. Santa Monica, Calif.: Getty Center for the History of Art and Humanities.

Schneekloth, Linda H., and Robert G. Shibley. 1995. *Placemaking: The Art and Practice of Building Communities.* New York: John Wiley and Sons.

Schön, Donald A. 1983. *The Reflective Practitioner: How Professionals Think in Action.* New York: Basic Books.

———. 1987. *Educating the Reflective Practitioner.* San Francisco: Jossey-Bass.

Schumacher, E. F. 1973. *Small Is Beautiful: Economics As If People Mattered.* New York: Harper and Row.

Schwartz, Peter. 1991. *The Art of the Long View: Planning for the Future in an Uncertain World.* New York: Doubleday Currency Books.

Scolari, Massimo. 1985. "Elements for History of Axonometry." *Architectural Design* 55, nos. 5–6: 73–78.

Scully, Vincent. 1991. "Marvelous Fountainheads: Louis I. Kahn, Travel Drawings." *Lotus International* 68: 48–63.

Seamon, David. 1987. "Phenomenology and Environment-Behavior Research." In *Advances in Environment, Behavior, and Design,* edited by Ervin H. Zube and Gary T. Moore, 3–27. New York: Plenum Press.

Seamon, David, and Robert Mugerauer, eds. 1985. *Dwelling, Place, and Environment: Towards a Phenomenology of Person and World.* Dordrecht, Netherlands: Martinus Nijhoff.

SEMCOG. 1991. *The "Business as Usual" Trend Future: The Data Base.* Detroit: Southeast Michigan Council of Governments.

Semper, Gottfried. [1851] 1989. *The Four Elements of Architecture and Other Writings.* Translated by Harry F. Mallgrave and Wolfgang Herrmann. Cambridge: Cambridge University Press. Originally published as *Die Vier Elemente der Baukunst: Ein Beitrag zur vergleichenden Baukunde.* Braunschweig: Vieweg, 1851.

———. [1860–1863] 1977. *Der Stil in den technischen und tektonischen Künsten, oder Praktische Ästhetik.* 2 vols. Munich: F. Bruckmann, 2d ed.; Munich, Bruckmann, 1878; reprint, Mittenwald, 1977.

Sennett, Richard. 1976. *The Fall of Public Man.* New York: Knopf.

Shackelford, George Green. 1995. *Thomas Jefferson's Travels, 1784–1789.* Baltimore: Johns Hopkins University Press.

Shumway, David R., and Ellen Messer-Davidow. 1991. "Disciplinarity: An Introduction." *Poetics Today* 12, no. 2 (summer): 201–25.

Sieder, Jill Jordan. 1996. "A Building of Her Own." In *U.S. News and World Report* 121, no. 15 (14 October): 66–68.

Sommer, Robert. 1969. *Personal Space: The Behavioral Basis of Design.* Englewood Cliffs, N.J.: Prentice-Hall International.

Spender, Dale, ed. 1981. "Introduction." In *Men's Studies Modified: The Impact of Feminism on the Academic Disciplines,* 1–9. New York: Pergamon Press.

Spivak, Gayatri Chakravorty. 1987. "French Feminism in an International Frame." In *In Other Worlds: Essays in Cultural Politics.* New York: Methuen.

———. 1997. "City, Country, Agency." In *Proceedings of the Theaters of Decolonization Conference, Chandigarh, January 6–10, 1995*, edited by Vikramaditya Prakash. Seattle, Wash.: Office of the Dean, College of Architecture and Urban Planning, University of Washington.

Sprengnether, Madelon, and C. W. Truesdale, eds. 1991. *The House on Via Gombito*. Minneapolis: New Rivers Press.

Stanton, Michael. 1985. "New York Rules, O.K.?" In *Art and Design* (London) 1, no. 3 (April): 42–46.

———. 1991. "Hedged Bets: Practical and Theoretical Equivocation during the Reagan Years." In *Modulus 21: Politics and Architecture*. New York: Princeton Architectural Press.

———. 1998a. "Dissipated Scandals: On Avant-gardism and Parlour Revolutions in Architecture." *Archis* 8 (August): 64–73.

———. 1998b. "Of Mice and Monsters: A Response to Bart Lootsma." *Archis* 10 (October): 66–69.

Stengers, Isabelle, and Judith Schlanger. 1991. *Les concepts scientifiques: Invention et pouvoir*. Paris: Gallimard.

Stirling, S. R. 1990. "Towards an Ecological World View." In *Ethics of Environment and Development: Global Challenge, International Response*, edited by J. Ronald Engel and Joan Gibb Engel, 77–86. Tucson: University of Arizona Press.

Strauss, M. 1984. "Cultural Leadership and the Avant-garde." In *Leadership: Multidisciplinary Perspectives*, edited by Barbara Kellerman, 179–97. Englewood Cliffs, N.J.: Prentice-Hall.

Summers, David. 1991. "Real Metaphor: Towards a Redefinition of the 'Conceptual' Image." In *Visual Theory: Painting and Interpretation*, edited by Norman Bryson, Michael Ann Holly, and Keith Moxey. New York: HarperCollins.

Summerson, John N. [1949] 1963. "Viollet-le-Duc and the Rational Point of View." In *Heavenly Mansions and Other Essays on Architecture*, 135–58. New York: W. W. Norton. Originally published in London: Cresset Press, 1949.

Surin, Kenneth. 1995. "On Producing the Concept of a Global Culture." In *Nations, Identities, Cultures*, edited by V. Y. Mudimbe. Special issue of *South Atlantic Quarterly* 94: 1179–99.

Sutton, Sharon Egretta. 1991. "Finding Our Voice in the Dominant Key." In *African American Architects in Current Practice*, edited by Jack Travis, 12–14. New York: Princeton Architectural Press.

———. 1992. "Power, Knowledge, and the Art of Leadership." *Progressive Architecture* 73, no. 5 (May): 65–68.

———. 1993. "The Progress of Architecture." *Progressive Architecture* 74, no. 10 (October): 76–79.

Sykes, Charles J. 1988. *Profscam: Professors and the Demise of Higher Education*. Washington, D.C.: Regnery Gateway.

Tafuri, Manfredo. 1976. *Architecture and Utopia: Design and Capitalist Development.* Translated by Barbara Luigia La Penta. Cambridge: MIT Press.

———. 1980. *Theories and History of Architecture.* Translated by Giorgio Verrecchia. New York: Harper and Row.

———. 1987. *The Sphere and the Labyrinth: Avant-Gardes and Architecture from Piranesi to the 1970s.* Translated by Pellegrino d'Acierno and Robert Connolly. Cambridge: MIT Press.

Taylor, Brian Brace. 1992. *Raj Rewal.* London: Mimar Publications.

Taylor, Charles. 1991. *The Ethics of Authenticity.* Cambridge: Harvard University Press.

Teymur, Necdet. 1992. *Architectural Education: Issues in Educational Practice and Policy.* London: ?uestion Press.

Tharu, Susie, and K. Lalitha, eds. 1991. *Women Writing in India: 600 B.C. to the Present.* New York: Feminist Press at the City University of New York.

Tillotson, G. H. R. 1989. *The Tradition of Indian Architecture: Continuity, Controversy, and Change since 1850.* New Haven, Conn.: Yale University Press.

Tinling, Marion, ed. 1993. *With Women's Eyes: Visitors to the New World, 1775–1918.* Hamden, Conn.: Archon Books.

Trimpi, Wesley. 1983. *Muses of One Mind: The Literary Analysis of Experience and Its Continuity.* Princeton, N.J.: Princeton University Press.

Tuan, Yi-fu. 1989. *Morality and Imagination: Paradoxes of Progress.* Madison: University of Wisconsin Press.

U.S. Department of Commerce. 1996. "Employed Civilians by Occupation, Sex, Race, and Hispanic Origin, Table 637." *Statistical Abstract of the United States.* Washington, D.C.: Government Printing Office

Van den Abbeele, Georges. 1992. *Travel as Metaphor: From Montaigne to Rousseau.* Minneapolis: University of Minnesota Press.

Van der Ryn, Sim, and Peter Calthorpe. 1986. *Sustainable Communities: A New Design Synthesis for Cities, Suburbs, and Towns.* San Francisco: Sierra Club Books.

Varnelis, Kazys, ed. 1999. "Critical Historiography and the End of Theory." Thematic group of articles in *Journal of Architectural Education* 52, no. 4 (May): 195–225.

Vattimo, Gianni. 1988. *The End of Modernity: Nihilism and Hermeneutics in Postmodern Culture.* Baltimore: Johns Hopkins University Press.

Venturi, Robert, Denise Scott Brown, and Steven Izenour. 1972. *Learning from Las Vegas: The Forgotten Symbolism of Architectural Form.* Rev. ed. Cambridge: MIT Press.

Vernant, Jean Pierre. 1983. "Prometheus and the Technological Function." In *Myth and Thought among the Greeks,* 237–47. London: Routledge and Kegan Paul.

Vidler, Anthony. [1976] 1996. "The Third Typology." Originally published in *Oppositions* 7 (winter): 1–4. Reprinted in Nesbitt 1996, 260–63.

————. 1992. *The Architectural Uncanny: Essays in the Modern Unhomely.* Cambridge: MIT Press.

Viollet-le-Duc, Eugène-Emmanuel. [1854–1868] 1979. *Dictionnaire raisonné de l'architecture française du XIe au XVIe siècle.* 10 vols. Paris: Morel; reprint, Paris: Saint-Julien-du-Sancey, 1979.

————. 1987. *Lectures on Architecture.* Translated by Benjamin Bucknall. New York: Dover.

Virilio, Paul. 1993. "The Interface." *Lotus International* 75: 126.

Vitruvius, 1960. *Vitruvius: The Ten Books on Architecture.* Translated by Morris Hicky Morgan. New York: Dover.

————. 1970. *Vitruvius on Architecture.* Translated by Frank Granger. Cambridge: Harvard University Press.

Voegelin, Eric. 1957. *Plato and Aristotle.* Baton Rouge: Louisiana State University Press.

————. 1973. "On Classical Studies." *Modern Age* 17: 2–8.

Voltaire. 1930. *Candide.* New York: Williams, Belasco and Meyers.

Wallerstein, Immanuel (commission chair), V. Y. Mudimbe, ed. [1996] 1997. *Open the Social Sciences: Report of the Gulbenkian Commission on Restructuring of the Social Sciences.* Palo Alto, Calif.: Stanford University Press.

Watson, Donald. 1994. "The Notion of Critical Practices: Roles for Educators in Continuing Education." Proceedings of the 82d Annual ACSA Meeting. Washington, D.C.: Association of Collegiate Schools of Architecture.

————. 1996. *Environmental Design Charrette Workbook.* Washington, D.C.: AIA/Rizzoli Publications.

————. 1999. "Improving Practice through Knowledge and Research." *Architectural Research Quarterly* 3, no. 1:9–13.

Weber, Samuel. 1987. "The Limits of Professionalism." In *Institution and Interpretation.* Minneapolis: University of Minnesota Press.

Weinsheimer, Joel. 1991. "The Question of the Classic." In *Philosophical Hermeneutics and Literary Theory.* New Haven, Conn.: Yale University Press.

Wener, Richard, and Françoise Szigetti, eds. 1988. *Cumulative Index to the Proceedings of the Environmental Design Research Association: Volumes 1–18, 1969–1987.* Washington, D.C.: EDRA.

White, Stephen. 1993. *Building in the Garden: The Architecture of Joseph Allen Stein in India and California.* Delhi and New York: Oxford University Press.

Whitehead, Alfred North. 1959. *Science and the Modern World.* New York: New American Library.

Wigley, Mark. 1995. [Untitled contribution]. In Eisenman et al. 1995, 90.

Williams, Raymond. 1977. *Marxism and Literature.* Oxford: Oxford University Press.

Wilshire, Bruce. 1990. *The Moral Collapse of the University: Professionalism, Purity, and Alienation.* Albany: State University of New York Press.

Wilson, Edward O. 1992. *The Diversity of Life.* Cambridge: Belknap Press of Harvard University Press.

———. 1993. "Is Humanity Suicidal? We're Flirting with Extinction of Our Species." *New York Times Magazine,* 30 May, 24.

Wirth, Louis. 1936. Preface to *Ideology and Utopia: An Introduction to the Sociology of Knowledge,* by Karl Mannheim. New York: Harcourt, Brace and World.

———. 1969. "Urbanism as a Way of Life." In *Classic Essays on the Culture of Cities,* edited by Richard Sennett, 143–64. New York: Appleton-Century-Crofts. Originally published in *American Journal of Sociology* 44 (1938).

Wittgenstein, Ludwig. 1961. *Tractatus Logico-Philosophicus.* Translated by D. F. Pears and B. F. McGuinness. London: Routledge.

Zeisel, John. 1981. *Inquiry by Design: Tools for Environment-Behavior Research.* Monterey, Calif.: Brooks/Cole.

Žižek, Slavoj, ed. 1994. *Mapping Ideology.* London: Verso.

Contributors

Sherry Ahrentzen is professor of architecture at the University of Wisconsin–Milwaukee. Her teaching and scholarship focus on how architecture can be more responsive to social change and conditions in American culture, particularly those affecting women and marginalized groups. Her research on new forms of housing that better address the social and economic diversity of U.S. households has been published extensively in journals and magazines. With Karen A. Franck, she coedited *New Households, New Housing*.

Stanford Anderson is professor of history and architecture and head of the Department of Architecture at the Massachusetts Institute of Technology. He was a fellow of the Institute for Architecture and Urban Studies, where he codirected the project that resulted in his edited volume *On Streets*. Among his many publications, the most recent is his monograph on the German architect Peter Behrens.

Carol Burns is a faculty member of the Harvard University Graduate School of Design and a principal at Taylor MacDougall Burns Architects, specializing in projects for urban, community-based, and educational institutions. Currently she is a housing fellow at Harvard Joint Center for Housing Studies. Her research focuses on the post–World War II era, relating architectural theory to professional and social practices and to evolving urban form. She has written about issues in housing, about professional practice and education, and about site issues in design. Her current work on housing and mobility connects the residential environment to physical, spatial, economic, and social mobility. She received a teaching award from Harvard students and the AIA National Education Honors Award.

W. Russell Ellis is professor of architecture at the University of California, Berkeley. He served as assistant dean of the College of Environmental Design at the University of California, Berkeley, from 1975 to 1977, and was Vice Chancellor for Undergraduate Affairs from 1989 to 1995. He has also taught at the University of California, Riverside; Pitzer College; the State University of New York at Old Westbury; and Yale University. Among other works, he coedited *Architects' People* (with Dana Cuff), which deals with architects' and planners' conceptions of the people who occupy their designs and plans.

Thomas Fisher is dean of the College of Architecture and Landscape Architecture at the University of Minnesota. He previously served as the editorial director of *Progressive Architecture* magazine, as well as in various roles in architectural firms and in state government. He is currently a coeditor of *Architectural Research Quarterly* and the author of *In the Scheme of Things: Alternative Thinking on the Practice of Architecture* (Minnesota, 2000).

Linda N. Groat is professor of architecture at the University of Michigan. She has published widely on meaning in contemporary architecture, frequently incorporating empirical methodologies. Recently she and Sherry Ahrentzen have completed research on the status of women and minorities in architecture, and they are working on a book titled *Roll Over, Roark: The Myriad Meanings, Visions, and Experiences of Architecture in the Lives of Students.*

Kay Bea Jones is associate professor of architecture at the Austin E. Knowlton School of Architecture at The Ohio State University, where she has directed studies in Italy since 1985. She is educated in the fine arts, architecture, and women's studies, and her architectural scholarship is inspired by photography, drawing, and critical writing. She regularly contributes to *Journal of Architectural Education* and is currently designing cohousing for single-parent university students.

David Leatherbarrow is professor of architecture and chair of the Ph.D. program in architecture at the University of Pennsylvania. He has written and edited numerous texts, including *Uncommon Ground: Architecture, Technology, and Topography; The Roots of Architectural Invention: Site, Enclosure, Materials*; and, with Mohsen Mostafavi, *On Weathering: The Life of Buildings in Time.*

A. G. Krishna Menon completed his undergraduate studies in architecture in India, followed by postgraduate work in architecture at the Illinois Institute of Technology, Chicago, and in urban planning at Columbia University. He has been writing, teaching, and practicing professionally in New Delhi since 1972. He has made significant contributions in the field of urban conservation of historic cities and was associated with the establishment of the TVB School of Habitat Studies, a school of architecture in New Delhi, where he is now director.

Andrzej Piotrowski is associate professor of architecture at the University of Minnesota. Born in Poland, he graduated from the Department of Architecture at Warsaw Polytechnic. He is a registered architect in Poland and has practiced in both Poland and the United States. His scholarship focuses on the history and theory of architectural representation. He is currently working on a book on representation and knowledge in architecture.

Julia Williams Robinson is professor of architecture at the University of Minnesota, where she teaches architectural design and theory. In addition to being a registered architect, she has expertise in anthropology, which she has applied in writing and research on building types, especially housing. She has written numerous publications on design methods and recently worked on architectural programming, design, and building evaluation (completing the research-build cycle) for the Department of Natural Resources of the State of Minnesota. Her commitment to the discipline through architectural research has been reflected at the national level through her service on the executive board of the Architectural Research Centers Consortium, which she chaired from 1992 to 1994.

Garth Rockcastle is professor of architecture at the University of Minnesota. His architectural design work as principal of Meyer, Scherer, and Rockcastle focuses on arts and university facilities, workplace design, and custom residential architecture; his work is frequently honored and widely published. He has written, edited, and published scholarly work and reviews in journals (such as *VIA, Architectural Research Quarterly, Public Art Review, Architectural Record,* and *Progressive Architecture*) and books (including *Introduction to Environmental Design* and *Encyclopedia of Twentieth-Century Architecture*). He is currently working on two books, *Seven Hinges: Essays on Ethics and Aesthetics in Architecture* and *Heinz Tesar: Projects, Notebooks, and Buildings*.

Michael Stanton has won the Young Architect's Award from Architectural League of New York, the Biennial Steedman Prize, and design awards from the ACSA and *Progressive Architecture*. He has been a fellow in architecture at the American Academy in Rome and was the first Aga Khan Traveling Fellow in 1980. He founded and directed eleven international workshops in Venice and Barcelona with the Institute for Advanced Architectural Studies and also founded programs for Tulane and the University of Minnesota. The recipient of three grants from Graham Foundation, he has lectured and exhibited his work extensively throughout the Americas and Europe, and he has taught at several schools, including Tulane University in New Orleans and the Royal Danish Academy in Copenhagen. He is now teaching at the American University of Beirut.

Sharon Egretta Sutton is professor of architecture and director of CEEDS (Center for Environment, Education, and Design Studies) at the University of Washington. Her research focuses on the study of youth, culture, and the environment. Her most recent book, *Weaving a Tapestry of Resistance,* is based on data collected during an evaluation of a K–12 urban design program she founded while at the University of Michigan. Formerly a Kellogg National Fellow as well as a Danforth Fellow, she is a distinguished professor of the Association of Collegiate Schools of Architecture and a fellow in the American Institute of Architects. She has degrees in music, architecture, psychology, and philosophy.

David J. T. Vanderburgh teaches architectural design, theory, and history at the Université Catholique de Louvain, Belgium. He directs a small research group, THAV (Théorie et Histoire de l'Architecture et de la Ville), concerned with historical and theoretical modernity. His recent publications include articles on arcades, architectural reform, and the theory of metaphor. He is currently working on a book proposal about architecture and reform in Europe and North America.

Donald Watson is an architect with a consulting practice based in Trumbull, Connecticut, and clinical professor of architecture at Rensselaer Polytechnic Institute. His research and professional projects have received numerous national and international awards. He is author of five reference books in architecture, most recently *AIA Handbook of Energy Design* and *Environmental Design Charrette Workbook,* and he served as editor in chief of the seventh edition of *Time-Saver Standards for Architectural Design Data.*

Index